Ultimate Selenium WebDriver for Test Automation

Build and Implement Automated Web Testing Frameworks Using Java, Selenium WebDriver and Selenium Grid for E-Commerce, Healthcare, EdTech, Banking, and SAAS

Robin Gupta

www.orangeava.com

First published: March 2024

Published by: Orange Education Pvt Ltd, AVA™

Address: 9, Daryaganj, Delhi, 110002

ISBN: 978-81-96994-76-1

www.orangeava.com

Dedicated To

My two families:

Parents (Late Mrs. VijayLaxmi Gupta, Mr. Rakesh Kumar Gupta), Wife (Sneha Singh), Daughter (Natasha Gupta), and my siblings' families

Selenium open-source community

Foreword

In some ways, you can view writing code as an act of collaborative art. Just as no two people would say the same thing if asked to describe a sunrise, those same people will write code in different ways, even if the goal is same for both of them. The process of taking a description of what we want to do and converting it into code is a creative one. Although we might write code on our own as a hobby, in professional settings we work in teams, with each person on the team working on the part of the tapestry of the application that suits their strengths. Not only is the process artistic, but also collaborative.

The expression "if the only tool you have is a hammer, everything looks like a nail" is frequently used in software development circles. That's because, just as with any artistic endeavor, to develop stable software proficiently, one needs to learn about the tools that can be used, and the techniques that can be applied. It's not enough to know how to use a tool, we need to know *when* to use it. So, not only is software development a collaborative artistic endeavor, but also one where we need to know tools and techniques in order to work effectively.

But there's a problem. How do we learn a new tool or technique? How do we begin to understand how and where to use it? After all, we've been writing software for a long time, so there must be a large body of tools and techniques to draw from.

Let's take the field of writing web apps. Tim Berners-Lee published the first website while working at CERN in December 1990. Originally, web pages were static and simple. When Netscape introduced Javascript to the world, these simple, static pages became a little more interesting. When Microsoft introduced XmlHTTPRequest, it became possible for pages to request information from web servers without needing to reload. In 1999, Darci DiNucci introduced the world to the phrase "Web 2.0", but it didn't become a widespread phrase until the early 2000s.

The early 2000s was when we saw an explosion of creativity on the Web. Sites suddenly went from being relatively static to being incredibly dynamic. The technologies powering Web 2.0 enabled sites like Google Maps to exist. And that explosion of creativity continues to this day, with websites becoming ever more complex, dynamic, and capable.

As the Web has grown, so has the tooling.

In 2004, Jason Huggins started the Selenium project. In 2011, we released Selenium 2, and Selenium 3 followed in 2016. Most recently, Selenium 4 was released in 2021, a full ten years after the world was introduced to the WebDriver APIs. Over those many years, the tool has grown and adapted to the changing world around it, and the community has gathered a wealth of knowledge and experience, not only about Selenium, but also how to use it, and get the most out of it.

This brings me to the book.

You hold in your hands a book that is ostensibly about Selenium. Except it's about far more than that. You see, in this book, Robin takes us on a journey from neophyte to master tester, introducing us not only to the tool that is Selenium, but also to the context in which it can be used. This book provides a distillation of many of the current "best practices" that many teams have adopted when using Selenium, particularly the Java bindings. Those are practices that have evolved over many years, and have been shown to be effective time and again.

Just as a paintbrush is most useful when there is a canvas and paint, so Selenium is most useful when used with test frameworks, design patterns, and logging. And just as there are many ways in which a paintbrush can apply paint to the canvas, so Selenium has many interesting capabilities and APIs. In this metaphor, Robin is the art teacher, wherein he starts gently, introducing us to Selenium through its IDE, and then builds upon that, chapter after chapter. Each step of the way, he provides supporting information and concepts.

So, even if this book is about Selenium Test Automation, when you've finished reading it, you'll be familiar with different kinds of tests, testing in general, design patterns, and other tools and frameworks which can be used with Selenium.

When you've finished reading it, you'll be better able to participate in the wildly entertaining collaborative art project we call software development, and that's a wonderful thing.

Simon Mavi Stewart

Creator of WebDriver

Selenium Project Lead 2009-2021

Coeditor of the WebDriver and WebDriver Bidi W3C specifications

London, January 2024

About the Author

Robin is a versatile engineering leader with over 15 years of experience in software delivery across startups, scale-ups, and enterprises. With a metrics-driven approach, he has elevated the engineering maturity of Dev/QA/DevOps teams for diverse domains such as BFSI, EdTech, Retail, and Developer Experience. Experienced in multiple tech stacks, Robin's hands-on leadership style yields positive results. Beyond work, he mentors at ADPList and Plato, contributes to open-source projects like Selenium, created TestZeus (the only open-source test automation framework for Salesforce), and has authored courses. He is also recognized as a speaker at international events such as Dreamforce (by Salesforce) and Selenium Conference. Balancing responsibilities as a dad at home and M.O.M (Manager of Managers) at the office, Robin excels in both personal and professional realms.

For more details, visit www.robin-gupta.com

About the Technical Reviewer

Shreya Singh Patel has been on an automation adventure for nearly a decade, building rock-solid testing frameworks with Selenium and Java like a tech architect conjuring bug-resistant fortresses. But her repertoire doesn't end there! She works on API automation, mobile automation, database, and load testing. Every mastered technology adds another vibrant thread to her ever-expanding skillset.

She has been working in the IT industry for over 7 years on various automation projects, also witnessing the rise in demand for automation in each industry, not just IT.

But she is not just about conquering bugs, she's about lighting the way for others. Witnessing the "Aha!" moments when her mentored manual testers transform into automation heroes fuels her passion more than any squashed superbug. She currently mentors colleagues, guiding them through code and frameworks until they write their own automation victories.

She actively volunteers as Internship Operation Head for both summer and winter internships at Internity Foundation, a startup. Her passion for mentorship shines through as she guides interns, sharing her knowledge and empowering them to build their own careers in the exciting world of automation.

That's why this book review opportunity feels like destiny. It's a chance for her to share her hard-won knowledge, acting as a friendly translator through the sometimes-confusing world of Selenium for eager beginners. Imagine her as a bridge, connecting complex code to wide-eyed minds, and empowering them to embark on their own testing adventures.

Acknowledgements

First and foremost, I want to express my gratitude to the team at Orange AVA. Without their help and support, this book would not have been possible. I also want to thank Shreya Singh Patel, who performed the technical review and, paradoxically, acted as the tester of a book on the topic of test automation.

Andrew Knight (passionately called The Automation Panda) and Ivan Harris (CPTO at Provar) have patiently answered my questions about writing a book - thank you, folks. Special recognition goes to Tristan Lombard (a.k.a Stage Mom) for keeping me on track during the writing process and guiding me to do the right things, not the easy things.

This book has hidden treasures across the chapters in the form of quotes from industry leaders and open-source contributors. I want to thank these luminaries for giving away these pearls of wisdom.

A big thanks to Simon Stewart (creator of WebDriver) for writing the foreword to this book and lighting the path for many engineers like me.

2023 was a rough year for me, so I want to express my gratitude to my wife for supporting me at every stage of this writing journey.

Preface

Once upon a time, in a land not so far away, I was chatting with my friend about a certification exam for a test automation tool that I had taken. He was telling me about this new thing called Selenium. I was entirely skeptical of this new open-source technology, believing it was a fad bound to fade away. Lo and behold, Selenium has not only turned me around but also raised the bar for browser automation. Since its inception in 2004, Selenium has stood tall for an eternity in the technology domain, where trends rise and fall every six months.

Selenium is a powerful tool that allows you to automate web browser interactions, essentially teaching your computer to act like a robot. It is like having your own personal minion to carry out your tasks, including software testing, allowing you to focus on the more creative and strategic aspects of software delivery.

Whether you are a seasoned tester or just dipping your toes into the world of browser automation, buckle up and get ready for an adventure. In this book, we will explore the ins and outs of test automation using Selenium. This book is organized into 11 chapters, as outlined below:

Chapter 1 acts as an onboarding ramp to the Selenium ecosystem by covering the introduction to Selenium and detailed hands-on sections with Selenium IDE. This way readers can accelerate their learning journey while staying in the low-code mode.

Chapter 2 delves into the basics of Software Quality, Test Automation strategy, and Reporting. Before we dive deep into the ocean of Selenium test automation, it is imperative that we take a holy dip into the world of software testing and quality. This ensures that we do not waste our time automating the wrong tests and can really deliver on the promise of testing via automation.

Chapter 3 covers one of the most important topics in test automation – Locator strategies. Additionally, readers learn interactions with various web elements (such as clicking links and buttons), form submissions, and file uploads.

Chapter 4 explores advanced techniques for using Selenium WebDriver. With our newfound grip on Selenium WebDriver basics, readers also learn about various methods to tackle synchronization and wait strategies. This chapter sheds light on Shadow DOM, automation for Animations, and design patterns such as Page Objects and Screenplay patterns.

Chapter 5 acts as the backbone for our learning experience, as we build out a full-fledged Test Automation framework. Here, readers also learn about a very important testing framework – TestNG, for adding tests in an extensible way to the test automation framework.

Chapter 6 explores Distributed Test Automation, emphasizing the importance of scaling tests via Selenium Grid across machines and browsers.

Chapter 7 provides readers insight into the field of test automation for Software as A Service (SAAS) applications. Readers also learn about automating non-functional tests like Security and Performance, using our beloved tool Selenium.

Chapter 8 raises the bar of Selenium test automation with Behavior Driven Development (BDD). Wouldn't it be great if non-technical users could read and execute our Selenium tests? In the quest to answer this question, readers learn about Cucumber and add Gherkin-syntax tests to their arsenal.

Chapter 9 covers the new features in Selenium 4 and is a true milestone in the journey of Selenium. Readers get exposure to the full array of upgrades in Selenium, ranging from updates in the architecture characterized by the Bi-Directional (BiDi) protocol to cutting-edge features like network interception and relative locators.

Chapter 10 provides the readers with strategic topics such as the Return on Investment (ROI) of test automation and ways to tackle maintenance for automation codebase. The chapter also covers tactical skills like extending browser automation with Excel interactions. Readers conclude the chapter with key topics such as designing Data-driven and Keyword-driven frameworks.

Chapter 11 provides insights into the future of test automation, covering topic such as using Artificial Intelligence (AI) for Test automation and Prompt engineering. To ensure a holistic learning experience, the chapter also covers GIT basics. Given Selenium as an open-source project, readers will also learn ways to get involved in the open-source community and utilize its benefits.

Get a Free eBook

We hope you are enjoying your recently purchased book! Your feedback is incredibly valuable to us, and to all other readers looking for great books.

If you found this book helpful or enjoyable, we would truly appreciate it, if you could take a moment to leave a short review with a 5 star rating on Amazon. It helps us grow, and lets other readers discover our books.

As a thank you, we would love to send you a free digital copy of this book, and a **30%** discount code on your next cart value on our official websites:

www.orangeava.com

www.orangeava.in (For Indian Subcontinent)

☑ **Here's how:**

Leave a review for the book on Amazon.

Take a screenshot of your review, and send an email to **info@orangeava.com** (it can be just the confirmation screen).

Once, we receive your screenshot, we will send you the digital file, within 24 hours.

Thank you so much for your support – it means a lot to us!

Downloading the code bundles and colored images

Please follow the links or scan the QR codes to download the
Code Bundles and Images of the book:

https://github.com/ava-orange-education/Ultimate-Selenium-WebDriver-for-Test-Automation

The code bundles and images of the book are also hosted on
https://rebrand.ly/a0b09d

In case there's an update to the code, it will be updated on the existing GitHub repository.

Errata

We take immense pride in our work at **Orange Education Pvt Ltd,** and follow best practices to ensure the accuracy of our content to provide an indulging reading experience to our subscribers. Our readers are our mirrors, and we use their inputs to reflect and improve upon human errors, if any, that may have occurred during the publishing processes involved. To let us maintain the quality and help us reach out to any readers who might be having difficulties due to any unforeseen errors, please write to us at :

errata@orangeava.com

Your support, suggestions, and feedback are highly appreciated.

DID YOU KNOW

Did you know that Orange Education Pvt Ltd offers eBook versions of every book published, with PDF and ePub files available? You can upgrade to the eBook version at **www.orangeava.com** and as a print book customer, you are entitled to a discount on the eBook copy. Get in touch with us at: **info@orangeava.com** for more details.

At **www.orangeava.com**, you can also read a collection of free technical articles, sign up for a range of free newsletters, and receive exclusive discounts and offers on AVA™ Books and eBooks.

PIRACY

If you come across any illegal copies of our works in any form on the internet, we would be grateful if you would provide us with the location address or website name. Please contact us at **info@orangeava.com** with a link to the material.

ARE YOU INTERESTED IN AUTHORING WITH US?

If there is a topic that you have expertise in, and you are interested in either writing or contributing to a book, please write to us at **business@orangeava.com**. We are on a journey to help developers and tech professionals to gain insights on the present technological advancements and innovations happening across the globe and build a community that believes Knowledge is best acquired by sharing and learning with others. Please reach out to us to learn what our audience demands and how you can be part of this educational reform. We also welcome ideas from tech experts and help them build learning and development content for their domains.

REVIEWS

Please leave a review. Once you have read and used this book, why not leave a review on the site that you purchased it from? Potential readers can then see and use your unbiased opinion to make purchase decisions. We at Orange Education would love to know what you think about our products, and our authors can learn from your feedback. Thank you!

For more information about Orange Education, please visit **www.orangeava.com**.

Table of Contents

CHAPTER 1

Introduction to Selenium Test Automation

Introduction

As of 2023, there are approximately 1.5 billion websites on the world wide web, with around 200 million being very active. In this vast and ever-expanding digital landscape, Selenium Test Automation has emerged as an increasingly popular and indispensable tool in the realm of web application automation. As technology continues to evolve and the demand for efficient, reliable software intensifies, Selenium shines as a crucial resource for developers and quality assurance professionals. This first chapter serves as your portal to comprehending how Selenium can transform your testing approach, enhancing speed, accuracy, and versatility.

Our journey begins with an introduction to Selenium, highlighting its significance and why it has become the go-to choice for automated testing in diverse sectors such as healthcare, education, and finance. The true elegance of Selenium resides in its capability to emulate human interactions in a native fashion.

Then we will discuss Selenium IDE in detail, a browser extension that allows users to record, edit, and replay tests without writing any code. This way we can get a flavor of Selenium, without getting into too much detail. We will examine its limitations, as well as its advantages, and compare it with Selenium WebDriver.

By the end of this chapter, you will have a foundation in Selenium Test Automation, equipped with the knowledge to start your journey. So, let's embark on this exciting trail together and discover how Selenium can revolutionize the way you approach software test automation.

Note: The statistics at the beginning of this section are inspired from https://www.internetlivestats.com/total-number-of-websites/.

Structure

In this chapter, we will discuss the following topics:

- Introduction to Selenium
- Advantages of Selenium
- Getting started with Selenium
- Selenium IDE

Introduction to Selenium

Selenium is a browser automation tool that can help in automating various repetitive tasks such as web crawling, scraping, portal administration and most importantly software testing. The Selenium family of tools comprises three components:

- **Selenium WebDriver**: Selenium WebDriver refers to both the language bindings and the implementations of the individual browser-controlling code. This is commonly referred to as just WebDriver. Selenium WebDriver uses a "WebDriver" interface to interact with web browsers using language-specific bindings (like Java, Python, and .NET). This interface defines a set of methods to navigate between pages, interact with page elements (such as clicking buttons or filling in text fields), and perform other tasks. One of the key benefits of using Selenium WebDriver is that it allows you to write tests in a way that closely resembles how a human user interacts with a website. This makes it easier to write tests that accurately simulate real-world usage scenarios. Overall, Selenium WebDriver is a powerful tool for automating web application testing that offers a wide range of capabilities and flexibility for developers and testers. We will cover WebDriver in detail in *Chapter 3: Selenium WebDriver Basics.*
- **Selenium IDE**: Selenium IDE (Integrated Development Environment) is a browser-based tool that allows you to create, record, and playback automated tests for web applications. It is an open-source project that is available as a Firefox plugin and as a Chrome extension.

Selenium IDE provides a user-friendly interface that allows users to record interactions with a web application and convert them into automated tests. This is done by recording user interactions, such as clicks and keystrokes, and generating test scripts in a format called JSON.

Selenium IDE has several features that make it a useful tool for automated testing. For example, it allows you to add assertions to your tests to verify that specific elements on a web page are present or have certain properties. It also allows you to define variables and use flow control statements, making it possible to write complex tests.

One of the advantages of using Selenium IDE is that it allows non-technical users to create automated tests without having to write code. However, it also provides an option to export the recorded test script to different programming languages, such as Java or Python, so that technical users can customize and extend the tests as needed.

Overall, Selenium IDE is a useful tool for creating simple automated tests for web applications. While it may not have the same level of functionality and flexibility as Selenium WebDriver, it can still be a valuable tool for teams that are just starting with automated testing or for non-technical users who need to create and run tests quickly and easily.

- **Selenium GRID**: Selenium Grid is a tool that allows you to run Selenium tests in parallel across multiple machines and browsers. It is a server that enables you to distribute your tests across different machines, thereby reducing the time required to run the tests and increasing the efficiency of your testing process. Selenium Grid works by creating a hub that manages the distribution of tests to multiple nodes. Each node is a machine that has a specific configuration, such as a specific operating system, browser version, or screen resolution. By adding nodes with different configurations to the grid, you can test your web application across multiple environments, ensuring that it works correctly on all of them. When a test is executed on the Selenium Grid, it is sent to the hub, which then forwards it to an available node that matches the desired configuration. The node then runs the test and sends the results back to the hub. This process can be repeated with multiple nodes, allowing you to run tests in parallel and significantly reducing the time required to complete the testing process. Selenium Grid supports various programming languages such as Java, Python, Ruby, and C#. It also supports different browsers including Google Chrome, Mozilla Firefox, Safari, and Edge. If you want to scale by distributing and running tests on several machines and manage multiple environments from a central point, making it easy to run the tests against a vast combination of browsers/OS, then you want to use Selenium Grid. We will cover GRID in detail in Chapter 6: Distributed Test Automation.

Selenium: The Origin Story

In 2004, Jason Huggins and his team were tasked with filling timesheets at their organization. This timesheet portal had a caveat, every time a new row had to be added, the web application would make a server call increasing the wait time for the user. Jason thought of automating the application with JavaScript as he observed the task to be repetitive and manually time-consuming. He wrote a small utility to accomplish the task and it gained popularity within his team as it was simple to use and easily saved the user time and effort with using the timesheet application. As this utility was gaining momentum, Jason made a joke mocking a competitor saying that you can cure mercury poisoning by taking selenium supplements. The others that received the email took the name and ran with it. And since then, the project has been called Selenium.

> *Selenium has been used for over 20 years and is based on industry standards, backed by Microsoft, Google, Apple, and Mozilla. This extensive experience has enabled Selenium to develop a robust and flexible tool that can handle the complexities of the modern web. This flexibility enables developers to write solid tests that can handle the advanced features of the modern web. Selenium is also open-source, which means that it is free to use and can be customized to meet the user's specific needs. By leveraging Selenium, developers can write efficient and reliable tests that can help streamline the software development process.*
>
> - Diego Molina, Technical Lead at Selenium Project and Staff Software Engineer at Sauce Labs.

Advantages of Selenium

Selenium test automation has become an essential tool for software development companies as it offers several advantages over traditional manual testing methods. In this section, we will discuss the advantages of Selenium test automation and explore how it can improve the efficiency and effectiveness of your software testing process.

- **Faster Test Execution**: One of the most significant advantages of Selenium test automation is faster test execution. Automated tests run faster than manual tests, which saves time and increases the efficiency of the testing process. With Selenium, you can execute multiple tests in parallel, reducing the time required to complete the testing process. For example, a team of manual testers may take several days to complete a series of tests, whereas the same tests can be completed in a matter of hours using Selenium.
- **Improved Test Coverage**: Another advantage of Selenium test automation is improved test coverage. Automated tests can cover a wider range of scenarios and test cases than manual tests, which helps to identify more bugs and issues. Automated tests can also be run repeatedly without incurring additional costs, which means that you can test your application thoroughly without exceeding your testing budget. This ensures that your application is thoroughly tested before it is released to the market.
- **Increased accuracy**: Manual testing is prone to errors, but automated testing using Selenium is highly accurate. Automated tests are programmed to execute the same way every time, ensuring that the same steps are followed and the same data is entered. This means that the results of automated tests are highly reliable and can be used to identify issues with a high degree of confidence.
- **Cost savings**: Selenium test automation can also save money by reducing the need for manual testers. Automated tests can be run at any time, which means that testing can be performed outside of normal working hours. This can lead to significant cost savings, as manual testers would otherwise need to be paid overtime or additional wages. Automated tests can also be run repeatedly without incurring additional costs, which means that you can test your application thoroughly without exceeding your testing budget.
- **Flexibility**: Selenium test automation is highly flexible and can be customized to meet the specific needs of your software development process. Selenium supports a wide range of programming languages and tools, which means that it can be integrated into your existing software development process seamlessly. It can also be used to test a wide range of web applications, from simple websites to complex enterprise applications.

To illustrate the advantages of Selenium test automation, let's consider a hypothetical scenario. Imagine that you are developing an e-commerce website that needs to be tested thoroughly before it is released to the market. You have two options: manual testing or Selenium test automation.

Manual testing would require a team of testers to manually perform tests on the website. This would be time-consuming and expensive, as the team would need to be paid for their time. Additionally, manual testing is prone to errors, which means that the results may not be reliable.

In contrast, Selenium test automation would allow you to execute tests quickly and accurately. You could create automated tests that cover a wide range of scenarios and test cases, ensuring that the website is thoroughly tested before it is released to the market. Automated tests can be executed repeatedly, ensuring that any issues are identified and fixed before the website is released.

To further illustrate the advantages of Selenium test automation, let us consider a comparison table between manual testing and Selenium test automation:

	Repetitive manual checks	**Selenium Test Automation**
Test Speed	Slow	Fast
Test Coverage	Limited	Comprehensive
Accuracy	Prone to errors	Highly accurate
Cost	Expensive	Cost-effective
Flexibility	Limited	Highly flexible

***Table 1.1**: (Comparison of repetitive manual checks and automated selenium tests)*

Evidently, Selenium test automation offers several advantages over manual testing, including faster test execution, and efficient and effective test coverage with a pragmatic Return on investment.

Let us explore some more advantages of Selenium test automation in different domains as follows:

- **Consistency and Reliability**: One of the major advantages of Selenium test automation is consistency and reliability. In healthcare, for example, testing medical software is critical as a minor mistake can have serious implications. Automated tests provide a consistent and reliable way to test medical software. Automated tests can be written to simulate a wide range of user interactions, ensuring that all possible scenarios are tested.
- **Compliance with Regulations**: Healthcare, Edtech, and BFSI (Banking, Financial Services, and Insurance) domains have to comply with various regulations, and testing is an essential part of this process. Selenium

test automation can help ensure compliance by providing consistent and reliable tests. In the BFSI domain, for example, it is essential to test software that deals with financial transactions. Automated tests can simulate different financial transactions, such as online money transfers, credit card payments, and stock trading, to ensure that the software complies with industry regulations.

- **Faster Testing**: Selenium test automation can help speed up the testing process in all three domains. In Edtech, for example, automated tests can help test learning management systems, which are used to deliver online courses. Automated tests can simulate different student interactions, such as taking quizzes and submitting assignments. By automating these tests, the testing process can be completed faster and more efficiently.
- **Increased Test Coverage**: Selenium test automation can help increase test coverage in healthcare, Edtech, and BFSI domains. In healthcare, for example, automated tests can simulate different medical scenarios, such as patient data entry and medical record keeping. By automating these tests, testers can ensure that all possible scenarios are tested, improving the overall test coverage.
- **Cost Savings**: Selenium test automation can help save costs in all three domains. In BFSI, for example, automating tests for financial transactions can help reduce costs associated with manual testing. Automated tests can be executed repeatedly without incurring additional costs, ensuring that the testing process does not exceed the testing budget. Similarly, in Edtech, automating tests can help reduce the need for a large testing team, resulting in significant cost savings.
- **Improved Test Accuracy**: Selenium test automation can help improve test accuracy in all three domains. In Edtech, for example, automated tests can help ensure that online courses function correctly, and students are assessed accurately. Automated tests can be written to simulate different student interactions, such as taking quizzes and submitting assignments, ensuring that the course content is functioning correctly.

In conclusion, Selenium test automation provides numerous advantages in healthcare, Edtech, and BFSI domains. It helps ensure consistency and reliability, compliance with regulations, faster testing, increased test coverage, cost savings, and improved test accuracy. By automating tests, testers can ensure that all possible scenarios are tested, resulting in software that is reliable, efficient, and meets industry standards.

Getting started with Selenium

Getting started with Selenium could be easy or very easy depending on who you ask. For our case, we will ease into the topic with some hands-on experience with Selenium IDE and then switch things up in *Chapter 3: Selenium WebDriver Basics.*

As mentioned earlier, Selenium is an umbrella project with three components:

- Selenium WebDriver
- Selenium GRID
- Selenium IDE

We will look at getting started with a low code approach to Selenium and test automation with the usage of Selenium IDE so that you can easily create and run tests. After that, we will discuss the basics of Selenium WebDriver and how to use it to interact with web elements. You will learn how to locate elements using various methods such as ID, name, class, and XPath. We will also cover how to handle different types of web elements like text boxes, dropdowns, checkboxes, and radio buttons. Additionally, we will dive into advanced topics like how to work with frames, alerts, and windows. Finally, we will look at best practices for Selenium automation testing. This will allow us to write effective and maintainable tests that can be integrated into continuous integration pipelines.

Selenium IDE

Selenium IDE is a browser extension that allows you to record, edit, and replay tests without writing any code. It is a great tool for beginners who want to get started with Selenium quickly. To get started, you need to install Selenium IDE in your browser.

Note: From this point onwards, we will run various hands-on exercises and code examples. Kindly execute each and every one of these, as automation and programming can be only learnt by doing it, in a hands-on manner.

Once you have installed it, you can open it and start recording your tests. Isn't that simple enough, so let's go!

Prerequisites

Before you start, you will need the following:

- A computer running Windows, macOS, or Linux
- Google Chrome browser installed on your computer

The first step to start using Selenium IDE is to install the extension in the Chrome browser. To do this, follow these steps:

1. Open Chrome browser and go to the Chrome Web Store. The URL should be: **https://chrome.google.com/webstore/category/extensions**

   Note: Download Chrome extensions from reliable sources only. Selenium IDE chrome extension should be from seleniumhq.org.

2. Search for **`Selenium IDE`** in the search bar and press *`Enter`*.

Figure 1.1: *Selenium IDE plugin page on Chrome store*

3. Click on the **`Add to Chrome`** button and confirm the installation by clicking **`Add Extension.`**

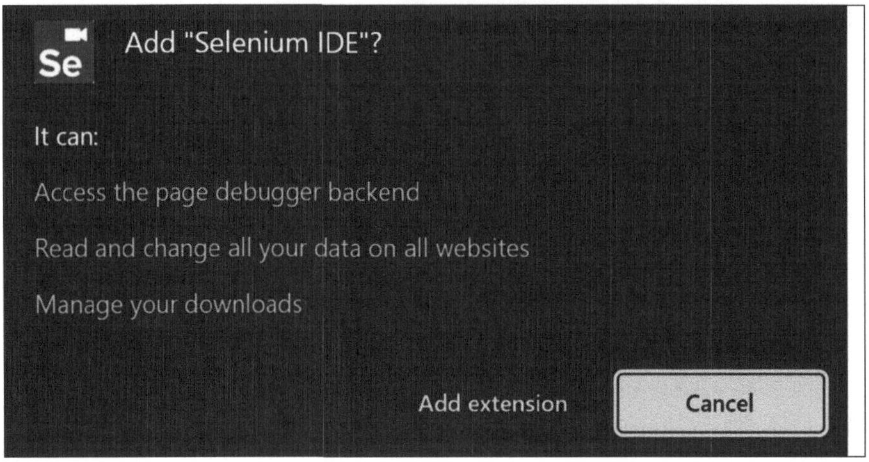

Figure 1.2: *Popup to confirm the plugin installation*

3. Wait for the extension to download and install.
4. You should now see the Selenium IDE icon in your Chrome toolbar.

   Note: If you encounter any issues during the installation process, try restarting your browser or clearing your cache.

Test Automation using IDE

Now that we have set up Selenium IDE, let us automate a simple use case:

1. Navigate to https://www.google.com and wait for the Newsletter popup.
2. Enter **`First Name`** as your name.
3. Enter **`Last Name`** as your last name.
4. Enter **`Email address`** as your email address.
5. Click on the **`Submit`** button.

In order to achieve automation for the above, let us follow the below steps:

1. Click on the **`Selenium IDE`** plugin icon.

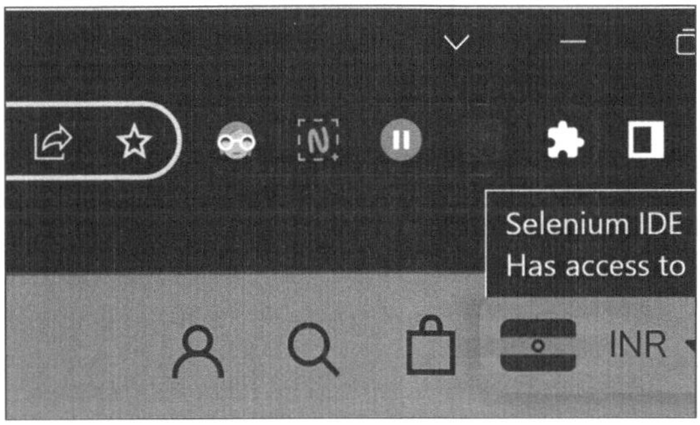

Figure 1.3: *Display of Selenium IDE as part of the Chrome extension panel*

2. Click on **`Record a new test in a new project`** in the resulting popup.

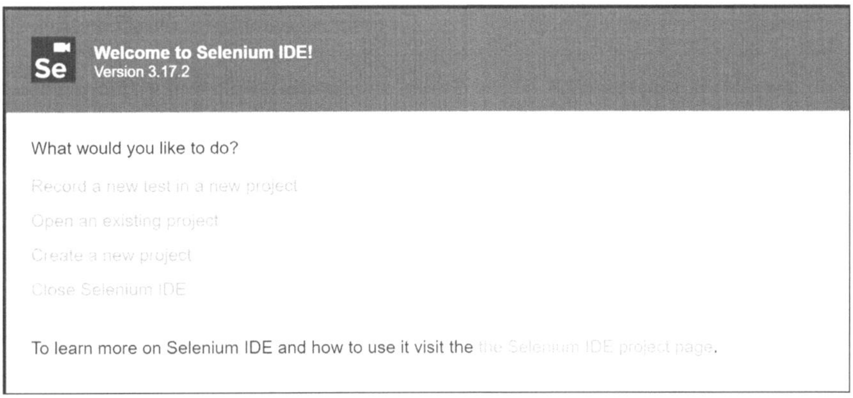

Figure 1.4: *Selenium IDE Welcome screen*

3. Enter the project name as **`Chapter_1`** in the resulting screen and press **`OK`**.

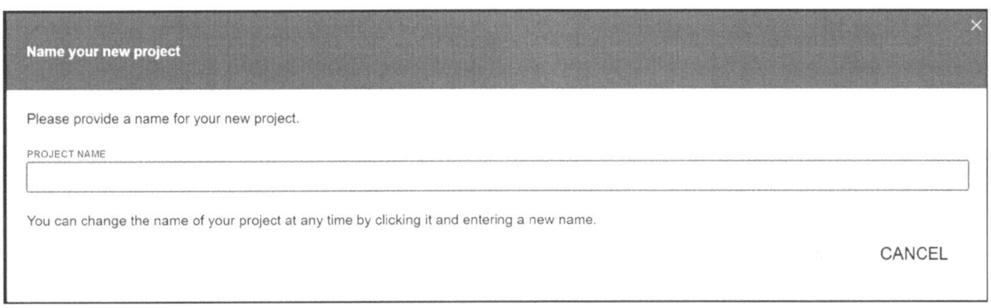

Figure 1.5: *New project creation screen*

4. After entering the Project name, we need to set the base URL for the application under test. From our sample test case above, it should be `https://orangeava.com/` in the next text box. Once you have entered the base URL, click on the **`START RECORDING`** button.

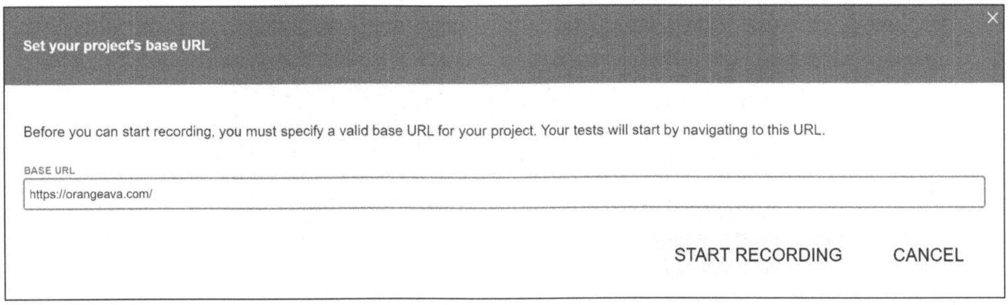

Figure 1.6: *Base URL Setup screen*

5. Clicking on the **`START RECORDING`** button, will open a new browser window and load the web page for Orange AVA publishers. Kindly notice the **`Selenium IDE is recording...`** overlay at the bottom, as it signifies that all user actions on this browser screen are being recorded by Selenium IDE. Fill up **`First Name`**, **`Last Name`**, **`Email`** fields and click on the **`Submit`** button.

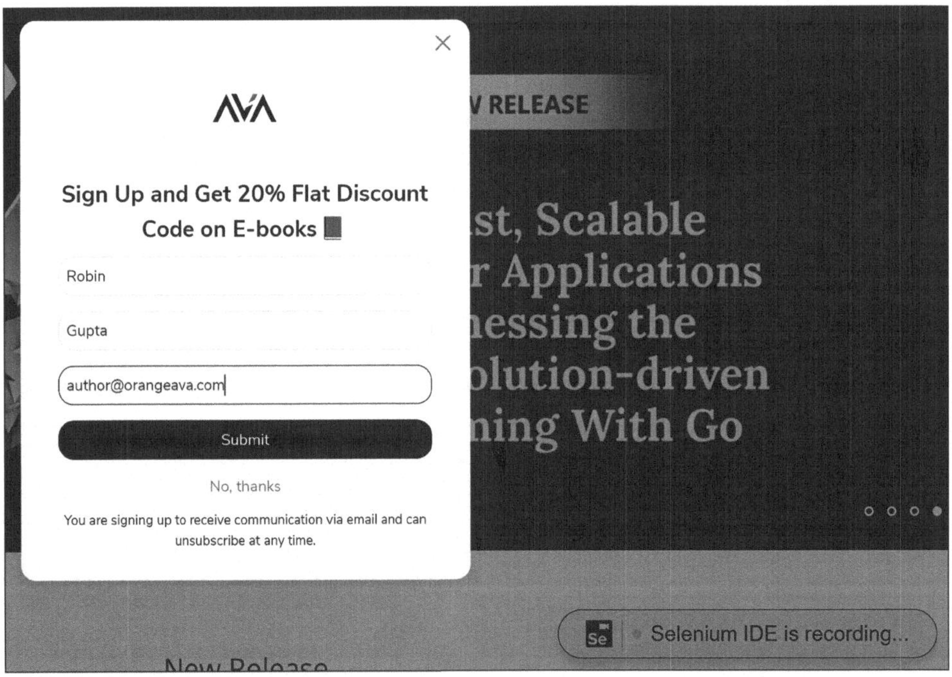

Figure 1.7: *Recording form entry steps on Orange AVA home page*

6. Navigate to Selenium IDE application window and click on **`Stop Recording`** button at the top-right location.

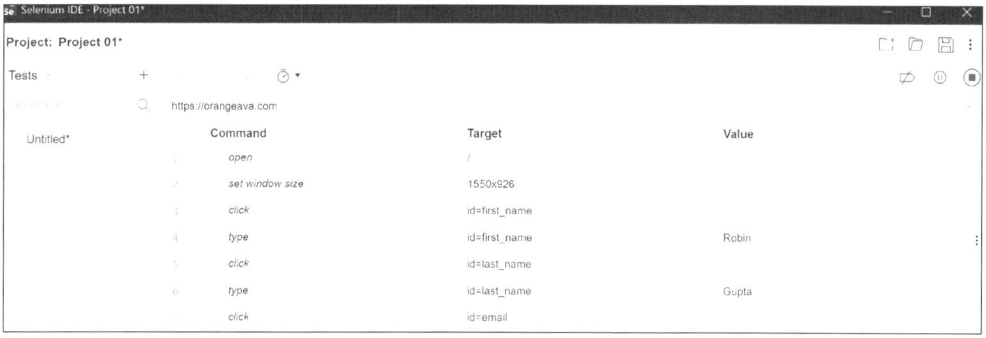

Figure 1.8: *Selenium IDE application window to stop recording*

7. Enter the Test name as **`Form Entry Test`** and click **`OK`**.

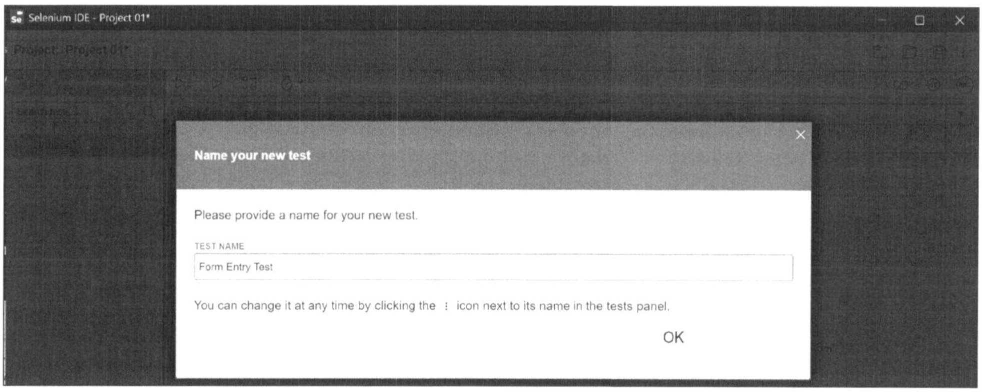

Figure 1.9: *New test naming screen*

8. On the Selenium IDE application click on the **`Run current test`** button from the top menu bar.

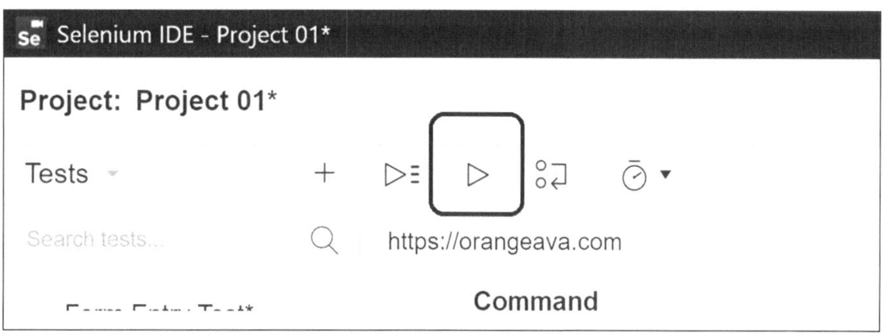

Figure 1.10: *Test execution using Run current test button*

Once you click the **`Run current test`** button, Selenium IDE will open the Chrome browser and replay all the steps recorded above.

Congrats! You have just automated and executed your first test case.

Note: If your test execution fails, do not be disheartened, as we will review the common pitfalls of web testing, debugging methods and limitations shortly.

IDE Walkthrough

Let us explore a few options and details on the **`Selenium IDE`** application.

The application window can be divided into three logical sections:

- **Test management**: The left-hand section can be utilized to create test suites for organizing tests, creating more tests or executing individual or cluster of test cases.

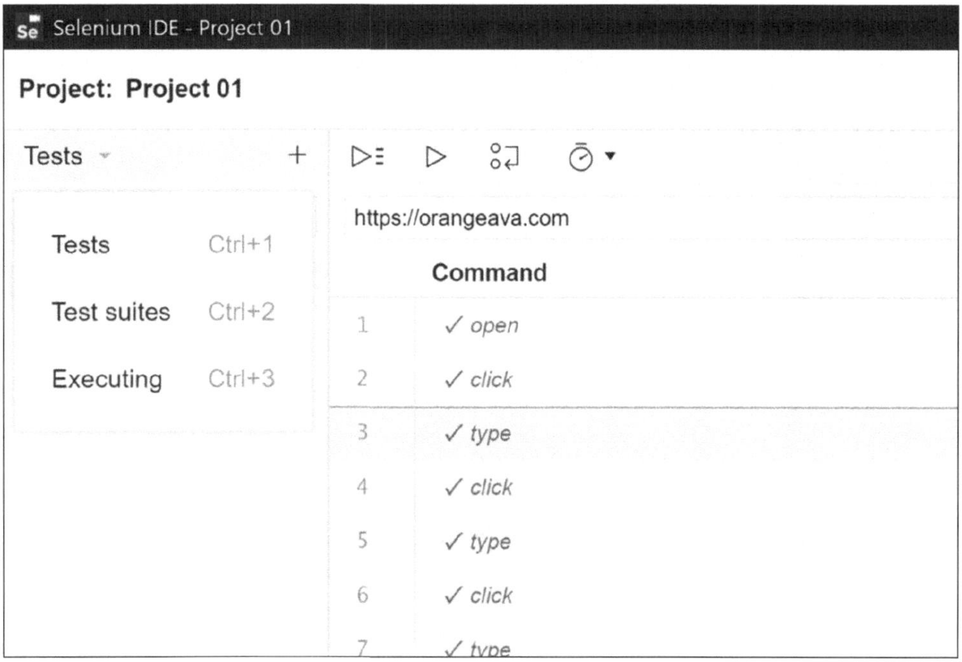

Figure 1.11: *Test management options in Selenium IDE*

- **Test Execution**: Users can execute the test steps with a variety of options here, including execution speed, pausing on exceptions, and changing commands or values as follows:

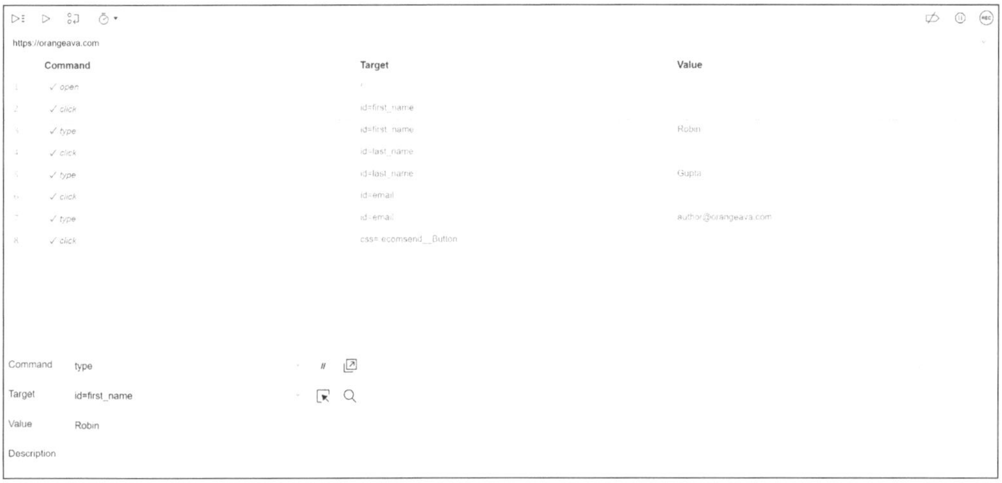

Figure 1.12: *Test execution options in Selenium IDE*

- **Logs and references**: Selenium IDE provides users with detailed execution logs for their steps, including the command executed, timestamp and any errors encountered. Users can also navigate to **`Reference`** tab and find a detailed explanation of the selected command.

Figure 1.13: *Selenium IDE Logs section*

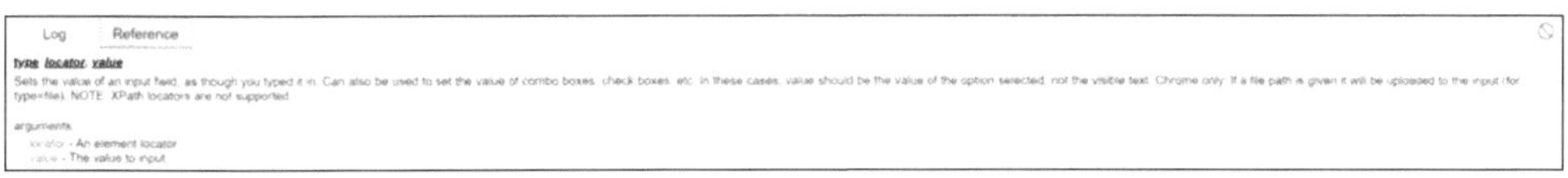

Figure 1.14: *Selenium IDE Reference section*

Debugging options

Selenium IDE comes with an array of debugging options that help you to identify and fix defects. Built-in debugging features like breakpoints and step-by-step execution help users to identify issues and enhance the efficiency of the testing process. Let us explore some of these options:

1. Breakpoints allow you to stop your test script at a specific line of code. This is useful if you have a long test script that is failing, especially if the

failure occurs near the end of the script. When a breakpoint is hit, the test script will stop running and you will be able to inspect the state of your application. You can then use the Step option to step through the code line by line, which can help you to pinpoint the source of the error. Breakpoints are a powerful debugging tool that can be used to find and fix errors in your test scripts. You can place a breakpoint in the Test script, by clicking on the numbers adjacent to the commands as follows:

***Figure 1.15**: Selenium IDE Reference section*

After placing the breakpoint, run your test and Selenium IDE will stop at the step with the breakpoint, so that user can inspect the web application's state and make corrective measures to the test script. This is especially useful for handling timeouts, popups and frames.

2. The **`Step over current command`** option allows you to run your test case one command at a time. This is very helpful for debugging, as it allows you to inspect exactly what is happening at each point in your test. This can be very useful for finding hard-to-reproduce bugs.
3. Selenium IDE also has a Pause on Exception option. When this option is enabled, the debugger will pause before a red message appears in the console or log. This allows you to inspect what is happening after something goes wrong.

In addition to the above, Selenium IDE also comes packed with some other debugging options which can be explored by clicking the three-dot icon to the right of any command as follows:

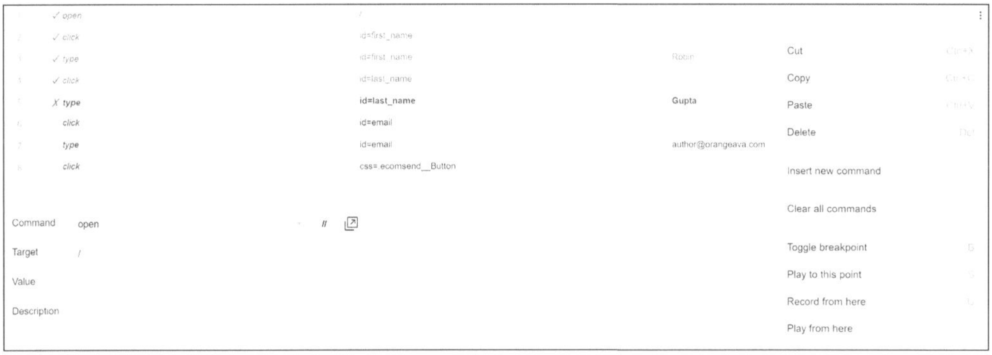

Figure 1.16: *Additional debugging and command level options*

1. **Play to this point**: This option starts the execution of the test case in a new browser and then pauses the execution, at the command, where this option is invoked. This option can be thought of as a combination of placing a breakpoint and then starting the execution of the test case.
2. **Record from here**: Assume that you would like to edit a long test case at the 11th step, due to a change in the flow, so rather than recording the whole flow again, you can activate the `Record from here` option, so that Selenium IDE can execute the test case till the 10th step in our example and then you can continue recording the updated flow.
3. **Play from here**: This option starts the execution in a new browser window, intending to execute the test case from the command, where the option is invoked.

Command Palette

Selenium IDE comes packed with 90+ commands like `Click`, `Set`, `Select`, and `Send Keys` to simulate common user actions on a web application. These commands can be utilized from the command drop down or by typing in the drop down as follows:

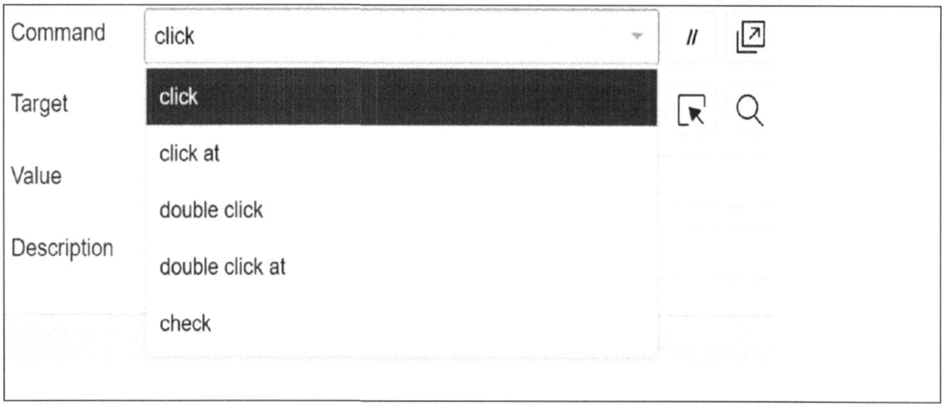

Figure 1.17: *Command selection in Selenium IDE*

Users can enable/disable the command by clicking on the `//` option next to the command drop down. Also, **`Add new window configuration`** can be utilized to simulate interactions with a new window if the command triggers opening a new browser window.

Target and Web elements

The **`Target`** option helps us choose the web elements on the web applications.

A web element is any visible or invisible part of a web page that can be interacted with by a user. This includes things like text boxes, buttons, links, images, and dropdown menus. When writing Selenium IDE tests, you will often need to interact with web elements. For example, you might need to enter text into a text box, click on a button, or select an item from a dropdown menu. To do this, you will need to use the **`Target`** to identify the web element and then perform the desired action.

There are several ways to identify web elements. You can use the element's ID, name, class, or other attributes. You can also use XPath or CSS selectors to identify web elements.

Once you have identified the web element, you can perform a variety of actions on it. You can send keys to it, click on it, or select it. You can also get the value of the element, or check whether it is enabled or disabled.

Web elements are an essential part of Selenium testing. By understanding how to identify and interact with web elements, you can write more effective and reliable tests.

Here are some examples of web elements:

- Text boxes allow users to enter text.
- Buttons perform an action when clicked.
- Links take users to a new page when clicked.
- Images display pictures.
- Dropdown menus allow users to select from a list of options.

When a user records a Selenium IDE test, it automatically captures the identifier for the web element, or the user has the following options to switch or update the identifiers:

1. Clicking on the **`Target`** dropdown, provides us with a list of web element identifiers that can be used to interact with the target web element as follows:

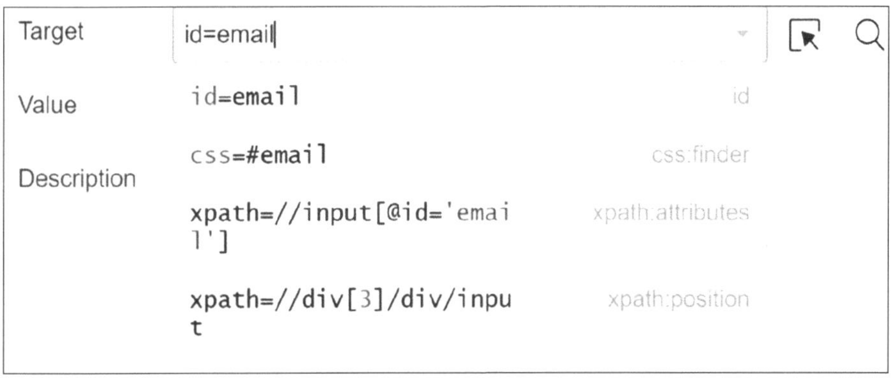

Figure 1.18: *Target selection in Selenium IDE*

Generally, **`id`** locators provide the most robust target selection strategies and are not prone to duplicates or changes. We will explore the target locator strategies such as CSS and Xpath in more detail in *Chapter 3: Selenium WebDriver Basics.*

Users can click on **`Select target in page`** to open the web application and select the web element for interaction. Last, but not the least, users can also click on **`Find target in page`** to find and highlight the web element on a web page, for closer inspection and debugging purposes.

Note: While recording a test script using Selenium IDE, users can right click on a web element and navigate to **`Selenium IDE`** sub menu item to open contextual actions such as Assert, Store, Verify and Wait For.

Additional Options

Selenium IDE has two additional controls for fine tuning test design and execution.

1. **Description field**: This field can be used to display a human readable format in the command list as follows:

Figure 1.19: *Setting the description for a command in Selenium IDE*

2. **Value field**: This field is used to enter the values into a target web element such as **`First Name`**, **`Last Name`** or **`Email.`** Users can manually enter the values or programmatically set the values using the **`store`** command. For example, if you use variables for the type command, take the following steps:

a. Create a **`store`** command to store a variable in Selenium IDE.

b. Right-click the row where the type command is and select **`Insert new command.`**

c. Click the new row that is inserted and select **`store`** from the command list.

d. Set the **`Value`** field with the variable name you want, such as username.

e. Leave the **`Target`** field blank or with a default value.

f. Click the row where the type command is again and change the Value field based on the variable name that you set in the last step.

g. Enclose the variable name in curly brackets ({}) and precede it with a dollar sign. Example as in *Figure 1.20*:

	Command	Target	Value
1	*open*	/	
2	*set window size*	1072x680	
3	*store*	demo	username
4	*type*	name=q	${username}

Figure 1.20: *Using a variable for a value field in Selenium IDE*

Conditional Logic

During the process of Selenium test automation, it is common to encounter scenarios where a set of commands must be executed only when certain conditions are met. For example, a user may need to consent to the use of cookies before proceeding with a test, or a newsletter subscription may need to be confirmed.

Selenium IDE supports conditional logic (or control flow) through conditional branching, which allows for changes in test behavior. It also supports looping through tests, where a set of commands can be executed repeatedly based on predefined criteria.

Some of the popular control flow commands that help with conditional branching and looping in Selenium IDE are:

- **`if:`** This command allows you to specify a block of code that will be executed only if the specified condition is true.
- **`else if:`** This command allows you to specify a block of code that will be executed only if the specified condition is true and the previous condition was false.
- **`else:`** This command allows you to specify a block of code that will be executed only if all the previous conditions were false.
- **`end:`** This command terminates the conditional command block. Without it the command block is incomplete and you will receive a helpful error message letting you know when trying to run your test.
- **`times:`** This command allows you to execute a block of code a specified number of times.
- **`do:`** This command allows you to execute a block of code repeatedly until a specified condition is met.
- **`repeat if:`** This command allows you to execute a block of code repeatedly until a specified condition is met, and then evaluate the condition again. The commands after the "**`do`**" will be executed first and then the expression

in the "`repeat if`" will be evaluated. If the expression returns true then the test will jump back to the "`do`" command and repeat the sequence

- **`while:`** This command allows you to execute a block of code repeatedly while a specified condition is met.
- **`forEach:`** This command allows you to iterate over a collection (e.g., a JS array) and reference each item in that collection while we do it.

By using these control flow commands, you can add more flexibility and complexity to your Selenium test automation scripts. This can help you to write more robust and reliable tests that can better mimic the behavior of real users.

Note: Selenium IDE enables users to re-use a test case. This can be enabled by adding a run command and the Target as the name of the test case, which needs to be reused as part of another test case. This can help in recording smaller flows such as logging into an application and reusing them as part of bigger flows.

Exporting the code

Users can export the either a test or suite of tests to WebDriver code by right-clicking on a test or a suite, selecting **`Export`**, choosing your target language, and clicking **`Export`**.

Here is a reference image for the **`Export`** option:

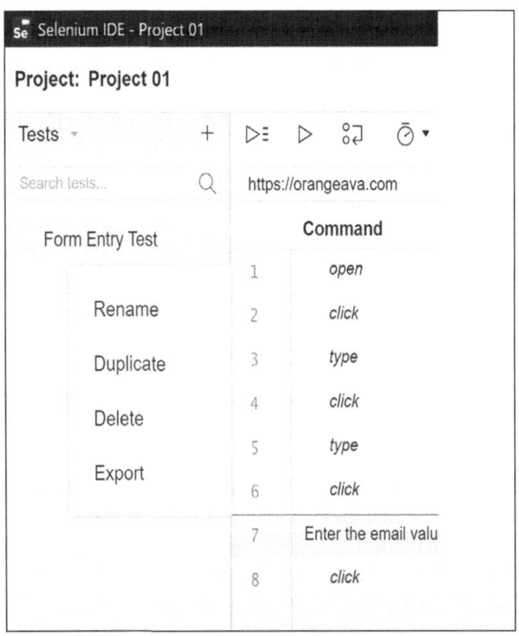

Figure 1.21: *Exporting code from Selenium IDE*

Currently Selenium IDE supports export in the following languages/frameworks:

- C# NUnit
- C# xUnit
- Java Junit
- JavaScript Mocha
- Python pytest
- Ruby RSpec

Clicking on the **Export** option provides us the following configurations:

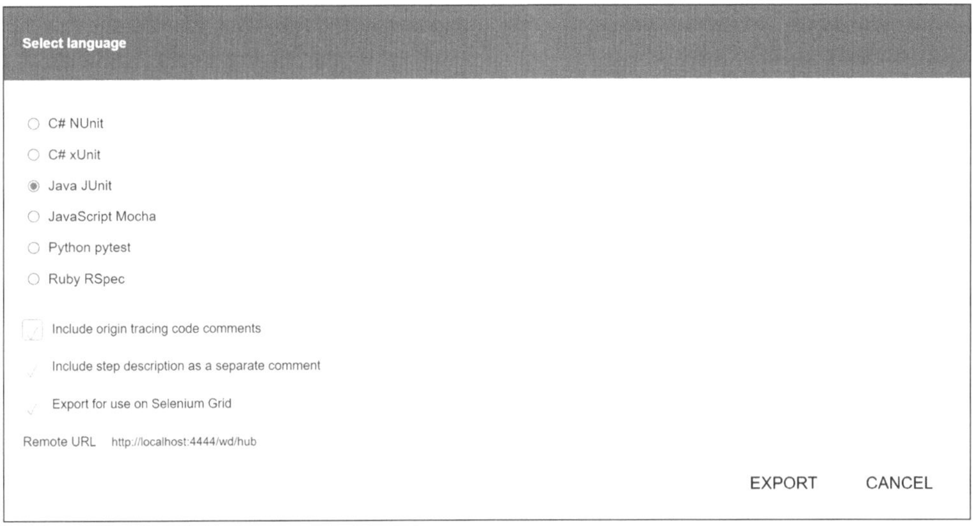

Figure 1.22: *Code export options from Selenium IDE*

In Figure 1.22, users have the following options:

1. **Include origin tracing code comments**: This option will place inline code comments in the exported file with details about the test step in Selenium IDE that generated it. Here is an example:

```
// Test name: Form Entry Test
// Step # | name | target | value
// 1 | open | / |
driver.get("https://orangeava.com/");
// 2 | click | id=first_name |
driver.findElement(By.id("first_name")).click();
```

2. **Include step description as a separate comment**: This option will place the `Description` as a commented code line in the output file as follows:

   ```
   // Enter the email value into the "email" field.
   driver.findElement(By.id("email")).sendKeys("author@orangeava.com");
   ```

3. **Export for use on Selenium Grid**: This option provides the user capability to run Selenium IDE tests on a Grid URL such as http://localhost:4444/wd/hub. And places the RemoteWebDriver configuration as follows:

   ```
   driver = new RemoteWebDriver(new URL("http://localhost:4444/wd/
   hub"), DesiredCapabilities.chrome());
   ```

Here is a snippet of the exported code in JAVA for reference:

```
public class FormEntryTestTest {
  private WebDriver driver;
  private Map<String, Object> vars;
  JavascriptExecutor js;
  @Before
  public void setUp() throws MalformedURLException {
    driver = new RemoteWebDriver(new URL("http://localhost:4444/wd/
hub"), DesiredCapabilities.chrome());
    js = (JavascriptExecutor) driver;
    vars = new HashMap<String, Object>();
  }
  @After
  public void tearDown() {
    driver.quit();
  }
  @Test
  public void formEntryTest() {
    // Test name: Form Entry Test
    // Step # | name | target | value
    // 1 | open | / |
    driver.get("https://orangeava.com/");
    // 2 | click | id=first_name |
    driver.findElement(By.id("first_name")).click();
```

```
    // 3 | type | id=first_name | Robin
    driver.findElement(By.id("first_name")).sendKeys("Robin");
    // 4 | click | id=last_name |
    driver.findElement(By.id("last_name")).click();
    // 5 | type | id=last_name | Gupta
    driver.findElement(By.id("last_name")).sendKeys("Gupta");
    // 6 | click | id=email |
    driver.findElement(By.id("email")).click();
    // 7 | type | id=email | author@orangeava.com
    // Enter the email value into the "email" field.
    driver.findElement(By.id("email")).sendKeys("author@orangeava.com");
    // 8 | click | css=.ecomsend__Button |
    driver.findElement(By.cssSelector(".ecomsend__Button")).click();
  }
}
```

Running on CLI

Selenium IDE can be utilized to run tests via the command line interface and as part of the build process. This capability can be utilized to run the tests in parallel and on Grid with minimal configuration. Here are some additional benefits of using Selenium IDE with the command line runner and Grid:

1. **Increased test speed**: Running tests in parallel and on Grid can significantly improve the speed of your test suite.
2. **Improved test coverage**: By running tests on a variety of browsers and devices, you can improve the coverage of your test suite.
3. **Reduced maintenance overhead**: The command line runner and Grid can help to reduce the maintenance overhead of your test suite.

In order to run Selenium IDE tests, we need to have a few pre-requisites installed as follows:

1. **node**: The Node.js programming language (version 8 or above)
2. **npm**: The NodeJS package manager which typically gets installed with "node"

3. **selenium-side-runner**: The Selenium IDE command line runner. Once you have "node" installed, you can install the "**`selenium-side-runner`**" with the following command on a terminal window:

   ```
   npm install -g selenium-side-runner
   ```

4. **Browser Driver**: Selenium communicates with each browser through a small binary application called a browser driver. Each browser has its own browser driver, which you can either download and add to your system path manually, or, you can use a package manager to install the latest version of the browser driver (recommended). A browser driver is a software program that allows Selenium to control a specific web browser. The browser driver communicates with the browser through a remote protocol, such as HTTP or HTTPS. This allows Selenium to send commands to the browser and receive information from the browser, such as the current page URL, the text of a web element, and the status of a web element.

Selenium supports a wide range of browser drivers, including drivers for Chrome, Firefox, Edge, Safari, and Internet Explorer. You can download the latest version of each browser driver from the Selenium website.

If you are using a package manager, such as npm or pip, you can use the package manager to install the latest version of the browser driver for your browser.

a. For Chrome, you can download Chromedriver using the below command on terminal:

   ```
   npm install -g chromedriver
   ```

b. For Microsoft Edge on a Windows PC, you can download the EdgeDriver using the following command on terminal:

   ```
   npm install -g edgedriver
   ```

c. For Firefox, you can download the geckoDriver using the below command on terminal:

   ```
   npm install -g geckodriver
   ```

Once you have setup the pre-requisites detailed in the above section, Selenium IDE tests can be run by calling the "**`selenium-side-runner`**" from the command line and targeting the **`.side`** project exported from Selenium IDE application. This can be accompalished by running the command as follows:

```
selenium-side-runner /path/to/your-project.side
```

This would run your tests by opening a Chrome browser and provides the output as follows:

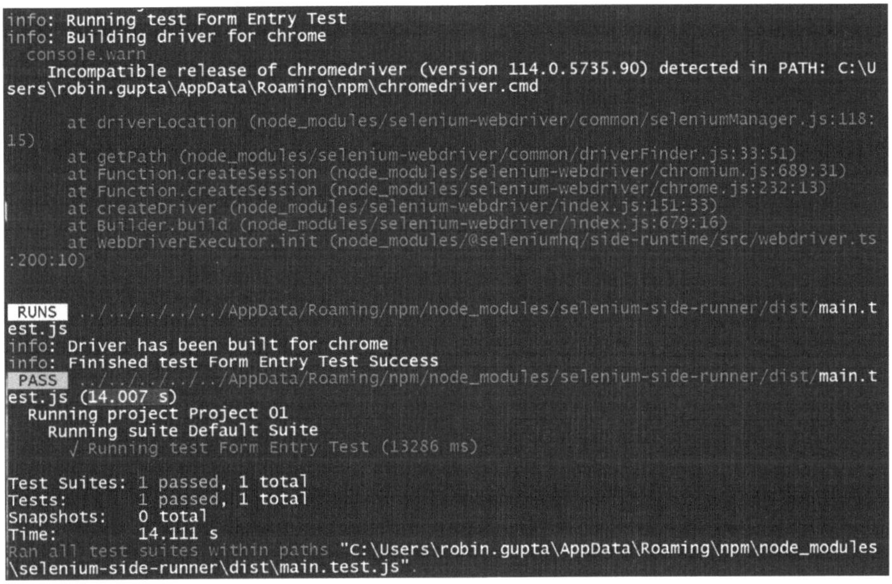

Figure 1.23: *Command line execution results from Selenium IDE Runner*

Configuring a browser: In order to change the browser to Chrome, Edge or Firefox, you can utilize the following command line options:

```
selenium-side-runner -c "browserName=chrome"
selenium-side-runner -c "browserName=edge"
selenium-side-runner -c "browserName=firefox"
```

Configuring a base URL: With the ability to specify a different base URL you can easily point your tests at different environments (e.g., local dev, test, staging, production). Here are some examples of how you might use different base URLs in your test cases:

- **Local development**: You might use a local development server to develop and test your web application. In this case, you would specify the URL of your local development server as the base URL for your test cases.
- **Testing**: You might use a testing server to test your web application before it is released to staging environment. In this case, you would specify the URL of your testing server as the base URL for your test cases.
- **Staging**: You might use a staging server to test your web application before it is released to production. In this case, you would specify the URL of your staging server as the base URL for your test cases.

- **Production**: You might use a production server to release your web application to the public. In this case, you would specify the URL of your production server as the base URL for your test cases.

The `base URL` can be changed via the command line runner as follows:

```
selenium-side-runner --base-url https://localhost
```

Writing test results to a file:

Selenium IDE users can execute the tests using command line interface, and write the detailed test results into a text compatible format. The following options can be used to output the test results:

1. `--output-directory` : This flag represents the target location where the results should be stored. This could be an absolute or a relative path.

2. `--output-format` : This flag represents the format of the output file. It can be:

   a. `jest`: For JSON output. This is also the default format. This option can be activated with the following usage:

   ```
   selenium-side-runner --output-directory=resultsfolder
   ```

   b. `junit`: For XML output. This option can be activated with the following usage:

   ```
   selenium-side-runner --output-directory=results --output-for-
   mat=junit
   ```

Key limitations and way forward

Selenium IDE, undoubtedly is a popular automation tool used to test web applications. However, it has its share of limitations that we will be discussing in detail in the subsequent sections.

One significant limitation of Selenium IDE is its inability to handle dynamic web elements. This is because it heavily relies on the recording and playback feature, which is unable to handle changes in a webpage's dynamic elements. As a result, test scripts may fail when web elements change, causing false positives or negatives.

Another limitation is the lack of programming support, which is a vital disadvantage for professional testers. The tool is meant for creating tests without the need for programming skills, but it becomes challenging to extend the script's functionality when required.

Selenium IDE may struggle with handling complex test scenarios that involve data-driven testing, parameterization, or interacting with databases or APIs.

When it comes to using Selenium IDE effectively, there are a few key strategies to keep in mind. First and foremost, always follow recording and playback best practices. This involves ensuring that tests are repeatable, and that you are capturing all the necessary steps. Additionally, be sure to understand element locators - this is crucial for making sure your tests are accurate and reliable.

Using assertions and verifications is another important part of effective Selenium IDE usage. These tools allow you to check that your tests are producing the expected results, and can help you quickly identify when things go wrong. Finally, it is important to create efficient test case workflows. This means organizing and prioritizing your tests, and making sure that everything is running as smoothly as possible.

In conclusion, while Selenium IDE is a powerful tool for automated testing, it does have some limitations. By using a programming language with Selenium WebDriver, a testing framework, and a debugger, you can overcome these limitations and create more powerful and maintainable tests.

> *Each iteration of Selenium IDE should hew closer to truly mirroring what a user is testing with their CI system. Version 2 was Firefox only and used emulated JS and some shady bridge internal patching. Version 3 supported Chrome and Firefox and used a web extension manifest 2 spec, and still used emulated JS. This was better because it supported local playback in more drivers, but both suffered from using JS for local playback, and webdriver for remote. Version 4 uses webdriver playback locally, and Electron as a binary, which means it comes with a driver built in. This is close to perfect, but there are still a few more flaws due to electron-chromedriver missing a few important APIs (setWindowSize and no support for window.prompt). By switching to bidi, we'll trade the Electron specific messaging APIs for Bidi based protocols, and that means we can run any driver with support for Bidi in local playback and recording, giving us support of all driver primitives and window builtins. That's the first goal, as that means the shared runtime of local playback can exactly mirror the shared runtime of CI playback, which is extremely important for these tools. After that, the goal will be to add hooks to let the IDE consume its own export formats via exit codes, persisted sessions, and local executions. The existing*

shared runtime is massively better than the emulated JS of before, but until we make export formats first priority in the IDE, we're basically disincentivizing the ecosystem. We want our runtime to be no more supported than java bindings, or a puppeteer format even if someone wanted to write that. Ultimately, the IDE exists as a tool for building e2e tests that will be played remotely later, and every step we take towards allowing the tool to ingest and support elements of that, whether it be the drivers and capabilities or the testing frameworks themselves, will be what decides its relevance into the future.

- Todd Tarsi, Open-source contributor, and maintainer on the Selenium IDE project.

Conclusion

As we wrap up this chapter on Selenium Test Automation, we've taken a deep dive into what makes Selenium such a useful tool for testing websites. It's like a Swiss Army knife for developers and testers, packed with different features like Selenium WebDriver, Selenium IDE, and Selenium Grid. Each of these has its own special role, from the WebDriver that drives your browser, to the IDE which lets you record and playback tests easily. We have seen how Selenium is not just powerful but also flexible, working across different browsers and supporting several programming languages.

We also explored how Selenium fits into real-life scenarios. It's not just about theory; Selenium is out there in the trenches, making a difference in industries like healthcare, education, and finance. We can use Selenium IDE to quickly validate automation scenarios and get a grip on web application automation.

In the next chapter on test automation, we delve into the essential aspects of software testing and its automation process. Beginning with an introduction to software testing, we explore the fundamentals and importance of ensuring software quality. The chapter then transitions into test automation, discussing its advantages and the tools used to streamline the testing process. We also cover test planning, which involves defining objectives, scope, and strategies for effective testing. Next, we examine test design, focusing on creating comprehensive test cases and scenarios that align with the software requirements. The chapter proceeds to discuss test execution and logging, highlighting the importance of tracking test results and identifying issues. Finally, we address test reporting, emphasizing the need to communicate test findings and insights to stakeholders for informed decision-making and continuous improvement.

Exercise

Hello champion, congrats on finishing *Chapter 1*, as we are just getting started. Let us tackle a hands-on exercise to deepen the understanding.

You need to automate the following scenario using Selenium IDE:

1. Navigate to https://orangeava.com/
2. Skip the pop up for sign up on home page by clicking the **`X`** button.
3. Click on the first book under **`New Release`** section.
4. Validate that the **`AVA`** logo at the top of the page has the correct URL for home page as https://orangeava.com/
5. After the execution, results should be stored in a JSON file via the execution from CLI.

Chapter 2
Fundamentals of Test Automation

Introduction

Welcome to the world of software testing, where we ensure that a software product is error-free, meets user requirements, and delivers a seamless user experience. Software testing is the process of evaluating a software application or system component for feedback and loopholes. Without it, our software would be like an unripe banana - you will not know what you are getting until you bite into it.

Picture this: You have just spent months developing a ground-breaking new software application. You are excited to release it to the world, but there is one crucial step you cannot afford to skip: software testing and automation. It is the unsung hero of the tech world, ensuring that your masterpiece is ready for prime time. In this chapter, we will dive into the world of software testing, exploring test planning, measurements, and management. So, whether you are a quality professional, a software engineer, or a curious learner, buckle up and get ready to learn the basics of software quality and automation!

Structure

In this chapter, we will discuss the following topics:

- Introduction to Quality
- Supercharge your Quality Journey with Automation
- Test Automation Strategy

- Test Designing for Automation
- Test Execution and Logging
- Reporting and Measurements

Introduction to Quality

The American National Standards Institute (ANSI) and the American Society for Quality (ASQ) define quality as follows:

> *The totality of features and characteristics of a product or service that bears on its ability to satisfy given needs.*

Let us break this down. Assume that you have joined a new job. On the first day of the job, you saw your new boss using a shiny expensive mobile phone. So, you aspire to buy an expensive mobile phone, from that day onwards. A year later, you buy an expensive mobile phone from your savings. On the second day itself, your phone starts hanging and freezing up. What will be your thoughts at this moment? "If only, the phone manufacturer had given a good **quality** phone."

Before we move forward, take a moment, and fill the following statement:

Quality for me means -

____

As you can observe, quality can be:

- Easy to observe but tough to measure.
- Influenced by the observer's own biases and perspectives.

Software quality refers to the degree to which a software product or system meets specified requirements and satisfies the needs and expectations of its users. It encompasses various attributes and characteristics that contribute to the overall excellence of software, ensuring its reliability, usability, maintainability, and efficiency. Achieving high software quality is vital for delivering a product that performs as intended and provides a satisfactory user experience.

You can think of software testers as **astronauts**, both peer into vast spaces, looking for the uncommon, uncovering risks while working tirelessly to improve our "quality" of life.

In the fast-paced world of software, deploying software without proper testing can be detrimental to your product, business, and reputation. Hence, software testing has become a crucial step in software development lifecycles. It is not enough to develop features or launch software products haphazardly; we need to ensure that they are of high quality and problem-free.

There are several key aspects that contribute to software quality, including:

- **Functionality**: The software should provide the features and capabilities required by the users.
- **Reliability**: The software should operate consistently and accurately under various conditions.
- **Usability:** The software should be easy to learn, use, and understand.
- **Efficiency:** The software should make optimal use of system resources, such as memory and processing power.
- **Maintainability**: The software should be easy to modify and update as needed.
- **Portability**: The software should be able to run on different platforms and environments.

These are just a few examples of software quality attributes, and achieving a high level of quality requires considering and balancing various other factors based on the specific context and requirements of the software project. By prioritizing software quality, organizations can enhance user satisfaction, reduce maintenance costs, and improve the overall success of their software products.

Several models have been proposed to help software engineers understand and measure software quality. Some of the most widely used models include:

- **ISO/IEC 25010:2011 Software Quality Model**: The ISO/IEC 25010:2011 Software Quality Model is an international standard that defines a set of quality characteristics and sub-characteristics for software products. This model is based on the premise that software quality can be measured by evaluating the product's ability to satisfy the needs of its users, as well as its adherence to specified requirements.
- **McCall's Quality Model**: McCall's Quality Model, proposed by James McCall in the 1970s, is one of the earliest software quality models. It identifies 11 quality factors that contribute to software quality, including correctness, reliability, efficiency, integrity, usability, maintainability, flexibility, testability, portability, reusability, and interoperability.
- **Boehm's Quality Model**: Boehm's Quality Model, developed by Barry Boehm in the 1980s, is another widely used software quality model. It focuses on three main aspects of software quality: product operation, product revision, and product transition. Each of these aspects is further

divided into sub-factors, such as correctness, reliability, efficiency, maintainability, and portability.

- **Dromey's Quality Model**: Dromey's Quality Model, proposed by R. Geoff Dromey in the 1990s, is a more recent approach to software quality. It emphasizes the importance of understanding the relationships between software quality attributes and the underlying software components. This model helps software engineers identify and address potential quality issues at the component level, leading to improved overall software quality.

As quality is highly contextual, it is possible for teams to follow all the above models and still see deviations in end-user expectations, resulting in production bugs.

Quality is important for both businesses and consumers. For businesses, quality can lead to increased sales, profits, and market share. It can also help businesses to build customer loyalty and improve their reputation. For consumers, quality can lead to satisfaction, safety, and peace of mind. Quality is also not absolute and is a constant journey, with feedback loops and conscious design decisions. As per Aristotle:

Quality is not an act; it is a habit.

Software Testing

Software testing is a crucial process in the software development lifecycle that involves evaluating and verifying the functionality, quality, and performance of a software application. It is performed to identify risks, defects, errors, or discrepancies between expected and actual results. The primary goal of software testing is to ensure that the software meets the specified requirements and operates smoothly for end users.

There are various types and techniques of software testing, some of which include:

- **Unit Testing**: This involves testing individual units or components of the software to ensure they function correctly in isolation. It focuses on validating the smallest testable parts of the software, such as functions or methods.

    Example: Testing a function that calculates the sum of two numbers by providing different inputs and verifying if the output matches the expected result.

- **Integration Testing**: This verifies the interactions between different software components to ensure they work together correctly. It aims to detect defects that may arise due to the integration of various modules or subsystems.

  Example: Testing the interaction between a payment module and an inventory management module to ensure that orders are correctly deducted from the inventory when payments are made.

- **System Testing**: This evaluates the behavior and performance of the entire software system as a whole. It verifies if the system meets the specified requirements and performs as expected in different scenarios.

  Example: Testing an e-commerce website by simulating user interactions such as browsing products, adding items to the cart, and completing the checkout process to ensure all functionalities work seamlessly.

- **Acceptance Testing**: This type of testing is performed to determine whether the software meets the expectations and requirements of the end users or stakeholders. It validates if the software is ready for deployment and use in a real-world environment.

  Example: Conducting user acceptance testing on a newly developed mobile application by involving a group of targeted end users to ensure it meets their needs and preferences.

- **Performance Testing**: This focuses on evaluating the software's responsiveness, scalability, and stability under different workloads and conditions. It aims to identify performance bottlenecks and ensure the software can handle expected user loads.

  Example: Stress testing a web server by simulating a large number of concurrent user requests to assess its performance and determine if it can handle the expected traffic without crashing or slowing down.

These are just a few examples of software testing types, and there are several others, such as regression testing, security testing, usability testing, and more. The choice of testing techniques and approaches depends on the specific requirements, constraints, and objectives of the software development project.

Software testing is critical, as it saves time, money, and curtails frustrations for developers and end-users alike. It is like a risk check - no one wants to pay for a substandard product. By testing software, we ensure that it is ready to handle user-input, conforms to business requirements, and performs the required task without breaking down. Even the slightest bug can cause significant problems, hence the importance of testing software before deployment.

In the fast-paced world of software, deploying software without proper testing can be detrimental to your product, business, and reputation. Hence, software testing has become a crucial step in software development lifecycles. It is not enough to develop features or launch software products haphazardly; we need to ensure that they are of high quality and problem-free.

Supercharge your Quality Journey with Automation

Traditionally, software testing has been a tedious, time-consuming, and expensive process that requires a significant investment. Manual testing methods can lead to human errors, inconsistencies in testing, and a longer time-to-market. Hence, automating software testing has become a necessity in the software development world.

Test automation enables businesses to test software much quicker, more efficiently, and with higher accuracy than traditional methods. Automation also helps in saving costs, improving quality assurance, and increasing test coverage, making it a clear winner alongside the manual testing process.

Integrating test automation with agile software development methods ensures greater transparency in the software development process and early detection of bugs, leading to a quicker resolution. With user-friendly tools, simplified maintenance, and training available, it is an easy solution for businesses to take advantage of.

Overall, automated software testing is becoming a necessity in this ever-changing digital world, where innovation drives growth. Stay ahead of the competition by embracing automated software testing and reap the benefits of leaner and quicker testing cycles, an increased frequency of deployments, and a greater ability to innovate.

Let us take an example: You are the CEO of a large software company. Your team has developed an exemplar website to sell online books around test automation. In this case, the primary use case for the website is the ability for the user to search for a title, add it to cart and complete the check-out use case. Isn't that pretty simple, and it would take under 5 minutes for your engineer to verify? Now, this same process needs to be repeated for all the sections of the website. And mind you, the website is supposed to function well on major browsers like Google Chrome and Firefox. After the first successful launch of the website, your team needs to ensure that the basic smoke scenarios like checkout, user registration, search, and listings work well on devices across a variety of network conditions, geographies, browsers, and mobile views. The combinatorial scenarios grow exponentially with every feature and quickly raise the heartbeat of you as the CEO as well. This is where test automation can help you achieve quality at scale, and match the velocity of development, by automated checking of regression features in order to balance agility and quality.

Test Automation brings along a bundle of benefits as follows:

- **Enhanced Test Coverage**: Let us face it - traditional testing methods can be tedious and time-consuming. Not to mention, manual testing can be prone to subjective errors. Test automation allows for enhanced test coverage, including repetitive testing, improved regression testing, and greater device coverage. With the ability to run tests continuously and parallelly, you can identify bugs early in the development process and avoid costly delays. Imagine having the ability to test across various devices, operating systems, and browsers - that is the kind of power test automation brings to the table. By automating your testing, you can ensure your product works seamlessly across all platforms and configurations. And let us not forget about the time savings! Automated tests run much faster than manual tests, allowing you to cover more ground in less time. Additionally, with the ability to run tests more frequently without requiring additional human resources, your testing process becomes much more efficient. Test automation is reliable, consistent, and, most importantly, saves you time and money. By enabling faster testing, improving test coverage, and enhancing the quality of your product, test automation can help keep your business ahead of the competition.
- **Early Detection of Bugs:** Nobody likes bugs, except maybe entomologists. But for the rest of us, bugs are a menace. Traditional testing methods are manual and, as such, prone to human error. Bugs can go undetected for days, weeks, months, and in some cases, even years. Want to know what is worse than finding a bug? Finding multiple bugs. Want to know what is even worse? Finding multiple bugs late in the development process. This is why you need test automation. It facilitates the early detection of bugs, which means faster troubleshooting, more comprehensive testing, and improved feedback loops. Bugs cannot hide from automated testing tools, and neither can their loyal companion, glitches.

Automated testing tools can run multiple tests simultaneously, making it easier to detect bugs early in the development process. This kind of testing and early detection is crucial to producing a superior product. Imagine releasing a new app only to have a user write a review saying, "App keeps crashing. Would not recommend." Yikes. With test automation, you can avoid all that. You can spot bugs and glitches before they become bigger issues, and that means a more stable, reliable, and trustworthy product for your clients.

> *In its 20 years of existence, Selenium has been a trailblazer in the change of making test automation a realistic way of continuously documenting our intent. While Selenium drives the browser and is extended by various libraries and frameworks for testing, it also creates a pathway to learn programming one library and api at a time, growing within the main language without a limit.*
>
> *Test automation helps us keep track of what we had to keep it around; ad it helps us simulate more complex scenarios from our future. It brings together the attended and unattended tasks of testing and serves as an asset that stays when people leave. As long as we make it worthwhile.*
>
> \- Maaret Pyhäjärvi, Testing Specialist and Development Manager at Vaisala. Project Leadership Committee member at the Selenium Project.

The advantages of test automation go beyond just early detection of bugs. Automated testing saves significant time and effort compared to manual testing. After all, manual testing is a tedious task, and humans are prone to overlook or miss bugs due to fatigue or lack of attention. On the other hand, automation ensures a more thorough and accurate testing process.

Test automation not only speeds up the bug detection process but also simplifies the work of engineers. Manually testing every feature and functionality of an application is a daunting task, but automated tests make it easier for engineers to verify and validate code changes. Furthermore, by automating tests, engineers can execute tests more frequently, ensuring that the newly added features do not negatively impact the existing functionalities of an application.

In summary, test automation ensures accurate and timely detection of bugs, simplifies the work of engineers, saves time and effort, and helps produce a superior product. So, if you want your application to be stable, reliable, and bug-free, consider investing in test automation tools and strategies.

- **Integration with Development Process:** Integrating test automation with the development process is a crucial step in improving the efficiency and accuracy of software testing. When done correctly, this integration can lead to a seamless collaboration between development and testing teams, resulting in project success.

One of the benefits of test automation is its ability to integrate with agile methodologies, making it easy to execute tests throughout the development stage. With this integration, there is improved collaboration between the development and testing teams, ensuring that the software meets the desired quality standards.

Apart from improved collaboration, this integration also brings greater transparency to the development process. Teams can track and monitor the progress of tests and identify potential roadblocks upfront. This allows for faster troubleshooting and ultimately enables faster delivery of high-quality software.

In summary, integrating test automation with the development process is critical for software development success. It allows for seamless collaboration between teams, brings greater transparency, and ultimately improves the accuracy and efficiency of the testing process.

- **Reliability:** We've all heard the phrase, "human error." There is no denying that manual testing is subject to such error. By implementing test automation into your business's testing process, you reduce the error factor in repetitive tasks and create a more reliable testing environment. Automated testing provides consistent results time and time again, which means fewer discrepancies and errors. It also dramatically lowers the likelihood of testing failure, which any business or developer can undoubtedly agree, is a massive win. When you invest time, effort and resources in automation, your business, your team, and your customers will thank you.
- **Stay Ahead of the Competition:** Want to outdo your competitors? Test automation is the way to go. You will enjoy leaner and quicker testing cycles, deploy more frequently, and innovate faster. Automated tools perform tasks faster and with fewer errors. As a result, you will cut down on testing time and quickly get your product to your customers.

In summary, test automation is the key to achieving increased efficiency, improved quality assurance, reduced costs, and reduced Go-To-Market times. With enhanced test coverage, early detection of bugs, and seamless integration with development processes, businesses can stay ahead of the competition. Furthermore, with user-friendly tools like Selenium, simplified maintenance, and reliability, businesses can enjoy consistency and lower failure rates. Above all, test automation has become a critical component that helps businesses innovate by streamlining testing procedures while reducing deployment times. This is why businesses need to incorporate test automation into their systems and keep themselves updated with new technologies and advancements while ensuring continuous testing and making automation an integral part of their software development lifecycle.

Test Automation Strategy

In today's fast-paced software development landscape, test automation has become a critical component of ensuring quality and efficiency. A well-defined test automation strategy can help organizations streamline their testing efforts, increase test coverage, reduce time-to-market, and improve overall software reliability. This section delves into the key elements of a robust test automation strategy, including test data management, scope of testing, reusable assets, resources, timelines, and risks. We will explore each topic in detail and provide examples to illustrate their significance.

- **Test Data Management**

Test data management (TDM) is a crucial aspect of a test automation strategy, as it ensures that the right data is available for testing at the right time. TDM involves the creation, storage, and maintenance of test data, which can be used to validate the functionality, performance, and security of the software.

- **Data Generation**: Test data can be generated using various methods, such as manual data entry, data masking, synthetic data generation, and data sub-setting. Each method has its advantages and drawbacks, so it is essential to choose the most suitable approach based on the specific requirements of the project.

  Example: In a banking application, synthetic data generation can be used to create realistic customer profiles, transaction histories, and account balances without exposing sensitive customer information.

- **Data Storage:** Test data should be stored in a centralized repository, which can be accessed by all team members involved in the testing process. This ensures consistency and reduces the risk of data duplication or corruption.

  Example: A cloud-based storage solution can be used to store test data, allowing testers to access the data from anywhere and at any time.

- **Data Maintenance**: Regular maintenance of test data is essential to ensure its accuracy and relevance. This includes updating the data to reflect changes in the application, removing obsolete data, and ensuring data integrity.

Example: In an e-commerce application, test data should be updated regularly to include new products, price changes, and promotional offers.

- **Scope of Testing**

Defining the scope of testing is a critical step in developing a test automation strategy. It involves identifying the areas of the application that will be tested, the types of tests to be performed, and the test automation tools and frameworks to be used.

- **Test Coverage**: Test coverage refers to the extent to which the application is tested. It is essential to strike a balance between thorough testing and efficient use of resources. A risk-based approach can be used to prioritize the testing of critical functionalities and high-risk areas of the application.

  Example: In a healthcare application, the functionality related to patient data management and treatment plans should be prioritized for testing, as any errors in these areas could have severe consequences.

- **Test Types**: Various types of tests can be automated, such as functional testing, performance testing, security testing, and regression testing. The choice of test types depends on the specific requirements of the project and the available resources.

  Example: In a mobile application, functional testing can be automated to validate the user interface and navigation, while performance testing can be automated to measure the application's response time and resource usage.

- **Test Automation Tools and Frameworks**: The selection of test automation tools and frameworks is a critical factor in the success of a test automation strategy. Factors to consider when choosing a tool or framework include ease of use, compatibility with the application's technology stack, and the availability of support and documentation.

  Example: Selenium is a popular test automation tool for web applications, while Appium is widely used for mobile application testing.

- **Reusable Assets**

Reusable assets are components of the test automation process that can be used across multiple projects or testing scenarios. These assets can help reduce the time and effort required to develop and maintain test scripts, thereby improving the efficiency of the test automation process.

- **Test Scripts**: Test scripts are the code that drives the test automation process. By creating modular and reusable test scripts, testers can reduce the time and effort required to develop new test cases and update existing ones.

  Example: In a content management system, a reusable test script can be created to validate the functionality of the login process, which can then be used across multiple test cases.

- **Test Data**: As mentioned earlier, test data should be stored in a centralized repository, making it easy to reuse across different test cases and projects.

- **Test Automation Frameworks**: Test automation frameworks provide a structured approach to test automation, making it easier to develop, maintain, and reuse test scripts. Popular test automation frameworks include data-driven, keyword-driven, and hybrid frameworks.

  Example: A data-driven framework can be used to test an e-commerce application, allowing testers to easily update test data, and run multiple test cases with different input values.

- **Resources**

A successful test automation strategy requires the right mix of resources, including skilled personnel, hardware, and software.

- **Personnel:** Test automation requires skilled professionals who arc proficient in programming languages, test automation tools, and testing methodologies. It is essential to invest in training and upskilling team members to ensure they have the necessary skills to execute the test automation strategy effectively.

  Example: A team of testers proficient in Java and Selenium can be trained to automate the testing of a web application.

- **Hardware**: Test automation may require additional hardware resources, such as test servers, storage devices, and networking equipment. It is essential to plan for these resources and ensure they are available when needed.

  Example: A performance testing project may require dedicated test servers to simulate high levels of user traffic and measure the application's response time.

- **Software**: In addition to test automation tools and frameworks, other software resources may be required, such as version control systems, continuous integration tools, and test management tools.

Example: A test management tool can be used to manage test cases, track test execution, and generate test reports.

- **Timelines**

Test automation can help reduce the overall testing cycle time, but it is essential to plan and allocate sufficient time for each phase of the test automation process.

  - **Test Planning**: The test planning phase involves defining the scope of testing, selecting test automation tools and frameworks, and identifying the resources required for the project. This phase should be completed before the start of the test automation process to ensure a smooth and efficient execution.
  - **Test Development**: The test development phase involves creating test scripts, test data, and other test assets. The time required for this phase depends on the complexity of the application and the skills of the test automation team.
  - **Test Execution**: The test execution phase involves running the automated test scripts and analyzing the test results. The time required for this phase depends on the number of test cases, the performance of the test automation tools, and the availability of hardware resources.
  - **Test Maintenance:** The test maintenance phase involves updating test scripts and test data to reflect changes in the application and addressing any issues identified during the test execution phase. This phase is ongoing and should be factored into the overall test automation timeline.

- **Risks**

Test automation can help improve the quality of the software, but it also introduces new risks that need to be managed effectively.

  - **Overreliance on Automation**: Test automation should complement manual testing, not replace it entirely. It is essential to strike a balance between automated and manual testing to ensure comprehensive test coverage.
  - **Inadequate Test Coverage**: Test automation can sometimes lead to inadequate test coverage, especially if the focus is on automating a large number of test cases rather than prioritizing critical functionalities and high-risk areas.
  - **Test Script Maintenance**: Test scripts need to be updated regularly to reflect changes in the application, which can be time-consuming and resource-intensive. It is essential to plan for test script maintenance and allocate sufficient resources to this task.

- **Tool and Framework Limitations**: Test automation tools and frameworks may have limitations that can impact the effectiveness of the test automation process. It is essential to be aware of these limitations and develop strategies to mitigate their impact.

A well-defined test automation strategy is essential for the successful implementation of test automation in any software development project. By carefully considering the key components discussed in this article, organizations can develop a comprehensive test automation strategy that delivers tangible benefits in terms of improved software quality, reduced testing cycle time, and efficient use of resources.

Test Designing for Automation

Test case design is a crucial aspect of software testing, ensuring that systems function as intended and meet user expectations. To create effective test cases, it is essential to consider various characteristics that contribute to their quality and thoroughness. In this section, we present a mnemonic, "**TEST CASE**," which encapsulates key characteristics to remember when designing test cases. Each letter represents a characteristic, accompanied by practical examples to illustrate their importance.

Thoroughness:

When designing test cases, it is vital to cover all possible scenarios and conditions. Consider a banking application where users can perform transactions. A thorough test case would examine scenarios such as normal transfers, failed transfers, insufficient funds, and concurrent transactions to ensure the system handles each situation correctly. In a nutshell, the tests should cover the positive and negative scenarios.

Effectiveness:

Test cases should effectively assess the desired functionality or behavior of the system. For instance, in an e-commerce website, an effective test case might involve verifying that the checkout process completes successfully, including adding items to the cart, applying discounts, selecting shipping options, and processing payments without any errors. An ineffective test case would not focus on the core business problem of the application under test.

Specificity:

To achieve clarity and precision, each test case should focus on a specific aspect or feature of the system. For example, in a social media application, a specific test case could target the feature of posting a status update, covering elements such as character limits, visibility settings, and multimedia attachments. This aspect also highlights the fact that a test case should be atomic. So, that one test case targets only one area of the application and should be as modular as possible.

Traceability:

Test cases should be linked to requirements or user stories to maintain traceability throughout the testing process. By establishing traceability, testers can easily track the progress and coverage of their testing efforts. For instance, if a requirement specifies that a banking application should allow users to set up recurring bill payments, a test case should be created to validate this requirement.

Clarity:

Clarity is essential when designing test cases. Testers should strive to create test cases that are clear and easy to understand by anyone executing them. This clarity helps prevent confusion and ensures consistency in the testing process. For example, a clear test case for a file management system would specify the steps to create a new folder, verify that it appears in the directory, and confirm that files can be successfully moved into the folder.

Accuracy:

Accurate test cases are crucial for reliable testing. Testers need to ensure that the expected results and actual results align precisely. For instance, when testing a search engine, an accurate test case would involve entering a specific keyword and verifying that the search results display relevant pages ranked according to their relevance.

Sustainable:

A sustainable test case can be maintained and reused over time. This is important because it can help to save time and money in the long run. In simple words, a test case should be repeatable so that its automation can bring scalable gains. Our initial example of a book checkout process is an example of a sustainable test case.

Efficiency:

Efficiency is a crucial aspect of test case design to ensure optimal use of time and resources. Test cases should be designed to be executed in a timely manner. For example, in a search engine application, an efficient test case would focus on validating search functionality across different devices and browsers without unnecessarily repeating steps or redundant verifications.

Here is a creative mnemonic to remember the characteristics of a test case:

T - **Thoroughness**: Ensure the test case covers all possible scenarios and conditions.

E - **Effectiveness**: The test case should accurately assess the desired functionality or behavior.

S - **Specificity**: Each test case should focus on a specific aspect or feature of the system.

T - **Traceability**: Test cases should be linked to requirements or user stories for easy tracking.

C - **Clarity**: The test case should be clear and easy to understand by anyone executing it.

A - **Accuracy**: The expected results and actual results should match precisely.

S - **Sustainability**: Consider the ability of the test case to handle varying data loads or system sizes.

E - **Efficiency**: Test cases should be designed to be executed in a timely manner.

Identifying test scenarios for automation testing is another key step in the automation test design process. Test scenarios should be selected based on their criticality, test frequency, and the amount of time taken to execute them manually. By automating frequently executed and critical test scenarios, the testing process can be made more efficient and reliable.

In order to design effective test cases, it is important to keep in mind some Tips for Effective Test Case Design. Firstly, test cases should be designed in a way that ensures maximum code coverage. Secondly, tests should be designed to be independent of each other. Thirdly, the test steps should be easy to understand and implement. Finally, test cases should be designed in such a way that they can be easily maintained in the long run.

Test Design Methodologies

There are various ways of designing tests and as explained earlier, the context of the business application matters more than anything else, when it comes to software testing. Test design methodologies can be sliced based on application layer, such as Black box testing, Whitebox testing and Gray box testing. Or we can have domain level design such as Pair wise testing or Risk-based testing. Also, multiple design methodologies can be combined to have deep coverage of the application under test.

Risk-Based testing

Risk-Based Testing (RBT) is an approach that aims to minimize risks associated with a project or product by identifying potential risks, assigning severity levels to each identified risk, and prioritizing test cases accordingly. This prioritization ensures that high-severity defects are addressed while meeting the requirements. RBT allows organizations to focus their testing efforts on critical areas, make informed decisions about resource allocation, and enhance the overall success of the application under development.

Advantages of RBT:

- **Efficient Resource Allocation**: By prioritizing test cases based on risk severity, RBT optimizes the allocation of time and effort during the testing phase. This results in improved timelines for completion and reduced costs, as resources are directed to areas with higher risk levels.
- **Early Issue Identification and Resolution**: RBT promotes early identification and resolution of issues by focusing on high-risk areas. By testing critical functionalities and components early on, potential defects are identified sooner, reducing the overall duration of the debugging process.
- **Collaboration among Team Members**: RBT encourages collaboration among team members from different roles, such as developers, business analysts, QA teams, and stakeholders. This collaborative effort ensures that all parties work towards common goals, such as delivering quality applications on time, meeting customer expectations, and addressing critical risks effectively.

Limitations of RBT:

- **Accurate Risk Assessment**: The effectiveness of RBT relies heavily on accurate risk assessment. If data is limited or incomplete, identifying, and prioritizing risks can be challenging. Organizations need to invest time and effort in gathering relevant information to ensure the validity of risk assessments.
- **Upfront Effort for Risk Model Establishment**: Implementing RBT in large projects with complex systems and dependencies requires establishing a clear and comprehensive risk model. This upfront effort may involve analyzing the project's scope, identifying potential risks, and determining

their severity levels. It can be time-consuming, especially in projects with numerous variables to consider.

- **Changes to Processes and Toolsets**: Adopting RBT may require significant changes to existing processes and toolsets, especially if an organization's software engineering practices are not mature in terms of risk management. Implementing RBT might involve multiple meetings, discussions, approvals, and potential additional expenses for acquiring or updating testing tools. Training requirements may also arise to ensure the team members are equipped with the necessary skills.

Despite these considerations, Risk-Based Testing remains a valuable approach for organizations seeking to improve their software development lifecycle. By addressing high-risk areas proactively, organizations can reduce the impact of critical defects, enhance the quality of their applications, and ultimately deliver better products to customers.

Here is how to calculate the risk in a risk-based testing approach:

- Identify the risks. This can be done by brainstorming with the development team, stakeholders, and testers.
- Assess the likelihood and impact of each risk. The likelihood of a risk is the probability that it will occur. The impact of a risk is determined by the severity of the consequences, if it does occur.
- Calculate the risk score. The risk score is the product of the likelihood and impact of a risk.
- Prioritize the risks. The risks with the highest risk scores should be prioritized for testing.

Here is an example of how to calculate the risk score for a risk:

- Likelihood: The risk is likely to occur.
- Impact: The impact of the risk is severe.
- Risk score: Likelihood * Impact = 10

Note: It is advisable to have a relative score of 1 to 10 for getting the conversations started, as collaboration and team-work are the gist of these discussions.

Here is a table that shows the risk scores for a few different risks:

Risk	Likelihood	Impact	Risk Score
User input validation	Likely	Severe	10
Data corruption	Possible	Moderate	6
Security vulnerability	Unlikely	Mild	2

Table 2.1: *Example of risk calculation*

As you can see, the risk score for the user input validation risk is the highest. This means that this risk should be prioritized for testing.

It is important to note that the risk-based testing approach is not a one-size-fits-all solution. The specific steps involved in the process may vary depending on the specific project and the team involved. However, the general principles outlined above can be applied to any project.

Here are some additional tips for calculating risk in a risk-based testing approach:

- Consider the experience of the development team and testers when assessing the likelihood and impact of risks.
- Use historical data to help you assess the likelihood of risks.
- Consider the cost of testing when prioritizing risks.
- Be flexible and willing to adjust your risk assessment as the project progresses.

Pair-wise Testing

Let us consider a deceptively simple example: a manufacturing automation system under test that has 20 controls, each with 10 possible settings, pose a total of 1020 (100,000,000,000,000,000,000) combinations, which is far more than a software tester would be able to test in a lifetime. Surprisingly, we can check all pairs of these values with only 180 tests if they are carefully constructed using a pair-wise design principle. Promising and elusive as it is, a tool so powerful, which if implemented accurately can save the most complex systems under test from impending paralysis of quality analysis.

Suppose we want to demonstrate that a new software application works correctly on PCs that use the Windows or Linux operating systems, Intel or AMD processors, and the IPv4 or IPv6 protocols. This is a total of $2 \times 2 \times 2 = 8$ possibilities, but, as the following table shows, only four tests are required to test every component interacting with every other component at least once. In this most basic combinatorial method, known as pairwise testing, at least one of the four tests covers all possible pairs ($t = 2$) of values among the three parameters. Note that while the set of four test cases tests for all pairs of possible values–for example, OS = Linux and protocol = IPv4–several combinations of three specific values are not tested–for example, OS = Windows, CPU = Intel, and protocol = IPv6. Even though pairwise testing is not exhaustive, it is useful because it can check for simple, potentially problematic interactions with relatively few tests.

Test Case	OS	CPU	Protocol
1	Windows	Intel	IPv4
2	Windows	AMD	IPv6
3	Linux	Intel	IPv6
4	Linux	AMD	IPv4

Table 2.2: *Combination of tests using pair-wise principle*

The reduction in test set size from eight to four shown in *Table* 2.2 is not that impressive, but consider a larger example: a manufacturing automation system that has 20 controls, each with 10 possible settings—a total of 1020 combinations, which is far more than a software tester would be able to test in a lifetime. Surprisingly, we can check all pairs of these values with only 180 tests if they are carefully constructed.

Whenever pairwise testing is discussed, it would be wise to shed some light on Orthogonal test design patterns too. A novice test designer might add that these are two faces of the same coin, but a true seasoned master understands the difference and can employ the right method as a medicine for the delusional test design dilemma.

The key ingredient for orthogonal kind of testing is a covering array, a mathematical object that covers all t-way combinations of parameter values at least once. For the pairwise testing example in *Table* 2.2, t = 2, and it is relatively easy to generate tests that cover all pairs of parameter values. Generating covering arrays for complex interactions is much harder, but new algorithms make it possible to generate covering arrays orders of magnitude faster than previous algorithms, making up to six-way covering arrays tractable for many applications. *Figure* 2.1 shows a covering array for all three-way interactions of 10 binary parameters in only 13 tests. Note that any three columns, selected in any order, contain all eight possible values of three parameters: 000,001,010,011, 100,101,110,111.

Test \ Parameters	1	2	3	4	5	6	7	8	9	10
1	0	0	0	0	0	0	0	0	0	0
2	1	1	1	1	1	1	1	1	1	1
3	1	1	1	0	1	0	0	0	0	1
4	1	0	1	1	0	1	0	1	0	0
5	1	0	0	0	1	1	1	0	0	0
6	0	1	1	0	0	1	0	0	1	0
7	0	0	1	0	1	0	1	1	1	0
8	1	1	0	1	0	0	1	0	1	0
9	0	0	0	1	1	1	0	0	1	1
10	0	0	1	1	0	0	1	0	0	1
11	0	1	0	1	1	0	0	1	0	0
12	1	0	0	0	0	0	0	1	1	1
13	0	1	0	0	0	1	1	1	0	1

Figure 2.1: *Three-way covering array for 10 parameters with two values each*

What are the pragmatic implications of being able to achieve 100 percent three-way coverage in 13 test cases on real-world software testing projects? Assuming that there are 10 defects in this hypothetical application and that 9 are identified through the 13 tests indicated, testing these 13 cases would find 71 times more defects per test case [(9/13)/(10/1,024)] than testing exhaustively and uncovering all 10.

There are multiple open source and free tools available for usage and further exploration of combinatorial testing:

- ACT from NIST: https://csrc.nist.gov/projects/automated-combinatorial-testing-for-software
- PICT from Microsoft: https://github.com/microsoft/pict

In the context of this book, we will focus on black box functional test automation, assuming that the reader has prioritized the right set of automation tests.

Test Execution and Logging

Execution and logging are critical components of any successful software development project. Yet many teams struggle to execute tests effectively and log results accurately. In this section, we'll explore what test execution and logging entail, why they matter, and best practices for implementing them in your own projects. First things first - what do we mean when we talk about "test execution"? Simply put, it is the process of running test cases against software applications to identify defects and ensure functionality. This can be done manually (by a human tester) or automatically using tools like Selenium. Regardless of how you approach testing, the end goal is the same - to catch bugs early on and improve overall product quality. But why does test execution matter? Isn't code review enough to catch errors before release? While code reviews are certainly important, they alone cannot replace the rigor of automated testing. Testing helps uncover issues that may not be immediately apparent during manual inspections, such as complex interactions between different parts of the application. By catching these issues early on, development teams can save time and money down the line, avoid negative customer feedback, and reduce the risk of costly recalls or reputation damage. So now that we understand why test execution matters, let us bite into some best practices for getting started. In order to explain the concept of test execution, let us consider a burger with multiple layers as follows:

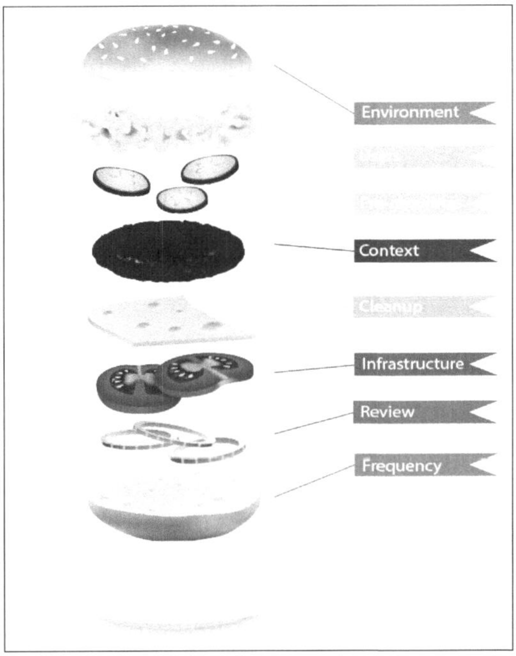

Figure 2.2: *Visualization for components of Test execution*

- **Environment**: In software testing, different environments are used to create distinct and controlled settings for testing activities. Each environment serves a specific purpose and is designed to meet the needs of different stages of the software development lifecycle. The most common environments include local, development (dev), staging, and production environments. The local environment is where developers and testers perform their initial development and testing activities. It is typically set up on an individual's local machine or workstation. The development environment, often referred to as the dev environment, is a shared environment used by the development team to integrate their individual changes into a cohesive system. The staging environment is a replica of the production environment that closely resembles the production setup. It is used for comprehensive testing before the software is deployed to the production environment. The staging environment allows testers to simulate real-world scenarios and perform end-to-end testing, including user acceptance testing (UAT), performance testing, and security testing. The production environment is the live environment where the software is deployed and made available to end-users. It is the actual working environment that serves the application to real users. Testing activities in the production environment are limited to monitoring and capturing feedback to ensure the software is running smoothly and any critical issues are promptly addressed.

- **Test user**: A test user, also known as a test account or test persona, is a user profile created specifically for testing purposes. Test users mimic real end-users and are used to simulate different scenarios, interactions, and roles within the software system. By using test users, testers can evaluate the application's functionality, security, and user experience under various user roles and permissions. Example: In an e-commerce application, test users can be created to represent different types of customers, such as a regular user, a premium user, and an admin user. These test users can then be used to verify the functionality of features like product browsing, cart management, checkout process, and order tracking from different user perspectives.
- **Pre-requisites and data setup**: Pre-requisites and data setup refer to the necessary conditions and data that need to be in place before executing a test. This includes configuring the system, setting up test data, and ensuring any required dependencies or prerequisites are met. Proper pre-requisites and data setup are crucial to ensure accurate and meaningful test results. Example: Suppose you are testing a banking application's fund transfer feature. The pre-requisites may include creating two test user accounts, each with a sufficient balance, and establishing a connection with a test database. Additionally, test data setup might involve populating the test database with sample transactions and verifying the initial account balances.
- **Context**: In software testing, context refers to the specific conditions, configurations, and scenarios in which testing is performed. It encompasses the understanding of the system's purpose, intended users, business rules, constraints, and any external factors that influence the testing process. Considering the context helps testers tailor their testing approach and prioritize their efforts effectively. Example: Testing an e-learning platform will have a different context than testing a financial trading system. The e-learning platform may require emphasis on

usability, course enrolment, and assessment functionalities. On the other hand, the financial trading system would focus on real-time data updates, transaction processing, and security aspects like trade execution and order validation.

- **Purging and cleanup**: Purging and cleanup refer to the process of removing any residual artifacts, temporary files, or test data generated during testing. It ensures that the testing environment remains clean, free from clutter, and ready for subsequent testing cycles. Proper purging and cleanup prevent interference between different test runs and minimize the risk of false positives or false negatives. Example: After executing a test suite on a web application, the purging and cleanup process may involve deleting temporary files, clearing browser caches, and resetting the application's database to its initial state. This ensures that any artifacts or data generated during the previous test run do not affect subsequent tests.
- **Infrastructure and tooling**: Infrastructure and tooling refer to the hardware, software, and tools necessary for conducting testing activities effectively. This includes test management tools, test automation frameworks, virtual machines, physical devices, and any other resources required to support the testing process. A robust and well-configured infrastructure, along with appropriate tooling, enables efficient and scalable testing. Example: For mobile application testing, infrastructure and tooling may involve having access to a range of physical devices or employing cloud-based mobile device testing platforms. Additionally, using tcst management tools like Jira, TestRail, or Azure DevOps can help streamline test planning, execution, and reporting activities.
- **Updates and review**: Updates and review refer to the periodic evaluation and refinement of test artifacts, including test cases, test plans, and test scripts. It is essential to update test artifacts to align with evolving requirements, bug fixes, and changes in the software under test. Regular review of test artifacts ensures their accuracy, completeness, and effectiveness in achieving the testing objectives. Example: Suppose a software application undergoes a significant update, including the addition of new features and modifications to existing functionalities. In such cases, the test artifacts, such as test cases, need to be updated or reviewed to cover the changes adequately. This helps ensure that the tests remain relevant and provide reliable coverage of the updated application.
- **Frequency**: Frequency refers to the regularity or frequency at which testing activities are performed. The frequency of testing can vary depending on project timelines, software development methodologies (for example, Agile, Waterfall), and the criticality of the system. Determining

the appropriate frequency of testing ensures the timely identification of defects and helps maintain product quality throughout the development lifecycle. Example: In an Agile development environment, testing activities are usually performed in short iterations or sprints, with frequent testing cycles conducted for each increment of the software. On the other hand, in a Waterfall model, testing activities are often concentrated toward the end of the development phase, with fewer iterations and longer intervals between testing cycles. Frequency can also be dependent on the context of the application, so for example, an e-commerce website might require the execution of daily automated checks to verify the state of inventory and orders.

Logging

In the context of software test automation, logging refers to the process of capturing and recording relevant information, events, and messages during the execution of automated tests. Logging plays a crucial role in providing visibility into the test execution flow, identifying issues or failures, and aiding in troubleshooting and debugging. It enables testers and developers to analyze the test results, trace the sequence of events, and understand the behavior of the system under test.

Importance of Logging

Logging is essential in test automation as it helps in the following ways:

- **Debugging and Troubleshooting**: Logging provides valuable insights into the execution flow, allowing testers to identify the root causes of failures or unexpected behavior during test runs. It assists in narrowing down issues by providing contextual information.
- **Test Execution Analysis**: Logging captures details about the test execution process, including timestamps, test case statuses, input data, and intermediate outputs. It helps testers analyze the results, track test progress, and assess the overall test coverage.
- **Reproducing Failures**: When a test fails, logs can provide a detailed account of the steps leading to the failure. Testers can use this information to reproduce the failure scenario, investigate the underlying cause, and facilitate bug fixing.
- **Auditing and Compliance**: Logging is often required to meet regulatory or compliance standards. It helps maintain an audit trail by recording important events, actions, and outcomes during the testing process.

Let us consider a scenario where a test automation framework is being used to test a login functionality of a web application. Here is an example of how logging can be used:

```
# Verify login success
    if login_successful:
        logger.info("Login successful")
    else:
        logger.error("Login failed")


    logger.info("Test case completed: login success")
```

As we can see, logging can be enabled at various levels such as "`error`" or "`info`". We will cover more details about logging tools, and application in frameworks in *Chapter 5: Test Automation Framework*. Also, do not hesitate to reach out to fellow developers or quality assurance experts for advice on how to improve your test execution process. The software community is vast and knowledgeable, so do not be afraid to ask questions! In conclusion, test execution and logging are critical components of modern software development. By following these best practices, you can help ensure that your applications are tested thoroughly and released with confidence. So, take the time to thoughtfully execute your tests, log results accurately, and collaborate with others in the process. You will be glad you did!

Reporting and Measurements

Understanding the importance of test reporting and measurements is a crucial aspect of software quality assurance. Accurate and actionable results allow stakeholders to make informed decisions, prioritize issues, and plan their release cycles. However, collecting, analyzing, and presenting data could be a complex task. It requires careful planning, attention to detail, and a well-defined set of key metrics. In this section, we will learn about various best practices, techniques, and challenges associated with successful test reporting and measurements. So, let us jump right in!

- **Define clear objectives:** The first step to effective test reporting is defining clear objectives, which should align with the overall project goals. This helps to avoid unnecessary information and ensures that the results obtained are actionable. For instance, defining objectives such as 'Test website loading speed and page performance on various devices' versus 'Test website performance' makes a significant difference in the resulting data.

- **Choose the right tools:** The tools used for reporting should suit the project's scope and objectives. Incompatibility of tools can lead to inaccuracies, which can result in waste of time and resources. The appropriate tools should provide accurate and comprehensive data, support data analysis, and representation. The range of reporting tools can vary from log files all the way up to commercial software such as Tableau.
- **Automate reporting:** Automating test reporting saves time and resources while ensuring consistency and accuracy. This is because it minimizes the possibility of human errors and ensures that the information generated is consistent with the testing criteria. Automation can also generate real-time reports, making it easy to track progress and implement corrective actions when necessary. In later sections, we will explore the automated reports via build management tools such as JENKINS.
- **Maintain consistency:** Maintaining consistency throughout the testing cycle ensures that the results obtained are reliable and can be used for further analysis. For instance, using the same test cases repeatedly saves time and resources and provides a baseline for comparison. Additionally, consistency enables teams to track significant changes in the software's performance and provide insights into the effectiveness of corrective measures.
- **Trend Analysis:** Tracking trends is a crucial aspect of test reporting and measurements. It helps identify patterns and spot anomalies early on. Understanding the significance of trends is paramount, as it gives an indication of where the testing effort is headed. This holds true for both positive and negative trends. The benefits of trend analysis are manifold; it enables stakeholders to identify areas of improvement and provides insights into the effectiveness of the testing process.

  Commonly tracked trends could include metrics like defect density, pass rate, and test coverage. These metrics not only help to measure the current testing status but also give an idea of the future testing effort required. Proper tracking of trends ensures that deviations can be detected early, thus mitigating the risk of cost and schedule overruns.
- **Data visualization:** Have you ever tried reading through a report filled with dry, complex data? It's not a pleasant experience. Not only is it difficult to understand, but it's also easy to miss important trends and patterns. This is where data visualization comes in.

  Data visualization is the practice of presenting large amounts of data in a graphical or pictorial format. It helps in presenting complex data in a more digestible and understandable format. Wouldn't it be great if we could take all that dry data and turn it into something visually appealing, making trends and patterns more apparent?

There are several types of visualizations used for data presentation. Some common types of visualizations include bar charts, line charts, pie charts, scatter plots, heat maps, and many more. Choosing the right visualization method is crucial in effectively conveying your data message to your audience. Here is an example of a visualization from a freemium tool (ReportPortal):

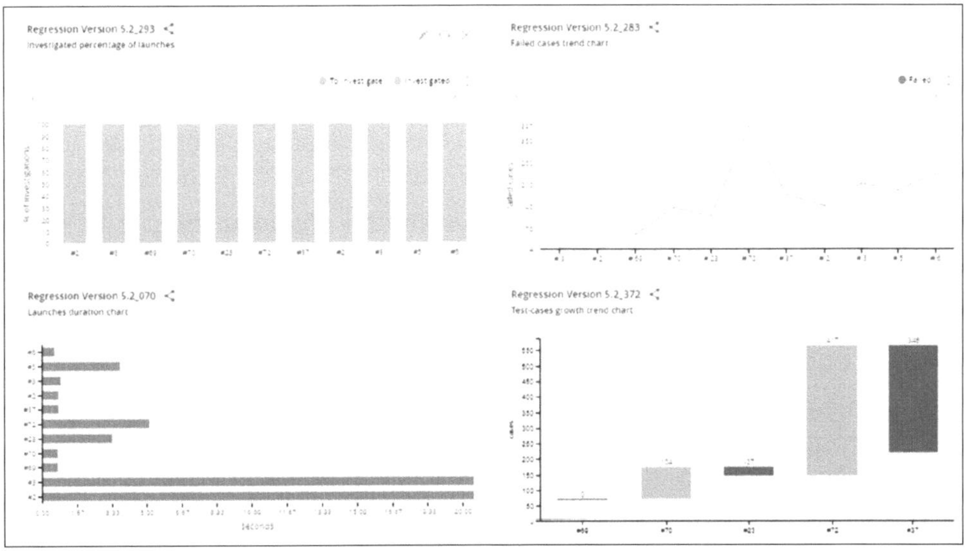

Figure 2.3: *Data visualization example from ReportPortal tool*

"Reports in test automation are as crucial as the tests themselves. Without someone to analyze these results, automation is like a performance in an empty theater. It's not just about running tests; it's about understanding and acting on the outcomes."

"To truly gauge the effectiveness of your test automation, you must measure its results. The insights gained from test failures are the metrics that quantify your progress and guide your path forward. In the world of automation, measurement is the key to mastery."

"The power of test automation lies not just in executing tests, but in the stories told by the reports. If no one is looking at the

results, you're missing out on the narrative of your software's performance and the opportunities to refine it."

- Dmitriy (Dzmitry Humianiuk) Gumeniuk – CEO at ReportPortal.io

---

The selection of appropriate automation testing metrics depends on the specific objectives of the business and team. When implementing automated testing for the first time, it is crucial to choose a metric that accurately measures the value of automation. Consider the following key factors when selecting automation testing metrics:

- **Alignment with Corporate Objectives**: The chosen automation metrics should align with the primary goals of the organization. For example, if the company prioritizes timely software delivery, selecting metrics that track test progress against predetermined success criteria would be beneficial.
- **Incremental Improvement of QA Team's Performance**: The metrics chosen should enable the organization to identify areas of ineffectiveness and gradually improve over time. To evaluate progress, it is important to establish a baseline and measure against it. This allows the team to track their advancements and make incremental improvements.
- **Easily executable**: Having too complex a metric like "Test Relevance" can be confusing to both implement and explain. It can be simpler to create bite-sized metrics that are intuitive and can be summed up to explain the bigger picture.

Test Automation Coverage

Test Automation Coverage is a sample test metrics that can be used for measuring your test automation efforts. It measures the extent to which the test suite is automated in relation to the overall scope of testing. It evaluates the percentage of test cases or functionalities that are automated compared to the total number of test cases or functionalities.

Suppose a project has 100 test cases, out of which 80 are automated. The test automation coverage would be 80%.

Advantages:

- **Improved Test Efficiency**: Test automation coverage helps identify the proportion of test cases automated, allowing teams to gauge the efficiency of the automation efforts. Higher coverage indicates a larger number of test cases executed swiftly, reducing testing time.

- **Increased Test Coverage**: Automation coverage highlights the areas covered by automated tests, enabling teams to ensure comprehensive testing across different functionalities, reducing the risk of critical bugs slipping through.
- **Scalability and Reusability**: By tracking automation coverage, teams can identify areas with low coverage and focus on automating those test cases. As the coverage improves, the test suite becomes more scalable and reusable, allowing teams to efficiently handle future releases and iterations.

Limitations:

- **Bias towards High-Risk Areas**: Test automation coverage may have a tendency to focus more on high-risk or critical areas, potentially leaving less critical functionalities with lower coverage. This requires a careful assessment of the application to ensure comprehensive coverage across all areas.
- **Maintenance Challenges**: As test automation coverage expands, the maintenance effort associated with automated tests also increases. Teams need to invest time and resources in maintaining and updating test scripts to keep up with changes in the application.

Test reporting and measurements are vital aspects of the software testing process, enabling effective communication, data-driven decision-making, and continuous improvement. By understanding their significance, following best practices, generating reports at appropriate intervals, and sharing them through suitable channels, you can enhance collaboration, track progress, and ensure the delivery of high-quality software projects. Remember, a well-crafted test report is a powerful tool for conveying information and fostering transparency in the testing process.

Conclusion

We have provided a comprehensive exploration of the essential topics that lay the groundwork for successful test automation. We began by understanding the importance of quality and how automation can supercharge the journey towards achieving it. We then delved into the intricacies of test automation strategy, emphasizing the significance of careful planning and consideration of various factors.

The chapter further enlightened us on the art of test designing for automation, highlighting the best practices and techniques to create effective and efficient automated tests. We explored the critical aspects of test execution and logging, understanding how to execute automated tests seamlessly and capture relevant information for analysis and debugging purposes.

Moreover, we discussed the significance of reporting and measurements in test automation, recognizing their role in providing valuable insights into the quality of the software under test. By leveraging comprehensive reports and accurate measurements, we can make data-driven decisions to further enhance our testing processes and improve overall software quality.

Armed with this knowledge, you are now equipped to embark on your test automation journey with a solid foundation. Remember, quality is a continuous endeavor, and test automation is a powerful ally that enables us to achieve higher levels of efficiency, accuracy, and effectiveness. By applying the principles and techniques covered in this chapter, you can elevate your testing practices and contribute to the development of exceptional software products.

In the upcoming chapter, we will continue our journey towards test automation with Selenium basics, its architecture, locator strategies, and common interaction patterns (like clicking a button or sending inputs to text fields on a webpage). We will also look at different ways of interacting with a web page and a few troubleshooting techniques for Selenium WebDriver, to lay a solid foundation about selenium test automation.

Exercise

Having acquired a solid understanding of software quality and test automation fundamentals, it is time to put your knowledge to the test. Presented here are several exercise questions designed to help you reinforce your learning:

- Note down five scenarios in the Google Maps application (or similar), for which automated checks are better than manual testing.
- Calculate the number of possible scenarios for testing a form field with five dropdown fields (each dropdown field has two possible values). Hint: Use the concepts from combinatorial testing.
- When designing automation tests, what factors should be considered to ensure reliable and maintainable automated test scripts?
- What should be a few metrics and measurements in software testing, and how do they help assess product quality for you?
- How can continuous integration and continuous testing practices contribute to achieving higher software quality levels?

CHAPTER 3

Selenium WebDriver Basics

Introduction

In this comprehensive chapter, we embark on an exciting journey to master web automation using WebDriver. As a pivotal tool in browser automation, WebDriver offers language-specific bindings for precise and efficient web interactions. We start by exploring the architecture of WebDriver, learning how it serves as a bridge between programming languages and browsers like Chrome and Firefox. This understanding is crucial as we delve into WebDriver's capabilities, including clicking elements, filling forms, and navigating web pages. Our journey covers the basics of setting up WebDriver, followed by hands-on practice with essential web tasks.

As we progress, the chapter introduces the challenges of managing multiple browser windows and frames, a skill akin to navigating different rooms within a complex building. Mastering this aspect of WebDriver ensures seamless transitions and interactions within web applications. Additionally, we focus on common HTML elements–the fundamental components of web pages. You'll learn to automate interactions with various elements like buttons, dropdowns, and forms. This includes handling form submissions and file uploads, replicating user actions in an automated manner.

To cement your learning, the chapter provides practical exercises, such as automating a shopping cart process on a website. These real-world scenarios enhance your understanding of WebDriver's applications beyond standard testing, preparing you for diverse automation challenges. By the end of this chapter, you'll be equipped with the knowledge and skills to efficiently automate complex web tasks, opening doors to advanced web automation techniques in further chapters.

Structure

In this chapter, we will discuss the following topics:

- WebDriver Architecture
- Setup and Basic Interaction
- Locators and Web Elements
- Different Locator Strategies
- Interactions with Web Elements
- Handling Frames and Windows
- Common HTML Elements
- Form Submissions and File Uploads

WebDriver Architecture

Let us jump into the heart of web browser automation with the Selenium WebDriver API. Selenium WebDriver offers a comprehensive set of language-specific bindings that empower you to control web browsers precisely and efficiently, in a manner that aligns with their intended functionality.

By leveraging Selenium WebDriver, you gain the capability to interact with web browsers programmatically, enabling seamless automation of browser-based tasks and tests. The collection of language-specific bindings provided by Selenium WebDriver ensures compatibility with various programming languages, such as Java, Python, C#, and more, enabling you to work with the language you are most comfortable and proficient in.

Selenium WebDriver functions as a bridge between your chosen programming language and the underlying browser drivers. The browser drivers, such as ChromeDriver, GeckoDriver, and SafariDriver, act as intermediaries, facilitating communication between Selenium WebDriver and the web browsers themselves. This architecture allows you to harness the full potential of Selenium WebDriver, as it provides a standardized and consistent interface for browser automation across different platforms.

With Selenium WebDriver, you can effortlessly create and execute test scripts that perform a wide range of actions, including clicking elements, filling in forms, navigating through web pages, and validating expected behaviors. The WebDriver API, an essential component of Selenium WebDriver, offers a rich set of methods and interfaces for locating web elements, performing actions on them, and synchronizing with the browser's state. This ensures that your test scripts interact with web elements accurately and reliably.

Selenium WebDriver refers to both the language bindings and the implementations of the individual browser-controlling code. This is commonly referred to as just **WebDriver.**

Have you ever thought about who decides the standards for creating web browsers and other web technologies like HTML, CSS, and many more? The **World Wide Web Consortium** (W3C) develops international Web standards. W3C's Web standards are called W3C Recommendations and are followed by browser vendors to implement features like accessibility, text video descriptions, and user agents. Additionally, these might include browsers, browser extensions, media players, readers, and other applications that render web content.

The latest version of Selenium WebDriver architecture is based on the W3C (World Wide Web Consortium) WebDriver protocol and therefore integrates very well with all the major web browsers (as they follow the W3C standards as well).

So, let's understand how Selenium WebDriver talks to the browser and performs the interactions:

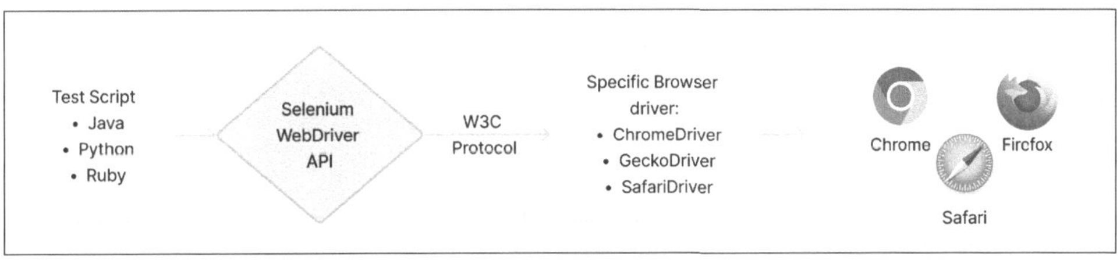

Figure 3.1: *Communication between test script and web browsers using Selenium*

In Selenium 4, the architecture involves three main components that work together to automate web browsers. Let us break down these components in a simple and detailed manner:

- **Selenium Client and WebDriver Language Bindings**: Selenium is an API (Application Programming Interface) that provides commands for automating web browsers. The Selenium Client is a separate part that allows us to interact with the Selenium API. WebDriver Language Bindings are specific to different programming languages (Java, C#, Python, Ruby, and JavaScript), providing the same Selenium commands in each language.
- **Browser Drivers**: The browser drivers serve as intermediaries between the Selenium Client and WebDriver Language Bindings, and the web

browsers. The first function of the Browser Drivers is to receive requests from the Selenium Client and WebDriver Language Bindings and pass them to the web browser. The Browser drivers are responsible for controlling the browser, acting as proxies for communication. The second function of the browser drivers is to receive responses from the browser and pass them back to the Selenium Client and WebDriver Language Bindings. The drivers utilize the W3C WebDriver Protocol, and most of them are developed by the respective browser vendors.

- **Web Browsers**: In our test scripts, we can use various web browsers, such as Chrome, Firefox, Safari, and Edge. These browsers are where all the Selenium commands are executed, performing the desired actions and interactions.

  When a request is sent from the browser driver to the browser, the browser processes the command and sends back a response to the driver.

The overall process involves the Selenium Client and WebDriver Language Bindings sending commands to the Browser Drivers, which then pass them to the web browsers. The browsers execute the commands and send back responses to the Browser Drivers, which in turn deliver them to the Selenium Client and WebDriver Language Bindings.

Enough talking, let us look at some technical examples and solidify our understanding.

Prerequisites

kindly ensure that the following prerequisites are present on your computer:

1. Download the latest ChromeDriver from https://chromedriver.chromium.org/home.
2. Unzip the files from the downloaded package.
3. Start a ChromeDriver session by executing the following command, assuming that the executable is in the current directory
   a. For Mac, open a shell window and run `./chromedriver`
   b. For Windows run `chromedriver.bat`

This would result in a window as follows:

Figure 3.2: *ChromeDriver started on port 9515*

Now in the same directory (where you have extracted and run ChromeDriver), open a shell window and run the following CURL request:

```
curl -XPOST http://localhost:9515/session -d
'{"desiredCapabilities":{"browserName":"chrome"}}'
```

Voila! A Chrome window should have been opened by ChromeDriver. Isn't that amazing?

Let us deconstruct, what just happened:

1. **`curl`**: This is a command-line tool used to send HTTP requests.
2. **`-XPOST`**: This option specifies the HTTP method of the request, which in this case is a POST request. POST is used to send data to the server.
3. **`http://localhost:9515/session`**: This is the URL to which the request is being sent. In this case, it is http://localhost:9515/session, indicating that the request is being sent to the local server running on port 9515.
4. **`-d`**: This option is used to specify the data that should be included in the request. The data is provided as a string enclosed in single quotes ('). In this case, the data being sent is `{"desiredCapabilities":{"browserName":"chrome"}}`, which is a JSON object.
5. **`{"desiredCapabilities":{"browserName":"chrome"}}`**: This is the JSON payload of the request. It specifies the desired capabilities for the session that will be created on the server. In this case, it specifies that the desired browser is Google Chrome **`("browserName":"chrome").`**

Overall, this CURL request is used to create a new session on the local server running on port 9515 and specifies that the desired browser for the session is Google Chrome.

Important thing to note here is that we just simulated an API call to ChromeDriver, and requested it to start a chrome browser session. Selenium follows the same mechanism to communicate with ChromeDriver and emulate user behavior like opening a chrome browser, finding web elements like buttons and links, and performing web actions like clicks, inputs, and drag and drops.

What good is a blank new page on the chrome browser? So, let us go further in our example and try to open a web page. After running the previous CURL command, you would get the command line window as follows:

```
$ curl -XPOST http://localhost:9515/session -d '{"desiredCapabilities":{"browserName
":"chrome"}}'
  % Total    % Received % Xferd  Average Speed   Time    Time     Time  Current
                                 Dload  Upload   Total   Spent    Left  Speed
100  1235  100  1187  100    48   1675     67 --:--:-- --:--:-- --:--:--  1744{"sess
ionId":"6b257ac33000601200ff0a283d9b05ab","status":0,"value":{"acceptInsecureCerts":
false,"acceptSslCerts":false,"browserConnectionEnabled":false,"browserName":"chrome"
,"chrome":{"chromedriverVersion":"114.0.5735.90 (386bc09e8f4f2e025eddae123f36f626309
6ae49-refs/branch-heads/5735@{#1052})","userDataDir":"C:\\Users\\robin.gupta\\AppDat
a\\Local\\Temp\\scoped_dir26224_1698763582"},"cssSelectorsEnabled":true,"databaseEna
bled":false,"goog:chromeOptions":{"debuggerAddress":"localhost:52030"},"handlesAlert
s":true,"hasTouchScreen":false,"javascriptEnabled":true,"locationContextEnabled":tru
e,"mobileEmulationEnabled":false,"nativeEvents":true,"networkConnectionEnabled":fals
e,"pageLoadStrategy":"normal","platform":"Windows","proxy":{},"rotatable":false,"set
WindowRect":true,"strictFileInteractability":false,"takesHeapSnapshot":true,"takesSc
reenshot":true,"timeouts":{"implicit":0,"pageLoad":300000,"script":30000},"unexpecte
dAlertBehaviour":"ignore","version":"114.0.5735.134","webStorageEnabled":true,"webau
thn:extension:credBlob":true,"webauthn:extension:largeBlob":true,"webauthn:extension
:minPinLength":true,"webauthn:extension:prf":true,"webauthn:virtualAuthenticators":t
rue}}
```

Figure 3.3: *Command output from CURL*

As part of the preceding output, note down the **Session ID** as **`6b257ac33000601200ff0a283d9b05ab.`**

This is the session ID corresponding to the browser session we have created above.

Run the following command in the same shell window as above, by replacing the session ID from your command line output:

```
curl http://localhost:9515/session/6b257ac33000601200ff0a283d9b05ab/url
-d '{"url":"http://google.com/"}'
```

This will open the Google home page in the web browser opened from the last command. And that is how we can instruct ChromeDriver to navigate to any web site.

If only, we didn't have to run these cryptic CURL commands to do simple operations like opening web browsers and navigating to URLs. And that is where Selenium comes to the rescue.

As you observed, we can communicate to a web browser via a browser driver (ChromeDriver in our example) using a simple REST API call. ChromeDriver follows the W3C WebDriver spec. There are tons of things you can do with it, but performing more advanced tasks without a tool like Selenium WebDriver can be quite difficult.

So now, let us perform the same example of opening a browser and navigating to a website using Selenium WebDriver.

Setup and Basic Interaction

Before we dive into the depths of Selenium, kindly ensure that the following prerequisites are present on your computer:

1. Eclipse (or similar Integrated Development Environment). It can be downloaded from https://www.eclipse.org/downloads/. Also, the following plugins should be installed:
    a. Maven : https://www.eclipse.org/m2e/
    b. TestNG : https://testng.org/doc/eclipse.html
    c. EGit plugins : https://eclipse.dev/egit/download/
2. Apache Maven. It can be downloaded from https://maven.apache.org/download.cgi. Also, ensure that the environment variables are setup for your computer.
3. JAVA JDK (version 11 or greater). You can download Amazon Corretto 17, the Amazon version of OpenJDK from here: https://docs.aws.amazon.com/corretto/index.html

Now, import the code for all chapters from the following GitHub location:

https://github.com/ava-orange-education/Ultimate-Selenium-WebDriver-for-Test-Automation

We will cover Git basics in *Chapter 11: Way Forward.*

TestNG is a beginner-friendly testing framework for Java that helps developers and testers create and manage automated tests easily. It provides powerful features like test parallelization, test grouping, and test dependencies, making test execution more efficient and organized. With TestNG, you can write test methods using simple annotations, such as "`@Test`," to mark them as test cases. It also supports data-driven testing, where you can run the same test with different sets of data. TestNG generates detailed test reports, making it effortless to identify test failures and track the overall test status. Its user-friendly approach and integration with build tools like Maven and Gradle make TestNG a popular choice for test automation in Java projects. Whether you are new to testing or a seasoned professional, TestNG offers a straightforward yet powerful framework for reliable and maintainable test automation.

Maven is an easy-to-understand build automation and project management tool for Java projects. It simplifies the process of building, managing dependencies, and organizing code. With Maven, you define your project's configuration in a simple XML file called **pom.xml**. This file contains information about your project, its dependencies, and how to build it. When you run Maven, it automatically downloads the required libraries and compiles your code, creating a structured output. Maven also supports various plugins that allow you to run tests, package your application, and deploy it to servers easily. Its user-friendly approach and standardized project structure make Maven a widely used tool for Java developers, as it saves time and ensures consistent builds across different environments.

Note: We will explore TestNG and Maven in more detail in *Chapter 5: Test Automation Framework.*

Once you have the preceding code downloaded, navigate to **Chapter03_3.java** at **src/test/java/chapter3** location:

```
package testscripts;
import org.openqa.selenium.WebDriver;
import org.openqa.selenium.chrome.ChromeDriver;
public class Chapter03_3 {
public static void main(String[] args) throws Exception {
// Creating a webdriver instance
WebDriver driver = new ChromeDriver();
//Navigating to Google home page
driver.get("https://www.google.com");
driver.quit();
}
}
```

Now open the context menu for this program (by right-clicking it);

and select **Run as Java application**.

This will run the program, and open a Chrome browser with www.google.com web page. Congrats! You have created and run your first Selenium Test Automation script.

Let us understand, what is happening here.

1. **`import org.openqa.selenium.WebDriver;`**

   This line imports the `WebDriver` class from the **`org.openqa.selenium`** package, which is a part of the Selenium WebDriver library. The `WebDriver` class provides methods and interfaces to interact with web browsers.

2. **`import org.openqa.selenium.chrome.ChromeDriver;`**

   This line imports the **`ChromeDriver`** class from the **`org.openqa.selenium.chrome`** package. The **`ChromeDriver`** class is a specific implementation of the **`WebDriver`** interface for the Google Chrome browser.

3. **`public class Chapter03_3 {`**

   This line declares a public class named **`Chapter03_3.`** This is the main class where the program execution starts.

4. **`public static void main(String[] args) throws Exception {`**

   This line declares the `main` method, which is the entry point for the program. It takes an array of strings **`(args)`** as an argument and may throw an exception. The **`throws Exception`** clause indicates that any exceptions raised within the **`main`** method will be propagated upwards.

5. **`WebDriver driver = new ChromeDriver();`**

   This line creates a new instance of the **`ChromeDriver`** class and assigns it to a variable named **`driver`**. This instance represents the Chrome browser and provides methods to control it.

6. **`driver.get("https://www.google.com");`**

   This line uses the `get` method of the **`WebDriver`** interface to navigate the Chrome browser to the specified URL, which is "https://www.google.com".

   It opens the Google homepage in the Chrome browser. This does the same thing as the CURL POST request we had earlier seen for opening the browser using commands in the shell window.

7. **`driver.quit();`**

   This line quits the driver instance and closes the browser window.

   That's it! This program sets up the ChromeDriver, opens a Chrome browser window, and navigates to the Google homepage using Selenium WebDriver.

Let us go into a bit more detail about step 5:

```
WebDriver driver = new ChromeDriver()
```

In the preceding line, we create an instance of ChromeDriver and assign it to the **driver** variable, effectively creating a connection between the WebDriver interface and the Chrome browser.

This is where run-time polymorphism comes into play. The WebDriver interface acts as a blueprint or contract that defines a set of methods that can be used to control any web browser. By assigning the ChromeDriver object (which implements the WebDriver interface) to the **driver** variable of type WebDriver, we're using run-time polymorphism to create an object of the ChromeDriver type, which can be used to interact with the browser opened by Selenium.

Finally, we call **driver.quit()** to quit all WebDriver instances (including any child windows, if opened).

Note: **driver.close()** is used to close the current browser window, while **driver.quit()** is used to terminate the WebDriver and close all browser windows associated with the WebDriver session. If you want to end the WebDriver session completely, it is recommended to use **driver.quit()** to ensure all browser windows are closed properly and resources are released.

If you write "driver." in your IDE and explore the autocomplete suggestions, you can see that all the methods for interacting with a browser can be found here, as follows:

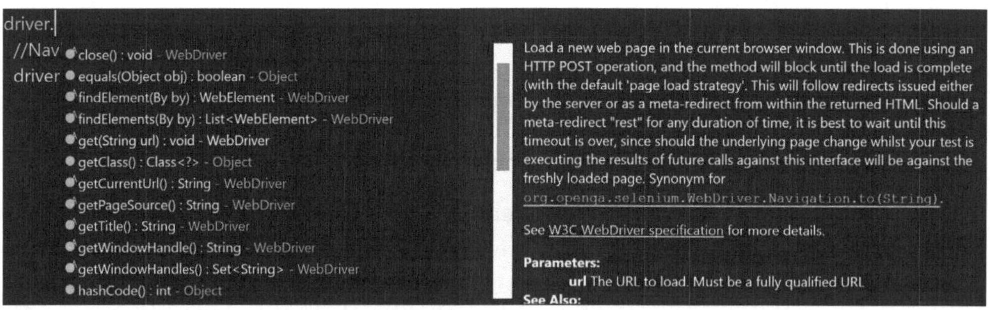

Figure 3.4: *Methods implemented in ChromeDriver for WebDriver interface*

Note: For the setup and reference in this book, we will refer to Selenium WebDriver API for JAVA (Stable Version 4.11.0).

In older versions of Selenium, we had to set the path to Chromedriver (and similar), using System properties. With Selenium version 4.6.0 onwards, **Selenium Manager** is bundled with its bindings, which downloads and sets up the browser drivers automatically, behind the scenes. So that automation engineers don't have to struggle with browser driver versions.

> *Selenium Manager is a command-line tool implemented in Rust that provides automated driver and browser management for Selenium. It is shipped and fully integrated with each release of the Selenium bindings languages (i.e., Java, JavaScript, Python, Ruby, and C#). This way, before a Selenium session starts, Selenium Manager automatically discovers, downloads, and caches the drivers required by Selenium (e.g., chromedriver, geckodriver, msedgedriver, etc.) when these drivers are unavailable. In addition, Selenium Manager automatically discovers, downloads, and caches the major browsers that can be used in a Selenium session, i.e., Chrome (using Chrome-for-Testing -CfT-), Firefox, and Edge, when these browsers are not installed in the local system.*
>
> - Boni Garcia, Open-source committer at Selenium project and the creator and maintainer of several projects belonging to its ecosystem, such as WebDriverManager, Selenium-Jupiter, and BrowserWatcher.

Locators and Web Elements

So, what are Selenium Locators, you ask? Well, my curious friend, Selenium Locators are like the GPS coordinates that help us locate and interact with specific elements on a web page. Without them, navigating the realm of web testing would be like trying to find a needle in a haystack. Let us take a simple example of the following web page:

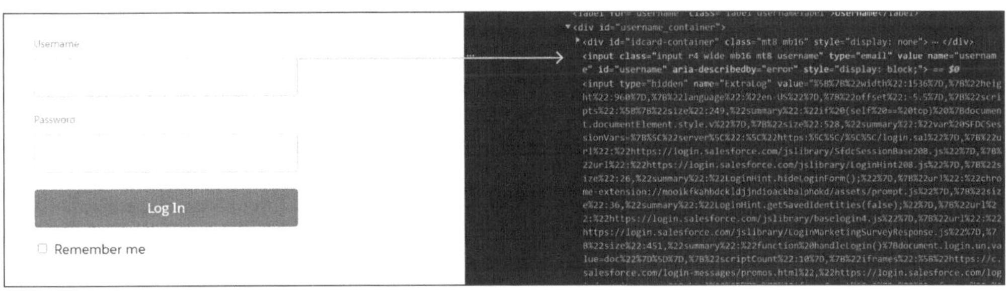

***Figure 3.5**: HTML representation of an input field on a web page*

The **Username** field on the left is made up of the HTML code on the right. Now, while we can read the webpages and identify the **Username** field, and fill it; just think how will a software (like Selenium) see and interact with such a web element?

Yes, you guessed it right: By utilizing the power of locators. Locators grant you the ability to fill in the fields, click buttons, and access any web element on a web page.

Note: You can view the source code of any web element on a web page (like a link or a button), by right-clicking it and selecting `Inspect element` on the context menu. Alternatively, you can press F12 on your keyboard to bring up Chrome Developer tools as well.

So how do locators work? To understand the concept of a locator which acts as the GPS (Global Positioning System) coordinates, we need to visualize the HTML as a map (*Figure* 3.6).

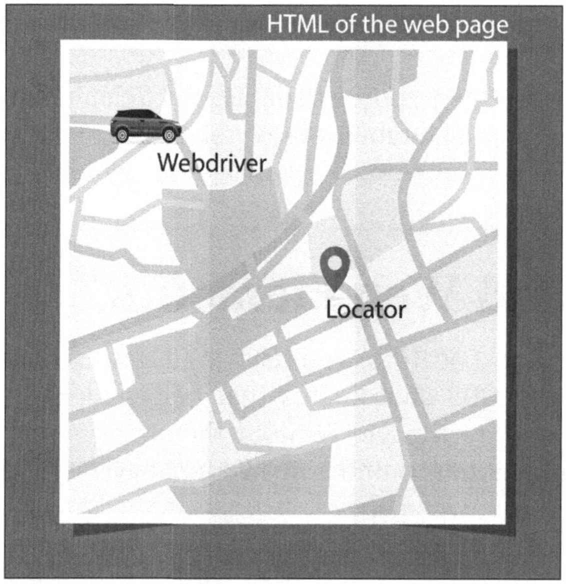

***Figure* 3.6**: *Representation of Document Object Model, WebDriver, and Locator*

Imagine you are going on a road trip, and you want to find a specific location. To do that, you use a GPS (Global Positioning System) that gives you coordinates (latitude and longitude) to reach your destination accurately. Similarly, in web development and testing, we have something called "**locators**," which act like GPS coordinates but for finding specific elements on a web page.

When we think of a web page as a map, just like a map has different locations with unique addresses, a web page has elements like buttons, text fields, images, and more. Each of these elements has its unique address, known as a "**locator.**"

When we interact with a web page using automation tools (like Selenium), we need to tell the tool how to find these elements accurately. That is where locators come into play. They provide specific instructions to locate the elements on the web page.

There are various types of locators, such as:

- `ID`: It is like a building's unique ID number on a map. Each element on a web page can have a unique ID, making it easy to find.
- `Name`: Like a street name, elements can have names. This can help us locate them when there is no unique ID.
- `XPath:` Think of it as a precise route drawn on the map. XPath provides the exact path to an element in the Document Object Model (DOM).
- `CSS Selector`: It is like using certain patterns or colors to locate elements on a map. CSS selectors help find elements based on their styles and attributes.

By using these locators, automation tools can navigate through the web page, click buttons, fill in forms, and perform various actions, just like a GPS guides you on your road trip.

So, the concept of locators acts as a virtual GPS for web pages, allowing automation tools to find and interact with specific elements, making web testing and development more efficient and accurate.

Another key concept touched on above is the **Document Object Model**. The DOM is a cross-platform interface that allows representing XML-like documents (for example, web pages, based on HTML) in a tree structure. Imagine a small web page with different parts, like the title, headings, links, and so on. The DOM creates a tree with each part of the web page represented as a "node" or "element" in the tree. For example, the title of the page will be a node, the heading will be a node, and links will be nodes too.

Every element in the web page, like the tags you see in HTML **(`<html>`, `<head>`, `<body>`, `<a>`,** and so on), becomes a node in the DOM tree. And each important detail, like the **`charset`** or **`href`**, becomes a property of that node. Additionally, the content you see inside these tags is also stored in the tree. So, the text you read on a web page is also part of the DOM tree.

Consider the HTML file as follows:

```
<!DOCTYPE html>
<html lang="en">

<head>
```

```
  <meta charset="UTF-8" />
  <meta name="viewport" content="width=device-width, initial-scale=1.0" />
  <link rel="stylesheet" href="style.css" />
  <title>Browser</title>
</head>
<body>
  <h1>
Selenium</h1>
  <p>
   Best Tool Ever
  </p>
</body>
</html>
```

Its DOM presentation can be visualized as follows:

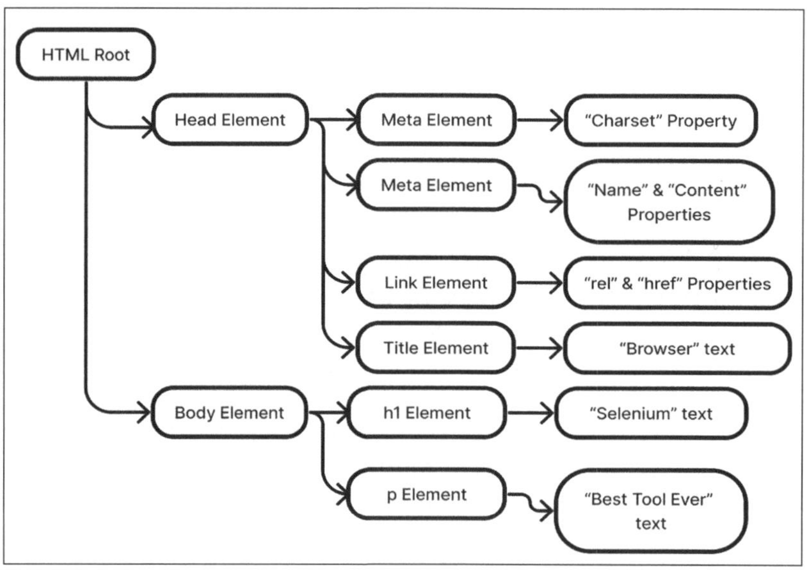

Figure 3.7: *Visual representation of Document Object Model*

WebElement

Selenium WebDriver exposes two key methods to locate "WebElement" (an abstraction of various elements like links, buttons, input fields, dropdowns, and so on) on the HTML page.

- **findElement():** This method is used to locate a single element on the web page based on a specific criterion. It searches through the Document Object Model (DOM), which is like a tree representing the web page's structure. When you call this method with a particular **By** parameter (location strategy), it looks for the first occurrence of an element that matches that criterion.

  For example, you can use **By.id** to find an element with a specific ID or **By.name** to locate an element by its name attribute.

  If the method finds a match, it returns that element so you can interact with it through your automation code. However, if the element is not found, it may throw an exception (like NoSuchElementException) or return a null value, depending on how it is implemented.
- **findElements():** This method is similar to the previous one, but it returns a list of elements instead of a single element. So, if you want to find multiple elements that match a specific criterion, you can use this method. For instance, if you want to find all the links on a page, you can use **By.tagName('a')** as the **By** parameter, and it will return a list containing all the link elements on the page.

Using **findElement** and locator strategies such as **id**, **class** or **XPath** we can locate and interact with web elements on a web page. Let us explore a few examples to solidify our understanding:

Example of using locators:

Open the **Chapter03_id_Locator.java** from the downloaded codebase earlier and focus on the given line:

```
WebElement inputfield = driver.findElement(By.id("username"));
```

We declare a new variable called **inputfield** to store information about a specific element on a web page. It uses the **driver** to search for an element on the web page with a unique **id** attribute equal to **username**. When the element is found, it assigns that information to the **inputfield** variable, so you can interact with it or perform actions on it later in the code.

As we can note in this Java class, there is no **public static void main(String[] args)** statement, as this class is modelled as a TestNG statement by employing the **@Test(priority = 1)** statement. The **@Test** annotation tells TestNG, that we are setting up the Java class as a TestNG test.

Note: To run a TestNG test, you can right click the editor window and click **Run As > TestNG Test** option. Alternatively, you can press *Alt+Shift+X*, N from keyboard.

When we run the code example from **`Chapter03_id_Locator.java`** as a TestNG test; the location of the web element on the screen is printed. Here is the sample console output:

```
[RemoteTestNG] detected TestNG version 7.4.0

Jul 30, 2023 6:26:05 PM org.openqa.selenium.remote.service.DriverSer-
vice$Builder getLogOutput

INFO: Driver logs no longer sent to console by default; https://www.se-
lenium.dev/documentation/webdriver/drivers/service/#setting-log-output

SLF4J: Failed to load class "org.slf4j.impl.StaticLoggerBinder".

SLF4J: Defaulting to no-operation (NOP) logger implementation

SLF4J: See http://www.slf4j.org/codes.html#StaticLoggerBinder for fur-
ther details.

Jul 30, 2023 6:26:07 PM org.openqa.selenium.devtools.CdpVersionFinder
findNearestMatch

WARNING: Unable to find an exact match for CDP version 115, so returning
the closest version found: 114

Location of the input field on screen is(90, 281)

PASSED: idLocatorExample


===============================================

    Default test

    Tests run: 1, Failures: 0, Skips: 0

===============================================


===============================================

Default suite

Total tests run: 1, Passes: 1, Failures: 0, Skips: 0

===============================================
```

Note: If you observe errors and test failures, kindly do not proceed further until this basic test passes. Common issues at this stage might be the internet connection or the location of the ChromeDriver not being set up correctly. More details around debugging automation tests, can be found in *Chapter 11: Way Forward.*

Here are a few more examples of other locators for your reference:

- **`Name`**: We can use the NAME attribute available with the element in a web page to locate it. Generally, the NAME property should be unique for an element on the web page. This example can be found in the **`Chapter03_name_Locator.java`** file.

  ```
  WebElement inputfield = driver.findElement(By.name("username"));
  ```

- **`linkText`**: When we want to find a link on a web page, we can use the link text locator. The link text is simply the text that you see on the link. So, if we have a link on the web page, we can use the link text to identify it.

  For example, let's say we have the following HTML snippet on the web page:

  ```
  <a class="button secondary" id="signup_link"
  href="https://www.salesforce.com/form/trial/freetrial.
  jsp?d=70130000000Enus">Try for Free</a>
  ```

  We locate the link using the **`driver.findElement(By.linkText())`** method, passing the link text **`Try for Free`** as the parameter to the **`linkText()`** method.

  ```
  WebElement tryforfreelink = driver.findElement(By.linkText("Try
  for Free"));
  ```

  Once we have the link element in the link variable, we can interact with it. In this example, we get the location of the "Try for Free" link, on the sample page.

- **`partialLinkText`**: We can use **`partialLinkText`** to locate a web element using part of the text in the link as below:

  ```
  WebElement tryforfreelink = driver.findElement(By.partialLink
  Text("for Free"));
  ```

Different Locator Strategies

In the world of web development, modern web pages are dynamic and complex, featuring intricate structures and frequently changing attributes. While basic locators like id, name, and linkText are useful for simple web elements, they may not suffice when dealing with more challenging scenarios. To overcome these challenges, we turn to the powerful XPath and CSS locator strategies in Selenium WebDriver.

Xpath Locators

XPath stands for XML path, which is a powerful language used to traverse and query XML-like structures, including the DOM of web pages. It provides an efficient way to specify the location of elements, making it a popular choice for web automation. XPath allows us to precisely navigate the Document Object Model (DOM) and locate elements based on their relationships, attributes, and text content. Let's understand the XPath concept using an example:

1. Navigate to https://orangeava.com/ in Chrome browser. And dismiss the sign-up pop-up to go to the home page.
2. Press the F12 function key on your keyboard. This will bring up the Chrome developer console.
3. Press the *Ctrl+f* key combination. This will present a small search bar at the bottom of the Chrome developer console.
4. Type the string `//input` in the search bar. And it should display as follows:

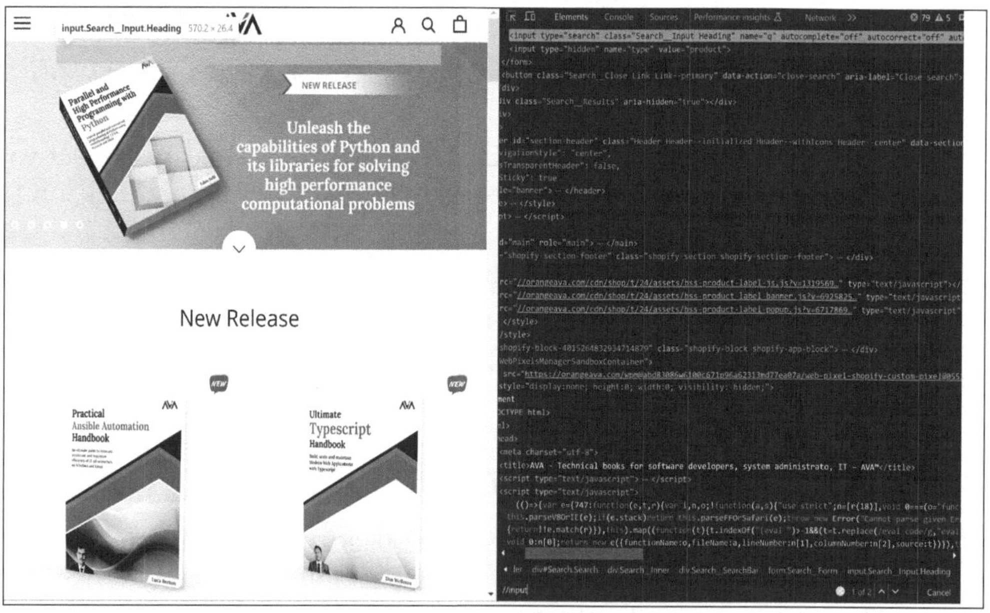

Figure 3.8: *Searching XPath using Chrome Developer Tools*

As we can observe here, the search string `//input` has found two results on the HTML and has highlighted the first result on the view port for us. Wow, how did that happen?

Let us look back at the Maps example we had seen earlier in (*Figure* 3.6), where WebDriver was represented as a car, the HTML presentation as a map, and the locator as the location pin. On this map, each building is represented by a unique location pin (locator). Your mission is to find all the buildings relative to any location on the map. Now, XPath comes to your rescue as your GPS for this unique map! You can use the `//` operator to search for buildings (elements) anywhere on the map, regardless of their position. This is like having a magical bird's-eye view of the entire city from above, allowing you to spot all the buildings, even if they are hidden behind other structures.

For example with **`//building`** as the XPath expression, you are essentially telling your GPS (XPath) to find all the elements with the tag **`building`** anywhere on the map. In XPath locators, the `//` operator is called the double forward slash, and it is used to select elements in a document from the current node regardless of their position in the HTML or XML structure. It allows you to search for nodes throughout the entire document, not just within a specific path.

> *Locators in the automation script are as important as the wheels for a Car.*
>
> *No matter how good engine or design your car has but if tyres get punctured it can't run. Similarly no matter how good script you have written if any locator get changed, script will fail. So having knowledge of locators and writing stable locator is very important.*
>
> - Sanjay Kumar, creator of SelectorsHub.

Open the **`Example1.HTML`** file in Chrome browser from **`src/main/resources`** location in the codebase downloaded from GitHub. Right click the opened web page, and click **`Inspect`** to open the Chrome Developer portal. Press *Ctrl+f* to open the search pane as earlier, for searching XPaths. And follow along with the following examples. Here is the HTML file for your reference:

```
<html>
  <body>
    <div id = '1461'>
      <p>Hello, World!</p>
    </div>
    <div>
      <p>Another paragraph.</p>
```

```
    </div>
  </body>
</html>
```

Now, let us say you want to select all the **p** elements in the document. You can use the **//** operator in your XPath expression like this:

```
//p
```

However, many times the element you would need will be hidden in complex sub-structures and you might need to use more than just the **//** operator. Here are a few more tools and examples for your rescue:

Attributes

Attributes are additional pieces of information associated with HTML elements. In XPath, you can use attributes to identify elements uniquely or to filter elements based on specific criteria.

Example: Selecting an element by its ID attribute in DOM.

To select the first **div** element with the **id** attribute equal to **'1461'**, you can use the following XPath expression: **//div[@id='1461']**

Axes

Axes define the relationship between elements in a document and allow you to navigate through different parts of the HTML tree. They help you select elements based on their position relative to other elements.

Example: Using the **ancestor** axis to select the ancestor **div** of the **p** element.

To select the **div** element that is the ancestor of the **p** element with the text **Hello, World!**, you can use the following XPath expression: `//p[text()='Hello, World!']/ancestor::div`

This expression reads as follows: "Select the **div** element that is an ancestor of the **p** element with the text '**Hello, World!**'"

Operators

XPath also supports various operators to combine expressions or compare values.

Example: Using the **`and`** operator to combine multiple conditions.

To select the **`div`** element that has the **`id`** attribute equal to **`'1461'`** and contains the text **`Hello, World!,`** you can use the following XPath expression: `//div[@id='1461' and p[text()='Hello, World!']]`

This expression reads as follows: "Select the **`div`** element that has the **`id`** attribute equal to **`'1461'`** and contains a **`p`** element with the text **`'Hello, World!'`**"

Let us explore more examples using combinations of axes, parameters, operators, and predicates. Open the **`Example2.HTML`** file in Chrome browser from **`src/main/resources`** location in the codebase downloaded from GitHub.

Right-click the opened web page, and click **`Inspect`** to open the Chrome Developer portal. Press *Ctrl+f* to open the search pane as earlier, for searching XPaths. And follow along with the following examples. Here is the HTML file for your reference:

```
<html>
  <body>
    <div id='1461'>
      <p>Hello, World!</p>
      <p>Another paragraph.</p>
    </div>
    <div>
      <p>Hello, XPath!</p>
      <span>Some text in a span.</span>
    </div>
    <div class='special'>
      <p>Special paragraph.</p>
    </div>
  </body>
</html>
```

Combining Axes with Predicates: Using the **`descendant`** axis with a predicate to select all **`p`** elements inside the **`div`** with the ID attribute equal to **`'1461'`:**

```
//div[@id='1461']/descendant::p
```

Explanation: This expression reads as follows: "Select all **`p`** elements that are descendants of the **`div`** element with the ID attribute equal to **`'1461'`**." It will return both **`p`** elements inside the first **`div`** because they meet the criteria.

Using Operators and Predicates: Using the **`or`** operator with predicates to select **`p`** elements containing either **`Hello`** or **`XPath`**:

```
//p[contains(text(),'Hello') or contains(text(),'XPath')]
```

Explanation: This expression reads as follows: "Select all **`p`** elements that contain the text **`Hello`** OR **`XPath`**."

It will return the first and third **`p`** elements because both contain either **`Hello`** or **`XPath`** in their text.

Combining Axes, Operators, and Predicates: Using the **`descendant`** axis, **`contains`** function, and **`not`** operator to select **`p`** elements with text that do not contain the word **`paragraph`**: `//p[not(contains(text(),'paragraph'))]`

Explanation: This expression reads as follows: "Select all **`p`** elements that do NOT contain the text **`paragraph`** among their descendants." It will return the second **`p`** element because it does not contain the word **`paragraph`** in its text.

Using Attributes, Axes, and Predicates: Using the **`following-sibling`** axis with the **`id`** attribute and a predicate to select the **`div`** element that comes after the **`div`** with the ID attribute equal to **`'1461'`**: `//div[@id='1461']/following-sibling::div[1]`

Explanation: This expression reads as follows: "Select the first **`div`** element that is a following sibling of the **`div`** with the ID attribute equal to **`'1461'`**."

It will return the second **`div`** element because it is the first sibling that comes after the **`div`** with ID **`'1461'`**.

Now that you have become an XPath samurai, slicing, and dicing your way through HTML, let us use these concepts to find a few web elements using Selenium.

Open the **`Chapter03_xpathlocator.java`** file as follows and run it as a TestNG test:

```
package testscripts;
import java.util.List;
import org.openqa.selenium.By;
import org.openqa.selenium.WebDriver;
import org.openqa.selenium.WebElement;
import org.openqa.selenium.chrome.ChromeDriver;
import org.testng.annotations.Test;
```

```
public class Chapter03_name_XPathlocator {
@Test(priority = 1)
public void XPathLocatorExample() throws Exception {
// Creating a webdriver instance
WebDriver driver = new ChromeDriver();
//Navigating to Salesforce Login page
driver.get("https://login.salesforce.com/");
WebElement inputfield = driver.findElement(By.XPath("//input[@id='
username']"));
System.out.println("Location of the input field on screen is
" +inputfield.getLocation());
List<WebElement> links = driver.findElements(By.XPath("//a"));
System.out.println("Count of all the links is " +links.size());
driver.quit();
}}
```

In the preceding Java class, the following lines are elemental for understanding the use of XPaths for locating web elements:

```
WebElement inputfield = driver.findElement(By.XPath("//input[@id='
username']"));
System.out.println("Location of the input field on screen is
" +inputfield.getLocation());
```

In these lines, we are using Selenium WebDriver to find an element on a web page with the help of an XPath expression. The XPath expression used here is `//input[@id='username']`. It means we are looking for an **`input`** element that has the attribute id with the value **`username`.** The **`driver.findElement`** method locates the first matching element on the web page based on the XPath expression and stores it in the variable **`inputfield`** of type **`WebElement`**. This allows us to print the location of it on the screen.

```
List<WebElement> links = driver.findElements(By.XPath("//a"));
System.out.println("Count of all the links is " +links.size());
```

In these lines, we are using Selenium WebDriver to find multiple elements on the web page with the help of an XPath expression. The XPath expression used here is **`//a`**. It means we are looking for all a elements (hyperlinks) on the web page. The **`driver.findElements`** method locates all matching elements based on the XPath expression and stores them in a list of **`WebElement`** objects named **`links`**.

The **links.size()** method returns the number of elements present in the **links** list, which corresponds to the number of hyperlinks found on the page.

CSS locators

CSS stands for Cascading Style sheets and can become the backbone of any locator strategy. CSS locators use a concise and expressive syntax like CSS (Cascading Style Sheets) to identify elements based on their attributes, classes, IDs, or position in the document tree. Just like in CSS, you can use different types of selectors to target specific elements, making it easy to access the elements you need straightforwardly and efficiently.

There are various types of CSS locators, including:

1. **Element Selector**: Targets elements based on their tag name (for example, **div**, **p**, **a**).
2. **Class Selector**: Targets elements based on their class attribute (for example, **.classname**).
3. **ID Selector**: Targets elements based on their ID attribute (for example, **#elementID**).
4. **Attribute Selector**: Targets elements based on any attribute and its value (for example, **"[attribute='value']")**.
5. **Descendant Selector**: Targets elements that are descendants of a specific parent element (for example, **parent descendant**).
6. **Child Selector**: Targets elements that are direct children of a specific parent element (for example, **parent > child**).

Let's explore some common formats for CSS locators along with HTML snippets.

Create the following HTML file or open it from **Example3.HTML** in your downloaded source code:

```
<html>
  <body>
    <div class="container">
      <h1>Welcome to CSS Locators</h1>
      <p class="highlight">This is a paragraph.</p>
      <p>This is another paragraph.</p>
      <ul>
```

```
        <li>Item 1</li>
        <li>Item 2</li>
      </ul>
    </div>
  </body>
</html>
```

Now follow these steps to check CSS locators in the console:

1. Press F12 to open up Chrome DevTools.
2. Switch to the Console panel.
3. Type in CSS selectors like **`$$("h1")`** to evaluate and validate.
4. Check results returned from console execution - If elements are matched, they will be returned in a list. Otherwise, an empty list [ ] is shown.

***Figure 3.9**: Finding CSS locators in the Chrome Dev Console*

Try the following examples of CSS selectors:

`Element Selector:` The element selector targets elements based on their tag name.

Example: Select the **`h1`** element.

CSS Locator: **`h1`**

Explanation: This CSS locator will select the **`h1`** element, which is **`Welcome to CSS Locators`**.

`Class Selector`: The class selector targets elements based on their class attribute.

Example: Select the element with the class **`highlight`**.

CSS Locator: **`.highlight`**

Explanation: This CSS locator will select the **`p`** element with the class **`highlight`**, which is **`This is a paragraph`**.

`Descendant Selector:` The descendant selector selects elements that are descendants of a specific parent element.

Example 4: Select all **`li`** elements inside the **`ul`** element.

CSS Locator: **`ul li`**

Explanation: This CSS locator will select both **`li`** elements, **`Item 1`** and **`Item 2`**, which are descendants of the **`ul`** element.

`Child Selector`: The child selector selects elements that are direct children of a specific parent element.

Example 5: Select all **`li`** elements that are direct children of the **`ul`** element.

CSS Locator: **`ul > li`**

Explanation: This CSS locator will select both **`li`** elements, **`Item 1`** and **`Item 2`**, which are direct children of the **`ul`** element.

`Attribute Selector`: The attribute selector targets elements based on their attributes.

Example 6: Select all elements with the **`class`** attribute.

CSS Locator: **`[class]`**

Explanation: This CSS locator will select both the **`div`** and **`p`** elements, as both have the **`class`** attribute.

What is theory, without practical? Let us use the preceding concepts around CSS locators to find a few web elements using Selenium.

Open the **`Chapter03_CSSlocator.java`** file as follows and run it as a TestNG test:
package testscripts;

```
import org.openqa.selenium.By;
import org.openqa.selenium.WebDriver;
import org.openqa.selenium.WebElement;
import org.openqa.selenium.chrome.ChromeDriver;
import org.testng.annotations.Test;
public class Chapter03_name_CSSlocator {
@Test(priority = 1)
```

```
public void CSSPathLocatorExample() throws Exception {
// Creating a webdriver instance
WebDriver driver = new ChromeDriver();
//Navigating to Salesforce Login page
driver.get("https://login.salesforce.com/");
WebElement inputfield = driver.findElement(By.cssSelector("input.r4.wide.
mb16.mt8.username"));
System.out.println("Location of the input field on screen is " +input-
field.getLocation());
driver.quit();
}
}
```

In simple words, the given line of code **`WebElement inputfield = driver.findElement(By.cssSelector("input.r4.wide.mb16.mt8.username"));`** searches for an `input` element with multiple CSS classes assigned to it, such as **`r4, wide, mb16, mt8,`** and **`username`**. The **`driver.findElement()`** method is used to search for the element, and the **`By.cssSelector()`** method specifies the search criteria using a CSS selector. The CSS selector provided is **`input.r4.wide.mb16.mt8.username`**, which targets an **`input`** element that has all the mentioned CSS classes. Once the element is found, it is stored in the `inputfield` variable, allowing you to perform various actions on this element later in the code, such as printing the location of the web element on the screen.

Note: While choosing a locator strategy, remember that while CSS locators are faster than XPaths, the latter offers bidirectional traversal in the DOM tree via axes (like **`ancestor`** or **`following-sibling`**) and better readability as well.

Interactions with Web Elements

Just like navigating a map using a trusty vehicle, we have already learned how to navigate HTML using the powerful WebDriver and locate web elements with various locator strategies. Now, it is time to take our journey to the next level by learning how to perform actions like clicks and more on these web elements.

Buckle up as we explore various kinds of interactions with web elements such as clicks, drag and drop, typing, and web navigation.

To explore all the options available on a web element, we can simply try the auto-complete on IDE as follows:

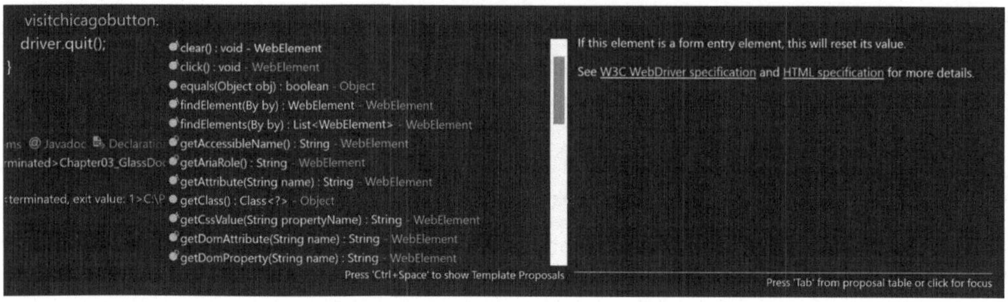

Figure 3.10: *Available methods for a web element*

Let us take a closer look at the various methods and operations available to us at the web element level.

click

The **`click()`** method is used to click an element. If this causes a new page to load, you should discard all references to this element and any further operations performed on this element will throw a **`StaleElementReferenceException`**. There are some preconditions for an element to be clicked. The element must be visible, and it must have a height and width greater than 0.

Open the **`Chapter03_ButtonClick.java`** class in the downloaded repository as follows:

```
WebDriver driver = new ChromeDriver();
//Navigating to Salesforce login page
driver.get("https://login.salesforce.com/");
WebElement loginbutton = driver.findElement(By.xpath("//input[@id='
Login']"));
//Attempting a click on the button
loginbutton.click();
driver.quit();
```

In the given Java Selenium code, we first initialize a ChromeDriver session to launch a web browser. Then, we navigate to the Salesforce login page using the **`get()`** method with the URL https://login.salesforce.com/. Next, we locate the login button on the page using the **`findElement()`** method and XPath expression. Upon finding the button, we attempt to click it using the **`click()`** method. Finally, after completing the interaction, we quit the WebDriver, close the browser and end the automation session. In summary, the code automates the process of accessing the Salesforce login page, locating the login button, and attempting to click it before ending the browser session.

isDisplayed

The **isDisplayed()** method is used to check if a web element is visible on the web page.

It returns a boolean value: true if the element is visible, and false if it is hidden or not present in the DOM.

Open the **Chapter03_IsDisplayed.java** class in the downloaded repository as follows:

```
WebDriver driver = new ChromeDriver();
//Navigating to Salesforce login page
driver.get("https://login.salesforce.com/");
WebElement loginbutton = driver.findElement(By.xpath("//input[@id='
Login']"));
//Checking if the element is displayed
System.out.println( "Is the button displayed ? "+loginbutton.is
Displayed());
driver.quit();
```

The print statement here displays **"Is the button displayed ? true"** showing that the button is displayed.

isEnabled

The **isEnabled()** method is used to check if a web element is enabled or disabled for user interaction. It returns a boolean value: true if the element is enabled, and false if it is disabled.

Open the **Chapter03_IsEnabled.java** class in the downloaded repository as below:

```
WebDriver driver = new ChromeDriver();
//Navigating to Salesforce login page
driver.get("https://login.salesforce.com/");
WebElement loginbutton = driver.findElement(By.xpath("//input[@id='
Login']"));
```

```
//Checking if the element is enabled
System.out.println( "Is the button enabled ? "+loginbutton.isEnabled());
driver.quit();
```

The print statement here displays **"Is the button enabled ? true"** showing that the button is enabled.

Note: **isEnabled()** and **isDisplayed()** are very good combinations for checking the availability of the web elements for interactions like clicks and more. Think of it as checking if the shop is displayed on the street and open before proceeding for shopping inside it.

getAttribute

The **getAttribute()** method is used to retrieve the value of a specified attribute of a web element. It is often used to extract information from an element, such as getting the value of an input field, the **"href"** of a link, or the **"src"** of an image.

Open and run the **Chapter03_getAttribute.java** class in the downloaded repository as follows:

```
//Navigating to Salesforce login page
driver.get("https://login.salesforce.com/");
WebElement loginbutton = driver.findElement(By.xpath("//input[@id='
Login']"));
//Getting the name attribute
System.out.println( "Value of the name attribute is :  "+loginbutton.
getAttribute("name"));
driver.quit();
```

The print statement here displays **"Value of the name attribute is : Login"** showing the name attribute. The reference HTML for the login button is as follows:

```
<input class="button r4 wide primary" type="submit" id="Login"
name="Login" value="Log In">
```

getText

The **getText()** method is used to retrieve the visible text of a web element (as rendered by the web browser and not hidden by CSS). It is commonly used to extract the content of headings, paragraphs, or labels on a web page.

Open and run the **Chapter03_getText.java** class in the downloaded repository as follows:

```
//Navigating to Salesforce login page
driver.get("https://login.salesforce.com/");
WebElement tryforfreebutton = driver.findElement(By.xpath("//a[@id='
signup_link']"));
//Getting the text value
System.out.println( "Value of the text is :  "+tryforfreebutton.
getText());
driver.quit();
```

The print statement here displays **"Value of the text is : Try for Free"** showing the text for the signup button. Its HTML is presented for reference as follows:

```
<a class="button secondary" id="signup_link"
href="https://www.salesforce.com/form/trial/freetrial.
jsp?d=70130000000Enus">Try for Free</a>
```

sendKeys

The **sendKeys()** method is used to simulate keyboard input into a text field or element.

It is commonly used to enter text, perform keyboard shortcuts, or interact with input fields.

Open and run the **Chapter03_sendKeys.java** class in the downloaded repository as follows:

```
//Navigating to Salesforce login page
driver.get("https://login.salesforce.com/");
WebElement usernameinput = driver.findElement(By.xpath("//input[@id='us-
ername']"));
//setting the text value
usernameinput.sendKeys("reader@orangeava.com");
thread.sleep(3000);
driver.quit();
```

The **sendKeys()** command is essentially telling Selenium WebDriver to find the input field, represented by usernameInput, and simulate the action of typing `reader@orangeava.com` into that field. This is a common action in web automation, often used to fill out login forms or input fields on web pages during testing.

Another thing to note here is the command: thread.sleep(3000).

In Selenium test automation using Java, the command `Thread.sleep()` is used to introduce a pause or wait in the test script for a specified duration. The duration is given in milliseconds. In this case, the command pauses the execution of the test script for 3000 milliseconds, which is equivalent to 3 seconds.

The `Thread.sleep()` method is part of the Java language, and it suspends the execution of the current thread, allowing other tasks to run in the meantime. It is commonly used in test automation to introduce a delay or wait for specific scenarios, such as waiting for a page to load, waiting for an element to become visible, or adding some time buffer between test steps.

However, it is essential to use `Thread.sleep()` with caution. While it can be useful in certain situations, it is not the recommended way to handle waits in Selenium test automation. Using explicit waits provided by Selenium's `WebDriverWait` class or `ExpectedConditions` is a more reliable and efficient approach as it allows the test to wait for specific conditions to be met rather than just a fixed duration. We will explore the waiting strategies in detail in our next chapter.

Excessive use of `Thread.sleep()` can slow down test execution unnecessarily and make the test script less maintainable. It may lead to longer test execution times and false positives in case of delays or variations in web application response times.

In our example, `Thread.sleep(3000)` is a command used to introduce a pause in test automation scripts for a specific duration. However, it is generally recommended to use explicit waits provided by Selenium WebDriver to handle waits and synchronization more effectively and efficiently. We have used `Thread.sleep()` to slow down the test script, so that we can observe that the text is being input to the login field.

clear

The `clear()` method is used to clear the text or reset the value of an input field. It is typically used before entering new data into the field. If this element is a form entry element, this will reset its value.

Open and run the **Chapter03_clear.java** class in the downloaded repository as follows:

```
//Navigating to Salesforce login page
driver.get("https://login.salesforce.com/");
WebElement usernameinput = driver.findElement(By.xpath("//input[@id='
username']"));
//setting the text value
usernameinput.sendKeys("reader@orangeava.com");
Thread.sleep(3000);
usernameinput.clear();
Thread.sleep(3000);
driver.quit();
```

The given commands are used to interact with the login input web element, enter text, clear the input field, and introduce pauses in the test script, for us to observe the interactions.

Here is a summary of key web interactions available in tabular format for reference:

Method	Description
`clear()`	Clears the text or resets the value of an input field.
`click()`	Simulates a click action on a web element, like buttons or links.
`findElement(By by)`	Finds and returns the first web element that matches the given locator strategy (**By**).
`findElements(By by)`	Finds and returns a list of all web elements that match the given locator strategy (**By**).
`getAccessibleName()`	Gets the accessible name attribute value of a web element, which is useful for accessibility testing.
`getAriaRole()`	Gets the ARIA role attribute value of a web element, which is helpful for accessibility-related testing.

getAttribute(String name)	Gets the value of the specified attribute of a web element, like **href** or **value**.
getCssValue(String property)	Gets the computed value of the specified CSS property of a web element, like **color** or **font-size**.
getDomAttribute(String name)	Gets the value of a DOM attribute of a web element, like **class** or **id.**
getDomProperty(String name)	Gets the value of a DOM property of a web element, like **textContent** or **innerText.**
getLocation()	Gets the location of the top-left corner of a web element on the page.
getRect()	Gets the size and position of a web element as a rectangle.
getShadowRoot()	Gets the shadow root of a web element that uses shadow DOM, if available.
getSize()	Gets the size (width and height) of a web element.
getTagName()	Gets the HTML tag name of a web element, like **div** or **input.**
getText()	Gets the visible text of a web element, like the content of headings or paragraphs.
isDisplayed()	Checks if a web element is visible on the page.
isEnabled()	Checks if a web element is enabled or disabled for user interaction.
isSelected()	Checks if a web element is selected, typically used for checkboxes or radio buttons.
sendKeys (CharSequence... key	Simulates typing or sending keyboard input to an input field or web element.
submit()	Submits a form, typically used on input elements within a form.

***Table 3.1**: Summary of web element methods*

Handling Frames and Windows

In the realm of Selenium test automation, browser windows and frames add an extra layer of complexity to our journey. Browser windows are like portals to different parts of the web, and frames are like intricate paintings within these portals. As testers, we must adeptly navigate between multiple windows and frames, switching contexts seamlessly to interact with the desired content. Whether it's handling pop-up windows, iFrames, or framesets, understanding the art of window management ensures we can effectively manipulate and validate elements across these digital canvases. This skill empowers us to create robust and comprehensive tests that encompass the intricacies of modern web applications.

iframes

In HTML, an iframe (short for inline frame) is an element that allows you to embed another HTML document within the current document. It essentially creates a window within a window, allowing you to display content from another source or website within your own webpage. iframes are commonly used for embedding videos, maps, advertisements, or other external content seamlessly into a web page.

Example HTML:

```
<iframe src="https://www.youtube.com/embed/your-video-id"></iframe>
```

Navigate to the URL https://www.w3schools.com/tags/tryit.asp?filename=tryhtml_table_test and try inspecting the table element with Chrome developer tools.

Observe the following image, table being displayed is within an iframe, we cannot locate or recognize that by just looking at it. So when we do a right-click the table, we can see additional options such as **`View frame source`** or **`Reload frame`**, proving the point that the web element under question (table in our example), is within an iframe.

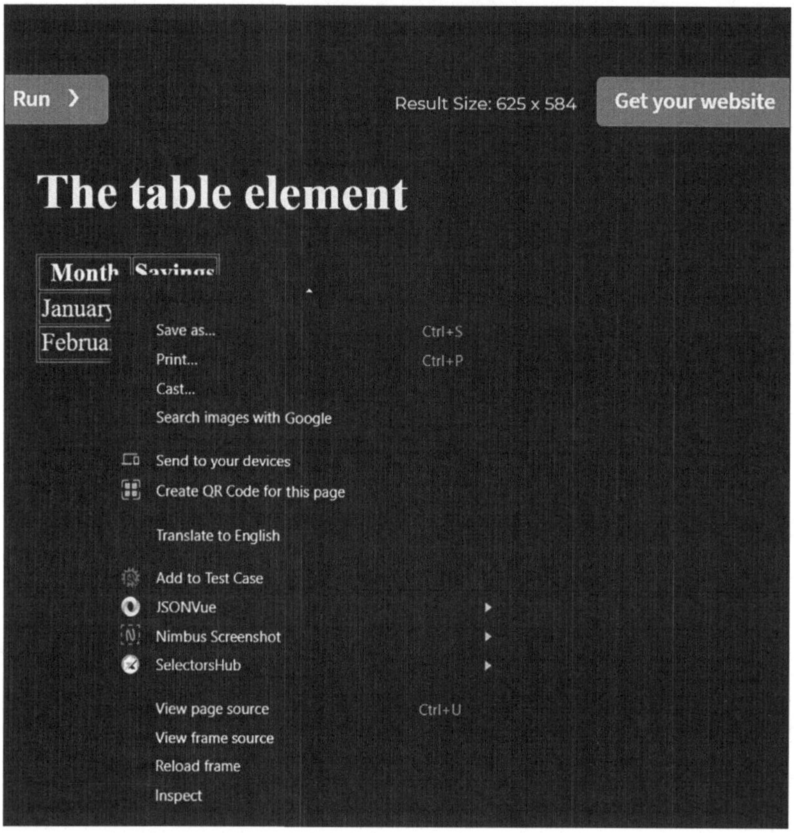

***Figure 3.11**: Contextual menu for iframes*

Interacting with iframes in Selenium using Java involves switching the WebDriver's focus to the iframe so that you can interact with elements inside it. There are three ways to handle iframes, including:

- **`By Index`**: You can switch to an iframe by its index number. The index starts from 0 and increments for each iframe present on the page. This method is useful when there is a single iframe or iframes that have a consistent order. Open and run the **`Chapter03_iframeInteraction.java`** file and observe the following lines:

```
driver.get("https://www.w3schools.com/tags/tryit.asp?filename=
tryhtml_table_test");

driver.switchTo().frame(0);

Thread.sleep(10000);

WebElement columnheader1 = driver.findElement(By.xpath("//th
[normalize-space()='Month']"));
```

```
//getting the text value
System.out.println("First Column header is " + columnheader1.
getText());
// Switch back to the main page
driver.switchTo().defaultContent();
```

Here we switch to the first iframe using the command **driver.switchTo().frame(0);** and then grab the web element for column header from inside of it. The xpath **("//th[normalize-space()='Month']")])** is used to locate a **<th>** (table header) element whose text content is **Month**, considering leading and trailing whitespaces are removed. Once, we get the web element's text, we can optionally switch back to the default content using **driver.switchTo().defaultContent();**.

- **By Name or ID:** You can switch to an iframe by its name or ID attribute. iframes with unique names or IDs can be easily targeted using this method.

Example:

```
WebDriver driver = new ChromeDriver();
driver.get("https://example.com");

// Switch to the iframe using its name or ID
driver.switchTo().frame("frameNameOrId");

// Perform actions inside the iframe
WebElement elementInsideiframe = driver.findElement(By.id("elemen-
tId"));
elementInsideiframe.sendKeys("Hello, iframe!");

// Switch back to the main page
driver.switchTo().defaultContent();
```

- **By Web Element:** If you have already located the iframe element using **findElement()** or any other method, you can directly switch to it using the **switchTo().frame()** method with the WebElement.

Example:

```
WebDriver driver = new ChromeDriver();
driver.get("https://example.com");
```

```
// Locate the iframe element
WebElement iframeElement = driver.findElement(By.id("iframeId"));

// Switch to the iframe using the WebElement
driver.switchTo().frame(iframeElement);

// Perform actions inside the iframe
WebElement elementInsideiframe = driver.findElement(By.id("elemen-
tId"));
elementInsideiframe.click();

// Switch back to the main page
driver.switchTo().defaultContent();
```

Note: After performing actions inside an iframe, it is essential to switch back to the main page using **`driver.switchTo().defaultContent()`** to interact with elements outside the iframe. Additionally, ensure that the iframe is loaded before switching to it (by using wait strategies or **`Thread.sleep()`** statements); otherwise, a `**NoSuchFrameException**` may be thrown.

Window Management

Window management in Selenium test automation refers to the process of handling multiple browser windows or tabs that may open during test execution. When interacting with web applications, actions like clicking links, and buttons, or opening new pages can lead to the opening of new windows or tabs. It is essential to switch between these windows to interact with their content.

Selenium provides methods to manage windows and tabs effectively. The primary methods used for window management are **`getWindowHandles(), switchTo().window(),`** and **`close().`**

Let's explore window management using Java and Selenium with examples from real websites. Consider a scenario of clicking a button that opens a new tab, and we need to switch between the original and new tabs.

Open and run the **`Chapter03_newTabInteraction.java`** file and observe the following code:

```
//Navigating to W3 website
driver.get("https://www.w3schools.com/tags/tryit.asp?filename=tryhtml_a_
target");
driver.switchTo().frame(0);
Thread.sleep(10000);
WebElement tablink = driver.findElement(By.xpath
("//a[normalize-space()='Visit W3Schools!']"));
tablink.click();
// Get the handles of all open tabs
String parentTabHandle = driver.getWindowHandle();
System.out.println("window handle of the parent tab is :"+parentTabHandle);
        for (String tabHandle : driver.getWindowHandles()) {
            if (!tabHandle.equals(parentTabHandle)) {
                driver.switchTo().window(tabHandle);
                 Thread.sleep(5000);
                break;
            }
        }
// Perform actions in the new tab
System.out.println("tab handle of the new tab is :"+parentTabHandle);
System.out.println("Title of the new tab: " + driver.getTitle());
// Switch back to the parent tab
driver.switchTo().window(parentTabHandle);
Thread.sleep(5000);
// Perform actions in the parent tab
System.out.println("Title of the parent tab: " + driver.getTitle());
```

In our example, we start by obtaining the current window handle using **`driver.getWindowHandle()`.** When a new window or tab is opened, we use **`driver.getWindowHandles()`** to get the handles of all open windows or tabs. We then iterate through the handles to find the new window or tab. Once located, we use **`driver.switchTo().window(windowHandle)`** to switch the focus to the new window or tab. After performing actions in the new window or tab, we can close it using **`driver.close()`** and switch back to the parent window or tab using **`driver.switchTo().window(parentWindowHandle)`.**

The same methodology can be followed for switching between windows in the browser.

Consider a scenario of clicking a link opens a new window, and we need to interact with elements in both the original and new windows. We can accomplish the same with the following code:

```
driver.get("https://www.example.com");
// Click on a link that opens a new window
driver.findElement(By.linkText("Open New Window")).click();
// Get the handles of all open windows
String parentWindowHandle = driver.getWindowHandle();
        for (String windowHandle : driver.getWindowHandles()) {
            if (!windowHandle.equals(parentWindowHandle)) {
                driver.switchTo().window(windowHandle);
                break;
            }
        }
        // Perform actions in the new window
System.out.println("Title of the new window: " + driver.getTitle());
// Close the new window and switch back to the parent window
driver.close();
driver.switchTo().window(parentWindowHandle);
// Perform actions in the parent window
System.out.println("Title of the parent window: " + driver.getTitle());
driver.quit();
    }
}
```

Common HTML Elements

Common HTML elements are the building blocks of web pages and form the foundation of web development. These elements are standardized and widely used across websites to structure and display content. Some of the most common HTML elements include headings (**<h1>** to **<h6>**), paragraphs (**<p>**), links (**<a>**), images (**<img>**), lists (**<ul>, <ol>, <li>**), tables (**<table>**, **<tr>**, **<td>**), forms (**<form>, <input>, <textarea>, <button>**), and more. These elements enable developers to organize and present information in a structured manner, making it easier for users to navigate and comprehend the content. Whether it's displaying text, images, or interactive elements, mastering these common HTML elements is essential for anyone involved in web development, design, or test automation, as they provide the backbone for creating rich and user-friendly web experiences.

Table

We briefly observed interactions with a table in our last section around iframes. Let us delve a bit deeper into the topic of interacting with HTML tables. Tables in HTML are used to organize data in rows and columns. They are a fundamental element for displaying structured information and are widely used to present tabular data. Tables consist of the **`<table>`, `<tr>`, `<th>`,** and **`<td>`** elements. **`<tr>`** represents a table row, **`<th>`** represents a table header cell, and **`<td>`** represents a regular data cell.

Example HTML:

```
<!DOCTYPE html>
<html>
<head>
<style>
table, th, td {
  border: 1px solid black;
}
</style>
</head>
<body>

<h1>The table element</h1>

<table>
  <tr>
    <th>Month</th>
    <th>Savings</th>
  </tr>
```

```
  <tr>
    <td>January</td>
    <td>$100</td>
  </tr>
  <tr>
    <td>February</td>
    <td>$80</td>
  </tr>
</table>


</body>
</html>
```

Open and run the **Chapter03_TableInteraction.java** file and observe the following code:

```
WebDriver driver = new ChromeDriver();
//Navigating to W3 website    driver.get("https://www.w3schools.com/
tags/tryit.asp?filename=tryhtml_table_test");
driver.switchTo().frame(0);
Thread.sleep(10000);
// Locate the table element
WebElement tableElement = driver.findElement(By.xpath("//table"));
// Access all rows within the table
List<WebElement> rows = tableElement.findElements(By.tagName("tr"));
// Loop through rows and access cells (columns)
for (WebElement row : rows) {
      List<WebElement> cells = row.findElements(By.tagName("td"));
       // Accessing data from each cell and printing it
          for (WebElement cell : cells) {
                System.out.print(cell.getText() + "\t");
          }
            System.out.println(); // Move to the next row
       }
```

```
        driver.quit();
}
```

In this example, we locate the table with xpath **`//table`** using **`driver.findElement(By.xpath("//table"));`**. Then, we access the rows and cells of the table using **`findElements(By.tagName("tr"))`** and **`findElements(By.tagName("td"))`**, respectively. Finally, we extract the data from each cell using **`getText()`** and print it to the console.

This way, you can automate HTML tables and perform various actions, such as data validation, filtering, or interacting with specific cells based on your testing requirements.

Select

The **`<select>`** element in HTML is used to create dropdown lists, also known as select dropdowns. It allows users to choose an option from a list of predefined options. The dropdown list contains one or more **`<option>`** elements that represent the selectable items. The selected option can be identified using the selected attribute in the `<option>` tag.

Example HTML:

```
<label for="cars">Choose a car:</label>
  <select name="cars" id="cars">
    <option value="volvo">Volvo</option>
    <option value="saab">Saab</option>
    <option value="opel">Opel</option>
    <option value="audi">Audi</option>
  </select>
```

Open the **`Chapter03_SelectInteraction.java`** file and observe the following code:

```
//Navigating to W3 website
driver.get("https://www.w3schools.com/tags/tryit.asp?filename=tryhtml_
select");
driver.switchTo().frame(0);
Thread.sleep(10000);
// Locate the <select> element by its ID
WebElement selectElement = driver.findElement(By.id("cars"));
```

```
// Create a Select object using the <select> element
Select select = new Select(selectElement);
// 1. Select option by visible text
select.selectByVisibleText("Volvo");
// 2. Select option by value
// select.selectByValue("saab");
// 3. Select option by index (0-based index)
// select.selectByIndex(2);
// Perform other actions if needed
// For example, to get the selected option text:
String selectedOption = select.getFirstSelectedOption().getText();
System.out.println("Selected option: " + selectedOption);
// Close the browser
driver.quit();
```

In this example, we use the **findElement()** method to locate the **<select>** element by its ID **cars**. Then, we create a Select object using the **<select>** element. You can select an option from the dropdown using any of the three methods provided by the Select class: **selectByVisibleText(), selectByValue(), or selectByIndex().** Simply uncomment the desired method and comment on the others based on how you want to select the option.

Radio button

Radio buttons are used to provide a list of mutually exclusive options to users. Only one option can be selected at a time from the group. Radio buttons are created using the **<input>** element with the **type="radio"** attribute. Each radio button should have a unique name attribute to group them.

Open and run the **Chapter03_RadioInteraction.java** file and observe the following code:

```
//Navigating to W3 website
driver.get("https://www.w3schools.com/tags/tryit.asp?filename=tryhtml5_
input_type_radio");
driver.switchTo().frame(0);
Thread.sleep(10000);
// Locate the radio buttons by their IDs
WebElement htmlRadio = driver.findElement(By.id("html"));
```

```
WebElement cssRadio = driver.findElement(By.id("css"));
WebElement javascriptRadio = driver.findElement(By.id("javascript"));
// Click on the radio button to select it
cssRadio.click();
// Perform other actions if needed
// For example, to check if a radio button is selected:
boolean isHtmlSelected = htmlRadio.isSelected();
System.out.println("Is HTML radio button selected? " + isHtmlSelected);
// Close the browser
driver.quit();
```

In this example, we use the **findElement()** method to locate the radio buttons by their IDs **("html", "css", and "javascript").** You can also locate them using other attributes like name or value, depending on the specific HTML structure. Then, we use the **click()** method to select the radio button **CSS.** You can change the selection to any other radio button by calling **click()** on the respective WebElement.

Drag and Drop

Drag and drop is a common user interaction in web applications where a user clicks and holds on an element, drags it to a new location, and then drops it there. Automating drag and drop interactions using Selenium involves using specialized actions from the Actions class provided by WebDriver.

Open the **Chapter03_DragAndDropInteraction.java** file and observe the following code:

```
 //Navigating to W3 website
 driver.get("https://www.w3schools.com/html/html5_draganddrop.asp");
Thread.sleep(5000);
// Locate the source and target elements
WebElement sourceElement = driver.findElement(By.xpath("//div[@
id='main']//img[@id='drag1']"));
WebElement targetElement = driver.findElement(By.id("div2"));
//Creating object of Actions class to build composite actions
Actions builder = new Actions(driver);
//Performing the drag and drop action
builder.dragAndDrop(sourceElement, targetElement).build().perform();
```

The **dragAndDrop()** method is part of the Actions class and is used to perform the drag and drop action. It takes two parameters: **sourceElement** and **targetElement**.

- **sourceElement:** This is the element that we want to drag and move.
- **targetElement:** This is the element where we want to drop the **sourceElement.**

The **build()** method is used to compile all the actions created by the Actions class into a single composite action. It is generally used when multiple actions need to be performed sequentially.

Finally, the **perform()** method is called to execute the composite action. It triggers the actual drag and drop operation, moving the sourceElement to the specified location represented by the targetElement.

Calendar

Calendars are commonly used in web applications for date selection. They allow users to pick a date from a visual calendar view. There are various JavaScript libraries and plugins available to create interactive and user-friendly calendars. Calendars can be implemented using custom HTML, CSS, and JavaScript or by using third-party calendar libraries like jQuery UI Datepicker.

Open and run the **Chapter03_CalendarInteraction.java** file and observe the following code:

```
// Locate the date element using XPath (Replace with appropriate locator strategy)
WebElement dateinputelement =
driver.findElement(By.xpath("//input[@id='datepicker']"));
dateinputelement.click();
Thread.sleep(3000);
WebElement dateElement = driver.findElement(By.xpath
("//a[@data-date=\"5\"]"));
// Click on the date element to select the date
dateElement.click();
Thread.sleep(3000);
// Optionally, perform actions after selecting the date
// For example, you can verify the selected date by getting the
element's text
```

```
String selectedDate = dateElement.getText();
System.out.println("Selected Date: " + selectedDate);
```

Here we first click the date input element to pop up the calendar widget and then select the date as **5** using the following code:

```
WebElement dateElement = driver.findElement(By.xpath("//a[@data
-date=\"5\"]"));
// Click on the date element to select the date
dateElement.click();
```

Depending on the webpage and the actual use case, you may need to adapt the XPath expressions to locate the elements properly.

Form Submissions and File Uploads

Forms are commonly used on web pages to gather user inputs, such as login credentials or registration details. Selenium provides methods to interact with form elements like text fields, checkboxes, and radio buttons to fill in the required information.

After entering the necessary data, the **submit()** method can be used on the form element to trigger the form submission process. This action is akin to clicking the **Submit** button on a web page, and it sends the data to the server for processing. Proper handling of form submissions ensures that user interactions and data submissions are accurately automated during test scenarios.

Open and run the **Chapter03_FormSubmission.java** file and observe the following lines:

```
//Navigating to OrangeHRM demo login page
driver.get("https://opensource-demo.orangehrmlive.com/web/index.php/
auth/login");
Thread.sleep(3000);
WebElement username = driver.findElement(By.xpath("//input[@placeholder
='Username']"));
username.sendKeys("Admin");
WebElement password = driver.findElement(By.xpath("//input[@placeholder
='Password']"));
password.sendKeys("admin123");
WebElement loginbutton = driver.findElement(By.xpath("//button[@
type='submit']"));
```

```
loginbutton.submit();
Thread.sleep(3000);
//Checking if the home page is displayed
System.out.println( "URL of the dashboard is  "+driver.getCurrentUrl());
```

Here the code automates the login process for the OrangeHRM demo application, enters the username and password, clicks the login button, and then verifies if the dashboard page is displayed by printing its URL navigates to the home page dashboard of the demo site using the user name, password and submitting the login form.

File upload functionality is another critical aspect of web applications, allowing users to upload files, such as images or documents. Selenium supports file uploads using the **sendKeys()** method, which allows specifying the file path of the file to be uploaded. This method works for **<input type="file">** elements, enabling test automation to simulate user interactions when selecting and uploading files. Robust handling of file uploads ensures that applications can handle various file formats and user inputs effectively during automated testing.

Example HTML:

```
<html>
<body>


<h1>File upload</h1>


<p>Show a file-select field which allows a file to be chosen for upload:</p>
<form action="/action_page.php">
  <label for="myfile">Select a file:</label>
  <input type="file" id="myfile" name="myfile"><br><br>
  <input type="submit" value="Submit">
</form>
</body>
</html>
```

We can upload a file to the referenced HTML via the Selenium code in **Chapter03_FileUpload.java** file as follows:

```
//Navigating to W3 website
driver.get("https://www.w3schools.com/html/tryit.asp?filename=tryhtml_
input_file");
driver.switchTo().frame(0);
Thread.sleep(10000);
// Locate the upload input button
WebElement uploadinput = driver.findElement(By.xpath("//input[@id='
myfile']"));
WebElement submitbutton = driver.findElement(By.xpath("//input
[@value='Submit']"));
String filePath = "C:\\Users\\robin.gupta\\OneDrive\\Desktop\\Project
70\\chromedriver_win32\\file.txt";
uploadinput.sendKeys(filePath);
// Wait for the file to be uploaded and perform further actions
// (e.g., verify successful upload or check for error messages)
// Click on the submit button to select it
submitbutton.click();
```

Note: While we have relied upon the manual creation of xpaths and other locators, there are numerous tools available on the Chrome plugin store to generate Xpaths and other locators. One example of such tool is **`Selectorshub,`** which can be used to generate relative XPaths in an efficient manner.

Few Use Cases on Automation

Just think about the power you wield as an automation rockstar. In addition to software test automation, you can now also automate non-testing scenarios as follows:

Web Scraping for Fun

Ever wondered how many cats are up for adoption in your city? With Selenium test automation, you can create a web scraping tool to visit animal shelter websites, extract the number of adorable feline friends available, and present the data in a cat-tastic way! You might even build a purr-fect dashboard to keep track of the fluctuating cat population.

Automated Price Tracker

Love online shopping? Let Selenium do the bargain hunting for you! Build a nifty price tracker that visits your favorite e-commerce websites, checks the prices of your desired items, and alerts you when they drop to a level that won't break the bank. Who knew automated shopping could be so much fun?

Virtual Plant Nurturer

Do you have a green thumb, but not much time? With Selenium, you can create a virtual plant nurturer that visits gardening websites, fetches tips on caring for your beloved plants, and sends you gentle reminders to water, fertilize, and pamper your green leafy pals. Happy plants, happy you!

Remember, while these use cases are fun and light-hearted, they also showcase the versatility and creativity of Selenium automation beyond traditional testing scenarios.

Conclusion

If you have reached here and run the code examples successfully, you deserve a pat on the back. You have learned how to automate web applications via interactions with common web elements. In this chapter, we dived into the foundation of WebDriver, a tool that helps automate web tasks. We learned about locators, which are like detectives finding hidden things on web pages, and web elements, which are like the things we want to interact with. Think of it as a conductor leading a music symphony, making clicks, inputs, and checks flow smoothly.

Throughout this chapter, we not only explored how to use everyday website parts for automation but also tackled trickier tasks. We faced challenges like sending forms and uploading files, all with skill. We also learned how to smoothly switch between different parts of a website.

In the next chapter, we will build on top of our knowledge of the basics of web interactions with deeper concepts around page object patterns, which involve creating separate classes for each web page, encapsulating web elements and their operations; dynamic web elements that change during runtime, requiring flexible locators and waiting mechanisms, and the Screenplay Pattern, which models test scenarios as user interactions, using reusable actions and promoting a user-centric approach to test automation.

Exercise

Automate the navigation to https://orangeava.com/ and add a book to the cart.

Here are the sample steps:

1. Browse to https://orangeava.com/
2. Fill in the sign-up pop on home page or click the **`X`** button to skip it
3. Click the first book on the book list
4. On the book detail page, click **`ADD TO CART`** button
5. Click the **`CHECKOUT`** button to navigate to the Shipping information page.

Chapter 4

Advanced Selenium Techniques

Introduction

Welcome to a thrilling chapter where we delve into the pulsating heart of advanced Selenium techniques! Imagine you're embarking on an adventure in the vast and ever-changing world of web automation. This chapter is your trusty map, guiding you through the maze of dynamic web elements and complex user interactions. First, we'll dive into the realm of Synchronization and Wait Strategies. Just like a skilled conductor ensures each musician in an orchestra plays in harmony, these strategies help your automation scripts perform flawlessly in the unpredictable tempo of web applications. Learn the art of syncing your tests seamlessly with dynamic web behavior, employing implicit and explicit waits, and customizing strategies for flawless execution. Our exploration continues with the powerful Page Object Model (POM), enabling you to organize your scripts elegantly and enhance maintainability. Lastly, embrace the innovative Screenplay Pattern, where tests become stories, actors enact actions, and your testing journey becomes more readable, reusable, and scalable.

Prepare to elevate your Selenium game as we delve into these advanced techniques. From conquering dynamic locators to mastering synchronization, and from POM's structured elegance to the magic of the Screenplay Pattern, this chapter equips you with the tools to navigate intricate testing landscapes with confidence and expertise.

Structure

In this chapter, we will discuss the following topics:

- Synchronization and wait strategies
- Shadow DOM
- Animations and moving elements
- JavaScript Executor
- Page object model
- Screenplay pattern

Synchronization and Wait Strategies

In the ever-evolving landscape of web applications, the immediate loading of elements is not always guaranteed. A myriad of factors can contribute to delayed element availability, presenting potential challenges for automation. These loading issues arise due to a variety of reasons, each requiring unique solutions to ensure reliable and accurate test automation.

- **Delay in Rendering**: Web pages may consist of complex structures, intricate styling, and dynamic content. These factors can lead to a delay in rendering elements, causing them to appear on the page after a certain amount of time.
- **AJAX Requests**: Asynchronous JavaScript and XML (AJAX) requests are used to fetch data from a server without reloading the entire page. Elements dependent on these requests might take time to load as the data is fetched in the background.
- **Animations**: Modern websites often feature animations that add a dynamic flair. Elements tied to animations might only become interactable once the animations are complete. This is analogous to the excessive Flash (a legacy Adobe technology) content on web pages.
- **Dynamic Content Loading**: Content, especially images or ads, might be loaded dynamically after the initial page load. This can lead to delays in the availability of certain elements.
- **Network Latency**: Variability in network speeds can lead to inconsistencies in element loading times across different users and environments.
- **JavaScript Execution Time**: Heavy JavaScript usage can lead to increased execution time for actions. If automation attempts to interact with an element before JavaScript execution is complete, the element might not yet be ready for interaction.

- **Backend Processing**: Some elements might rely on backend processing or data retrieval, leading to delays in their availability. This can be aggravated by poor coding standards, complexity and density of the backend code.
- **Server performance and location**: Sometimes the backend server might be clogged up with requests, like an ecommerce application acting slow on the sale days. Or the servers might be located at a geographically far location from the requestor's location.
- **Lack of caching**: Majority of modern web applications suffer with inadequate caching techniques, such as client-side caching or database caching. This can cause degradation for the browsing experience.

Synchronization is the linchpin that addresses these loading issues. It is a practice where automation code is programmed to wait until specific conditions are met before proceeding with the next action. By employing synchronization, you mitigate the risks of encountering errors due to interactions with elements that have not fully loaded. This ensures the stability and reliability of your automation scripts, particularly in the face of the challenges posed by dynamic web elements and varying loading times.

Imagine a group of trapeze artists performing a breathtaking aerial routine.

Each artist swings, flips, and catches with impeccable timing, creating a seamless and mesmerizing spectacle. This coordination is like the synchronization we implement in Selenium automation.

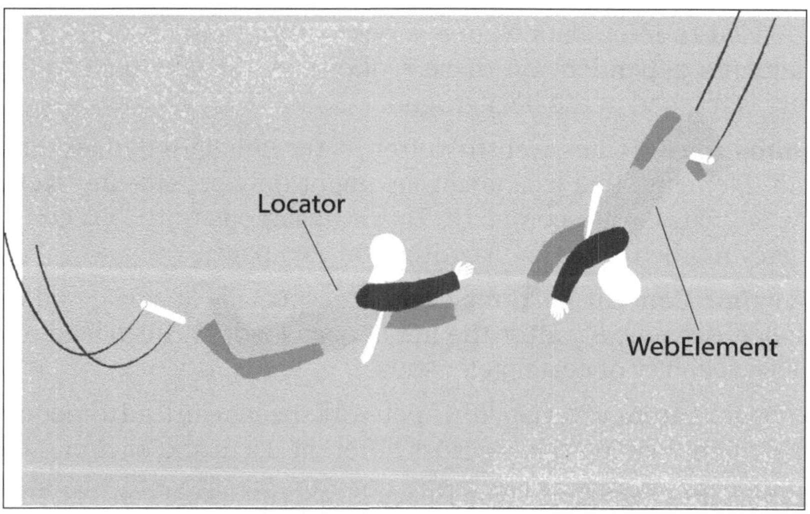

Figure 4.1: *Visual presentation of synchronization*

In the context of web automation, consider a scenario where you are automating a dynamic webpage with various elements that load at different times due to animations, AJAX requests, or other delays. It is like the trapeze artists preparing to perform their aerial acts, but not all of them are in position yet. If you were to command an action without waiting for the elements to fully load, your automation script might fail, just like a trapeze artist attempting a catch before their partner is ready.

Synchronization in Selenium is like a choreographer ensuring that each trapeze artist is in the right position before the routine advances. You employ techniques like implicit and explicit waits, polling, and custom conditions to ensure that your automation script does not proceed until the required elements are fully loaded and ready to interact with. This synchronization prevents errors and creates a smooth flow in your automation, just as the trapeze artists' coordination creates a flawless aerial performance.

So, just as the trapeze artists synchronize their moves for a stunning routine, Selenium's synchronization techniques ensure that your automation script flows seamlessly through the dynamic landscape of web elements, guaranteeing accurate and reliable interactions.

In technical words, if you try to click a button and maybe the internet is slow, the button might not show up on the webpage completely. In Selenium, this would cause an error message to pop up, saying that the button is not visible. It's similar to a trapeze artist trying to jump before the other person is ready to catch them.

In the context of browser automation, a significant challenge revolves around ensuring that the web application is in the right state to execute specific Selenium commands effectively. This often leads to a situation where there is a race between the browser getting into the desired state and the Selenium code executing.

Sometimes the browser wins, and everything works as planned; other times, the Selenium code is quicker, resulting in unexpected behavior. This dynamic interplay is a major reason for unreliable tests, often referred to as "flaky tests."

Note: "*Test flakiness*" in test automation refers to the inconsistent behavior of a test script. It results in unpredictable pass or fail outcomes across different test executions, often due to timing issues poor locator strategies, or environmental variations. Flaky tests undermine the reliability of test results and can lead to false positives or negatives.

Here are some other exceptions from WebDriver, to explain potential issues with synchronization of test execution or poor locator strategies:

- **`NoSuchElementException:`** When the automation script tries to locate an element that is not present in the DOM, this exception is thrown. It can also occur when attempting to interact with an element before it is fully loaded.
- **`StaleElementReferenceException:`** This exception arises when an element is no longer attached to the DOM, usually due to a page refresh or navigation. It can happen when trying to interact with an element that has become stale.
- **`ElementNotInteractableException:`** When an element is present in the DOM but is not in a state that can be interacted with (e.g., not visible or disabled), this exception occurs. It's common when attempting to click or send keys to an element that's not ready for interaction.
- **`ElementClickInterceptedException:`** If another element covers the target element at the time of click action, this exception is thrown. It can occur when dynamic elements overlap or animations are in progress.

And so, the big question is how do we handle synchronization issues?

Selenium offers a big answer in the form of waiting strategies to solve most (if not all) synchronization issues. These strategies come in 3 forms:

- Implicit
- Explicit
- Fluent

Let us take an example. Navigate to the web address:

https://ava-orange-education.github.io/Ultimate-Selenium-WebDriver-for-Test-Automation/docs/Chapter3_Waits.html

Click the **`Wait 1 second to get an input box`** button, to get an input box displayed on the UI (user interface). However, did you notice that the input box does not come right away as you click the button? It takes a while (one second) to get displayed.

If we had to automate this click and check the presence of the input box, our locator and web element might land in the "trapeze situation" as explained earlier, and would have resulted in a **`NoSuchElementException`** or similar. So how do we automate such scenarios? Can we use **`Thread.sleep()`** methods? Because we know that the input box will become visible in 1 second after clicking the button. Yes, we can add **`Thread.sleep()`** methods, however, these methods are often considered a code smell in Test Automation for several reasons. Firstly, they introduce unnecessary pauses in your code, making your automation slower than it needs to be. For instance, let us say you are automating a login process. If you put a `Thread.sleep(5000)` after entering the username and another after entering the password, you are adding a 10-second delay even though the browser might have already moved on. It is like waiting for a green light at a traffic junction when the light is already green!

As `Thread.sleep()` is not very smart, it waits for a fixed time, but what if the element you are waiting for loads faster or slower than expected? If you set a sleep for 5 seconds but the element loads in just 2 seconds, you are wasting 3 seconds of your precious test execution time. On the other hand, if it takes more than 5 seconds, your test will fail.

Moreover, using `Thread.sleep()` makes your tests more prone to flakiness. Imagine running the same test on different machines or in different network conditions. If the element loads quickly on one machine but slowly on another, your test might pass on one machine and fail on the other, even if the application is working fine.

Waiting Strategies

Wait strategies in Selenium are essential techniques used to handle timing and synchronization issues when automating web applications. These strategies ensure that your automation code interacts with elements only when they are fully loaded and ready for interaction. Waiting mechanisms prevent errors and flakiness caused by elements not being available or visible at the time of interaction.

Wait strategies are crucial for dealing with real-world scenarios where web elements might load at varying speeds, due to network latency or dynamic page rendering. By employing effective wait strategies, you enhance the reliability and stability of your test automation scripts, reducing the chances of encountering timing-related errors and ensuring successful test outcomes.

Implicit Waits

Implicit waits in Selenium are a way to manage the timing of test execution. It is like giving Selenium some “patience” for the web element to appear, before interacting with it. When you set an implicit wait, Selenium will wait for a specified amount of time before throwing an exception if an element is not immediately found. This wait is applied globally to all elements in the test for a session, making it a simple way to handle synchronization issues.

The default value for the implicit wait is `0` and as soon as the element is located, the driver will return the element reference and the code will continue executing, so a larger implicit wait value won't necessarily increase the duration of the session. Here's how you can use implicit waits in Java with Selenium:

```
// Set an implicit wait of 10 seconds
driver.manage().timeouts().implicitlyWait(10, TimeUnit.SECONDS);
```

Note: The polling time for implicit waits is 500 milliseconds counted till the timeout is provided as an argument.

Open the **`Chapter04_ImplicitWaits.java`** class in the **`chapter4`** package and focus on the following lines:

```
// Navigating to sample page
driver.get("https://ava-orange-education.github.io/Ultimate-Selenium
-WebDriver-for-Test-Automation/docs/Chapter3_Waits.html");
// Setting up Implicit wait
driver.manage().timeouts().implicitlyWait(Duration.ofSeconds(3));
WebElement inputboxbutton = driver.findElement(By.id("implicitbutton"));
inputboxbutton.click();
WebElement inputbox = driver.findElement(By.id("inputbox"));
System.out.println("Tag name of the displayed box on screen is " + in-
putbox.getTagName());
inputbox.sendKeys("Input value in the box");
```

In the given Selenium code, an implicit wait of 3 seconds is established (for the entirety of the session) to allow the WebDriver time to wait for elements to load before throwing an error. The script starts by locating and clicking a button element with the ID **"`implicitbutton.`"** Following the button click, it identifies an input element with the ID **"`inputbox`"** and retrieves its tag name, indicating its type. Subsequently, the code simulates entering the text **"`Input value in the box`"** into the input field. Through these steps, the implicit wait enhances test stability by ensuring that elements have sufficient time to load before interactions, contributing to reliable test automation.

Implicit waits can help us solve the synchronization to some extent, however, they come with some limitations, such as:

- **Limited Applicability**: Implicit waits are global by design. Other synchronization requirements, such as waiting for a certain condition or a particular state of an element, cannot be effectively addressed using implicit waits alone.
- **Binary Outcome**: The outcome of an implicit wait is binary – it either returns an element if found within the specified timeout or an error if not found. This doesn't provide additional information about the state of the element or any intermediate conditions during the wait.
- **Scope**: Implicit waits lack flexibility as they can only be set as a global timeout for the entire session. This limitation prevents finer control over waiting times for different elements or scenarios, which may be necessary for optimal test execution.

Explicit Waits

Explicit waits are a synchronization strategy that pauses the execution of your code until certain expected conditions are met. These conditions can be anything from the visibility of an element to its click-ability, presence, or specific attribute values. Explicit waits are particularly useful when dealing with dynamic web applications, AJAX-based content loading, and scenarios where elements appear or change state after a certain user action.

Let us go back to the "trapeze" example for a few moments. Imagine that if we had to write the pseudo algorithm for the trapeze artists to jump and get caught in the air by their partner, it would involve a sequence of steps that mimic the synchronization challenges faced in test automation. For example:

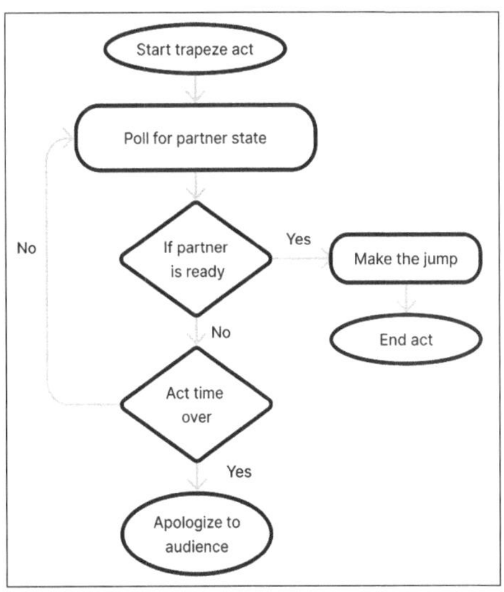

Figure 4.2: *Pseudo algorithm for trapeze act*

Explicit waits work in the same way, where WebDriver polls for the success of a certain condition and waits for its completion or timeout, to proceed with the execution or throw an exception.

Let us dive into the code to gain a practical understanding of the explicit wait strategy. Open **Chapter04_ExplicitWait.java** from the downloaded codebase, and focus on the following lines:

```
// Navigating to sample page

driver.get("https://ava-orange-education.github.io/Ultimate-Selenium
-WebDriver-for-Test-Automation/docs/Chapter3_Waits.html");

WebElement yellowcirclebutton = driver.findElement
(By.id("explicitbutton"));

yellowcirclebutton.click();

// Setting up Explicit wait

Wait<WebDriver> wait = new WebDriverWait(driver, Duration.ofSeconds(10));

wait.until(ExpectedConditions.visibilityOfElementLocated(By.cssSelector
(".circle")));

WebElement yellowcircle = driver.findElement(By.cssSelector(".circle"));

// Asserting if the yellow circle is displayed on screen

Assert.assertTrue(yellowcircle.isDisplayed(), "Yellow circle is not
displayed");

driver.quit();
```

An Explicit Wait is set up using the **WebDriverWait** class to make the script wait for a specific condition to be met. The purpose of this wait is to ensure that the script doesn't proceed until the condition is satisfied. The expected condition, in this case, is defined using the **ExpectedConditions.visibilityOfElementLocated()** method. This method expects a locator (in this case, a CSS selector) as an argument and returns a condition that waits until the element identified by the locator becomes visible. The **WebDriverWait** class is provided with the WebDriver instance (driver) and the maximum time to wait (timeout) for the condition to be met. Here, a timeout of 10 seconds is specified using **Duration.ofSeconds(10).**

Note: **Assert.assertTrue(...)** is a method provided by TestNG's Assert class. It's used to assert that a given condition is true. If the condition is true, the test continues executing. If the condition is false, the test is marked as failed, and the specified failure message is displayed. We have covered more details on TestNG library in the next chapter.

In the context of the preceding code, the line **`Assert.assertTrue(yellowcircle.isDisplayed(), "Yellow circle is not displayed")`** is a verification step that uses TestNG's assertion mechanism to check whether a certain condition is true or not. This assertion is used to validate whether the yellow circle element on the webpage is displayed or not.

Here is the sample output from the console for the TestNG Assert statement:

```
PASSED: explicitWaitExample

===============================================
    Default test
    Tests run: 1, Failures: 0, Skips: 0
===============================================


===============================================
Default suite
Total tests run: 1, Passes: 1, Failures: 0, Skips: 0
===============================================
```

Explicit waits are a valuable tool in Selenium test automation. They provide the precision and control needed to ensure reliable test scripts, especially in dynamic web environments. However, careful consideration of conditions and timeouts is essential to strike a balance between reliability and efficiency.

Explicit waits offer several key benefits:

- **Precision**: Unlike implicit waits, explicit waits only apply to specific conditions for targeted elements. This allows for more granular control over synchronization.
- **Dynamic Timeouts**: You can define different timeout durations for different elements, scenarios, or actions, ensuring optimal synchronization without unnecessary delays.
- **Customizable Expected Conditions**: The **`ExpectedConditions`** class provides a range of built-in conditions (for example, **`visibilityOf`**, **`elementToBeClickable`**) that you can use, or you can create your custom conditions.

Note: It is not advised to use both implicit and explicit waits in the same script or session. As explicit waits are more reliable and customizable, practically most of the standard test automation frameworks incorporate it as a thumb rule.

Fluent Waits

Fluent waits extend the concept of explicit waits by providing the user with the option of customizing various attributes of the waiting strategy such as polling times, exception handling and expected conditions. Fluent waits enable a smoother flow of execution, especially in scenarios where elements might undergo dynamic changes.

In the case of Explicit wait, this polling frequency is by default 500 milliseconds. Using Fluent wait, you can change this polling frequency based on your needs, i.e., you can tell your script to keep checking on an element after every 'x' seconds.

Let us dive into the code to gain a practical understanding of the fluent wait strategy. Open **`Chapter04_FluentWait.java`** from the downloaded codebase, and focus on the following lines:

```
// Setting up Fluent wait

Wait<WebDriver> wait = new FluentWait<>(driver).withTimeout(Duration.
ofSeconds(10))

.pollingEvery(Duration.ofMillis(250)).ignoring(NoSuchElementException.
class);

wait.until(ExpectedConditions.visibilityOfElementLocated(By.cssSelector
(".circle")));
```

In the given lines of code, a Fluent wait is being established for the WebDriver instance. Fluent waits offer a dynamic synchronization strategy, and here, it's configured to wait for a maximum timeout of 10 seconds. During this time, it will poll for the presence of a specific web element defined by the CSS selector **`".circle"`.** The polling interval is set to 250 milliseconds, meaning that the wait will check for the element's presence every 250 milliseconds. The "ignoring" method is used to specify that the wait should ignore the **`NoSuchElementException`** exception, which commonly occurs when an element is not found. The **`until`** method then waits until the specified condition is met, which in this case is the visibility of the element located by the CSS selector. Once the condition is fulfilled or the timeout is reached, the code execution will continue.

This setup ensures that the script progresses only when the desired element becomes visible within the specified time frame, enhancing the reliability and stability of the test automation process.

Fluent waits provide additional customizations such as:

- **Customizable Polling Interval**: One of the key advantages of fluent waits is the ability to change how often the code is evaluated. This can be crucial in scenarios where elements appear at varying intervals.
- **Handling Specific Exceptions**: You can specify which exceptions should be handled automatically during polling. This enhances the resilience of your script, making it more adaptable to changing conditions.

Fluent waits equip testers with a potent tool for handling synchronization issues in selenium test automation. Their customizable nature, combined with the ability to implement fallback mechanisms, empowers testers to build resilient and reliable automation scripts that gracefully handle dynamic web elements. While they have their limitations, when used judiciously, fluent waits enhance the robustness and stability of the testing process.

Shadow DOM

Shadow DOM is a web technology that allows the encapsulation of HTML elements and their styles, scripts, and markup within a boundary called a "shadow root." It enables creating isolated DOM subtrees inside a web page's main DOM, providing a level of compartmentalization and separation between the main page's components and those encapsulated within the shadow DOM.

This is especially useful for building complex web components that have their own styles and behaviors without conflicting with the rest of the page's elements.

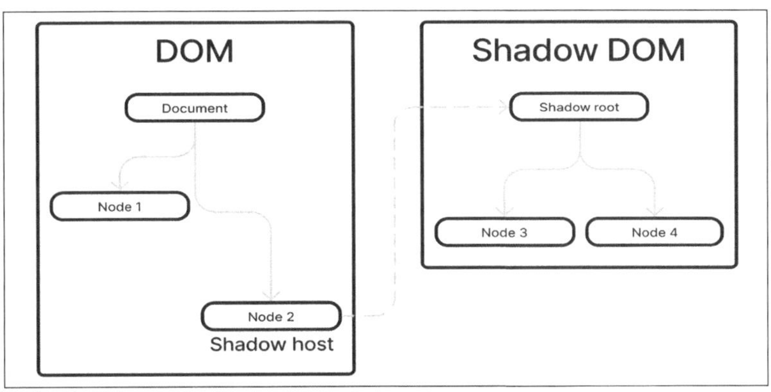

***Figure 4.3**: Visual representation of Shadow DOM*

Let us understand the preceding example with a technical example. Navigate to https://ava-orange-education.github.io/Ultimate-Selenium-WebDriver-for-Test-Automation/docs/Chapter4_ShadowDOM.html .

Here, try inspecting the input box. Notice anything new? The input box is set up inside a shadow DOM. So if we try entering the values as per the following code, we will get a **NoSuchElementException**.

```
// Navigating to sample page
driver.get("https://ava-orange-education.github.io/Ultimate-Selenium
-WebDriver-for-Test-Automation/docs/Chapter4_ShadowDOM.html");
// Erroneous navigation
WebElement inputfield = driver.findElement(By.id("shadowinput"));
inputfield.sendKeys("Test input value");
```

So how can we automate Shadow root? With the release of Selenium WebDriver's version 4.0.0 and above, the **getShadowRoot()** method was introduced and helps locate Shadow root elements. As per the documentation, the **getShadowRoot()** method returns a representation of an element's Shadow root for accessing the Shadow DOM of a web component. In case Shadow root is not found, it will throw **NoSuchShadowRootException**.

Open and run the **Chapter04_ShadowDOM.java** class in the downloaded codebase. Focus on the following lines:

```
WebElement shadowHost = driver.findElement(By.id("shadow_host"));
SearchContext shadowRoot = shadowHost.getShadowRoot();
WebElement inputfield = shadowRoot.findElement(By.cssSelector
(".shadowinput"));
inputfield.sendKeys("Test input value");
```

The first step involves locating a web element with the id **"shadow_host,"** which is presumably the host element for the Shadow DOM. This element is obtained using the **findElement** method.

Once the host element is located, the **getShadowRoot** method is invoked on it. This method is used to access the Shadow DOM of the host element, returning a **SearchContext** object that represents the root of the Shadow DOM subtree. This enables interaction with elements encapsulated within the Shadow DOM.

Subsequently, within the Shadow DOM context, another web element is located using the **findElement** method with a CSS selector of **".shadowinput".** Finally, the `sendKeys` method is applied to this input field, simulating the action of entering the text "Test input value".

Animations and moving elements

In the dynamic landscape of web applications, animations and moving elements have become commonplace, adding a visually engaging touch to user interfaces.

However, automating tests involving animations and moving elements can be a bit tricky due to the asynchronous nature of these effects. In this section, we will delve into the challenges posed by animations and moving elements in test automation and explore strategies to effectively automate such scenarios using Selenium WebDriver and Java.

Animations and moving elements introduce unpredictability to the timing of element visibility and interactions. This can lead to test flakiness and false negatives, where tests fail intermittently due to timing misalignment. Additionally, animations might cause elements to shift position on the page, leading to incorrect locators and unexpected element states. Handling these challenges requires a combination of synchronization techniques and smart locator strategies.

Let us understand the automation for moving elements, with a scenario which can cause proverbial butterflies in an automation engineer's belly. Navigate to the web URL https://ava-orange-education.github.io/Ultimate-Selenium-WebDriver-for-Test-Automation/docs/Chapter4_Butterfly.html .

Watching the butterflies here is beautiful, isn't it? Additionally, they swarm towards the mouse location with a mesmerizing effect. And if you click on the screen, they sort of disperse and then re-align to follow the mouse pointer.

When we do a right click and try to inspect these little critters is when we see the real beauty (or the beast) of this animation:

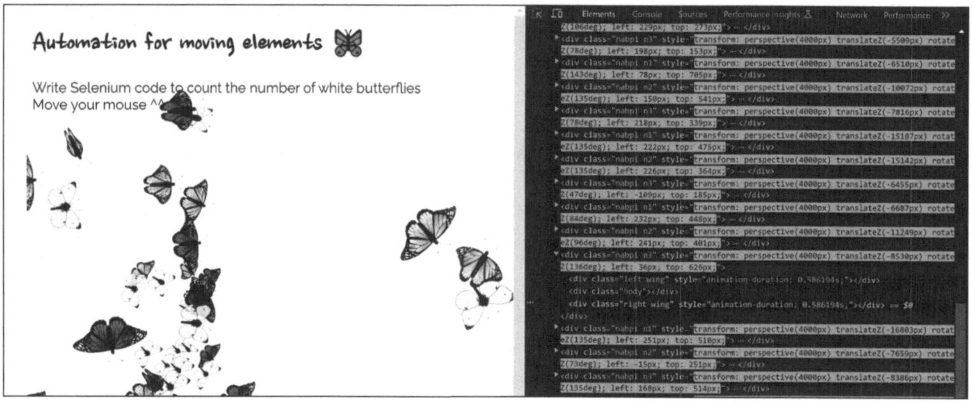

***Figure 4.4**: HTML view for Chapter4_Butterfly web page.*

Let us assume that the task at hand is to write a selenium script for counting the white butterflies from the kaleidoscope (it is the official term for a group of butterflies).

As we can observe there are a couple of challenges in automating the scenario at hand:

- The loading time for butterflies' animation depends on the network speed and host machine.
- The butterflies themselves are not static, so inspecting their attributes (for locators) can be tedious.
- The style attributes for the butterfly's components keep changing, based on its animation properties.

Just like any complicated programming problem, let us break down the preceding challenges into discrete steps:

1. Use of explicit waits for dynamically waiting for the butterflies after the page loads.
2. Pausing the animation for butterflies to inspect their DOM properties.
3. Understanding the patterns in DOM properties, to craft dynamic locators.

As we have covered the first step (around explicit waits) in detail in the previous sections, we will focus on the second step of the solution set directly, for pausing the animation.

We can pause the animation using a special debugger on the parent element. The steps will be as follows:

1. Right-click on the element.
2. Select **`Inspect`** (Elements tab will open with the selected element highlighted).
3. Right-click the highlighted HTML.
4. Go to Break on and select the type of breakpoint.
    a. Subtree modification breakpoints will break the execution of any event whenever a child element of a selected node is modified. The modification can be a removal, addition, or change in child content.
    b. Node Removal Breakpoints are triggered when an element is removed from the DOM tree.
    c. Attribute modification breakpoints are used for debugging changes to attributes in an element. They are triggered when an attribute is changed, added, or removed.

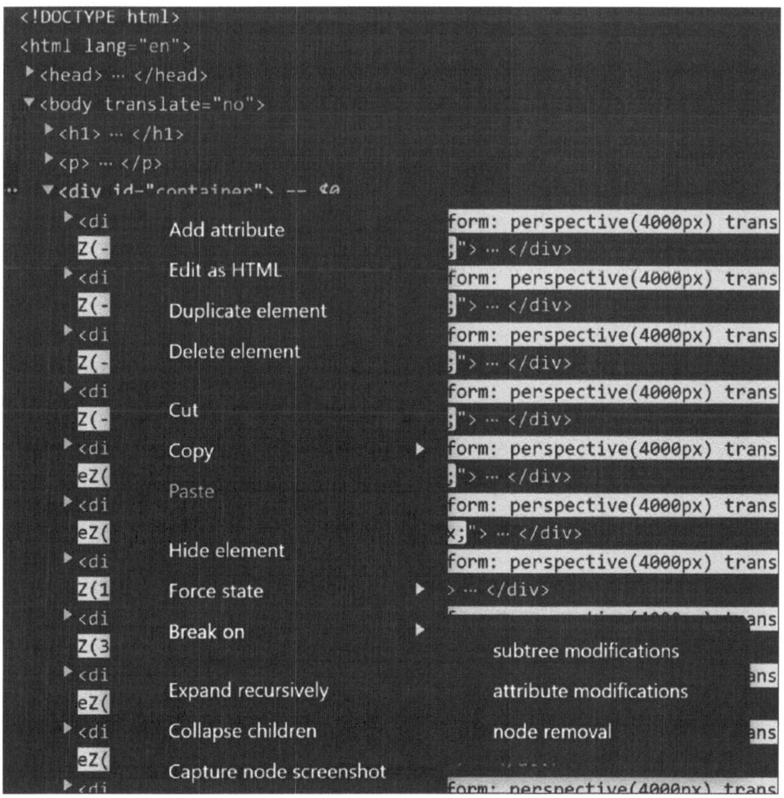

Figure 4.5: *Adding breakpoints to DOM nodes*

We will be using the **Attribute modification Breakpoint** option to pause the butterfly animation as we can observe that the style attribute is changing dynamically for the animation.

Once the animation is paused, we can calmly inspect the web elements, understand the pattern, and write the dynamic locators for the white butterflies.

Open the **Chapter04_AnimationAutomation.java** in the downloaded codebase and execute the file to get a hands-on learning experience. Focus on the following lines for a deeper understanding of automating animations on web pages:

```
// Dynamic wait for butterfly animation to appear
Wait<WebDriver> wait = new WebDriverWait(driver, Duration.ofSeconds(5));
wait.until(ExpectedConditions.visibilityOfElementLocated(By.xpath
("//div[@class=\"nabpi n1\"]")));
// Fetching count of all white butterflies in a list
List<WebElement> whitebutterflylist = driver.findElements(By.xpath
("//div[@class=\"nabpi n1\"]"));
System.out.println("Count of white butterflies is : " + whitebutterflylist.
size());
```

In this piece of Selenium code, we are employing dynamic waiting to ensure the appearance of a butterfly animation on a web page. We initiate a **WebDriverWait** with a timeout of 5 seconds, specifying that we are waiting for the visibility of a specific element characterized by its XPath. The **ExpectedConditions.visibilityOfElementLocated** ensures that the animation element becomes visible before proceeding. Once the animation is visible, we proceed to fetch all instances of the animation element with a particular class, representing white butterflies, and store them in a list named **whitebutterflylist**. By using **driver.findElements** with the appropriate XPath, we accumulate all occurrences of the animation element. Finally, we print the count of white butterflies on the web page using the size of the **whitebutterflylist.**

Note: While these strategies can help mitigate challenges, it's important to note that some animations might be too complex to handle reliably through automation. In such cases, manual testing or collaboration with developers might be necessary.

JavaScript Executor

JavaScript Executor is a powerful feature in Selenium that enables the execution of JavaScript code within the context of a web page. It bridges the gap between

Selenium's automation capabilities and the dynamic nature of modern web applications. By providing direct access to the browser's JavaScript engine, JavaScript Executor allows testers and developers to perform various actions that might be challenging or impossible using standard Selenium methods alone.

Modern web applications often heavily rely on JavaScript to create dynamic user interfaces, update content without refreshing the page, and handle asynchronous operations. While Selenium provides a robust set of methods for interacting with HTML elements, there are scenarios where these methods fall short due to the dynamic nature of the web. This is where the JavaScript Executor comes into play.

With JavaScript Executor, you can manipulate the Document Object Model (DOM) directly, trigger events, modify styles, and even retrieve values that might not be exposed through Selenium's APIs. This capability is particularly useful when dealing with hidden elements, implementing scrolling behavior, interacting with complex dropdowns, validating content updates, and more. Here are a few practical use cases for our consideration:

- **Scrolling**: You can scroll a webpage to bring a specific element into view. This is especially valuable when dealing with lengthy pages or lazy-loaded content.
- **Handling Hidden Elements**: Hidden elements, which are not directly accessible by Selenium, can be interacted with using JavaScript Executor.
- **Changing Styles**: You can dynamically change the CSS styles of elements to simulate user interactions or manipulate visual aspects of the page.
- **Validation**: By executing JavaScript code to verify the presence of specific content or elements, you can enhance the accuracy of your tests.

Open the **`Chapter04_JSExecutor.java`** class and focus on the following lines for a code sample around JavaScript Executor:

```
// Navigating to sample page
driver.get("https://googlechromelabs.github.io/chrome-for-testing/");
//Utilizing JavaScript Executor to scroll to the Canary header on Chrome
for testing page
WebElement canaryheader = driver.findElement(By.xpath("//h2[text()='
Canary']"));
((JavascriptExecutor) driver).executeScript("arguments[0].scrollIntoView
(true);", canaryheader);
// Thread sleep added only for
```

```
reader's reference and verification of the
// actions performed above
Thread.sleep(2000);
// Utilizing JavaScript Executor to add a border to the header identified
above
((JavascriptExecutor) driver).executeScript("arguments[0].style.border
='15px solid red';", canaryheader);
//Thread sleep added only for reader's reference and verification of the
actions performed above
Thread.sleep(5000);
driver.quit();
```

The provided code navigates to a webpage and utilizes the JavaScript Executor feature in Selenium to perform actions on elements. Initially, the code opens a webpage using the **`driver.get()`** method. Then, it finds the "Canary" header element on the page and uses the **`scrollIntoView()`** JavaScript method to bring it into view. After a brief pause for reader verification, the code further employs JavaScript Executor to add a red border of 15 pixels to the header element. Another pause is added for verification before the browser window is closed using **`driver.quit()`**. This code showcases how JavaScript Executor can be used to interact with web elements and manipulate their appearance in the browser.

While JavaScript Executor offers significant flexibility, it's important to exercise caution when using it. Overuse of JavaScript Executor can lead to code that is less maintainable and readable. Moreover, JavaScript-based interactions might not work consistently across all browsers, as different browsers have varying levels of JavaScript support and behavior.

JavaScript Executor is a valuable tool in Selenium's arsenal, enabling testers to overcome challenges posed by dynamic web applications. By smartly utilizing its capabilities, you can enhance your test scripts' accuracy and comprehensiveness, leading to more effective and robust test automation for complicated scenarios.

Page Objects

At its core, a Page Object is a design pattern that helps you represent each web page of your application as a separate class in your test automation framework. This class encapsulates all the elements, actions, and interactions related to that specific page. By doing so, you create a clear separation between your test scripts and the underlying structure of your web application.

Before we get into the specifics of implementation, let us explore the problem domain a little more. Here is an example code snippet from the Login page we had seen earlier:

```
WebElement loginbutton = driver.findElement(By.xpath("//input[@id='
Login']"));
//Attempting a click on the button
loginbutton.click();
```

Can you list the problems with scaling up the preceding type of code with thousands of test cases?

For example, if we had to write the preceding login code for a thousand test cases, we would have to repeat the same locator and corresponding interaction code for all of them. In case the **`id`** for the web element changes from **`Login`** to **`Signin`**, then we would have to update the locators in all the thousand test cases. Additionally, different engineers might use slightly different locators or interaction methods for the same element. This inconsistency can make your test scripts confusing, unreliable, and difficult to understand. The disadvantages become even more pronounced as your test suite expands.

In order to handle the preceding problems, Page object design patterns are utilized to provide a layer of abstraction and centralization for re-usable web elements and corresponding interactions. Here are other advantages of the Page object design pattern:

- **Modularity and Reusability**: With Page Objects, you encapsulate the elements and interactions of each page into separate classes. This modularity enables easy reuse of code across different tests and even projects, reducing redundancy and enhancing maintainability.
- **Abstraction**: Page Objects abstract away the complexities of the underlying HTML structure. Test scripts interact with these Page Objects using simple and meaningful methods, making the scripts more readable and less dependent on the technical details.
- **Maintenance**: When your application's UI changes, you only need to update the corresponding Page Object class. The changes are localized, ensuring that your test scripts remain unaffected, reducing maintenance efforts and saving time.

Interestingly, the Page object design pattern follows the "DRY" principle. The "Don't Repeat Yourself" (DRY) design principle is a fundamental concept in software engineering that promotes code reusability and maintainability. The essence of the DRY principle can be summarized as "Every piece of knowledge or logic should have a single, unambiguous representation within a system."

In simpler terms, the DRY principle encourages developers to avoid duplicating code or logic throughout their codebase. Instead of writing the same code in multiple places, the idea is to create a single source of truth for a particular piece of functionality, and then reference or reuse it whenever needed.

Let us walk through the process of creating a Page Object using a simple example in Java.

1. **Create a New Class**: For each web page you want to automate, create a new class. Name the class according to the page's purpose, like **`LoginPage`** or **`HomePage`.**
2. **Locators and Elements**: Inside the Page Object class, define the web elements using various locators like IDs, XPaths, or CSS selectors. Use annotations such as **`@FindBy`** to link these elements to the actual web elements in the HTML.
3. **Methods**: Create methods that perform actions and interactions on the page. For instance, a **`LoginPage`** might have methods like **`enterUsername`,** **`enterPassword`,** and **`clickLoginButton`.**
4. **Return Types**: Methods in Page Objects could return the subsequent page or a confirmation of an action. This promotes a fluent and intuitive script structure.
5. **Instantiate in Scripts**: In your test scripts, instantiate the Page Object class. Interact with the page using the methods defined in the class. This separation of concerns makes the scripts concise and focused on the actual test logic.

Let us examine the preceding concepts in detail via code. First and foremost, open the OrangeHRMLoginPage.java file situated at the **`src/main/java/pageobjects`** location in the downloaded codebase. Here is the code for the Login page object:

```
public class OrangeHRMLoginPage {
protected WebDriver driver;


private By usernamelocator = By.xpath("//input[@placeholder='Username']");
private By passwordlocator = By.xpath("//input[@placeholder='Password']");
private By loginlocator = By.xpath("//button[@type='submit']");
```

```
public OrangeHRMLoginPage(WebDriver driver) {
      this.driver = driver;
      if (!driver.getTitle().equals("OrangeHRM")) {
            throw new IllegalStateException("This is the right Page,"
+ " current page is: " + driver.getCurrentUrl());
            }
      }


public OrangeHRMHomePage login(String userid, String passwordtext) {
      // Setting up Explicit wait
      Wait<WebDriver> wait = new WebDriverWait(driver, Duration.ofSec-
      onds(20));
      wait.until(ExpectedConditions.visibilityOfElementLocated(user-
      namelocator));
      // Typing the username
      driver.findElement(usernamelocator).sendKeys(userid);
      // Typing the password
      driver.findElement(passwordlocator).sendKeys(passwordtext);
      // Pressing the Login button
      driver.findElement(loginlocator).click();
      // Returning the instance of Homepage for fluent style of programming
      return new OrangeHRMHomePage(driver);


      }
}
```

As we can observe that there are three distinct parts comprising the **OrangeHRMLoginPage** class, each playing a pivotal role in keeping our test base "DRY":

- **Web Elements**: This section serves as a repository for all web elements that are integral to the login process. Here we store the locators in a variable of the type `By`. This can be later used in the method **`driver.findElement(By….)`** for interacting with the web element.
- **Constructor**: A crucial segment of the class, the constructor function plays a significant role in initiating the class. It requires an essential parameter - a WebDriver instance. This WebDriver instance functions as the driving force behind the interaction with the web browser. This

section employs a validation mechanism that scrutinizes the title of the web page being accessed. This is the only validation that a Page object class would generally have.

Note: Page object classes should not have any tests or assertions, and all of the business scenario related tests should be part of the Test class, to align with SOLID programming principles.

- **Page Specific Methods**: In the preceding case, the **`login`** method encapsulates the actions required to log in using the provided username and password, using explicit waits to ensure that the necessary elements are available before interacting with them. It then returns an instance of the next page for further test steps. This method helps in keeping the test code organized, readable, and maintainable by encapsulating login-related actions in a single method.

In order to solidify our understanding, let us look at another page object class. Open the **`OrangeHRMHomePage.java`** class and observe the following code:

```
public class OrangeHRMHomePage {
protected WebDriver driver;
private By profilebutton = By.xpath("//span[@class='oxd-userdropdown
-tab']");


public OrangeHRMHomePage(WebDriver driver) {
		this.driver = driver;
	}


public void clickProfileButton() {
// Setting up Explicit wait for the profile button
Wait<WebDriver> wait = new WebDriverWait(driver, Duration.ofSeconds(20));
wait.until(ExpectedConditions.visibilityOfElementLocated(profilebutton));
driver.findElement(profilebutton).click();


	}
}
```

Did you observe the same three components of the page object class again? It is as simple as locators (with the **`By`** mechanism), a constructor and methods contextual to the web page under consideration (with an appropriate waiting mechanism). The **`OrangeHRMHomePage`** class encapsulates the behavior of the home page of the OrangeHRM application. It includes methods to interact with page elements and perform actions such as clicking the profile button. The use of explicit waits ensures that the necessary elements are ready before interacting with them, promoting stable and reliable test automation.

Note: The SOLID design principles are a set of guidelines for creating more maintainable and flexible software. Each letter in SOLID stands for a different principle:

- **S** (Single Responsibility Principle): A class should have only one reason to change, meaning it should have a single, well-defined purpose.
- **O** (Open/Closed Principle): Software entities (classes, modules, etc.) should be open for extension but closed for modification. This encourages adding new features without changing the existing code.
- **L** (Liskov Substitution Principle): Subtypes should be substitutable for their base types without affecting the correctness of the program. In simpler terms, derived classes should be able to replace the base class without causing unexpected behavior.
- **I** (Interface Segregation Principle): Clients should not be forced to depend on interfaces they don't use. This principle promotes smaller, specific interfaces rather than large, general-purpose ones.
- **D** (Dependency Inversion Principle): High-level modules should not depend on low-level modules; both should depend on abstractions. Additionally, abstractions should not depend on details; details should depend on abstractions. This encourages a more flexible and decoupled architecture.

These principles help developers create code that is easier to understand, maintain, and adapt over time, contributing to better software design and development practices.

Page Factory

Selenium provides a default implementation for the Page factory in Java. Think of it as a Page object model that meets a factory design pattern. Here is how web elements are initiated using page factory methods provided by Selenium:

```
@FindBy(id = "username")
private WebElement usernameField;
```

```
@FindBy(id = "password")
private WebElement passwordField;

@FindBy(id = "submit")
private WebElement submitButton;
```

Notice the **@FindBy** annotation provided by Selenium for easing out the web element declaration process.

The second component of a page factory class is the constructor with initialization of the annotated web elements using the **PageFactory.initElements()** method as follows:

```
public LoginPage(WebDriver driver) {
    this.driver = driver;
    PageFactory.initElements(driver, this);
}
```

The third component of the class would be the page-specific methods such as logging into the application using the web elements defined:

```
public void login(String userid, String passwordtext) {
            username.sendKeys(userid);
            password.sendKeys(passwordtext);
            submitButton.click();


      }
```

Note: Page factory design pattern is not generally recommended for teams just starting with Test Automation. Additionally, Page Factory methods have been deprecated from some language bindings as well, like C#; due to issues with complex proxy mechanisms and reflections in code.

Therefore, page object design pattern is mostly used across test automation frameworks, however in some cases, based on the context and maturity of test automation team; page factory design pattern can be used as well.

Page Object limitations

Just like anything else, even the Page Object Model has its drawbacks when taken to the extreme. While this model is great for making test automation code organized and easy to manage, it is important to remember that it also has some downsides. Despite its benefits in making code more structured and maintainable, there are things we need to keep in mind. Consider the following screenshot for a flight booking site:

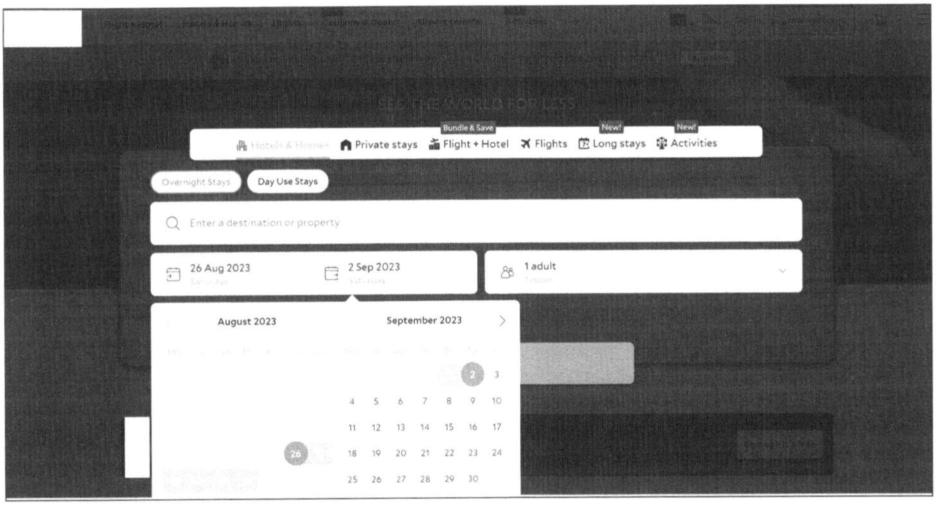

***Figure 4.6**: Representation of a complex web page.*

If we had to model the preceding home page into a page object class, it would have tens of locators ranging from links around destinations to date pickers, and hundreds of combinatorial methods like signing in, signing up, booking flights, hotels, both, or activities.

As the test suite grows, we can only imagine that the **`home page`** page object class would grow exponentially and might become a source of technical debt in the long term.

So, what should we do? Just like any codebase, we should fragment the **`home page`** page object class into further segments like Header – **`HeaderPageObject.java`**, Footer – **`FooterPageObject.java`**, Flights- **`FlightsPageObject.java`** etc. to ensure separation of concerns at the right level, while maintaining DRY principle.

For example, we can model the homepage as follows:

```
public class HomePage {
      protected WebDriver driver;
      private By brandicon = By.xpath("//img[@id='branicon.jpg']");
```

```
	public HomePage(WebDriver driver) {
		this.driver = driver;
	}

	public void clickBrandIcon() {
		driver.findElement(brandicon).click();

	}
}
```

This HomePage page object class can be extended by the various sections of the home page. For example, we can model the header component as follows:

```
public class HeaderComponent {
	protected WebDriver driver;
	private By flightslink = By.xpath("//a[@id='https://www.booking-site.com/flights']");

	public HeaderComponent (WebDriver driver) {
		this.driver = driver;
	}

	public void clickFlightsLink() {
		driver.findElement(flightslink).click();

	}
}
```

In this way, we can modularize our codebase to reduce redundancy and improve maintainability.

While Page Objects offer immense advantages, it's important to acknowledge their limitations. Creating and maintaining Page Objects requires additional upfront effort. If not managed properly, a high number of Page Objects can lead to code duplication and a bloated codebase. Similarly, on the other extreme Page object model is not Ideal for small projects. In smaller projects or proof-of-concept scenarios, the implementation of the Page Object Model might be overkill. It could introduce unnecessary complexity and overhead, making it more efficient to use simpler approaches.

In conclusion, Page Objects is a pivotal concept in Selenium test automation.

They empower you to create modular, maintainable, and efficient automation scripts, elevating the quality of your testing efforts. By investing time in designing and implementing robust Page Objects, you pave the way for a sustainable and scalable automation framework that will serve your testing needs effectively.

ScreenPlay pattern

The Screenplay Pattern is a powerful architectural design for organizing Selenium test automation code in a structured and modular manner. Unlike the traditional approach of scattering automation logic across test cases, the Screenplay Pattern emphasizes separation of concerns by breaking down the tests into distinct screens, actions, and tasks. The pattern promotes better readability, maintainability, and collaboration among team members. It encourages reusability and reduces code duplication by defining reusable tasks and interactions. Moreover, it enhances the abstraction level, making test cases easier to understand even for non-technical stakeholders.

Additionally, Screenplay Pattern is an approach to writing high-quality automated acceptance tests based on good software engineering principles such as the Single Responsibility Principle and the Open-Closed Principle. It is an innovative approach to writing high-quality automated acceptance tests that drives an effective use of abstraction, helps your test scenarios capture the business scenarios, and encourages good software engineering habits on your team.

Note: The Single Responsibility Principle (SRP) states that a class should have a single responsibility and thus only a single reason to change. This means that every class, module, or function in a program should have one responsibility/ purpose in a program. The Open-Closed Principle (OCP) states that software entities (classes, modules, functions, etc.) should be open for extension but closed for modification. This means that you should be able to extend a class's behavior without modifying it.

Before diving further into the Screenplay pattern, let's inspect a drawback with the Page object pattern:

Did you notice any issues with the preceding Login page object?

Hint: It's around the concept of the Single Responsibility principle.

The preceding page object class breaks the Single responsibility principle by housing two responsibilities as follows:

1. Declaring the web elements
2. Setting up the interactions with the web elements

```
public class OrangeHRMLoginPage {
    protected WebDriver driver;
    private By usernamelocator = By.xpath("//input[@placeholder='Username']");      1.
    private By passwordlocator = By.xpath("//input[@placeholder='Password']");
    private By loginlocator = By.xpath("//button[@type='submit']");

    public OrangeHRMLoginPage(WebDriver driver) {
        this.driver = driver;
        if (!driver.getTitle().equals("OrangeHRM")) {
            throw new IllegalStateException("This is not Log In Page," + " current page is: " + driver.getCurrentUrl());
        }
    }

    public OrangeHRMHomePage login(String userid, String passwordtext) throws InterruptedException {
        // Setting up Explicit wait
        Wait<WebDriver> wait = new WebDriverWait(driver, Duration.ofSeconds(20));
        wait.until(ExpectedConditions.visibilityOfElementLocated(usernamelocator));
        // Typing the username                                                          2.
        driver.findElement(usernamelocator).sendKeys(userid);
        // Typing the password
        driver.findElement(passwordlocator).sendKeys(passwordtext);
        // Pressing the Login button
        driver.findElement(loginlocator).click();
```

***Figure 4.7**: Breach of Single Responsibility principle with Page Object Class*

Screenplay pattern provides enhancements on top of page objects with separation of concerns and breaks down the responsibilities further with screen UIs, tasks, and actions.

As part of the Screenplay pattern, all tests are conceptualized as Actors performing Tasks using Actions on Screens.

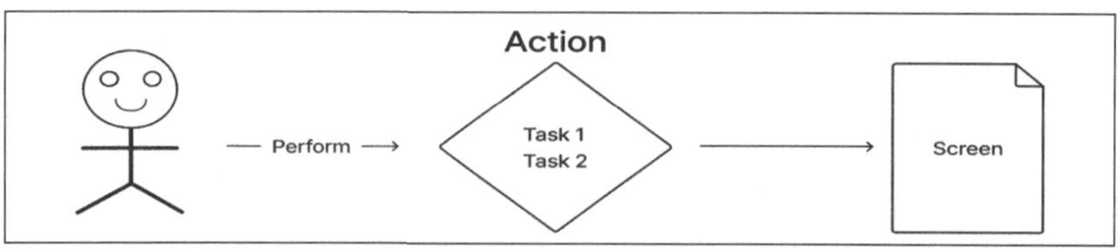

***Figure 4.8**: Visualization of Screenplay pattern*

In the preceding visualization, the "Actor" can be a human user (like you or me) or a system user (external API call to the system under test). The "Actions" could range from logging into a web application, comprising "Tasks" such as filling in a username/password and clicking the login button; to sending an email via an application. The "Screen" could be a web page, mobile screen, or desktop app.

When automating tests for any kind of software product, we must inevitably perform interactions with the software. As humans, we think of interactions in plain terms, like "fill out the form," "navigate to this page," or "find this record." When we write code to implement interactions, we often lose the intention behind them. For example, filling a form quickly becomes a series of sending keys, clicks, and waits with low-level Selenium calls.

Page objects can provide some structure to help, with locators for important elements and methods for interactions on those elements. However, coupling page structure with interactions forces us to focus more on the pages themselves rather than the behaviors in the software. They struggle to model multi-page workflows. Plus, page objects tend to have lots of duplicative code, such as a click method for each button, and oftentimes I've seen folks forget to add proper waiting conditions inside page object methods. Their design is completely freeform, so they can be difficult to understand when moving from project to project.

The Screenplay Pattern is a much better way to model interactions. With Screenplay, Actors use Abilities to perform Interactions. An Actor initiates interactions, just like a human tester. Abilities are tools that help the Actor do testing, such as Selenium WebDriver for browser automation. Interactions exercise behaviors in the software. They could be as low-level as clicking elements or scraping their text, and they may also be composed into much larger workflows. For example, we could create an interaction named "FillTheForm" that internally calls interactions for clicking and sending keys, which internally can have all the proper waiting. Screenplay maximizes reuse with readability. It puts emphasis on behavioral intention, rather than rote page structure.

If you want to use the Screenplay Pattern, check out Serenity BDD (Java), Serenity/JS (JavaScript), and Boa Constrictor (.NET/C#). Each of these projects provides a solid (and SOLID) implementation of the pattern as well as helpful documentation to learn more about it.

- Andrew Knight (The Automation Panda), Principal Architect at Cycle Labs and open-source contributor to the Boa Constrictor project.

Let us understand the preceding concept in detail using technical examples from our downloaded code base.

First and foremost, open the **`LoginUI.java`** class under the **`uiscreens`** package. It is as simple as:

```
public class LoginUI {


public static By usernamefield = By.xpath("//input[@placeholder='
Username']");

public static By passwordfield = By.xpath("//input[@placeholder='
Password']");

public static By submitbutton = By.xpath("//button[@type='submit']");


}
```

As you can observe, the java class is only composed of the relevant locators for the login page.

Note: Static variables and methods are used throughout the code snippets for the Screenplay pattern, for ease of use only. These should be updated with appropriate configuration as per project-specific requirements.

Similarly, open the HomePageUI.java class under the **`uiscreens`** package.

```
public class HomePageUI {


      public static By searchfield = By.xpath("//input[@placeholder='
      Search']");


}
```

Again, it only consists of the relevant locator for the home page. As we can see, that page object classes only contain the relevant locators under the Screenplay design pattern.

So where do we house our interactions?

The answer lies in Actions and Tasks.

For example, an actor or a user can log in to a web application using a combination of interactions such as entering the username, entering the password, and clicking the login or submit button. This is like how we had modelled the interactions as part of page object classes.

There is one key distinction in the approach here, that "Tasks" are broken into "Actions". For example, the "**`click`**" on a button, "**`wait`**" for a web element or "**`enter`**" the text into an input box could be discrete actions, which bundle up and make the "**`Login`**" task.

Let us open the **`Click.java`** class under the **`screenplayactions`** package, to get a detailed understanding of the abstractions at the "Action" level.

```
public class Click {


      public static void On(WebDriver driver, By locator) {
      driver.findElement(locator).click();
      }
```

It is as simple as taking in an instance of WebDriver and a locator to perform a click on the web element. This action could be used to click on any web element on the UI and can be reused across tasks and test cases.

Similarly, here are examples of other actions from the downloaded codebase:

Action to enter text into an input box:

```
public class Enter {


      public static void Text(WebDriver driver, By locator, String text) {
      driver.findElement(locator).sendKeys(text);
      }
```

Action to explicitly wait for a web element:

```
public class ExplicitWait {


public static void forElement(WebDriver driver, By locator, int time) {
      Wait<WebDriver> wait = new WebDriverWait(driver, Duration.of
      Seconds(time));
      wait.until(ExpectedConditions.visibilityOfElementLocated(locator));
      }
}
```

Action to open a web URL:

```
public class With {

	public static void URL(WebDriver driver, String URL) {
		driver.get(URL);
	}

}
```

Action to support assertion for a web element:

```
public class Assertion {

	public static boolean forSearch(WebDriver driver) {
		ExplicitWait.forElement(driver, HomePageUI.searchfield, 15);
		return driver.findElement(HomePageUI.searchfield).is
		Displayed();
	}}
```

These actions could be bundled into tasks for the actor to perform on the screen (web page in our case). Let us open the **Login.java** class under the **tasks** package in the downloaded codebase as follows:

```
public class Login {
	public static void As(WebDriver driver, String userid, String
passwordtext) throws InterruptedException {
		// Waiting for the home page to load
		ExplicitWait.forElement(driver, LoginUI.usernamefield, 15);
		// Typing the username
		Enter.Text(driver, LoginUI.usernamefield, userid);
		// Typing the password
		Enter.Text(driver, LoginUI.passwordfield, passwordtext);
		// Pressing the Login button
		Click.On(driver, LoginUI.submitbutton);

	}
}
```

This code represents a "**login**" task. It waits for the page to load, types the username and password into their respective fields, and clicks the login button to perform a login operation. It uses custom tasks like **ExplicitWait.forElement**, **Enter.Text**, and **Click.On** to make the code more organized and readable.

Based on the same principle, let us explore the task of opening a browser and navigating to a URL as well. This can be found in the **OpenBrowser.java** class as follows:

```
public class OpenBrowser {
	public static void navigate(WebDriver driver, String URL) {
		With.URL(driver, URL);


	}
}
```

As we can observe, the preceding code takes in a WebDriver instance and URL string to navigate to it using the **With.URL** task (which internally uses the **driver.get** method from Selenium).

Now let's sum up the preceding tasks into a test which opens the OrangeHRM sandbox application, logs into it and validates the **search** button on the home page.

Open and run the **Chapter04_OrangeHRMLoginTest_Screenplay.java** in the downloaded codebase as follows:

```
public class Chapter04_OrangeHRMLoginTest_Screenplay {
	@Test(priority = 1)
	public void loginTest() throws Exception {
		// Creating a webdriver instance
		WebDriver driver = new ChromeDriver();


		// Attempting the login action
		OpenBrowser.navigate(driver, "https://opensource-demo.
orangehrmlive.com/web/index.php/auth/login");
		Login.As(driver, "Admin", "admin123");
		Assert.assertTrue(Assertion.forSearch(driver));
		// Added Thread sleep just for demo purpose, so that user
can see if the homepage is displayed
```

```
            Thread.sleep(5000);
            driver.quit();
    }
}
```

In the provided code snippet, the Screenplay pattern is utilized to structure a test case for logging into the OrangeHRM application. Inside the **loginTest** method, a WebDriver instance is created using ChromeDriver, and the Screenplay pattern is followed to execute the login action. The **OpenBrowser.navigate** method directs the browser to the specified URL, and then the **Login.As** method performs the login with predefined credentials. An assertion from the **Assertion.forSearch** method validates the success of the login. While a **Thread.sleep** pause is added for demonstration purposes, it's important to note that real test automation would employ better synchronization methods. Finally, the browser is closed using **driver.quit().** The Screenplay pattern's organization of actions and interactions enhances the test's readability and maintainability, aligning with the best practices of test automation design.

The Screenplay Pattern is an innovative, user-centred approach to writing high-quality automated acceptance tests. It steers your team towards effectively using layers of abstraction, helps your test scenarios capture the business vocabulary of your domain, and encourages good testing and software engineering habits. Focusing on actors and their goals and incorporating your domain language into test scenarios improves team collaboration and alignment, enabling technical and business stakeholders to understand and readily contribute to the test automation process.

Serenity/JS implementation of the Screenplay Pattern enables developers to easily introduce this design approach even into existing test automation projects. Moreover, the framework provides integration libraries to facilitate various test automation types, including end-to-end, component, mobile and API testing, making it a versatile choice for different testing needs. Serenity/JS also provides reporting tools and code reuse patterns that facilitate sharing test code across projects and teams and reducing maintenance costs. Reference: https://serenity-js.org/handbook/design/screenplay-pattern/

- Jan Molak, Principal Consultant at smartcode Ltd. And Open-source contributor and author of Serenity/JS

To cement our understanding of the Screenplay pattern, here is a visualization:

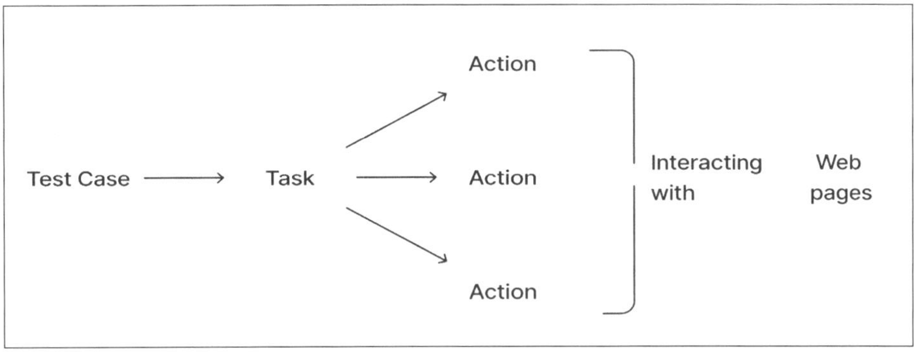

***Figure 4.9**: Visualization of a Test case as per Screenplay pattern.*

Note: Serenity BDD is a JAVA framework for implementing Screenplay patterns with pre-built methods and configurations.

Comparison of Screenplay and Page Object Design Patterns

The comparison of Screenplay and Page object design patterns is not an apples-to-apples comparison. We can think of it as the brightness setting on your computer's screen, with raw WebDriver calls on the extreme left and Screenplay on the extreme right in terms of relative abstraction and alignment to SOLID design principles.

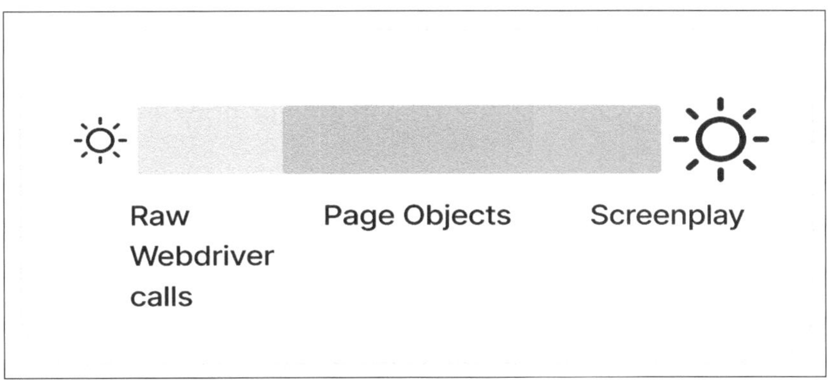

***Figure 4.10**: Conceptual comparison of various design patterns in Selenium*

Therefore, the best design pattern for your case depends on the business context of your team, processes, and technology stack. To make a better decision, here are some key parameters to be considered.

- **Application Complexity**: For simple applications, the Page Object Pattern offers simplicity. For complex applications with intricate user interactions, the Screenplay Pattern's modularity can be beneficial.
- **Team Expertise**: The Page Object Pattern suits teams new to test automation, while experienced teams might opt for the Screenplay Pattern's scalability.
- **Long-Term Goals**: If UI changes are frequent, or the application is expected to grow in complexity, Screenplay offers adaptability. Stable applications with minimal UI changes might favor Page Objects.
- **Non-Technical Communication**: The screenplay's narrative style can be valuable when sharing the automation tests with non-technical stakeholders.

Noted here are some of the strengths and weaknesses of both the Page object and Screenplay pattern to aid you in a detailed analysis.

Page Object Pattern

Strengths:

- **Simplicity and Ease**: The Page Object Pattern treats web pages as objects, providing a simple and intuitive way to represent UI elements and interactions.
- **Code Reusability:** Page Object classes can be reused across multiple tests, reducing code duplication and maintenance effort.
- **Maintainability**: UI changes only need to be updated in one place, ensuring changes are centralized and easily manageable.
- **Industry Recognition**: The Page Object Pattern is widely adopted and recognized, providing ample resources and prior experience for new team members.
- **Tool Support**: Many automation tools offer built-in support for the Page Object Pattern.

Weaknesses:

- **Complexity with Scaling**: For complex applications, the number of Page Objects can grow substantially, leading to maintenance challenges.
- **Brittleness:** Frequent UI changes can result in significant overhead in maintaining the Page Objects.
- **Test Duplication**: Poorly managed Page Objects might lead to duplicated code sequences across tests.

Screenplay Pattern

Strengths:

- **User-Centric Approach**: The Screenplay Pattern shifts focus from the system to user interactions, enabling a more intuitive representation of user journeys.
- **Modularity**: The pattern encourages creating small, reusable tasks and interactions, leading to modular and maintainable test code.
- **Expressiveness**: Tests written using Screenplay read like narratives, making them easier to understand and communicate to non-technical stakeholders.
- **Scalability**: The pattern scales well, allowing the combination of tasks to create complex interactions.

Weaknesses:

- **Learning Curve**: The Screenplay Pattern is more complex than the Page Object Pattern and requires a longer learning curve.
- **Overhead for Simplicity**: For simpler applications or tests, the Screenplay Pattern might introduce unnecessary complexity.
- **Limited Adoption**: The Screenplay Pattern is less widely adopted compared to the Page Object Pattern, resulting in fewer resources for learning and troubleshooting.

Both Page Object and Screenplay Patterns have distinct strengths and weaknesses. The choice depends on application complexity, team expertise, and long-term project goals. Effectiveness in implementation is key, so focus on using the chosen pattern well. Ultimately, our goal should be enhanced code readability, maintainability, and reusability, regardless of the selected pattern.

Conclusion

In this chapter, we've explored advanced Selenium techniques that significantly enhance web automation skills. The chapter covered synchronization and wait strategies, aiding in managing dynamic web pages smoothly. Patience truly is a virtue when it comes to web automation, and employing these techniques will make your scripts more reliable and stable.

We learned about manipulating elements within the Shadow DOM, addressing modern web applications. Animating elements, utilizing JavaScript Executor for executing custom scripts, and adopting the Page Object Model for organized automation were also discussed. The Screenplay Pattern highlighted the importance of reusable components as actions and tasks for comprehensive testing. These concepts collectively empower us to navigate complex automation scenarios with confidence, contributing effectively to testing adventures.

As part of our upcoming journey, we will explore how to build a test automation framework. We will start by digging into what testing frameworks are and how they help keep things consistent when we are testing all sorts of different cases. Then, we will dive into how Selenium teams up with TestNG and Maven, which is like a trio of tools that make creating, managing, and running tests super smooth. JENKINS will be our helper, who does a lot of the heavy lifting when it comes to testing and deploying software. And as we go along, we will learn why having clear and detailed test reports is a big deal, because it's more than just a summary – it's a crucial communication tool for stakeholders. Whether you are just getting started or you have been around the testing block, put on your tinkerer hats, as things are about to get exciting.

Exercise

As we gear up towards a full-fledged test automation framework, let us tackle an end-to-end flow on an e-commerce website using the concepts in this chapter.

Kindly automate the test flow as follows:

1. Navigate to https://orangeava.com/.
2. Click on the first book under the `New Release` section.
3. Capture the book price on the book detail page.
4. Click on the `ADD TO CART` button.
5. Verify that the book price displayed in the `Cart` section is the same as the value captured in Step 3.
6. The test case should interact with:
    a. Homepage Page object
    b. BookDetail Page object
    c. Cart Page object
7. All the Selenium waits utilized should be "explicit" in nature.
8. The test case should utilize the `Assert.assertTrue` method from the TestNG library for verification of the book price.

Chapter 5
Test Automation Framework

Introduction

Welcome to the delightful world of test automation, where we're going to bake a framework! In this chapter, we will combine the forces of Selenium WebDriver, locators, synchronization, Page Object Model, and software design patterns to setup a Test Automation Framework. A well-structured framework is the cornerstone of successful test automation, as it not only streamlines the testing process but also enhances maintainability and scalability. In this chapter, we'll explore the ingredients and steps to create a delicious testing framework from scratch. Just like a cake, it's essential to have a solid foundation, so we'll start with the framework basics – think of it as preparing the baking pan. But what's a cake without a special recipe? We'll delve into design patterns – these are like secret recipes that make your tests robust and easily scalable, just like adding a pinch of magic to your cake mix. To make our baking adventure even more exciting, we have Maven, a magic oven that helps manage all the ingredients (dependencies) effortlessly. TestNG, our trusty taste tester, will guide us in creating and organizing our cake layers (test cases). And what's a cake without some sprinkles on top? We'll also learn how to create scrumptious reports that tell the story of our baking journey. But don't forget to keep an eye on your cake as it bakes! We'll explore the concept of logging – it's like having an oven timer to make sure nothing gets overcooked. So, put on your apron, grab your whisk, and let's get started on this fun and mouthwatering adventure of baking a test automation cake from scratch. By the end of this chapter, you'll not only have your delicious framework but also your very first automated test up and running. Let's get baking!

Structure

In this chapter, we will discuss the following topics:

- Framework Basics
- Design Patterns
- Maven
- TestNG
- Test Reporting
- Logging
- Building a Framework
- Creating Automated Tests
- Continuous Integration/Continuous Delivery

Framework Basics

Raise your hand, if you have ever baked a cake, tried writing an essay, or learned how to drive.

Well, I cannot see you, but each of these skills requires the understanding of a few fundamental steps in a repeatable fashion to achieve a goal. And that is analogous to understanding what is a framework. So, let us first understand what is a framework, before getting to the building blocks of a framework.

Imagine you are about to bake a cake for the first time. You have a kitchen full of ingredients, but without a recipe, you are unsure about the quantities, the sequence, or even the techniques to use. Now, think of a recipe as a **framework** for baking. It provides a structured approach, detailing the ingredients you need, the quantities, the sequence of steps, and even the techniques to employ, like whisking or folding. By following this framework, you can consistently produce a delicious cake, even if you decide to tweak the flavor or add some personal touches.

Similarly, when you are tasked with writing an essay, you might have a plethora of ideas, arguments, and references. However, without a proper structure or guideline, your essay might come across as a jumbled collection of thoughts. Here, the classic essay structure – introduction, body, and conclusion – acts as a **framework**. It guides you on how to introduce your topic, present your arguments, and conclude your thoughts. By adhering to this structure, your essay becomes coherent, persuasive, and engaging, even if the topic or the arguments change.

A test automation framework is like a cooking recipe, where we pull in different tools and libraries to achieve a common goal in a repeatable fashion. In our case, the common goal is to automate the test cases in a scalable fashion.

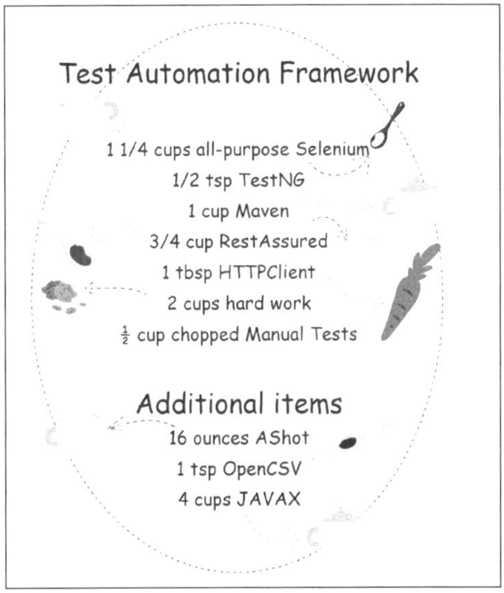

Figure 5.1: *Visualization for a framework*

Here are a few strong reasons to think about building a framework, when picking up scalable test automation as a goal:

- **Reusability of Code**: One of the main reasons to use a framework is to avoid redundancy. By using a framework, you can reuse code and test components across different test cases, thus reducing the time and effort required to develop and maintain test scripts.

Mental model: Imagine having a set of common operations like login, logout, or navigation that need to be tested frequently across different parts of an application. Without a framework, you would end up writing the same code for these operations repeatedly. With a framework, you can write the code once and reuse it wherever needed. The same applies for instantiating WebDriver as follows:

```
WebDriver driver = new ChromeDriver();
```

Let's say we have 1000 test cases, then we would need to instantiate the "driver" or write complicated code around garbage collection a thousand times. Wouldn't that be painful for the compiler and us? And this example brings us to the next factor:

- **Scalability**: Automated tests might start small, but they grow with the project. A well-designed framework allows you to scale up your testing efforts seamlessly.

Mental model: Consider a startup that began by launching one product but later expanded its range. If they had a robust test automation framework in place, they could easily scale their test scripts to cover the new products without having to reinvent the wheel.

- **Maintainability**: As applications evolve, so do their tests. An automation framework can make it easier to update test scripts, making maintenance less cumbersome.

Mental model: Let us say a web application underwent a design change where a button's locator changed. If tests were built without a framework, each test case referencing that button would need an update. In a structured framework, this change might be made in just one place, benefiting all relevant test cases. Reminds us of SOLID design principles and Page Object design patterns, right?

- **Consistency**: A framework ensures consistency in test script creation, execution, and reporting. This makes it easier for teams to understand, write, and review test cases.

Mental model: Consider two developers, me and you. Without a framework, I might name a test `testLoginFunction`, while you name it `verifyUserLogin`. With a standard approach in place, naming conventions and other procedures would be consistent, avoiding such discrepancies. Cheers for conflict resolution for us!

- **Improved Reporting**: Most frameworks offer ways to generate logs and reports, providing a structured way to understand test results.

Mental model: After executing a suite of 100 test cases, a tester wants to understand which ones failed and why. Instead of manually sifting through results, a framework could generate a clear report highlighting failures, making it easier to pinpoint issues.

- **Collaboration**: Frameworks can enhance collaboration among QA, developers, and non-technical stakeholders. Standardized test scripts, combined with shared tools and practices, make it easier for teams to work together.

Mental model: A non-technical product manager, Jane, wants to understand the test progress. A standardized framework could provide her with clear reports and dashboards, even if she doesn't dive into the actual code.

Now that we understand what is a test automation framework and its advantages, let us proceed with building one. Just like every recipe is different, targeting a certain taste profile; every test automation framework is custom-created for a certain team/application/software. For example, if we are only targeting integration and end-to-end UI tests, our test automation framework will have the components pertaining to API and Selenium test scripts.

Therefore, to build a framework (or any software for that matter), let's start with capturing some requirements.

Assume that our test automation framework will be used by a large multinational organization for automating their test cases. Now that is a good starting point, but let us understand some finer nuances for building this framework. So, here are some more requirements for our consideration:

1. We should be able to automate manual test scenarios, such as login to the application, creating records, verifying the record creation, and logging out.
2. Our framework should enable code reuse and follow SOLID principles. For example:
    a. WebDriver management (setup, initialization, and tear down)
    b. Relevant use of objects and "static" methods
3. We should be able to run the tests in parallel.
4. The test execution should be reported in a user-friendly manner.
5. The test logic should be separate from the test data.
6. Test logic should be loosely coupled with the details of interaction with the application.
7. Our framework should be highly maintainable.
8. The framework should be extensible by design. For example, we should be able to plugin libraries as required.
9. We should be able to group tests with minimum effort. For example, we can group tests around smoke testing to run together.
10. Traceability. For example, we should be able to capture screenshots on failure.

Now before we move onto the next section, take a few (or many) moments, and try solving the preceding puzzle with what you have learned so far. Here's a hint: Try breaking the problem into smaller parts and see how you can solve them individually.

Remember, system design and framework-building skills can get better only by practicing.

With that pinch of motivation, let us proceed with our problem at hand: designing a scalable, maintainable, and extensible test automation framework.

Any system design problem starts with a bucketing of the requirements, so that we can apply tools, libraries, and design patterns to solve each part of the problem.

Remember, you can only eat a pizza in slices, so let us slice and dice the problem into its parts and correlate them with some concepts we have explored earlier, with some new concepts.

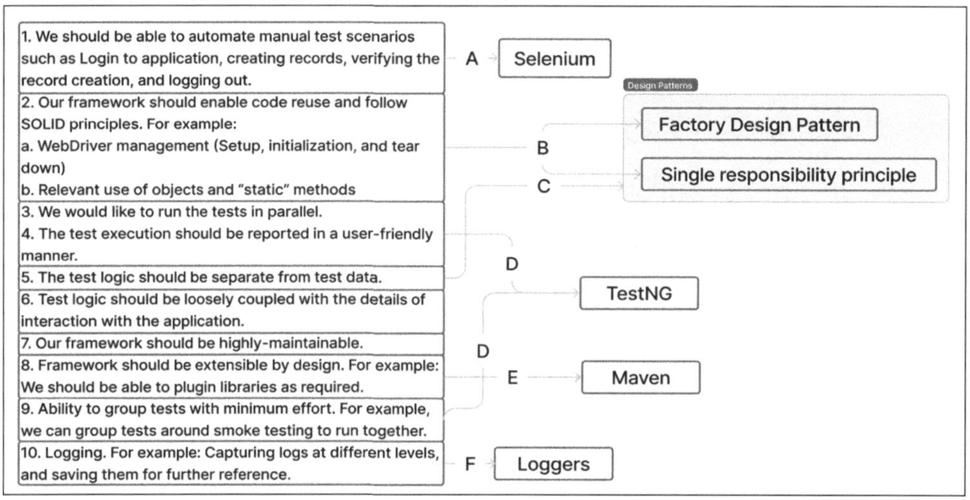

Figure 5.2: *Gathering the ingredients for a Test Automation Framework*

Take another moment and try matching the preceding solution with the one you have sketched, as requested. Don't be bothered if the solution in your head (or notebook) doesn't match the one above, as there is a cardinal rule in the realm of framework design: "No solution is perfect". While your solution might be flawed, the one we will design as per the above might be flawed as well. As long as it serves the purpose of teaching us the basics of framework design, we will be successful. Also, don't be intimidated by the arrows and boxes in *Figure* 5.2, we will zoom into each and every detail.

To start on a simple note, let us evaluate requirement 1 and arrow A.

To simulate the real use case for the framework, our sample test case will be along the lines of:

1. Navigating to the login page of the OrangeHRM demo app here: https://opensource-demo.orangehrmlive.com/web/index.php/auth/login
2. Entering credentials for user ID and password and logging to the application.
3. Clicking the **Profile** button.
4. Validating that the **Search** field is present on the home page.

For automating the preceding test case, we can use Selenium. A simple automation script for the scenario using Page objects can be as follows. As we have noted earlier, Page Object Model helps us centralize repeated code like locators and methods for a certain webpage or component of the web application. Here is a reference in the form of BadExample.java in downloaded codebase:

```
public class BadExample {
      @Test(priority = 1)
      public void loginTest() throws Exception {
            // Creating a webdriver instance
            WebDriver driver = new ChromeDriver();

            // Navigating to sample page
            driver.get("https://opensource-demo.orangehrmlive.com/web/
index.php/auth/login");
            //Instantiating page objects for login page and home page
            OrangeHRMLoginPage loginpage = new OrangeHRMLoginPage(driver);
            OrangeHRMHomePage homepage = new OrangeHRMHomePage(driver);
            //Test Steps
            loginpage.login("Admin", "admin123");
            homepage.clickProfileButton();
            String homepageURL = driver.getCurrentUrl();
            Assert.assertTrue(homepageURL.contains("dashboard"));
            driver.quit();
      }
}
```

Note: If you are using an older version of Selenium, you might need to setup the path for ChromeDriver, before instantiating WebDriver. As we are using Selenium v4.11, therefore ChromeDriver is also managed by Selenium Manager, which comes bundled with Selenium bindings.

Here is the reference code for **`OrangeHRMLoginPage`**, which can be found at **`src/main/java/pageobjects`** package:

```
public class OrangeHRMLoginPage {
	protected WebDriver driver;


	private By usernamelocator = By.xpath("//input[@placeholder='
	Username']");
	private By passwordlocator = By.xpath("//input[@placeholder='
	Password']");
	private By loginlocator = By.xpath("//button[@type='submit']");


	public OrangeHRMLoginPage(WebDriver driver) throws Interrupted
	Exception {
		this.driver = driver;
		// Validation for page
		Thread.sleep(5000);
		if (!driver.getTitle().equals("OrangeHRM")) {
			throw new IllegalStateException("This is not Log In
Page," + " current page is: " + driver.getCurrentUrl());
		}
	}


	public OrangeHRMHomePage login(String userid, String password-
text) throws InterruptedException {
		// Setting up Explicit wait
		Wait<WebDriver> wait = new WebDriverWait(driver, Duration.
ofSeconds(20));
		wait.until(ExpectedConditions.visibilityOfElementLocated
(usernamelocator));
		// Typing the username
		driver.findElement(usernamelocator).sendKeys(userid);
```

```
            // Typing the password
            driver.findElement(passwordlocator).sendKeys(passwordtext);
            // Pressing the Login button
            driver.findElement(loginlocator).click();
            // Returning the instance of Homepage for fluent style of
programming
            return new OrangeHRMHomePage(driver);
      }
}
```

And here is the code for OrangeHRMHomePage, which can be found at **src/main/java/pageobjects** package:

```
public class OrangeHRMHomePage {
      protected WebDriver driver;

      private By profilebutton = By.xpath("//span[@class='oxd-user
dropdown-tab']");

      public OrangeHRMHomePage(WebDriver driver) {
            this.driver = driver;
      }

      public void clickProfileButton() {
            // Setting up Explicit wait for the profile button
            Wait<WebDriver> wait = new WebDriverWait(driver, Duration.
ofSeconds(20));
            wait.until(ExpectedConditions.visibilityOfElementLocated
(profilebutton));
            driver.findElement(profilebutton).click();

      }
}
```

While this code satisfies requirement 1 and a few from requirement 2 from *Figure 5.2*, it breaks the others or does not fit very well. For example:

1. ChromeDriver instantiation is done as part of the test class. Wouldn't it be nice if we could have a more dynamic way of doing it?
2. The URLs and other test data are "hard-coded" in the test. What would happen if we were to change it? We would have to update all the test classes.
3. Page objects are instantiated as part of the test, breaking the single responsibility principle and making object management difficult across test cases.

How can we solve these limitations? Well, the answer lies in design patterns, dependency management, and good coding practices.

Design Patterns

Design patterns in programming are general reusable solutions to common problems encountered. When working with Selenium and Java for test automation, employing design patterns can significantly improve code maintainability, reusability, and readability. As part of our core requirement 2 and arrow B from *Figure* 5.2, here are some design patterns essential to our context:

Factory Design Pattern

The Factory pattern is used to create objects without specifying the exact class of object that will be created. This is useful in Selenium when you have different browsers to test on and want to create WebDriver instances accordingly for multiple test cases. Instead of creating objects directly in your code, you tell a "factory" what type of object you need, and it produces and gives you that object. It's like ordering a pizza - you choose the toppings (object type), and the pizza place (factory) makes the pizza (object) just for you. This pattern makes your code more flexible and easier to maintain because you can change the object creation process in one place (the factory) without affecting the rest of your code. Following is the sample code for a factory of WebDriver instances:

```
public class WebDriverFactory {
    public static WebDriver createDriver(String browserType) {
        WebDriver driver = null;
        switch (browserType.toLowerCase()) {
            case "chrome":
                driver = new ChromeDriver();
```

```
                break;
            case "firefox":
                driver = new FirefoxDriver();
                break;
            // ... other browsers
        }
        return driver;
    }
}
```

Now, instead of creating driver instances directly, you can use the factory:

```
WebDriver driver = WebDriverFactory.createDriver("chrome");
```

In this way, creating WebDriver instances becomes seamless and standardized.

From our **`Chapter05_BadExample.java`** class, we can easily observe that we should separate the WebDriver creation into a WebDriverFactory, and additionally, we could also cut out the page object initialization into a **`PageObjectFactory`**. As part of the "Building blocks of Framework" section, we will be exploring this concept in further detail.

Single Responsibility Principle (SRP)

SRP states that a class should have only one reason to change, meaning it should only have one responsibility. In Selenium, this is often seen in the separation of concerns between page objects, test data, test logic, or cutting out common methods into a utility class.

For instance, a Login Page Object may look like the following code, as we have seen earlier:

```
public class LoginPage {
    private WebDriver driver;
    private By usernameField = By.id("username");
    private By passwordField = By.id("password");
    private By loginButton = By.id("login");

    public LoginPage(WebDriver driver) {
        this.driver = driver;
```

```
    }

    public void enterUsername(String username) {
        driver.findElement(usernameField).sendKeys(username);
    }

    public void enterPassword(String password) {
        driver.findElement(passwordField).sendKeys(password);
    }

    public void clickLogin() {
        driver.findElement(loginButton).click();
    }
}
```

In this class, all methods are solely focused on interacting with the Login page, adhering to the SRP.

If we inspect the **`BadExample`** Java class previously mentioned, we might notice that the test class takes on the responsibilities of instantiating WebDriver, Page Objects, test logic, page interaction logic, and contains hard-coded data.

Ideally, we should cut down these responsibilities into separate classes for easier maintenance and code re-usability.

We will be using the concept of Single Responsibility Principle to not only divide the responsibilities of a test case versus page objects but also to cut out common methods across the framework.

Reflection in Java

Reflection is a feature in Java that lets you inspect and manipulate classes, interfaces, constructors, methods, and fields at runtime. This is useful in Selenium when dynamically loading page objects or other classes based on runtime conditions.

Imagine you're standing in front of a mirror. What you see is a reflection of yourself. Just like how you can see the details of your face, your clothes, and even any new freckles you might have, similarly, Java's reflection feature allows a program to inspect and examine its own inner details at runtime.

With Reflection, you can create instances of classes dynamically, making your framework more flexible and adaptable to changes:

```
Class<?> arrayListClass = ArrayList.class;
List<?> myList = (List<?>) arrayListClass.getDeclaredConstructor().
newInstance();
```

Let us understand the preceding two lines of code in more detail, as it will be instrumental in helping us create Page objects dynamically at run time.

Imagine you have a toy-making machine that can create any toy if you feed it the blueprint of that toy. But you are not sure which blueprint you will get each day.

The given code is doing something similar for creating a list:

```
Class<?> arrayListClass = ArrayList.class;
```

Here, we are getting the blueprint of the **ArrayList** toy. This blueprint is represented by the Class object mentioned earlier. By saying **ArrayList.class**, we're asking Java, "Hey, give me the blueprint for the **ArrayList** toy!"

```
List<?> myList = (List<?>) arrayListClass.getDeclaredConstructor().new-
Instance();
```

Now, we have the blueprint (**arrayListClass**), and we want to create an actual toy (**ArrayList** instance) from it. **getDeclaredConstructor()** is like setting the machine to the default mode to make the toy, meaning we're choosing the default way to construct our **ArrayList. newInstance()** is like pressing the **Start** button on the machine to finally create the toy.

(List<?>) before **arrayListClass...** is just making sure that what we get out of the machine is indeed a type of list. In other words, we're telling Java, "Hey, treat the toy you've just made as a type of list!"

So, in simple terms, this code is about getting a blueprint of an **ArrayList** and then using that blueprint to create an actual empty **ArrayList**.

In our framework, we will use reflection to dynamically create instances of Page objects at run time, which can be used to interact with web elements.

Maven

In our world of software development, systems are often reliant on third-party libraries or modules. These external libraries, referred to as "dependencies", empower developers by providing functionality that doesn't need to be built from scratch. Dependency management is the practice of controlling, organizing, and maintaining these third-party libraries. Think of it as the librarian for your codebase, ensuring that the correct book (library) versions are available and organized on the shelves.

For instance, consider a real-world analogy: baking a cake. The recipe may call for various ingredients like flour, sugar, and eggs. Imagine if these ingredients were continually changing – a different type of sugar or a unique blend of flour.

It would be challenging to achieve a consistent outcome without some form of management. In software terms, these ingredients are akin to libraries, and dependency management ensures the right ingredients, in the right quantity, are always available.

Effective dependency management is crucial to the stability and reliability of software projects. As software evolves, it's common for newer versions of dependencies to be released, and these may contain critical bug fixes or additional features. However, they may also introduce breaking changes, which can inadvertently introduce bugs or errors. Dependency management helps in ensuring that:

- All required libraries are present.
- Conflicts between library versions are resolved.
- The right versions of libraries are used.
- Upgrades to newer versions are smooth and controlled.

Let us review the requirements outlined in *Figure* 5.2, where framework extensibility is a core requirement for point 8 and arrow E. Therefore, dependency management becomes particularly significant. Selenium itself has numerous versions, and it integrates with various browser drivers and testing frameworks. Keeping everything in sync is essential for the stability of automation scripts.

Apache Maven, commonly referred to as Maven, is a powerful build and dependency management tool used widely in the Java ecosystem. With Maven, defining and retrieving dependencies becomes a standardized process.

POM file

Dependencies are specified in a "Project Object Model" or POM file (`pom.xml`). When a Maven command runs, it reads this file, fetches the required dependencies from repositories (centralized places where libraries are stored), and makes them available for the project.

```
<dependency>
    <groupId>org.seleniumhq.selenium</groupId>
    <artifactId>selenium-java</artifactId>
    <version>3.141.59</version>
</dependency>
```

The preceding snippet from a pom.xml tells Maven to fetch the Selenium library for Java of version 3.141.59.

Fun fact: Selenium project was maintaining the version numbers for a while, using the digits in the ratio of 22/7 (commonly referred to as Pi).

The **pom.xml** is the heart of a Maven project. It contains configuration details, project metadata, and, most importantly, the list of dependencies (like ingredients in a recipe).

Here's a basic structure:

```
<project>
    <modelVersion>4.0.0</modelVersion>
    <groupId>com.example</groupId>
    <artifactId>sample-project</artifactId>
    <version>1.0</version>

    <dependencies>
        <!-- List of dependencies go here -->
    </dependencies>
</project>
```

The key components are as follows:

- **groupId**, **artifactId**, and **version** define the unique identifier for the project.
- **<dependencies>** is where all the project dependencies are listed.

Kindly navigate to the **pom.xml** file in the downloaded codebase and observe the content and project's dependencies. The dependencies are listed as follows:

Parametrizing the version and then collating all the version numbers in one place as follows:

```
<properties>
                <testng.version>7.6.0</testng.version>
        </properties>

<dependency>
                        <groupId>org.testng</groupId>
                        <artifactId>testng</artifactId>
                        <version>${testng.version}</version>

                </dependency>
```

Or we could directly mention the version of dependency in an XML node as follows:

```
                <dependency>
                        <groupId>com.jayway.jsonpath</groupId>
                        <artifactId>json-path</artifactId>
                        <version>2.4.0</version>
                </dependency>
```

Let us zoom into the following section of our **pom.xml** file:

```
<profiles>
                <profile>
                        <id>all-tests</id>
                        <activation>
                                <activeByDefault>true</activeByDefault>
                        </activation>
                        <build>
                                <plugins>
                                        <plugin>
        <groupId>org.apache.maven.plugins</groupId>
                                                <artifactId>maven-compiler
-plugin</artifactId>
                                                <version>3.3</version>
                                        </plugin>
                                        <plugin>
```

```
<groupId>org.apache.maven.plugins</groupId>
                                        <artifactId>maven-surefire-
plugin</artifactId>
                                        <version>2.19</version>
                                        <configuration>
                                               <suiteXmlFiles>    <!--
Specify the TestNG XML file you want to run over here -->
      <suiteXmlFile>src/test/java/chapter5/testng.xml</suiteXmlFile>
                                               </suiteXmlFiles>
                                        </configuration>
                                 </plugin>
                          </plugins>
                   </build>
            </profile>
      </profiles>
```

This XML snippet sets up a default configuration called **all-tests**. When this configuration is active, it tells Maven how to handle Java code compilation and how to run tests. It uses two tools for this: the Maven Compiler Plugin for code compilation and the Maven Surefire Plugin for running tests. The code points to a specific way to run tests using a TestNG file, which will be explored in a further section. Essentially, this configuration ensures that the Java code is compiled, and tests are ready to be run in a TestNG XML file.

Directory Structure of a Maven Project

A Maven project follows a standard directory structure, which helps in organizing files and makes projects predictable:

```
sample-project
|
├── src
|   ├── main
|   |   └── java (contains the source code)
|   |
|   ├── test
|   |   └── java (contains the test code)
```

```
|
├── target (compiled bytecode and JARs will be here)
|
└── pom.xml
```

Maven Commands

Apache Maven operates via a sequence of commands, each designed to execute a particular task or a series of tasks within the build lifecycle. These commands, often referred to as Maven goals, dictate Maven's behavior at various stages of the project lifecycle. Let's delve deeper into some of the most commonly used Maven commands and their intricacies:

- **`mvn clean`**: The **`mvn clean`** command is analogous to spring-cleaning in a house. Over time, as you compile and build your project repeatedly, Maven accumulates generated files – like compiled bytecode in the form of .class files or packaged JARs. These reside within the **`target/`** directory.

  Executing **`mvn clean`** purges the **`target/`** directory, wiping out previous builds and ensuring a fresh start for subsequent builds. This is especially useful to ensure no stale artifacts are present and can prevent potential conflicts or confusion in later build stages.

- **`mvn install`**: The **`mvn install`** command is a multi-tasker. Its main objectives are:
  - Compiling the source code.
  - Executing any unit tests.
  - Packaging the compiled code into an artifact, such as a JAR.
  - Installing the packaged artifact into the local Maven repository.

The local Maven repository is like a cache on your computer where Maven stores downloaded dependencies and any artifacts generated from your projects. This local repository ensures that Maven doesn't have to repeatedly fetch popular dependencies from the central repository, speeding up builds.

The "`install`" goal, by placing the project's artifact into this repository, makes it accessible to other Maven projects on the same machine. This is particularly useful if you're developing multiple projects that depend on one another.

- **`mvn test`**: A cornerstone in the software development lifecycle, testing ensures the robustness and reliability of code. The **`mvn test`** command is Maven's gateway to this crucial phase. When you run this command:

- Source code gets compiled.
- Unit tests, typically written in frameworks like JUnit or TestNG, are executed.
- A report of the tests, detailing successes and failures is generated.

It's crucial to understand that **`mvn test`** only runs unit tests and doesn't package or install the project's artifacts. Its primary goal is to facilitate rapid feedback during development. If tests fail, the Maven build lifecycle stops at this phase, preventing potentially buggy code from advancing to packaging or deployment stages.

Maven's commands form the backbone of its functionality, guiding the build lifecycle from raw code to deployable artifacts. By understanding and effectively leveraging these commands, we can achieve a streamlined and efficient build process, ensuring high-quality software delivery.

Note: We can also chain multiple commands, such as "mvn clean install" test, to achieve multiple goals.

To run the commands, we can either do it through the GUI by activating the contextual menu (right-click on pom.xml file and select "Run As" for Eclipse IDE) or navigate to the location of pom.xml and trigger the commands via a terminal window (command prompt or shell) as follows:

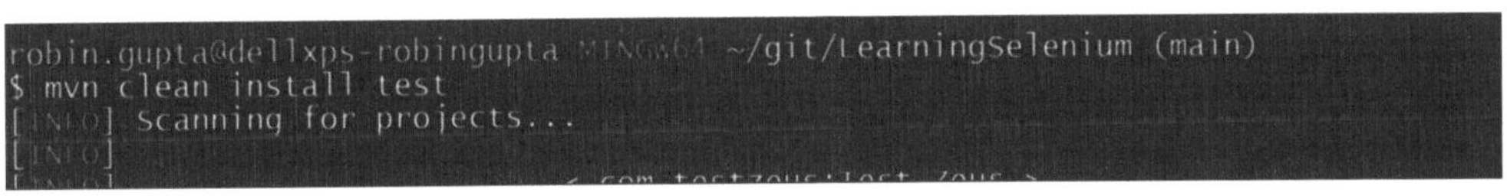

***Figure 5.3**: Maven command execution from Terminal*

Note: Trying out and using multiple dependencies via Maven can be very tempting; however, we must ensure that the dependencies added in pom.xml are safe and necessary to the requirements of the framework.

TestNG

Let us assume that we have to host a house party. As the host, our activities should be planned and executed in a certain order. Yes, hosting a dinner party and writing test automation might seem worlds apart, but they share an underlying principle: **organization**. Imagine you are hosting this dinner. You would first send out invites (initial setup), then clean and organize the venue (pre-test arrangements), serve the main course and dessert (execution of the main events), and finally, wind down the evening, thanking your guests and cleaning up (post-test activities). TestNG, a Java-based testing framework, helps you organize your test automation activities in a similar fashion, so that our goal of efficiency is successfully met.

TestNG, short for "Test Next Generation", is a testing framework that evolved to overcome the limitations of another popular Java testing framework: JUnit. With its flexibility, powerful features, and integrative capabilities, TestNG quickly became a favorite among Java professionals.

In our context, TestNG will help us resolve requirements numbered 3, 4, 9, and some parts of 5 from *Figure* 5.2, as we will observe in the following sections.

Installation

Before you whip up the dishes, you need to set up your kitchen. Similarly installing TestNG can be achieved by adding the following dependency to your pom.xml:

```
<dependency>
    <groupId>org.testng</groupId>
    <artifactId>testng</artifactId>
    <version>7.6.0</version>
    <scope>test</scope>
</dependency>
```

If we navigate to the pom.xml downloaded as part of the project, we can observe that it already includes an entry for TestNG as follows:

```
<testng.version>7.6.0</testng.version>
```

Note: For Eclipse IDE Users: Navigate to **`Eclipse Marketplace`**, search for **`TestNG,`** and install the plugin. This will provide additional capabilities such as running the tests from the GUI of Eclipse. Similar plugins can be installed for IntelliJ and other IDEs as well.

Annotations and their Execution Order

Annotations in TestNG serve as markers, guiding the execution flow. Let's learn their order using a storyline.

Imagine you're preparing for a big family dinner. Here's how you'd go about it, mapped to TestNG annotations:

@BeforeSuite: This runs before all the tests in the suite. Imagine cleaning the entire house before any preparation starts. Or setting up WebDriver instances in our case.

```
@BeforeSuite
public void cleanHouse() {
    System.out.println("House cleaned!");}
```

@BeforeTest: Performed in this suite before any test methods of classes available inside the <test> tag in testng.xml. For example: ensuring the kitchen is ready, even if you forgot to clean the house. Or in the case of test automation, ensuring that we delete all cookies before instrumenting any new tests. Additionally, in the following example, **alwaysRun = true** is used when we want to make sure a method always runs even if the parameters on which the method depends, fails.

```
@BeforeTest(alwaysRun = true)
public void prepKitchen() {
    System.out.println("Kitchen ready!");
}
```

@BeforeClass: Performed before the first examination method in the current class. Think of it as getting all the ingredients for a specific dish. Or instantiating page objects in our case.

```
@BeforeClass
public void getIngredients() {
    System.out.println("Ingredients fetched for the dish.");
}
```

@BeforeMethod: Performed before each test (@Test) method. In our dinner arrangement, this would be like laying out the cooking tools before cooking each part of the dish.

```
@BeforeMethod
public void layTools() {
    System.out.println("Cooking tools ready.");
}
```

@AfterMethod: Executed after each test (@Test) method. This is like cleaning the tools after cooking each part.

```
@AfterMethod
public void cleanTools() {
    System.out.println("Tools cleaned after cooking.");
}
```

@AfterClass: Executed after all test methods in the current class. This is like setting the dish on the table once it is ready.

```
@AfterClass
public void placeDish() {
    System.out.println("Dish placed on the table.");
}
```

@AfterSuite: Executed after all tests executed in this current suite. In our example, this would be like locking up the house and retiring for the night after dinner.

```
@AfterSuite
public void lockUp() {
    System.out.println("House locked. Good night!");
}
```

In short, here is the execution sequence of TestNG annotations:

Execution Sequence of TestNG Annotations

1. `BeforeSuite`
2. `BeforeTest`
3. `BeforeClass`
4. `BeforeMethod`
5. `Test`
6. `AfterMethod`
7. `AfterClass`
8. `AfterTest`
9. `AfterSuite`

This order of execution is of the essence. Just as you can't set a dish on the table before preparing it, you can't skip the execution order in TestNG.

Let us look at the **TestNG_ExecutionOrder** class (located at **src/test/java/chapter5/TESTNG_ExecutionOrder.java**) to get a hands-on experience with the order of events:

```
public class TestNG_ExecutionOrder {
      @BeforeSuite
      public void beforeSuite() {
            System.out.println("BeforeSuite: Clean the entire house.");
      }
      @BeforeTest(alwaysRun = true)
      public void beforeTest() {
            System.out.println("BeforeTest: Ensure the kitchen is
            ready.");
      }
      @BeforeClass
      public void beforeClass() {
            System.out.println("BeforeClass: Get all the ingredients
            for the dish.");
      }
      @BeforeMethod
      public void beforeMethod() {
            System.out.println("BeforeMethod: Lay out the cooking
            tools.");
      }
      @Test(groups = "starters")
      public void serveSalad() {
            System.out.println("Test: Serving salad as a starter.");
      }
      @Test(groups = "mains")
      public void servePasta() {
            System.out.println("Test: Serving pasta as a main
            course.");
      }
      @Test(groups = "desserts")
      public void serveIceCream() {
```

```
        System.out.println("Test: Serving ice cream for dessert.");
    }
    @AfterMethod
    public void afterMethod() {
        System.out.println("AfterMethod: Clean the cooking
        tools.");
    }
    @AfterClass
    public void afterClass() {
        System.out.println("AfterClass: Place the dish on the
        dining table.");
    }
    @AfterTest
    public void afterTest() {
        System.out.println("AfterTest: Turn off the kitchen
        lights.");
    }
    @AfterSuite
    public void afterSuite() {
        System.out.println("AfterSuite: Lock up the house and
        retire for the night.");
    }
    public static void main(String[] args) {
        // This is just a placeholder. Typically, TestNG tests are
        not run via a main
        // method.


// Instead, you'd run this using a TestNG runner (via testng.xml or di-
rectly
        // through your IDE's TestNG plugin).
        System.out.println("Run the test through TestNG runner.");
    }
}
```

Running and Debugging TestNG tests

TestNG is a powerful testing framework for Java, and Eclipse IDE provides an intuitive environment for running and debugging these tests. Here's how to effectively run and debug TestNG tests in Eclipse.

Running TestNG Tests

Running Tests: Eclipse makes running TestNG tests straightforward. To execute your tests, right-click on the test class or specific test method in the Project Explorer and select `Run As > TestNG Test`. This action initiates the execution of the tests.

Viewing Results: After running the tests, Eclipse displays the results in the 'TestNG' view. This section provides a detailed report of all executed tests, categorizing them into passed, failed, and skipped tests. You can click on each test to view more details, such as the stack trace for failed tests, which is crucial for initial troubleshooting.

Debugging TestNG Tests

Setting Breakpoints: Debugging in Eclipse starts with setting breakpoints. A breakpoint is a marker that you can set on a line of code where you want the execution to pause. To set a breakpoint, double-click on the left margin next to the line of code in your test class. A blue dot indicates that a breakpoint is set.

Initiating Debug Mode: To start debugging, right-click on the test class or method and choose `Debug As > TestNG Test.` This action launches the test in debug mode, and the execution will pause at the breakpoints you've set.

Using Debugging Tools: When the execution pauses at a breakpoint, Eclipse opens the `Debug` perspective. This view offers several powerful tools:

- **Stepping Controls**: These buttons in Eclipse's top menu bar allow you to step over to the next line of code, step into methods to see what's happening inside, or step out when you're done.
- **Variables View**: This shows the current value of variables in the scope where the execution is paused.
- **Expression Evaluation**: You can write and evaluate expressions on the fly, which is useful for checking how changes in code might affect the execution.
- **Identifying and Solving Issues**: As you step through your code, pay attention to the values in the 'Variables' view and the responses in the

'Console'. These clues can help you understand why a test might be failing and guide you to a solution.

Running and debugging TestNG tests in Eclipse is an efficient process that enhances your testing workflow. By leveraging Eclipse's straightforward run configuration and powerful debugging tools, you can quickly identify and resolve issues in your tests, ensuring more reliable and robust Java applications.

On the other hand, if you are using another IDE such as IntelliJ or VS Code, the concepts detailed above remain the same. And similar experience can be enabled via plugins and extensions from the respective IDE's marketplace.

@Factory and @DataProvider

TestNG also provides two very powerful annotations for data-driven testing, namely `@Factory` and `@DataProvider` for data-driven test automation.

`@Factory`: This annotation allows for the dynamic creation of test instances in TestNG. This is particularly useful when you want to run the same set of tests with different configurations or setups.

Imagine you're automating browser tests using Selenium. You want to run the same test on Chrome, Firefox, and Safari. Instead of creating separate test methods or classes for each browser, you can use the @Factory annotation as follows:

```
public class BrowserTestFactory {


    private String browser;


    public BrowserTestFactory(String browser) {
        this.browser = browser;
    }


    @Test
    public void openAndCloseBrowser() {
        WebDriver driver = new WebDriverFactory().getDriver(browser);
        driver.get("https://www.example.com");
        driver.quit();
    }
```

```
    @Factory
    public static Object[] createInstances() {
        return new Object[]{new BrowserTestFactory("chrome"), new
BrowserTestFactory("firefox"), new BrowserTestFactory("safari")};
    }
}
```

Here, the **@Factory** method creates three instances of **BrowserTestFactory**, each for a different browser. The **openAndCloseBrowser** test will be run for each browser.

@DataProvider: This annotation is used to supply data to a test method. This allows a single test method to be executed multiple times with different sets of data.

Suppose you have an e-commerce website and you want to automate the login functionality for multiple user accounts. Instead of writing separate tests for each user account, you can use the **@DataProvider** to feed the user credentials into a single test.

```
public class LoginTest {

    @Test(dataProvider = "credentialsProvider")
    public void testUserLogin(String username, String password) {
        WebDriver driver = new ChromeDriver();
        driver.get("https://www.e-commerce-site.com/login");

        WebElement usernameField = driver.findElement(By.id("username"));
        WebElement passwordField = driver.findElement(By.id("password"));
        WebElement loginButton = driver.findElement(By.id("loginButton"));

        usernameField.sendKeys(username);
        passwordField.sendKeys(password);
        loginButton.click();

        // Further assertions to validate login
        driver.quit();
```

```
    }

    @DataProvider(name = "credentialsProvider")
    public Object[][] provideCredentials() {
        return new Object[][]{
            {"user1", "password1"},
            {"user2", "password2"},
            {"user3", "password3"}
        };
    }
}
```

In the preceding example, the `testUserLogin` method will be run three times, once for each set of credentials provided by the `credentialsProvider`.

The `@Factory` and `@DataProvider` annotations provide powerful mechanisms to achieve flexibility and reusability in your tests, reducing the amount of repetitive code. When used with Selenium, they enable testers to handle varying test scenarios and configurations more efficiently. This not only makes the test code cleaner but also allows for easy scalability and maintainability.

testng.xml and Parallel execution

"testng.xml" is an XML configuration file that provides a centralized place to define test suites and tests. It offers various configuration options, which can be tailored based on testing requirements. When automating tests with Selenium, testng.xml becomes particularly valuable due to the following reasons:

- **Different Browsers and Environments**: You can define separate tests or suites to run on different browsers or environments.
- **Regression and Smoke Tests**: You can group tests as regression, smoke, and more, and choose which group to run based on your current requirement.
- **Parallel Execution**: If you're running your tests on a Selenium Grid or locally, you can execute tests in parallel across different sessions to speed up the execution.

Let us take a practical example to understand the utility of testng.xml in our context.

Suppose you are testing a web application, and you want to:

1. Run tests on both Chrome and Firefox browsers.
2. Avoid hard coding of the browser value in the test class.
3. Parallelize the execution.

Here's how you might set up your testng.xml (as per src/test/java/chapter5/testng.xml):

```
<?xml version="1.0" encoding="UTF-8"?>
<!DOCTYPE suite SYSTEM "https://testng.org/testng-1.0.dtd">
<suite name="Suite1" parallel="tests" thread-count="2">

  <test name="test on firefox">
  <parameter name="browser" value="firefox"></parameter>
    <classes>
      <class name="chapter5. Chapter05_LoginExample"/>
    </classes>
  </test> <!-- Test1 -->

  <test name="test on chrome">
  <parameter name="browser" value="chrome"></parameter>
    <classes>
      <class name="chapter5. Chapter05_LoginExample"/>
    </classes>
  </test> <!-- Test1 -->

</suite> <!-- Suite1 -->
```

The testng.xml file defines a test suite named `Suite1` and specifies that the tests within the suite should run in parallel. The `parallel="tests"` attribute signifies that the `<test>` elements should run concurrently, and the `thread-count="2"` attribute means that two threads will be allocated for this parallel execution.

Inside this suite, two `<test>` elements are defined:

- **test on firefox**: This sets a parameter named browser with the value **firefox** and indicates that the **LoginExample** class should be executed with this parameter.
- **test on chrome**: Similarly, this sets a parameter named browser with the value **chrome** and indicates the same **Chapter05_LoginExample** class should be executed.

Due to the parallel execution configuration, both these tests will run concurrently, each in its own thread.

The `@Parameters` annotation simplifies the process of configuring your tests to run under different conditions without modifying the test code. The parameter value is passed from testng.xml file to the `@Parameters` annotation in the test class .

This becomes particularly powerful in Selenium Test Automation where tests often need to be executed against different browsers, environments, or configurations. The use of externalized parameters through testng.xml ensures your test code remains clean, reusable, and maintainable.

Another common use case with Selenium test automation is the need to run tests on different environments or URLs. Imagine having a development, staging, and production environment for your application. Instead of hardcoding the environment URLs or creating separate test methods for each, you can utilize `@Parameters` to pass the environment URL dynamically.

Now, let us create the test class, where we can trigger the Chrome browser and Firefox browser tests in parallel as follows (reference code located at src/test/java/chapter5/LoginExample.java):

```
public class LoginExample {
      WebDriver driver = null;
      @Parameters("browser")
      @BeforeTest
      public void setUp(String browser) {
            if (browser.equalsIgnoreCase("chrome")) {
                  // initializing and starting the Chromebrowser
                  driver = new ChromeDriver();
            } else if (browser.equalsIgnoreCase("firefox")) {
                  // initializing and starting the Firefoxbrowser
                  driver = new FirefoxDriver();
```

```
        }
    }
    @Test(groups = { "regression" })
    public void test1() throws InterruptedException {

        System.out.println("Execution for Chrome browser");
        driver.get("https://orangeava.com/");
        Thread.sleep(3000);
    }
    @Test(groups = { "smoke" })
    public void test2() throws InterruptedException {
        System.out.println("Execution for Firefox browser");
        driver.get("https://orangeava.com/");
        Thread.sleep(3000);
    }
    @AfterTest
    public void tearDown() {
        driver.quit();
    }
}
```

So, now when you navigate to your IDE and run the testng.xml file as "Test Suite" (right-click and "`Run as TestNG Suite`" in the contextual menu of the IDE, or "`Alt+Shift+X, G`" as the keyboard shortcut in Eclipse), we can observe:

- Two threads will be allocated for parallel execution.
- In one thread, the `LoginExample` class's methods will be executed with the browser parameter set to `firefox`. The Firefox browser will be launched, and both `test1` and `test2` methods will execute sequentially, each opening the specified URL.
- Concurrently, in the second thread, the `LoginExample` class's methods will execute with the browser parameter set to `chrome`. The Chrome browser will be launched, and both `test1` and `test2` methods will execute in a similar fashion.

Note: TestNG executes different tests alphabetically. By default, test1 will run first, and after that test2, and finally test3.

In this way, we can parallelize or orchestrate various tests in our arsenal using TestNG annotations.

Assertions

In the world of test automation, the role of assertions is akin to a vigilant gatekeeper. Assertions keep a strict check on the expected behavior of an application, ensuring that the software's output aligns with what is anticipated. TestNG furnishes a dedicated "`Assert`" class for achieving this goal. This class contains a suite of static methods tailored for diverse validation needs. When combined with Selenium, these assertions become powerful tools to validate web page states, content, and interactions, thus solidifying the reliability of our applications. Let us look at the various methods provided in the TestNG library to assert that our applications behave as expected.

assertEquals

This method is used to compare the expected and actual values. If there's any mismatch, the test fails.

Here is the code example:

```
String expectedTitle = "Welcome to XYZ";

String actualTitle = driver.getTitle();

Assert.assertEquals(actualTitle, expectedTitle, "Page title doesn't
match the expected value.");
```

assertNotEquals

This method is used to ensure that expected and actual values are not the same. While this method looks trivial, it's particularly helpful in cases where certain default placeholders should have been replaced by actual content or values.

Here is the code example:

```
String defaultText = "Default";

String buttonText = driver.findElement(By.id("button")).getText();

Assert.assertNotEquals(buttonText, defaultText, "Button text shouldn't
be the default value.");
```

assertTrue

This method is used to validate that a particular condition is true. This is one of the most used methods, which is used to ensure that an expected condition is found to be true.

Here is the code example:

```
WebElement menu = driver.findElement(By.id("menu"));

boolean isMenuExpanded = menu.getAttribute("expanded").equals("true");

Assert.assertTrue(isMenuExpanded, "Menu should be in an expanded state.");
```

For example, this assertion can be used to check the states of elements, such as whether a dropdown menu is expanded after a user action.

assertFalse

This method is used to ensure that a condition turns out to be false. It's a handy assertion for cases where you expect certain elements not to be visible, especially after successful operations.

Here is the code example:

```
WebElement errorNotification = driver.findElement(By.id("errorNotification"));

boolean isNotificationVisible = errorNotification.isDisplayed();

Assert.assertFalse(isNotificationVisible, "Error notification should not be visible on a successful action.");
```

In test automation with TestNG and Selenium, assertions play a crucial role in verifying an application's behavior. Key methods include `assertEquals` to check if values match, `assertNotEquals` to ensure they differ, `assertTrue` to confirm a condition is true, and assertFalse to verify it's false. These assertions are vital for testing web page functionality, like confirming if menus are correctly expanded or error messages are hidden when expected.

Test Reporting

In our world of software testing, a substantial amount of time and effort is expended to ensure that applications function as intended. However, after a myriad of test cases are executed, how does one communicate the outcomes? Say hello to 'Test Reporting'.

Test reporting is the process of summarizing and presenting test execution results in a structured format.

It encapsulates the health of the tested application, detailing which tests passed, which failed, and why, giving a clear picture of the application's quality.

Imagine baking a cake and serving it, without checking if it's baked thoroughly to the core. Test reporting is not just about presenting results, it's a compass for stakeholders. It guides developers towards defects, aids management in decision-making, and provides testers with insights into areas of improvement and further inspection. Furthermore, when a test suite grows with the application's evolution, tracking the progress and pitfalls over time becomes essential. Reports serve as historical documents, charting the journey of an application's quality over time.

There are some very good tools like ReportPortal, which can be integrated into a test automation framework for generating world-class reports. In our case, to keep things simple, we will use the inbuilt capabilities of TestNG to produce reports from our automated test execution. After each test run, TestNG automatically generates a detailed HTML report. These reports are intuitive, providing a bird's eye view of the entire test execution, and diving deep into each test case, revealing the details of every success or failure.

Let us learn by a simple example Chapter05_TestNGReportExample test class located at src/test/java/chapter5:

```
@Test
public void sampleTest() {
    Assert.assertEquals(5, 5, "Sample test for demonstration.");
}
```

Upon executing this test with TestNG, an HTML report will be generated post-execution. Locating TestNG's reports is straightforward. After executing your test suite using TestNG, navigate to your project's root directory. Inside it, you will find a directory named 'test-output'. Open this directory, and you will spot an 'index.html' file. This file is the gateway to your test reports. Opening it in a web browser presents a comprehensive overview of the test execution.

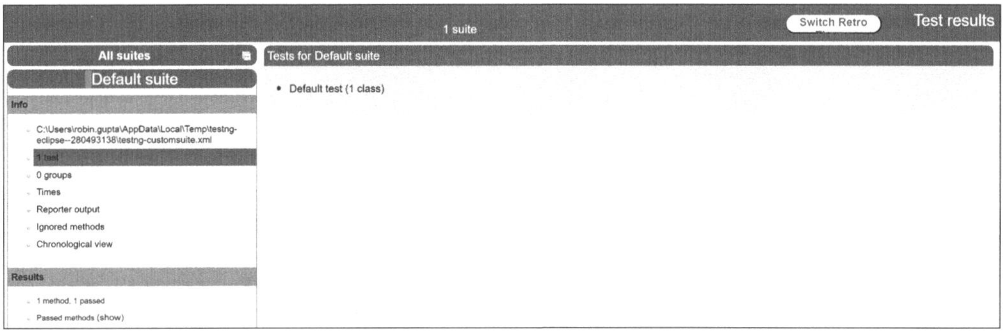

***Figure 5.4**: Sample report from TestNG*

As we can observe, the report provides details of all Test methods and the ones which have passed. If we click on the tabs like "Times", we can also observe the time it took for the execution of the test case. This data can be crucial in the performance tuning of the tests. In most of the practical use cases, you can use the "emailable-report.html" to share the details with the relevant stakeholders in the team as follows:

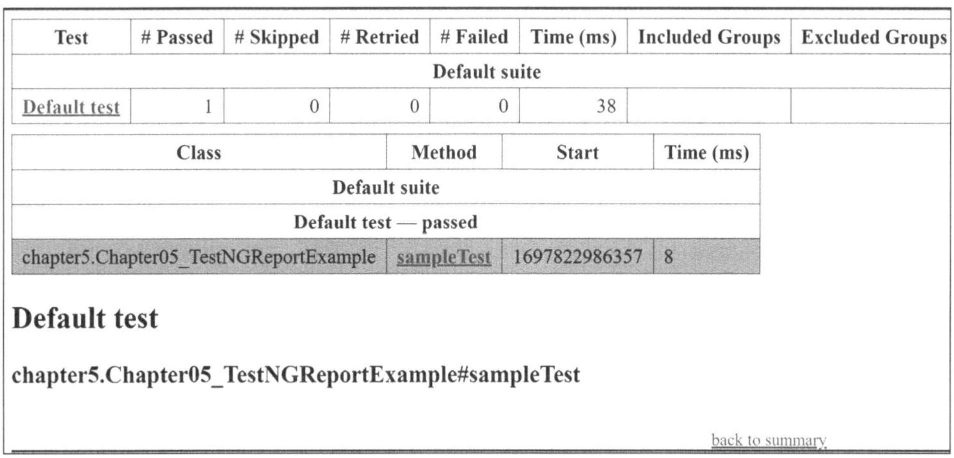

Test	# Passed	# Skipped	# Retried	# Failed	Time (ms)	Included Groups	Excluded Groups
Default suite							
Default test	1	0	0	0	38		

Class	Method	Start	Time (ms)
Default suite			
Default test — passed			
chapter5.Chapter05_TestNGReportExample	sampleTest	1697822986357	8

Default test

chapter5.Chapter05_TestNGReportExample#sampleTest

back to summary

***Figure 5.5**: Sample view of emailable-report.html*

Each test method that's executed has its own section, detailing parameters, start time, end time, and duration. In case of failures, TestNG thoughtfully captures the exception, displaying the stack trace, thus easing the debugging process.

Test reporting is the beacon that illuminates the path forward in software quality assurance. While TestNG provides a robust default reporting mechanism, the quest for comprehensive reporting might lead teams to integrate additional tools. Nonetheless, for those starting their journey in automation with TestNG, its inherent reporting offers a solid foundation. Remember, the core of reporting isn't just about numbers and charts, it's about clarity, insights, and informed decisions that guide software towards excellence.

Logging

Logging is like having a surveillance camera in a store; it records everything that happens, making it easier to figure out what went wrong in case of an incident. It helps developers identify errors, monitor system performance, and ensure that everything is functioning as it should. With logging, you have a history of system activity that can be invaluable for troubleshooting and optimizing performance.

Furthermore, logging acts as a form of documentation. It creates a trail of events, which can be crucial for security audits and compliance. In a way, it's the system's way of telling its story, providing insights that can help improve future operations.

So far, in our examples, we have been using the "`System.out.println()`" statement to print crucial information to the console for validating the execution of our programs. While this approach is good, it fails in a few places:

1. **Persisting the data**: Once a program is re-run or another one is run, the console is cleaned up, and we lose track of the earlier executions.
2. **Low clarity**: The console gets cluttered without timestamps and with output from multiple running threads.

To ensure that we can resolve the preceding problems and create an enterprise-grade framework, we can use an external library such as Log4J for our logging purposes.

Think of it as a sophisticated digital diary for your software. The latest version, Log4j2, is like a diary with added features such as bookmarks and color-coded pages that make it easier to navigate through the logs. It helps organize log messages, making it simpler and faster for developers to find the information they need.

Installation

Here's a snippet of how to add Log4j to your Maven project. In our case, this has already been added to the pom.xml file in the downloaded codebase:

```
<dependency>
                <groupId>org.apache.logging.log4j</groupId>
```

```
            <artifactId>log4j-api</artifactId>
            <version>2.16.0</version>
        </dependency>
        <dependency>
            <groupId>org.apache.logging.log4j</groupId>
            <artifactId>log4j-core</artifactId>
            <version>2.16.0</version>
        </dependency>
```

Configuration

Getting started with Log4j is like setting up a new diary. We need to get the diary, decide the format of entries, and start making entries. In technical terms, we add the Log4j library to our project (as previously mentioned), and then configure it via an XML file, as follows:

```
<?xml version="1.0" encoding="UTF-8"?>
<Configuration status="INFO">
    <Appenders>
        <File name="file" fileName="logs/app.log">
            <PatternLayout pattern="%d{yyyy-MM-dd HH:mm:ss.SSS} [%t]
%-5level %logger{36} - %msg%n" />
        </File>
    </Appenders>

    <Loggers>
        <Root level="info">
            <AppenderRef ref="file" />
        </Root>
    </Loggers>
</Configuration>
```

The same configuration XML can be found in the downloaded code base located at src/main/resources/log4j2.xml. This XML snippet is a setup guide for Log4j, instructing it on how to handle logging in a Java application. It specifies that Log4j should note down its own messages at the "INFO" level or higher. It designates a file named **logs/app.log** where all log messages will be recorded.

Each log message will have a specific format, showing the date, time, thread name, log level, logger name, and the actual message. The configuration ties everything together, ensuring that any important info (at the "INFO" level or higher) is logged to the specified file in the specified format, making it easier for engineers to review what happened during the application's run. Let us zoom into the `PatternLayout` node without getting intimidated by it:

- **`PatternLayout:`** This element defines the format of log messages. The pattern attribute specifies how log messages will be formatted.
- **`%d{yyyy-MM-dd HH:mm:ss.SSS}:`** This part formats the date and time of the log message.
- **`[%t]:`** This part logs the name of the thread that generated the log message.
- **`%-5level:`** This part logs the level of the log message (for example, INFO, ERROR) and pads it to 5 characters.
- **`%logger{36}:`** This part logs the name of the logger that generated the log message, truncated to 36 characters.
- **`%msg:`** This part logs the actual log message.
- **`%n:`** This part writes a newline character after each log message, ensuring that each message appears on a new line.

Log Levels

A natural question arises at this point: if we are logging information at the "**`INFO`**" level in the previous section, what are the other levels? Log4j offers six log levels by default, and each level is associated with an integer value:

- **`TRACE (600):`** This level is for very detailed information, such as when you step in or out of functions or check the values of variables in your code. It's like having a magnifying glass to see the tiny details of how your program is running.
- **`DEBUG (500):`** This level is used when you're building or testing your program. It gives you messages that help check if parts of your program are working right.
- **`INFO (400):`** This level logs general happenings during your program's normal run, such as when a user logs in or when your program talks to a database. It's like a journal of the main actions your program is taking.
- **`WARN (300):`** This level flags things that might not be wrong but could turn into problems. It's like a heads-up to check certain areas of your program.

- **ERROR (200):** This level logs when something goes wrong unexpectedly while your program is running. It's for noting down the unexpected hiccups.
- **FATAL (100):** This level is for major alarms, indicating something went very wrong that needs urgent fixing. It's like a loud siren signaling a serious issue in your program's core part.

For example, the preceding log levels can be implemented for an e-commerce system as follows:

```
logger.trace("Entering method processOrder().");
logger.debug("Received order with ID 12345.");
logger.info("Order shipped successfully.");
logger.warn("Potential security vulnerability detected in user input: '...'");
logger.error("Failed to process order. Error: {. . .}");
logger.fatal("System crashed. Shutting down...");
```

Let us cement our understanding by looking at a hands-on example. This is implemented in the Chapter05_LogExample class located at src/test/java/chapter5, as follows:

```
public class Chapter05_LogExample {
	@Test(priority = 1)
	public void loggerTest() throws Exception {
		final Logger = LogManager.getLogger();
		logger.trace("Entering method processOrder().");
		logger.debug("Received order with ID 12345.");
		logger.info("Order shipped successfully.");
		logger.warn("Potential security vulnerability detected in user
input: '...'");
		logger.error("Failed to process order. Error: {. . .}");
		logger.fatal("System crashed. Shutting down...");


	}
}
```

When we run the aforementioned as a TestNG test, we can observe the following log in the "**app.log**" file located in the "**logs**" folder, as follows:

```
2023-10-21 22:57:19.723 [main] INFO  chapter5.Chapter05_LogExample
- Order shipped successfully.

2023-10-21 22:57:19.725 [main] WARN  chapter5.Chapter05_LogExample
- Potential security vulnerability detected in user input: '...'

2023-10-21 22:57:19.725 [main] ERROR chapter5.Chapter05_LogExample
- Failed to process order. Error: {. . .}

2023-10-21 22:57:19.725 [main] FATAL chapter5.Chapter05_LogExample
- System crashed. Shutting down...
```

Did you observe that we had six commands in the JAVA class for various log levels, but the log file has only four of them registered?

Yes, this is due to the configuration for log level as "`INFO`", as we had set up earlier in the log4j2.xml configuration file. Therefore, our logger highlights the information above the "INFO" level.

Note: Take a minute and try changing the log level to "`Debug`" or "`Error`", running the test again, and observing the results. Remember, great software engineering skills emerge from curiosity and experimentation.

Building a Framework

Now that we have assembled the blocks of a framework, let us get to putting it together, so that our sum can be greater than the individual parts. If we were to think of our journey in automation as baking a cake, the framework would be our recipe book, detailing each step, each ingredient, and the end goal - a delectable, error-free software (or cake)!

Folder structure

Before we get to baking, or, in our case, making a Test Automation Framework, let us understand the kitchen, by walking through the folder structure of the downloaded code base.

As we can observe, the folder structure follows the standard Maven folder structure. Here's an explanation of the primary components:

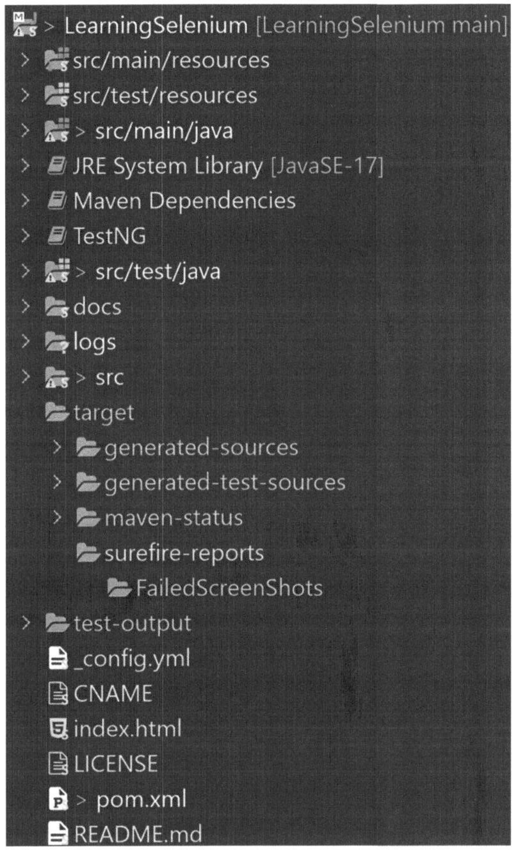

Figure 5.6: *Folder structure of the framework*

- **LearningSelenium**: This is the root directory of our project. It would be the name provided initially while cloning the code from Github repository.
- **src/main/java**: This directory contains the main application code for the project. However, in our context of a Selenium framework, this will include base classes, custom libraries, page objects, and other core code that the tests rely on.
- **src/main/resources**: This is where we'd put resources that the main application (or test code) might need, like configuration files or data files.
- **src/test/java**: This directory will house our Selenium test cases and related test classes.
- **src/test/resources**: Resources specifically needed for testing would go here. This might include test data, configuration files specifically for tests, and more.
- **JRE System Library [JavaSE-17]**: This shows that the project is using Java Standard Edition 17.

- **Maven Dependencies**: Libraries and dependencies managed by Maven. These can include Selenium libraries, testing frameworks like TestNG or JUnit, and any other libraries your tests or main code might need.
- **docs**: A folder that contains web documents for practicing waits, asynchronous elements, and Shadow DOM. This is just for presentation and will not be a part of a standard test automation framework.
- **logs**: As the name suggests, this directory is used to store log files generated during test execution.
- **target**: This is a standard Maven directory where compiled bytecode (`.class` files) and packaged builds (such as `.jar` or `.war` files) are placed. The sub-directories under `target` are as follows:
    - **generated-sources and generated-test-sources**: Folders for source code generated during the build process.
    - **maven-status**: Contains status information related to the Maven build.
    - **surefire-reports**: Surefire is a Maven plugin used for running tests. This directory would contain reports generated by Surefire after running the tests.
    - **FailedScreenShots**: This is a custom directory to store screenshots of failed test cases, a common practice in Selenium test automation to help with debugging.
- **test-output**: Directory that contains output from TestNG test executions.
- **README.md**: A markdown file that typically provides information about the project, how to set it up, run tests, and more.

This folder structure provides a clear separation of concerns, with distinct places for the main code, test code, resources, and outputs. It's a common setup for a Maven-based Java project with Selenium tests. If we zoom out for a minute, this test automation framework and mostly all others are combined of four layers:

1. **Test classes**: The classes representing test cases and verifying a certain piece of functionality from the application under test.
2. **Page objects**: Locators and application-specific methods for certain sections and pages on the web application.
3. **Data**: Test data, metadata, and logs.
4. **Helper classes**: These classes help in organizing the code, creating objects, and accessing data as required by test classes.

Now that we understand the kitchen well, let us take a closer look at the ingredients at the table:

- Maven for Dependency management.
- TestNG for test execution, reporting, and ordering of script execution.
- Selenium for browser automation.
- Design patterns to tie these ingredients together for building a scalable test automation framework.

Now, just as in baking a cake, adding the icing before baking, or mixing sugar after baking the batter would not help, therefore, even with our tools and libraries, the layering of these libraries and tools is very important to the craft of creating a framework.

Code smells

Code smells refer to patterns in software code that suggest potential problems, indicating areas where the code might need refactoring. They don't necessarily mean the code is wrong, but they can make the code harder to maintain or understand. Recognizing code smells helps developers keep their code clean and efficient.

Let us probe the following code, **`Chapter05_BadExample`** class, and look at some code smells or probing questions:

```
@Test(priority = 1)
Run | Debug
public void loginTest() throws Exception {

   // Creating a webdriver instance
A  WebDriver driver = new ChromeDriver();

   // Navigating to sample page
B  driver.get("https://opensource-demo.orangehrmlive.com/web/index.php/auth/login");
   // Instantiating page objects for login page and home page
   OrangeHRMLoginPage loginpage = new OrangeHRMLoginPage(driver);
C  OrangeHRMHomePage homepage = new OrangeHRMHomePage(driver);
   // Test Steps
D  loginpage.login("Admin", "admin123");
   homepage.clickProfileButton();
E  String homepageURL = driver.getCurrentUrl();
   Assert.assertTrue(homepageURL.contains("dashboard"));
F  driver.quit();
}
```

***Figure 5.7**: Sample test class with code smells*

A. Can we instantiate the WebDriver using a Factory design pattern, in a central location, which can supply WebDriver to all page objects and test scripts? Can we improve further and use TestNG annotations to dynamically set it up before any test class is run?

B. Should we have a central mechanism for common methods such as "driver.get"? So that custom implementations and waits can be added easily?

C. Can we instantiate the page objects using a Factory design pattern? So that we have less duplicated code?

D. Should we centralize the test data and related metadata into a standard structure such as JSON or another file format?

E. Rather than exposing raw WebDriver instances, can we pass them from a parent class?

F. Just as in point "A" above, can we improve the process by quitting WebDriver, after all the tests are run?

Think of these questions and connect them back to the concepts we have explored in this chapter, along with a pinch of OOPS (object-oriented programming structure).

In order to solve these code smells, we will try to build scalable components of a framework, and then connect them together in order to build a scalable, maintainable, and stable test automation framework.

Building blocks of framework

Alright, let's get started. We're going to proceed with the following basic components as our starting point. As we move forward, we'll carefully assess if these elements align with our needs and requirements and ensure that we're on the right track. So, let's begin by undertaking the following blocks:

1. Setting up a Base class, which can serve as the parent class for all test classes. It can cover core methods for TestNG, test data management, and logging. This can help us maximize code re-use as per OOPS concepts.

2. Using Factory design pattern for creating manufacturing plants of WebDriver and Page object instances. This can ensure scalability and low maintenance for the framework.

3. A Utility class for centralizing commonly used methods such as Date/ Time, interactions with frames, or Shadow DOM. This can reduce duplication in the code across page objects.

The aforementioned three-part design also helps us achieve separation of concerns, where Test classes are responsible for asserting the functional areas, whereas Page objects are responsible for the interactions with the application under test.

We can arrange these building blocks as per the following framework diagram:

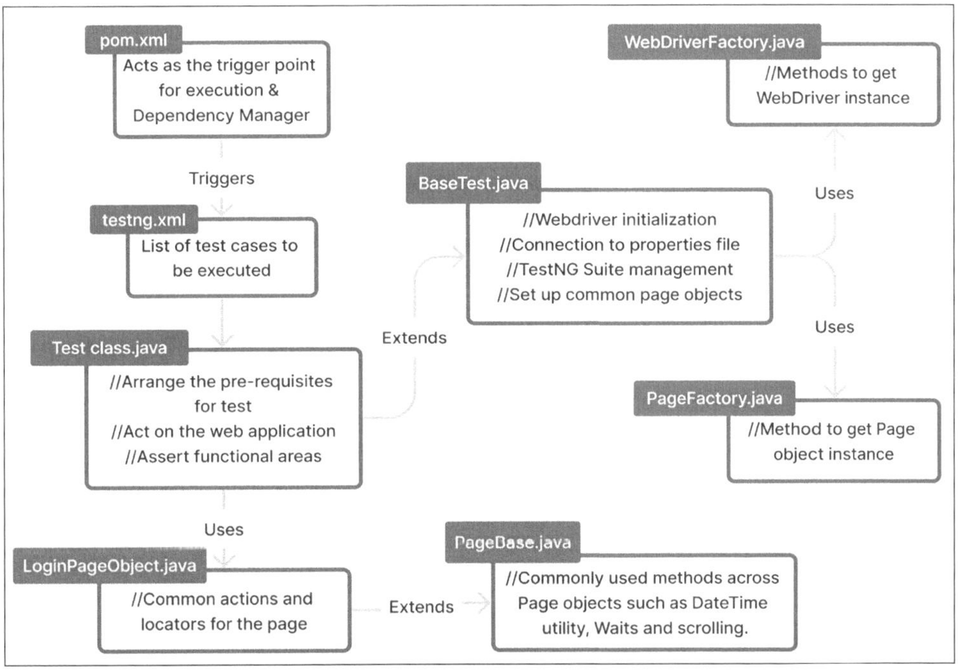

***Figure 5.8**: Visual presentation of the Test Automation Framework*

Now, let us explore these blocks in detail.

WebDriver Factory Class

We can start designing our framework by implementing a **factory design pattern** to standardize the WebDriver instantiation. The idea for this WebDriverFactory Java class is to create instances of WebDriver based on the specified template.

For example, we could create a WebDriver instance for Chrome and another one for Edge, based on the requirements of the Test case.

To dive deeper into the concept, open the WebDriverFactory class in the downloaded codebase located at src/main/java/base/WebDriverFactory.java.

The first main method here is the createInstance method responsible for creating the WebDriver instance to be used in test cases as follows:

```
public static WebDriver createInstance(URL hubUrl, String browserName)
throws IOException {
            WebDriver driver = null;
            try {
                  if (browserName.equalsIgnoreCase("firefox")) {
                        driver = new FirefoxDriver(createFirefox
                        Profile());
                  } else if (browserName.equalsIgnoreCase("chrome")) {
                        driver = new ChromeDriver();
                  } else if (browserName.equalsIgnoreCase("edge")) {
                        driver = new EdgeDriver();
                  } else if (browserName.equalsIgnoreCase("safari") &&
isSafariSupportedPlatform()) {
                        driver = new SafariDriver();
                  }


            }


            catch (Exception e) {
                  System.out.println("Error creating browser session
--" + e.getLocalizedMessage());
            }
            log.info("WebDriverFactory created an instance of WebDriver
for: " + browserName);
            return driver;
      }
```

This is the core factory method. This method, based on the browser name provided (browserName), decides which WebDriver instance to create (ChromeDriver, FirefoxDriver, EdgeDriver, or SafariDriver). The decision is made using a series of if-else statements. The factory method abstracts away the specifics of object creation and provides a single point of change if ever needed.

The other key aspects of the class are as follows:

- `static Logger log = LogManager.getLogger(WebDriverFactory.class);`

This line initializes a logger instance to log messages from this class.

- `static boolean isSafariSupportedPlatform() { ... }`

This method checks whether the current platform supports Safari. Safari is primarily supported on MAC OS.

- `static FirefoxOptions createFirefoxProfile() { ... }`

This method establishes a custom Firefox profile for Selenium testing, specifying how the browser should behave during test sessions. It restricts certain behaviors like pop-up display, sets maximum script run times, handles SSL certificate validations, and more. Similarly, in Selenium, `ChromeOptions` can be used to configure Chrome-specific behaviors, such as setting binary paths, disabling extensions, or running in headless mode. For a more browser-agnostic approach, `DesiredCapabilities` can be employed to specify browser settings such as proxy configurations or enabling JavaScript. Both `ChromeOptions` and `DesiredCapabilities` ensure a consistent and controlled environment for test execution across different browsers, enhancing the reliability of automated tests.

Here is an example of setting up Chrome options and desired capabilities:

```
ChromeOptions options = new ChromeOptions()
options.addArgument("start-maximized");
ChromeDriver driver = new ChromeDriver(options);
```

This would start the Chrome browser in maximized mode.

Note: We will cover ChromeOptions in more detail in the next chapter.

The benefits of using Factory design pattern in this context are as follows:

- Provides an abstraction between the client and the WebDriver classes.
- Centralizes the WebDriver object creation to one place, making the code more maintainable.
- It's easier to add support for new browsers in the future without affecting existing code.

Note: The Factory method isn't limited to just the createInstance method; the createFirefoxProfile can also be seen as a specialized Factory method that creates an instance of FirefoxOptions based on predefined settings.

PageFactory Class

Now that we have become an expert in the Factory design pattern, let us use the same concepts in setting up the factory for page objects. Navigate to the **PageFactory** class located at src/main/java/base/PageFactory.java as follows:

```
public class PageFactory {
	private WebDriver webDriver;
	public PageFactory(WebDriver webDriver) {
		this.webDriver = webDriver;
	}
	public Object getPageObject(String pageobject) {
		try {
			Constructor<?> c =
Class.forName(pageobject).getConstructor(WebDriver.class);
			return c.newInstance(webDriver);
		} catch (NoSuchMethodException e) {
			BaseTest.logger.error("No such method exception in
PageFactory");
			e.printStackTrace();
		} catch (SecurityException e) {
			BaseTest.logger.error("Security exception in
PageFactory");
			e.printStackTrace();
		} catch (ClassNotFoundException e) {
			BaseTest.logger.error("Class not found exception in
PageFactory");
			e.printStackTrace();
		} catch (InstantiationException e) {
			BaseTest.logger.error("Instantiation exception in
PageFactory");
			e.printStackTrace();
		} catch (IllegalAccessException e) {
			BaseTest.logger.error("Illegal Access exception in
PageFactory");
			e.printStackTrace();
```

```
            } catch (IllegalArgumentException e) {
                  BaseTest.logger.error("Illegal argument exception in
PageFactory");
                  e.printStackTrace();
            } catch (InvocationTargetException e) {
                  BaseTest.logger.error("Invocation Target exception in
PageFactory");
                  e.printStackTrace();
            }
            return null;
      }
}
```

The preceding code uses Java reflection to create a new instance of the class specified by the `pageobject` string. As explained earlier, Java reflection is a mechanism that allows us to examine and modify the structure of Java programs at runtime. It can be used to get information about classes, their fields, and methods, and to invoke methods and constructors.

In the preceding code, the `Class.forName()` method is used to get a `Class` object for the class specified by the `pageobject` string. The `getConstructor()` method on the `Class` object is then used to get a `Constructor` object for the constructor with the specified parameter list. In this case, the parameter list is `WebDriver.class`, which means that the constructor takes a `WebDriver` object as a parameter.

Finally, the `newInstance()` method on the `Constructor` object is used to create a new instance of the class, passing the `webDriver` object to the constructor.

So, the overall effect of the code is to create a new instance of the class specified by the `pageobject` string, passing the `webDriver` object to the constructor. This is useful for creating page object classes, which are classes that represent web pages and provide methods for interacting with those pages.

BaseTest Class

We can use the WebDriverFactory class to instantiate the WebDrivers for our test cases, but how can we scale it further and maximize the code reusability? How about setting up a base class for test cases, which can be used as the "Base" for centralizing activities around WebDriver instantiation (from the factory class mentioned earlier)? And maybe augmenting it with additional capabilities, such as test data creation/purging and ordering of test execution using TestNG. This way, all the test classes can inherit these capabilities from BaseTest, allowing us to maximize code reusability with object-oriented programming.

Please open the BaseTest class in the downloaded code (located at src/main/java/base) and refer to it actively as we explore the following details. It's a big one, but we will go through it slice by slice, just like a pizza.

Let us look at the first main component of this class:

```
@BeforeSuite(alwaysRun = true)
@Parameters({ "browserType" })
public void setupWebDriver(@Optional("chrome") String browserType)
throws IOException {
// Below lines can be uncommented to provide log level at fine grained
scale for
// debugging Selenium WebDriver
//SeleniumLogger seleniumLogger = new SeleniumLogger();
//seleniumLogger.setLevel(Level.FINE);
	if ((driver == null)) {
		logger.info("setupWebDriver()");
		driver = WebDriverFactory.createInstance(huburl, browserType);
		action = new Actions(driver);
		pageFactory = new PageFactory(driver);
		driver.manage().window().maximize();
		logger.info("Window width: " +
	driver.manage().window().getSize().getWidth());
		logger.info("Window height: " +
driver.manage().window().getSize().getHeight());
		}
	}
```

The preceding lines of code utilize the `createInstance` from `WebDriverFactory` class to create an instance of WebDriver based on the `@Optional("chrome")` parameter passed at run time. Don't bother about the "huburl", as we will shortly explore it with concepts around Selenium GRID in the next chapter.

`setupWebDriver` method does a couple of other interesting things as follows:

1. Sets up an instance of `action` object, which can be used by child objects (Test classes), for utilizing WebDriver's Actions class and interacting with web elements.
2. Instantiates a `pageFactory` object to be used later in the BaseTest class for the runtime initialization of Page objects using the factory design pattern.
3. Maximizes the newly opened browser window and captures the screen dimensions for reporting purposes.

The next section of code helps us delete cookies before every test, to ensure a clean state before starting the testing process:

```
@BeforeTest(alwaysRun = true)
public void cleanTestSetup() {
driver.manage().deleteAllCookies();
      }
```

The following section of code does a lot of heavy lifting:

```
@BeforeClass(alwaysRun = true)
protected void setUp() throws MessagingException {
// Set up the common page objects using Reflections concept
loginpage = (OrangeLoginPage) pageFactory.getPageObject(OrangeLoginPage.
class.getName());
homepage = (OrangeHRMHomePage) pageFactory.getPageObject(OrangeHRMHomeP-
age.class.getName());
// Below is code as reference for reading common data from properties file
// Kindly note that the uncommon data should be read in the specific test
class
orangehrmurl = (String) getStaticData().get("orangehrmloginurl");
orangehrmuserid = (String) getStaticData().get("orangehrmuserid");
orangehrmpassword = (String) getStaticData().get("orangehrmpassword");
// Setting up email utils object
// EmailUtils emu = new EmailUtils();
      }
```

This code snippet defines a setup method that is intended to be executed before a test class runs, as indicated by the @BeforeClass(alwaysRun = true) annotation. Within this method:

- **Page Object Setup using Reflection**: It initializes two-page objects, `loginpage` and `homepage`, from the classes `OrangeLoginPage` and `OrangeHRMHomePage`, respectively, using the concept of Reflection. The method `pageFactory.getPageObject` creates instances of these page objects based on their class names.
- **Reading Data from Properties File**: The method pulls common login data for the OrangeHRM application from a properties file. Specifically, it retrieves the URL for login, user ID, and password.

In essence, this method sets up the necessary preconditions and initial data before running a set of tests on the OrangeHRM application.

The following section of code helps us capture screenshots of the failed tests:

```
@AfterMethod(alwaysRun = true)
public void tearDownandCaptureScreenShot(Method method, ITestResult result)
{
// Method for taking screenshots on failure of the test case
if (ITestResult.FAILURE == result.getStatus()) {
        try {
                SimpleDateFormat simpleDateFormat = new
SimpleDateFormat("yyyyMMddhhmmss");
                String currentdatetime = simpleDateFormat.format(new Date());
                File source = captureScreenShot();
                FileUtils.copyFile(source, new File(System.getProperty
("user.dir")
                                                + "/target/surefire-reports/
FailedScreenShots/" + result.getName() + currentdatetime + ".png"));
                        logger.info("Screenshot taken");
                    } catch (Exception e) {


                    logger.info("Exception while taking screenshot " +
e.getMessage());
                    }
            }
```

```
            logger.info("************");
            logger.info("Ending Test  ---->" + method.getName());


    }
```

This code defines a method named `tearDownandCaptureScreenShot` that is intended to be executed after each test method completes, as indicated by the `@AfterMethod(alwaysRun = true)` annotation. The primary role of this method is to take a screenshot when a test case fails. This can be useful for debugging and recording the state of the application when an error occurs. The condition `if (ITestResult.FAILURE == result.getStatus())` checks if the test that just ran resulted in a failure. Our code captures screenshots of failure as follows:

- A `SimpleDateFormat` object is created to format the current date and time in the pattern `yyyyMMddhhmmss` (YearMonthDayHourMinuteSecond).
- The current date and time are then obtained and formatted using this pattern, giving a unique string `currentdatetime`.
- The `captureScreenShot()` method is called to take a screenshot, and the resulting file is saved as `source`.
- The `FileUtils.copyFile` method is used to save a copy of this screenshot to a specific directory within the project, naming it based on the failed test method's name and the current date-time, with a `.png` extension. This ensures that screenshots from different failed tests don't overwrite each other.
- If successful, a log entry "Screenshot taken" is recorded.

If any exception arises while taking or saving the screenshot, the catch block will log an appropriate message about the exception. Regardless of whether the test passed or failed, the method logs the end of the test using the test method's name.

Therefore, this method is a cleanup routine that captures and saves a screenshot if the test fails, providing visual evidence of the application's state at the time of the failure, and always logs the end of the test execution.

Following the above, our next snippet helps in purging session cookies and closing any additional browser windows:

```
@AfterClass(alwaysRun = true)
public void deleteAllCookies() {
// Handling windows after executing each class from Suite
```

```
            try {
                  String originalHandle = driver.getWindowHandle();
                  for (String handle : driver.getWindowHandles()) {
                        if (!handle.equals(originalHandle)) {
                              driver.switchTo().window(handle);
                              driver.close();
                        }
                  }
                  driver.switchTo().window(originalHandle);
            } catch (Exception e) {
                  logger.info("Error while closing child windows" +
e.getMessage());
            }
            logger.info("Clearing all browser cookies...");
            driver.manage().deleteAllCookies();
      }
```

The code defines a method `deleteAllCookies` that runs after all test methods in a class. It first closes any extra browser windows opened during testing, ensuring only the original window remains open. If any errors occur while closing these windows, they are logged. Lastly, the method clears all browser cookies to prepare for any following tests, ensuring a consistent starting environment.

Once we have managed the windows and cookies, we can jump up a level and purge the WebDriver instance for a clean exit from the test, as per the following code:

```
@AfterSuite(alwaysRun = true)
      public void quitWebDrivers() {
            logger.info("terminateWebDrivers()");
            try {
                  driver.close();
                  driver.quit();
                  // Setting driver to null for stopping persistent
use of driver
                  // session across browsers
                  driver = null;
```

```
            } catch (Exception e) {
                  // Sometime driver.quit() causes exception and not
nullifying the
                  // driver obj. Which stops next successful browser
                  launch
                  driver = null;
                  logger.error("Error quitting driver");
                  e.printStackTrace();
            }
      }
```

The preceding code describes a method, `quitWebDrivers`, set to execute after all test suites. It aims to gracefully terminate active browser sessions. Initially, it attempts to close the current browser window and then quit the browser driver. To avoid unintentional use of the same browser session in subsequent tests, the driver is set to null. If any issues arise during the closing or quitting process, the driver is still nullified, and an error is logged to record the exception.

BaseTest can be also used to house commonly used methods, such as `captureScreenShot()` as follows.

We will take a deeper look at this method in the following section on the `PageBase` class:

```
public File captureScreenShot() {
            return new PageBase(driver).takeScreenshot();
      }
```

As part of the BaseTest, we also implement the method to read data from the properties file as follows:

```
@Override
      public Properties getStaticData() { // Method to read data from
static data properties file
      if (staticData == null) {
            staticData = new Properties();
            InputStream input = null;
            try {
                  String filename = "staticdata.properties";
                  input =
```

```
BaseTest.class.getClassLoader().getResourceAsStream(filename);
                  if (input != null) {
      // load a properties file from class path, inside static method
                        staticData.load(input);
                        logger.info("staticdata.properties loaded
successfully");
                        }
                  } catch (IOException ex) {
                        logger.info("error loading staticdata.
properties" + ex.getMessage());
                  } finally {
                        if (input != null) {
                              try {
                                    input.close();
                                    logger.info("staticdata.properties
closed successfully");
                              } catch (IOException e) {
                                    logger.info(("error loading
staticdata.properties") + e.getMessage());
                              }
                        }
                  }
            }
            return staticData;
      }
```

The method `getStaticData` is designed to read data from a properties file named `staticdata.properties`. If the `staticData` object is not initialized (that is, `null`), a new `Properties` object is created for it. The method then attempts to load this file from the class path using the class loader of BaseTest class. If the file is successfully found, it's loaded into the `staticData` object, and a success message is logged. If there's an issue reading the file, an error message indicating the failure is logged. Finally, regardless of success or failure in loading the file, the method attempts to close the `InputStream` to free up resources and logs the status of this operation. If there's any exception during closing, that too is logged. The method then returns the `staticData` object, which contains the loaded properties or remains uninitialized if there was an error.

The BaseTest class is well-structured to support a robust test automation framework. It encapsulates common setup, teardown, and utility functions that will be shared across all test classes inheriting from it. This design promotes code reusability, maintainability, and a clear separation of concerns between setup, utility functions, and actual test logic.

PageBase Class

We have explored a parent class (BaseTest) for the test classes, so that common code can be housed together. But, what about our Page objects? For example, multiple page objects might require custom methods to select values as follows:

```
public void selectValue(WebElement ele, String value) {
Select select = new Select(ele);
      select.selectByValue(value);
      logger.info("Selected value : " + value);
      }
```

While we can set up such methods for the web interactions on each page object, it would cause maintenance issues in the long run. Therefore, as part of our test automation framework, we will be setting a "PageBase" class, which will act as a parent utility class for common methods around web interactions, such as selecting values, waits, scrolling, or even date/time utilities. As our page objects extend PageBase, all these methods are easily available for consumption at the page level. Please navigate to the **PageBase.java** class located at src/main/java/base, and let us explore a few utility methods here:

Code for getting the current date:

```
      public String getCurrentDate() {
            SimpleDateFormat simpleDateFormat = new SimpleDateFormat
("yyyy-MM-dd");
            String currentdatetime = simpleDateFormat.format(new Date());
            return currentdatetime;
      }
```

Code to refresh the web page:

```
public void refreshPage() {
            driver.navigate().refresh();
```

```
            logger.info("Page Refreshed");
      }
```

Code for waiting and clicking on an element:

```
public void waitAndClick(WebElement element) {
            // waiting for web element before clicking
            Wait<WebDriver> wait = new WebDriverWait(driver, Duration.
ofSeconds(10));
            wait.until(ExpectedConditions.elementToBeClickable(element));

            // Validating the element after ample waiting
            if (element.isDisplayed()) {
                  logger.info("Element found and clicked");
                  element.click();
            } else {
                  logger.info("Element Not Displayed " + element.
getText());
            }

      }
```

Code for taking screenshots:

```
public File takeScreenshot() {
            WebDriver augment = new Augmenter().augment(driver);
            return ((TakesScreenshot) augment).getScreenshotAs(Output-
Type.FILE);
      }
```

Creating Automated Tests

Now that we know what are the building blocks of the framework and how they fit together, let's use the provided design to create scalable and easy-to-maintain automated tests. At the high level, the steps are very simple:

1. Make the test class (it should inherit from the **`BaseTest`** class).
2. Use existing or make new page objects (they should inherit from the PageBase class).

3. If needed, add test data to the properties file.
4. Include the test class in testng.xml if suite-level execution is needed.

It's time to roll up our sleeves and create an automated test based on the framework. Please open the Chapter05_LoginTest.java test class as follows:

```
public class Chapter05_LoginTest extends BaseTest {
	@Test(priority = 1)
	public void loginTest() throws Exception {
		// Navigating to sample page
		loginpage.openHomepage(orangehrmurl);
		// Test Steps
		loginpage.login("Admin", "admin123");
		homepage.clickProfileButton();
		String homepageURL = loginpage.getCurrentURL();
		Assert.assertTrue(homepageURL.contains("dashboard"));
	}
}
```

Isn't it simple and elegant? Let us peel the layers on this class. First and foremost, the test class extends the `BaseTest` class so that it can inherit the Before/After ordering of setup and cleanup methods, common test data, page objects, and logging capabilities.

The following line uses the `LoginPage` page object and opens the login page using the `openHomepage` method inherited from the `PageBase` class. The value for URL comes from BaseTest, as part of common test data.

```
		loginpage.openHomepage(orangehrmurl);
```

The following line uses the page object method to perform the login action.

```
		loginpage.login("Admin", "admin123");
```

Similarly, we use the page object method to perform the click on the "profile" button. This way we have separated the concerns of testing the application and web interactions between the test class and page object class:

```
		homepage.clickProfileButton();
```

We can use the `getCurrentURL()` method from `PageBase` to capture the URL. As we have centralized such methods in `Pagebase`, all our Page object classes can inherit these capabilities from one central location.

```
String homepageURL = loginpage.getCurrentURL();
```

Last, but certainly not the least, we have the assertion at hand:

```
Assert.assertTrue(homepageURL.contains("dashboard"));
```

This way test class can be updated without impacting the methods and classes for web interactions.

To supplement the test class, we have noticed that we will require a Page object class, so it is worthwhile to quickly zoom into that area. Please open the **OrangeLoginPage** java class located at src/main/java/pageobjects:

```
public class OrangeLoginPage extends PageBase {
        protected WebDriver driver;
        private By usernamelocator = By.xpath("//input[@placeholder='
        Username']");
        private By passwordlocator = By.xpath("//input[@placeholder='
        Password']");
        private By loginlocator = By.xpath("//button[@type='submit']");
        public OrangeLoginPage(WebDriver webDriver) {
                super(webDriver);
                this.driver = webDriver;
        }
        public OrangeHRMHomePage login(String userid, String passwordtext)
throws InterruptedException {
                explicitWait(usernamelocator, 10);
                // We can optionally call driver methods directly here or
optionally use common
                // methods from PageBase
                driver.findElement(usernamelocator).sendKeys(userid);
                driver.findElement(passwordlocator).sendKeys(passwordtext);
                safeClick(loginlocator);
                // Returning the instance of Homepage for fluent style of
programming
```

```
            return new OrangeHRMHomePage(driver);
      }
}
```

This code defines the page object named **OrangeLoginPage**, which represents the login page of an application. This class inherits from our base class **PageBase**. Inside, there are locators to identify the username, password fields, and the login button on the webpage using their XPath. The class constructor initializes the web driver, which controls the browser actions. There's a login method provided that first waits for the username field to be available, then enters the provided username and password, clicks the login button, and subsequently navigates to the home page. This method returns an instance of the **OrangeHRMHomePage**, allowing for a continuous flow of actions.

Interestingly, Page object classes can use methods from **PageBase** class for common interactions or define their own custom methods for bespoke interactions. This way we can balance code re-usability and flexibility at page level.

To instantiate the page object class, we have added the following lines of code to **BaseTest** class:

```
protected OrangeLoginPage loginpage;
      loginpage = (OrangeLoginPage)
pageFactory.getPageObject(OrangeLoginPage.class.getName());
```

We follow the same process for creating the **OrangeHRMHomePage** class.

So, let us summarize all the preceding steps for authoring a new test in three simple pieces:

1. Start from the creation of the Test class.
2. Based on existing Page object classes, and the scope of the Test class, create new Page object classes.
3. Setup the Page object class in the BaseTest class, so that it's available for all the Test classes.

Once we are done with the preceding steps, we can add the Test class to testng.xml for execution as part of regression cycles. And yes, if the test execution fails, then the screenshot for the failed step can be found in the **FailedScreenShots** folder, and the logs can be located in the **app.log** file for debugging purposes.

Running tests via TestNG or Maven

Now that we have created our test case, it can be run in a couple of ways as follows:

1. **Running as an individual test case**: As mentioned earlier, this can be achieved by right-clicking on the test and using **`Run as TestNG Test`** option from the IDE, or the corresponding keyboard shortcuts. This option is most suitable when we need to run the test individually, as part of the test authoring phase.
2. **Running as part of a TestNG suite**: We can also run the test case by adding its corresponding entry to **`testng.xml`** suite file, and then using **`Run as TestNG Suite`** option from IDE. This option is most suitable when we need to run a bunch of tests together. This option can also be used as part of the build process or CI/CD pipeline, using the corresponding tools.
3. **Running as part of a Maven build**: Last but not the least, once we have added the tests to be run, as part of the testng.xml file, we can point to the testng.xml file from Maven pom.xml file and trigger it as part of the Maven build. From our pom.xml file, we can see the following segment:

```
<plugin>
        <groupId>org.apache.maven.plugins</groupId>
        <artifactId>maven-surefire-plugin</artifactId>
        <version>2.19</version>
        <configuration>
                <suiteXmlFiles>     <!-- Specify the TestNG XML file
you want to run over here -->
<!--
        <suiteXmlFile>src/test/java/chapter5/testng.xml</
suiteXmlFile> -->
<suiteXmlFile>src/test/java/chapter6/chapter6_testng.xml</
suiteXmlFile>
                </suiteXmlFiles>
        </configuration>
</plugin>
```

This segment from our Maven pom.xml file is configuring the Maven Surefire plugin, which is used primarily for running unit tests. The

groupId (org.apache.maven.plugins) and **artifactId (maven-surefire-plugin)** identify the plugin within the Maven ecosystem. The version tag specifies the version of the plugin, in this case, 2.19.

The configuration section is where the specific settings for the plugin are defined. Here, it includes **suiteXmlFiles**, which points to the TestNG XML files that describe the tests to be run. In this example, the file chapter6_testng.xml located in the **src/test/java/chapter6** directory is specified. This means that when Maven runs the Surefire plugin during the build process, it will execute the tests as defined in the **chapter6_testng.xml** file. The commented-out line **(<!-- -->)** is an example of how you might specify a different TestNG configuration file, but in this case, it's not active because it's commented out.

By following a few straightforward steps as above, such as creating test classes and using page objects, we can build tests that are easy to update and maintain. Adding tests to TestNG or running them through Maven helps fit testing neatly into our overall project, making sure everything works smoothly. In short, this approach is all about making our life easier when it comes to testing our software, ensuring that everything works well without a lot of hassle.

Continuous Integration/Continuous Delivery

Continuous Integration and Continuous Delivery (CI/CD) are key Developer-Operations (DevOps) practices that automate building, testing and deployment of software. In this section, we will learn how CI/CD enables executing Selenium tests automatically for every code change to detect issues early.

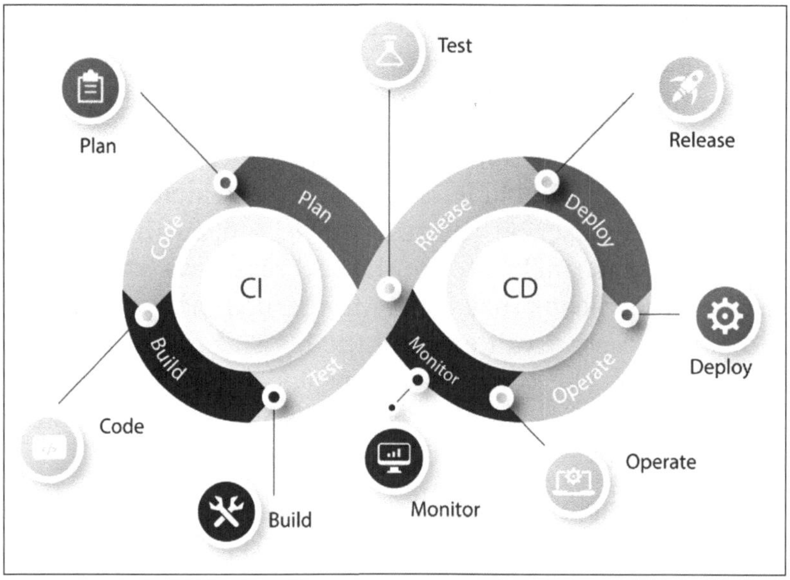

***Figure* 5.9**: *CI/CD lifecycle*

Continuous Integration means integrating code changes from different developers frequently by merging them into a shared code repository. With CI, developers commit code multiple times a day into the main branch. Each commit triggers an automated build and test process to provide rapid feedback. For example, when a developer makes a commit, automated tests run against the changes on a CI server like Jenkins. If any test fails, the team is alerted to fix it immediately. This tight feedback loop catches defects early before they multiply.

Continuous Delivery builds on CI by automating release processes. In addition to build and testing, CD pipelines automate deployment into staging and production environments. For example, after testing, the code is automatically deployed to a staging environment for further testing. The delivery pipeline orchestrates code deployment all the way to production in a sustainable manner.

Together, CI and CD form an automated software pipeline that improves quality and speed.

Benefits of CI/CD

Here are some benefits from implementing a CI/CD pipeline:

- Every commit trigger automated test execution
- Fast feedback within minutes
- Engineers fix issues immediately

- Consistent test environments using containers
- Scaling across distributed test infrastructure
- Deploy to staging and prod with confidence

CI/CD pipelines enable executing all Selenium tests automatically rather than sporadic manual testing. Developers get rapid feedback to code changes via test results. This catches defects early and improves quality.

Tools and Usage

Let's look at some popular tools used to build CI/CD pipelines:

- **Jenkins**: The de facto standard CI/CD server. Jenkins provides distributed test execution, scheduling, and integration with Selenium. The Selenium plugin allows triggering Selenium Grid tests.
- **Docker**: Container technology like Docker provides isolated, consistent environments to run tests reliably. No more "But it worked on my machine!" excuses.
- **Cloud Infrastructure**: Cloud providers like AWS make it easy to scale test infrastructure on demand. Cloud instances can be scripted to auto-scale up or down based on load.
- **TravisCI, CircleCI, GitLab**: There are hosted CI/CD platforms that provide pipelines without needing to maintain your own infrastructure. These can integrate with GitHub for commit-driven testing.

By leveraging CI/CD pipelines, teams can scale automated testing and improve software quality significantly. CI/CD paired with Selenium test automation frameworks unlocks huge advantages in product quality and team productivity. Gradually evolving your automation and workflows will allow you to harness its benefits.

> *Automation frameworks have come to a level wherein they are a commodity. Just as one buys a car or a bike, one can adopt an automation framework from the Open source world and use it. But people should take the time and effort to look under the hoods to see how an automation framework works.*
>
> *With TestNG, I look at it as my first gospel on learning concurrency in Java. I think this quote that I found on the internet sums it all "Threading isn't hard, locking is".*
>
> - Krishnan Mahadevan, Open-source contributor at the TestNG, Selenium, Simple-SSH and SeLion projects, among others.

Conclusion

In this chapter, we arrived at one of the peaks of our framework design and test automation journey. If you have made it this far, with all code examples working, you deserve a coffee, a pat on the back and perhaps a slice of cake. Since most of the test automation assignments will bank on these core concepts around TestNG, Maven, Page objects, SOLID principles, and Design patterns. It is worthwhile to review *Figures* 5.2, 5.7, and 5.8 to connect the mental dots and get a holistic picture of the problem statement and solution set before moving forward.

A robust framework is crucial for efficient test automation, ensuring easier testing, better maintainability, and scalability. While we explored these concepts in detail, in our next chapter, we will undertake cross-browser test automation as the next challenge and conquer it using Selenium GRID.

Now, it's time to roll up your sleeves and put on your thinking hat to solve the below exercise.

Exercises

Hello, aspiring framework designer, kindly automate the test case as follows:

1. Navigate to https://orangeava.com/
2. Click on the first book under the **`New Release`** section.
3. Capture the book price on the book detail page.
4. Click on the **`ADD TO CART`** button.
5. Verify that the book price displayed in the **`Cart`** section is the same as the value captured in Step 3 above.
6. Test case should utilize the **`Assert.assertTrue`** method from the TestNG library for verification of the book price.
7. Ensure that:
    a. Test Class extends BaseTest
    b. Page objects extend PageBase
    c. Execution for the Test Class from 7.a should be triggered from Maven using **`testng.xml`** file.

CHAPTER 6

Distributed Test Automation

Introduction

Google Chrome, Firefox, and Microsoft Edge have different release cycles. As of the public information available, Google Chrome has been releasing stable versions every four weeks, resulting in at least 10 to 12 releases per year. Firefox has been following a rapid release cycle, with new major version releases occurring on four-week cycles and Microsoft Edge has been releasing new major versions every 6-8 weeks, with an option for an Extended Stable release cycle for enterprise customers, resulting in around 6-9 major releases per year. Therefore, ensuring that your web applications function correctly across different browsers and browser versions becomes a significant challenge. Each browser has its unique quirks and behaviors, making cross-browser compatibility testing essential. As web applications grow larger and more complex, manually testing them across browsers can become incredibly time-consuming and resource-intensive.

This is where the concept of scaling test automation comes in. The goal of scaling automation is to increase the speed, efficiency, and coverage of testing by leveraging multiple resources in parallel. Some key ways to scale automated testing include distributing tests across multiple machines, executing tests concurrently, and integrating testing earlier in the development cycle.

Distributed execution involves splitting up large test suites and running different parts on multiple machines or environments simultaneously. This parallel execution dramatically reduces the total time taken to run all tests. Distributed testing also enables you to cover more test configurations and browsers through parallel cross-browser testing.

Selenium Grid is a powerful tool that helps enable distributed, parallel test execution. It allows you to spread your test suite across multiple machines and run tests concurrently. Selenium Grid manages the distribution of tests and aggregation of results from across these remote machines. This makes it much easier to scale automated testing.

In this chapter, we'll explore distributed testing with Selenium Grid, covering cross-browser compatibility behaviors, and diving into the world of scaled automation.

Structure

In this chapter, we will discuss the following topics:

- Cross-browser compatibility
- Handling browser-specific behaviors
- Selenium Grid
    - Setup and installation
    - Grid architecture
    - Roles
    - Security

Cross-browser Compatibility

Imagine you have developed a web application, and it works perfectly on your favorite browser. But when you open it on another browser, it is a completely different story. Elements are misaligned, buttons do not work, and your application is a mess. This is the essence of cross-browser compatibility challenges.

Cross-browser compatibility is the art of ensuring your web application functions consistently and correctly across various web browsers, such as Chrome, Firefox, Safari, and Edge. Each browser interprets web content differently, which can lead to visual discrepancies and functionality issues.

Let us take an example to tie this together. Kindly open the DifferentlyRenders.html file present at **`src/test/java/chapter6`** in the downloaded codebase in Chrome and Firefox browsers, respectively. Did you "know"-tice any differences? Wordplay aside, here we can notice the difference in rendering the same web page by two different browsers.

Figure 6.1: *Web page rendering in Chrome.*

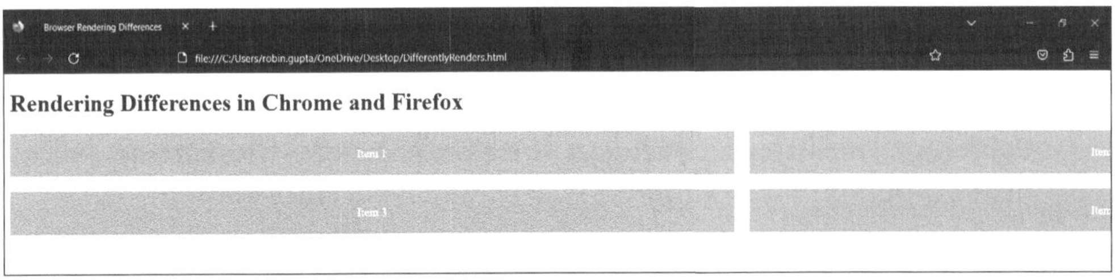

Figure 6.2: *Web page rendering in Firefox*

If we probe a little into the HTML content of the file, we can observe that the following lines are causing the mischievous difference in behavior:

```
/* Firefox-specific CSS */
        @-moz-document url-prefix() {
            .container {
                grid-template-columns: repeat(var(--grid-columns),
minmax(1000px, 1fr));
            }
```

In this example, we define a CSS variable, **`--grid-columns`**, which determines the number of grid columns. In Chrome, it renders as a 2-column grid, while in Firefox, it renders with a minimum column width of 1000px. This showcases the difference in rendering behavior between the two browsers, emphasizing how their rendering engines handle CSS grids and variables differently.

Web browsers are sophisticated pieces of software that play a crucial role in rendering web content for users. They follow a multi-step process to load and display web pages. To understand cross-browser compatibility, let's first understand how browsers load web pages by performing the following journey:

1. **URL Parsing**: When a user enters a URL in the address bar or clicks on a link, the browser starts by parsing the URL to identify the protocol (e.g., HTTP or HTTPS), domain name, and specific web page path. It then sends an HTTP request to the server hosting the web page.
2. **Server Response**: The server responds to the browser's request with HTML, CSS, JavaScript, and other assets that make up the web page. This response may also include metadata like response headers.
3. **Rendering**: The browser's rendering engine takes over, parsing the HTML to create the Document Object Model (DOM) and processing CSS to build the CSS Object Model (CSSOM). These two models are used to generate the render tree, which represents the web page's layout and content.
4. **Painting**: The browser renders the content onto the screen, painting pixels based on the computed styles and layout information.

The same process is followed by each browser to render the web pages. Then the question is, if the same process is followed by each browser, then how come the web pages end up looking and working differently on different browsers?

Yes, most of the answer lies in the rendering process.

Web browsers use rendering engines to interpret and display web content.

Let us consider the differences in the rendering engines of Firefox and Chrome.

Firefox and Chrome employ different rendering engines: Gecko and Blink, respectively. These engines have evolved independently, leading to variations in their rendering behavior and support for web standards.

- **Gecko (Firefox)**: Firefox uses the Gecko rendering engine, known for its open-source nature. Gecko is built to be modular and highly customizable, making it a preferred choice for privacy-focused browsers like Firefox. It often implements new web standards at a conservative pace, prioritizing privacy, stability, and compatibility.
- **Blink (Chrome):** Chrome utilizes the Blink rendering engine, which was originally a fork of the WebKit engine. Blink is designed for speed and efficiency, aiming to minimize page load times and maximize responsiveness. Google actively contributes to Blink, resulting in the rapid adoption of new web standards and experimental features.

Understanding how browsers load web pages and the differences in rendering engines is crucial for engineers. It helps ensure consistent and optimal user experiences across different browsers. As we have seen, Firefox's Gecko engine prioritizes stability and compatibility, while Chrome's Blink engine emphasizes speed and performance. The example provided serves as a practical illustration of these differences, highlighting the importance of testing web content in multiple browsers to ensure cross-browser compatibility.

Handling Browser-Specific Behaviors

Browser testing using Selenium poses unique challenges due to rapid release cycles and constant changes. Each browser has its own quirks and implementation differences that can cause flaky test failures if not handled properly. Additionally, with the advent of *Chrome for Testing* and auto-updating browsers, it is notoriously difficult to ensure constant quality for web applications. In this section, we take a deep dive into the most common browser-specific issues faced in Selenium testing and how to address them through detailed examples using Java.

Let us explore some of the typical browser-specific issues that need explicit handling:

- **JavaScript Errors**: Browsers use different JS engines like V8 (Chrome) and SpiderMonkey (Firefox). Certain JavaScript-heavy sites may work on one but throw errors on another.
- **Popup Windows**: The window opening API is not consistent across browsers. File upload dialogs, alerts and permissions popups need specialized handling codes for each browser.
- **Browser Crashes**: Each browser handles memory and resources differently. Certain sites or actions tend to crash specific browsers due to high memory usage or bugs.
- **Rendering Issues**: Browsers differ in their default CSS styling, conformity to standards and layout engines. Certain UIs may render incorrectly on browsers.
- **Certificate Errors**: Handling of invalid SSL certificates varies across browsers. Some may show verification popups that need programmatic handling.
- **Browser Dialogs**: Browsers have different permissions popups for location, notifications, microphone access, and so on. These need to be handled to avoid blocking execution.
- **Performance**: Browsers optimize and prioritize performance differently. Some older versions significantly lag behind newer ones.

- **Legacy Support**: Supporting dated browsers requires accounting for legacy features missing or behaving differently.

Handling Chrome Browser Issues Using Selenium

When working with automated testing in Chrome using Selenium, you may encounter common browser-specific issues that need to be addressed. Chrome offers a range of customizable options and configurations to tackle these challenges. Let's explore these options in detail to ensure a smoother and more reliable automation experience. Kindly open the `Chapter6_ChromeOptions` Java class at `src/test/java/chapter6` location, and run the following examples one by one, for a deeper understanding of the topic at hand.

Note: If you have installed the Eclipse IDE plugin for TestNG, you can run individual tests by clicking the `Run` button just below the @Test annotation. Similarly, tests can be run from Test Explorer in VS Code IDE by right-clicking in the code editor on a test and selecting `Run test` or by using the default Test Explorer shortcuts in Visual Studio IDE. Some of the shortcuts are context-based. This means that they run or debug tests based on where your cursor is in the code editor.

ChromeOptions

The `ChromeOptions` class is your gateway to configuring Chrome for automated testing. It allows you to set various preferences, arguments, and browser profiles during the initialization of the WebDriver. Here is how to use it:

```
// Create ChromeOptions instance
ChromeOptions options = new ChromeOptions();
// Add preferences and arguments
options.addArguments("--start-maximized"); // Maximize the browser window
options.addArguments("--disable-extensions"); // Disable Chrome extensions
options.addArguments("--incognito"); // Launch Chrome in incognito mode

// Initialize WebDriver with ChromeOptions
WebDriver driver = new ChromeDriver(options);
```

ChromeDriverService

The **ChromeDriverService** class allows you to exert even more control over your **ChromeDriver** instance. You can manage settings like the port on which **ChromeDriver** operates, additional command-line arguments, logs, and capabilities. It provides a way to fine-tune your Chrome automation setup.

```
// Setting the location for ChromeDriver logs, with a directory of your choice
            System.setProperty("webdriver.chrome.logfile",       "C:\\Users\\robin.gupta\\git\\LearningSelenium\\logs\\chromedriver.log"); // Create a ChromeDriverService instance

ChromeDriverService service = new ChromeDriverService.Builder()

    .usingPort(9515) // Specify the port for ChromeDriver

    .withVerbose(true) // Enable verbose logging

    .build();

// Initialize ChromeDriver with the service

WebDriver driver = new ChromeDriver(service);
```

Once we open the **chromedriver.log** file, we can observe the logs as follows:

```
[Starting ChromeDriver 118.0.5993.70 (e52f33f30b91b4ddfad649acddc39ab570473b86-refs/branch-heads/5993@{#1216}) on port 9515

Only local connections are allowed.

Please see https://chromedriver.chromium.org/security-considerations for suggestions on keeping ChromeDriver safe.

ChromeDriver[1698904712.337][INFO]: [bcc284602eea9fe9997ea575987454a6] COMMAND InitSession {

   "capabilities": {

      "firstMatch": [ {

         "browserName": "chrome",

         "goog:chromeOptions": {

            "args": [ "--remote-allow-origins=*" ],

            "binary": "C:\\Program

Files\\Google\\Chrome\\Application\\chrome.exe",

            "extensions": [  ]

         }

      } ]
```

```
    }
}. . . . . . . .
```

This is a very strong capability, which we should start utilizing early on. WebDriver logging can be very useful for running remote, distributed, and parallel tests.

Certificates

Chrome, by default, blocks access to sites with invalid SSL certificates. To disable this check and access insecure sites during testing, you can use **`setAcceptInsecureCerts(true)`** as part of your **`ChromeOptions`**. This capability must be used with caution, as browsing websites with an expired certificate could lead to security issues and unsafe experiences. However, if you are under pressure to run your smoke tests on your website, and the certificates have expired just in the nick of time, then this capability can help you bypass this limitation. For the following example, first, try opening https://expired.badssl.com/ in a normal browser. Did you notice the warning page from Chrome? Yes, this could be a hindrance to test automation If you know that the web application under test is safe for browsing. Now, try the example given here, and observe that our test automation script can bypass this limitation easily:

```
// Disable invalid certificate errors
ChromeOptions options = new ChromeOptions();
options.setAcceptInsecureCerts(true);
// Initialize WebDriver with ChromeOptions
WebDriver driver = new ChromeDriver(options);
driver.get("https://expired.badssl.com/");
```

Note: Kindly use this capability for trusted environments only.

Popups

Chrome often presents permission and alert popups that may disrupt your automated tests. To prevent these popups from interfering with your test execution, you can disable notifications and popup blocking using **`addArguments()`** in your `ChromeOptions`.

```
// Disable various popups
ChromeOptions options = new ChromeOptions();
options.addArguments("--disable-notifications");
options.addArguments("--disable-popup-blocking");
```

```
// Initialize WebDriver with ChromeOptions
WebDriver driver = new ChromeDriver(options);
```

Headless Mode

Headless mode allows you to run Chrome without a visible user interface. This can significantly improve test execution speed and efficiency, especially for automated test suites that run in the background. When you run the following code snippet in your IDE; well, you might notice no web browser opening, as we have gone **headless**.

```
// Enable headless mode
ChromeOptions options = new ChromeOptions();
options.addArguments("--headless");
options.addArguments("--disable-gpu"); // Necessary for some platforms
// Initialize WebDriver with ChromeOptions
WebDriver driver = new ChromeDriver(options);
```

Note: It would be helpful to combine this capability with the logging capability discussed before, to ensure that desired browser-level actions are being performed in the background.

Mobile Emulation

For mobile testing, you can emulate various mobile devices by setting screen size, user agent, and other characteristics. This helps in testing how your web application performs on different mobile devices.

```
// Emulate Pixel 2
ChromeOptions options = new ChromeOptions();
Map<String, String> mobileEmulation = new HashMap<>();
mobileEmulation.put("deviceName", "Pixel 2");
options.setExperimentalOption("mobileEmulation", mobileEmulation);

// Initialize WebDriver with ChromeOptions
WebDriver driver = new ChromeDriver(options);
```

When we run this code snippet, we can observe that the browser opens a mobile view and then loads the web application under test. This can be immensely helpful in performing responsive testing.

Note: Responsive testing is the process of evaluating a website's or web application's ability to adapt to various screen sizes and devices, such as desktops, tablets, and smartphones. It ensures that the content and layout of the site respond effectively to different screen dimensions, providing an optimal user experience regardless of the device used.

Localization

To test the localization of your web application, you can set the browser's language using **`addArguments()`** in **`ChromeOptions`**. This is useful for ensuring that your application displays content in different languages correctly.

```
// Set French browser language
ChromeOptions options = new ChromeOptions();
options.addArguments("--lang=fr");
// Initialize WebDriver with ChromeOptions
WebDriver driver = new ChromeDriver(options);
```

This capability can help with localization testing of the web application.

Note: Localization testing is the process of verifying that a software application or website functions correctly when adapted to different languages, cultures, and regions. It ensures that content, date formats, currency symbols, and other elements are culturally appropriate and accurately displayed for the target audience.

Improve loading times

You can fine-tune Chrome options to improve test performance by disabling resource-intensive features like images, JavaScript, and CSS. This can help speed up your test execution and make it more efficient.

```
// Disable images and JavaScript
ChromeOptions options = new ChromeOptions();
options.addArguments("--disable-javascript");
options.addArguments("--blink-settings=imagesEnabled=false");
// Initialize WebDriver with ChromeOptions
WebDriver driver = new ChromeDriver(options);
```

Note: This option is ideal for staging or UAT environments, as disabling Javascript and images might disable some features of the web application.

By using these features and techniques, you can have more control over your Chrome automation, address specific issues, and ensure your tests run smoothly in the Chrome browser.

Can you guess where should we set up these capabilities and options?

Yes, the answer is in the WebDriver factory. Based on our requirements, we can set these up in the WebDriverFactory java class at the **`src/main/base`** location, as discussed in the last chapter.

In this section, we explored common Chrome-specific issues in Selenium and how to mitigate them through **`ChromeOptions`**, **`ChromeDriverService`**, and targeted workarounds. Similar options classes exist for Firefox, Edge, and other browsers.

Now let us scale the problem before we come to a scalable solution. Imagine you have to launch an online store to sell sneakers. Your customers will use all sorts of different devices and web browsers, and each of those browsers has its own version. Checking your website on all of them by hand would be a total nightmare.

Let us look at a specific requirement to understand the problem better. Say, you want your online sneaker shop to work perfectly on the latest browser versions and the three most recent versions of Chrome, Firefox, and Edge. It should work smoothly on devices using Windows, Linux, and Mac OS. Plus, you have got fifty automated tests to make sure everything is working on all these systems.

Number of automated tests to be run: 50

Number of Browsers to be supported: $3 \times 4 = 12$ (Three browsers and 4 versions of each with the latest and the last three versions)

Number of OS to be supported: 3

Total number of browsers and OS combinations: $12 \times 3 = 36$

Therefore, the total test executions to be managed per cycle is the number of automated tests multiplied by OS/Browser combinations: $50 \times 36 = 1800$!

Now, while we have a scalable framework from the previous chapter, how can we ensure that our automated test executions are managed in a simple way? Running all 1800 tests sequentially on a single machine would take forever. And maintaining 36 different environments locally would give anyone nightmares!

This is where distributing our test execution comes in handy. What if we could split these 1800 tests across 10 different machines running different browsers and platforms?

By distributing the load across many parallel resources, we can reduce the overall execution time drastically. However, setting up and managing such a complex grid of machines manually would be extremely challenging. We would have to install browsers, configure tests, distribute load, aggregate results, and handle failures across dozens of independent machines. Doing this reliably requires an intelligent platform to coordinate everything.

This is where Selenium Grid fits in perfectly! It helps us easily set up a grid of machines for distributed, parallel, and scalable test execution.

Selenium Grid

Let's imagine a bakery that needs to bake thousands of cupcakes each day. At first, the baker tried doing this alone in a small kitchen. He could only bake a dozen cupcakes every hour! At this rate, it would take him weeks to bake the quantity needed daily.

The baker realized he couldn't scale his operations alone. So he came up with a plan - he opened several kitchens across the city and hired more bakers. Now, instead of just him, there were five bakers who could bake cupcakes in parallel across five kitchens.

By distributing the workload, the team could now bake hundreds of cupcakes each hour! The baker no longer had to spend weeks baking alone. Scaling operations through multiple resources allowed them to dramatically increase their productivity.

In the world of software testing, scaling automation works quite like how the baker scaled up his cupcake production. Different tests can be distributed across multiple machines and executed in parallel. This allows you to scale test coverage and speed.

However, running these distributed tests efficiently can be complex to manage manually. Here Selenium Grid comes in as the savior – it helps coordinate and distribute tests across multiple machines almost magically!

In this section, we will learn how Selenium Grid helps "bake" test automation at scale through distributed, parallel execution, just like how more kitchens and bakers helped our baker in the previous example. Selenium Grid is a tool that enables the parallel execution of tests across multiple browsers and platforms. It addresses the need for efficient cross-browser testing by allowing you to run tests on a grid of machines. This grid of machines could be composed of physical or virtual machines, but the principles of distributed test automation remain the same.

Setup and installation

Let us look at the ways of installing and setting up Selenium Grid. It can be done by downloading the JAR file from Selenium's GitHub repository. The latest Selenium Server jar file can be downloaded from https://github.com/SeleniumHQ/selenium/releases/latest . As we are using selenium-4.11.0, therefore we can use the following link to download the corresponding Selenium Server JAR file: https://github.com/SeleniumHQ/selenium/releases/download/selenium-4.11.0/selenium-server-4.11.0.jar

Once the JAR file is downloaded open a command line (or bash interface) in the folder where the JAR is downloaded, and run the following command:

```
java -jar selenium-server-4.11.0.jar --help
```

This will output the commands available for Selenium Grid, and each can be explored further with **`--help`** flag.

Grid architecture

Selenium Grid 4 is composed of the following components:

- **Node**: It is the most important component of the Selenium Grid, as it is where the WebDriver session runs. Each node has a set of capabilities, which define the browsers and operating systems that it can support. For example, a node might have the following capabilities: browserName: Chrome, version: 103, platform: Windows 10.
- **Router**: The Router in the Grid functions as the central hub for all external requests, directing them to their respective destinations. When a new session request arrives, it is sent to the Session Queue, and for requests linked to existing sessions, the Router queries the Session Map to identify the active Node for direct routing. This strategic load balancing ensures that requests are efficiently distributed to the most suitable components, avoiding overload on unnecessary ones, thus optimizing the system's performance.
- **Session Map**: The Session Map is like a database that remembers which session is running on which Node. When the Router needs to send a

request to the right node, it simply checks with the Session Map to find out where that session is. It's like a map that helps the Router deliver requests to the correct destination.

- **Session Queue**: The Session Queue is like a waiting room for new session requests, and it handles them in a first-come, first-served order. It has settings to manage how long requests can wait and how often the system checks if they've waited too long. When a new session request arrives, the Router places it in the queue and waits for a response. The Distributor, on the other hand, keeps an eye out for open slots to run new sessions. If a slot becomes available, it checks the queue for the oldest matching request and tries to create a new session. If the request matches a free slot's capabilities, it's assigned; otherwise, it goes back to the queue. If a request times out during retries, it's rejected. Once a session is successfully created, the Distributor shares the session details with the Session Queue, which then relays it back to the Router and finally to the client, ensuring a smooth process from request to session initiation.
- **Distributor**: The Distributor plays two important roles in the system. First, it registers and keeps an eye on all the Nodes in the network, confirming their existence and capabilities. Second, it regularly checks the Session Queue for any pending new session requests, finds the right Node to create the session, and tracks which Node is running that session through the Session Map. In simple terms, it ensures all the machines are accounted for and matches new tasks with the right ones.
- **Event Bus**: The Event Bus acts as the messenger connecting all the Grid components like Nodes, Distributors, Session Queues, and so on facilitating communication within the Grid.

Roles of Selenium Grid

Selenium Grid allows you to run your tests on multiple machines simultaneously. This can significantly speed up your test execution time, especially for large test suites. Selenium Grid helps us manage distributed test automation in three roles as follows:

- **Standalone**: All components on a single machine
- **Hub and Node**: Group the components on a single or multiple machines
- **Fully distributed**: Each component on a separate machine

Let us explore each one of these in detail.

Standalone

The Standalone mode, as the name suggests, encapsulates all the components of Selenium Grid within a single process. This makes it the most straightforward setup, ideal for quick and easy testing on a single machine. With a single command, you can spin up a fully functional Selenium Grid, ready to handle your testing needs. This is the easiest mode to set up and use, but it is not scalable.

All the components of the Grid and the node (responsible for running tests) are running on the same process. This mode is suited for developing or debugging tests locally, or checking out the setup in CI/CD tools for experimentation.

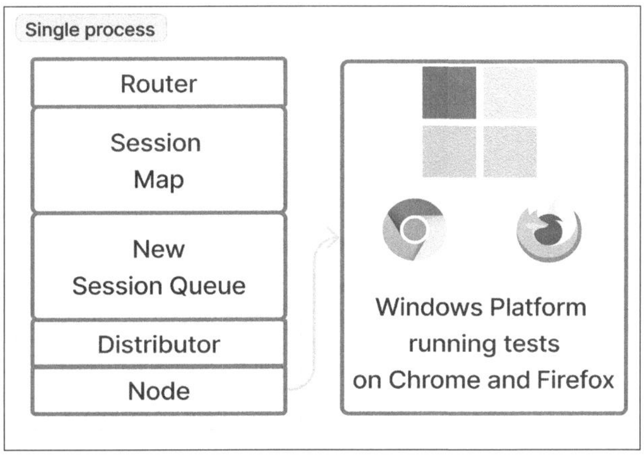

***Figure 6.3**: Grid components in Standalone mode*

To start the Grid in Standalone mode, kindly run the following command in the Command line (or bash terminal), where Grid JAR is downloaded:

```
java -jar selenium-server-4.11.0.jar standalone --selenium-manager true
```

Once we run the preceding command, by default, the Grid server will listen for RemoteWebDriver requests on http://localhost:4444. By default, the server will detect the available drivers that it can use from the System PATH. The flag **-selenium-manager true** helps us configure the drivers automatically in the build path. Now if you navigate to the URL http://localhost:4444 in your browser, we can observe that the following screen magically greets you:

Figure 6.4: *Selenium Grid UI screen*

This is the UI screen for visualizing and managing Grid processes and sessions. If we look closely at the numbers on browser icons (like 12 next to the chrome icon in *Figure* 6.4), we can find the number of maximum concurrent sessions we can run for each browser and operating system combination, in this Grid setup.

Note: By default, the maximum number of simultaneous sessions a Node can handle is constrained by the quantity of available CPUs. For instance, on a Node with 12 CPUs, it can simultaneously run up to 12 browser sessions, except for Safari, which is limited to one session.

If we navigate to the **`Sessions`** tab, we can notice a message as **`No running or queued sessions at the moment.`** So how can we get the sessions running on this Standalone node? It's pretty simple, we just need to point our tests to http://localhost:4444. Let us explore this process in detail. Open the WebDriverFactory class at **`src/mainjava/base`** location and uncomment the following lines:

```
else if (browserName.equalsIgnoreCase("chrome") && hubUrl != null) {
      DesiredCapabilities capabilities = new DesiredCapabilities();
      capabilities.setCapability("browserName", "chrome");
      driver = new RemoteWebDriver(hubUrl, capabilities);
```

In this code, we're telling Selenium Grid what we need for our automated test.

We create a set of "capabilities," which is like a list of requirements. In this case, we say we want to use the "chrome" browser. Then, we connect to Selenium Grid using the "hubUrl" and tell it to set up a remote WebDriver, which is like a remote-controlled browser that will run our test. The "capabilities" we defined earlier tell the remote WebDriver what kind of browser we want to use. So, it's like giving instructions to the Grid to start a Chrome browser for our test.

Similarly, navigate to the **`BaseTest`** class at **`src/mainjava/base`** location and uncomment the following lines:

```
try {
        huburl = new URI("http://localhost:4444").toURL();
        // Setup GRID URL here or from properties
        } catch (MalformedURLException ex) {
        logger.error("Received error in converting URI to URL for
Grid as " + ex.getMessage());}
```

Here we are setting up the Grid URL for usage in the following line in the BaseTest class:

```
driver = WebDriverFactory.createInstance(huburl, browserType);
```

Once the relevant sections are uncommented from WebDriverFactory and BaseTest as mentioned earlier, we can run the **`Chapter6_LoginTest`** java class at **`src/test/java/chapter6`** location as a TestNG test, and observe that a session is created for the Standalone Grid setup we have done:

***Figure 6.5**: Running session view on Selenium Grid UI*

Another way of running the Selenium Grid is by adding the Maven dependency for it in our pom.xml file and calling the corresponding methods in a Java class.

The Maven dependency can be set up as:

```
<dependency>
    <groupId>org.seleniumhq.selenium</groupId>
    <artifactId>selenium-grid</artifactId>
    <version>4.11.0</version>
</dependency>
```

This way we don't have to trigger the JAR file from the command line or terminal as per the preceding steps. And Grid can be invoked directly from our Java code as per **Chapter6_StandAloneGridTest** class at **src/test/java/chapter6** location:

```
final URL gridServerUrl;
int port = PortProber.findFreePort();
Main.main(new String[] { "standalone", "--port", String.valueOf(port) });
gridServerUrl = new URL(String.format("http://localhost:%d/", port));
RemoteWebDriver driver = new RemoteWebDriver(gridServerUrl, new
ChromeOptions());
// Navigating to sample page
driver.get("https://google.com");
```

In this snippet, we're setting up a standalone Grid server on a free port by finding an available port number. Then, we create a URL for this server at "localhost" on the chosen port. We launch a remote WebDriver that connects to this server using Chrome as the browser choice. After that, we navigate the WebDriver to the Google website. So, this code essentially sets up a local Selenium Grid server, connects to it with a Chrome browser, and opens the Google website for automated testing.

Hub and Node

The Hub and Node architecture introduce a distributed testing environment, where the Hub acts as the central coordinator and the Nodes are the execution machines. The Hub receives test requests and intelligently distributes them to available Nodes based on their capabilities. Picture a team of testers working on a complex web application. With Hub and Node mode, they can distribute their tests across multiple machines (physical or virtual), significantly reducing execution time and improving efficiency.

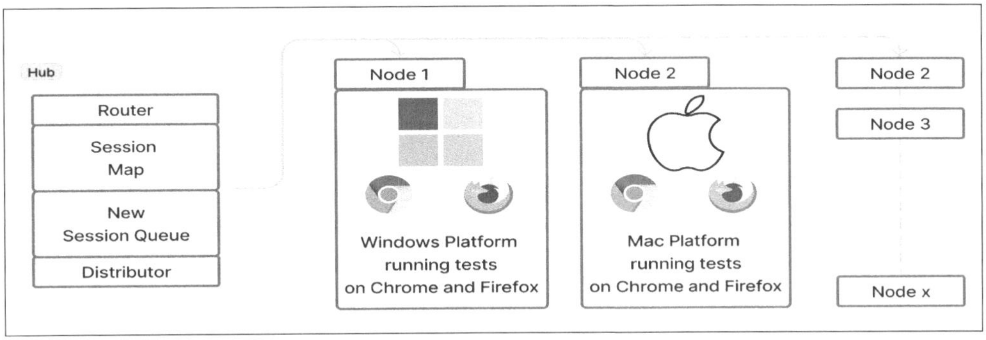

***Figure 6.6**: Grid components in Hub and Node modes*

As we can see in *Figure* 6.6, the Hub and Node model, helps us scale our tests across multiple nodes via operating system and browser combinations.

If given enough resources, this model can theoretically scale horizontally to support as many nodes as we want. This model is generally used across teams worldwide to create scalable test infrastructure.

Just like in the standalone mode, we can use the Selenium Grid JAR to initiate this mode from the command line. Initially, we launched the hub on a computer. After that, we can add one or more nodes on the same computer or different ones. It's all about setting up the hub and then connecting the nodes, making them work together.

To start a Hub session, kindly run the following command in the terminal window:

```
java -jar selenium-server-4.11.0.jar hub
```

This will start the Grid server in Hub mode. Now open a second terminal window and run the following command:

```
java -jar selenium-server-4.11.0.jar node
```

This command instructs Grid to start a node with the default port (5555).

Now, open a third terminal window and run the following command:

```
java -jar selenium-server-4.11.0.jar node --port 6666
```

Here we are instructing Grid to start a node with a specific port (6666). Consequently, when we open http://localhost:4444/ui# , we can observe that we have created two nodes as follows:

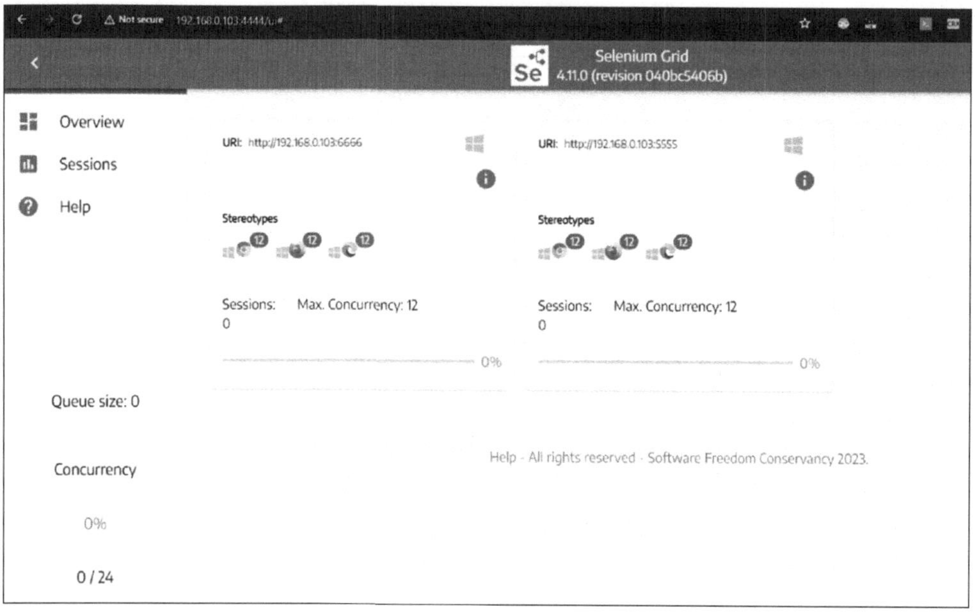

Figure 6.7: *Concurrent node sessions on Grid.*

Now, how do we run tests on these newly created nodes? Just as we did in the past section, by instantiating RemoteWebDriver instances against the Hub URL. Kindly open the **chromeGridTest** class at the **src/test/java/chapter6** location and run the tests as follows to cement your understanding:

```
@Test(priority = 1)
	public void chromeGridTest() throws Exception {
		WebDriver driver_chrome = new RemoteWebDriver(new 
URL("http://192.168.0.103:4444"), new ChromeOptions());
		// Navigating to sample page
		driver_chrome.get("https://google.com");
		Thread.sleep(3000);
		driver_chrome.quit();
	}
@Test(priority = 1)
	public void firefoxGridTest() throws Exception {
		FirefoxOptions options = new FirefoxOptions();
		WebDriver driver_firefox = new RemoteWebDriver(new 
URL("http://192.168.0.103:4444"), options);
		// Navigating to sample page
```

```
            driver_firefox.get("https://google.com");
            Thread.sleep(3000);
            driver_firefox.quit();
    }
```

In this code, there are two separate test methods. The first method, `chromeGridTest` is set up to run a test using the Chrome browser on a Selenium Grid. It connects to the Selenium Grid at the specified Hub URL, opens Google's website, waits for 3 seconds for display, and then closes the browser. The second method, `firefoxGridTest` does the same but uses the Firefox browser instead. It also connects to the same Selenium Grid URL, opens Google, waits, and closes the Firefox browser. The "Distributor" component of Grid distributes the sessions across available resources. These methods demonstrate how you can run tests on different browsers using Selenium Grid, making it convenient to test web applications across various platforms and configurations. Once we run the preceding test class, we can observe the sessions running in parallel as follows. These test methods demonstrate how we can run tests on different browsers using Selenium Grid, making it convenient to test web applications across various platforms and configurations.

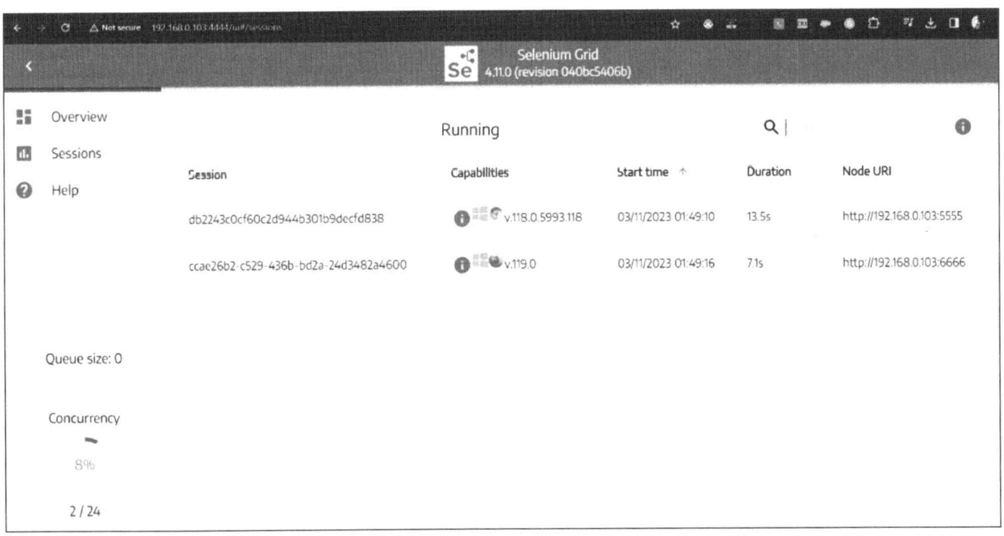

Figure 6.8: *Concurrent sessions running on two nodes in parallel using the Hub-Node model.*

In the preceding example, we are triggering the nodes on the same machine as the hub, but what if we need to trigger the node from a separate machine? Don't worry, you can use the following command to trigger a node from a different machine and register to a specific hub URL if the hub is using default ports:

```
java -jar selenium-server-4.0.0.jar node --hub http://<hub-ip>:4444
```

Can we also start a Hub-Node-based grid setup using Java code?

Yes, it can be done using the same pattern we illustrated in `Chapter6_StandAloneGridTest` class.

Fully distributed

The Fully Distributed mode takes the concept of distributed testing to the next level, decentralizing the Grid's components into separate processes. This enhances scalability and fault tolerance, making it ideal for large-scale testing scenarios. Imagine a large organization with a vast web application and a global team of testers. Fully Distributed mode empowers them to distribute tests across a network of machines, ensuring seamless testing even in the face of network disruptions or machine failures, to run hundreds of tests together.

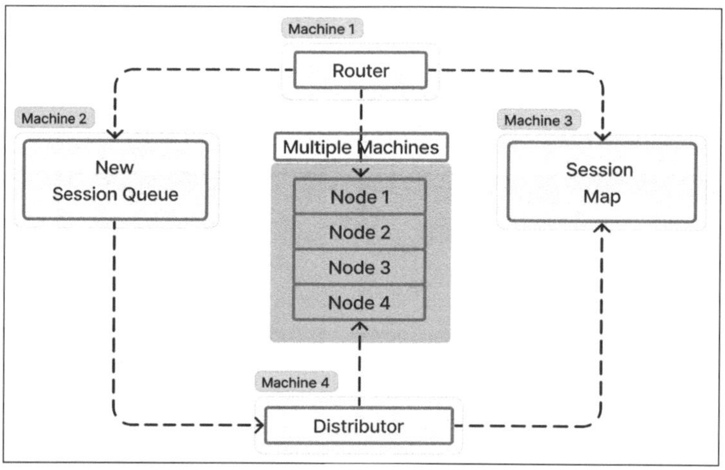

***Figure 6.9**: Distributed mode for Selenium Grid*

In distributed mode, Selenium Grid components run on separate machines for maximum scalability and reliability. The key components are:

- **Event Bus**: Enables internal communication between Grid components
- **Session Queue**: Holds new session requests
- **Session Map**: Maps session IDs to nodes
- **Distributor:** Assigns new sessions to nodes
- **Router:** Routes requests to Session Queue, Nodes or Session map. This is the single-entry point to the Grid
- **Nodes:** Execute browser tests

Each component needs to be started individually with the correct ports exposed for connectivity. In the following example, we will be running all the commands in the same machine using different terminal windows, but ideally, in a fully distributed mode, all the components are run on different machines to provide stability and scalability.

Let's look at starting each component in detail:

- **Event Bus**: The event bus facilitates inter-component communication in a Selenium Grid. We need to start this first on a central server. It uses ports 4442, 5557, and 4443 for publishing and subscribing events. The main event bus process runs on port 5557. It can be started by running the following command in the terminal:

  ```
  java -jar selenium-server-4.11.0.jar event-bus
  ```

- **Session Map:** The session map component maps active test sessions to nodes. It tracks which nodes are running which sessions. This runs on port 5556 and interacts with the event bus for notifications. We can start it using the terminal command as follows:

  ```
  java -jar selenium-server-4.11.0.jar sessions
  ```

- **Session Queue**: The session queue holds all new incoming test session requests. This is queried by the distributor to assign sessions. It runs on port 5559 by default. We can use the terminal command as follows:

  ```
  java -jar selenium-server-4.11.0.jar sessionqueue
  ```

- **Distributor:** The distributor is the brains of the Grid. It queries the session queue and assigns incoming sessions to nodes based on capabilities and load. It runs on port 5553 and interacts with all other components. We can start this component with the following command:

  ```
  java -jar selenium-server-4.11.0.jar distributor --sessions
  http://localhost:5556 --sessionqueue http://localhost:5559
  --bind-bus false
  ```

Note: We are using localhost in URLs like http://localhost:5556 as we are running all the components on the same machine. However, in practical scenarios, this would be changed to the URL of the machine, where the respective component is running.

- **Router**: The router routes all session requests - new ones go to the session queue and existing ones to nodes. Think of it as the heart of the Grid system, acting as the entry gate for the Grid, and controlling all the blood flow. It uses port 4444 by default. We can start it, using the terminal command as follows:

```
java -jar selenium-server-4.11.0.jar router --sessions http://
localhost:5556 --distributor http://localhost:5553 --sessionqueue
http://localhost:5559
```

- **Nodes**: Finally, we start the node machines that will execute the browser tests.

  Nodes run on port 5555 by default and register themselves with the distributor, similar to a Hub-Node grid. We can start these on multiple machines, using the terminal command as follows:

  ```
  java -jar selenium-server-4.11.0.jar node --selenium-manager true
  ```

Note: The node can be customized further with flags like max-sessions, log-level, **`--heartbeat-period`**, **`--session-timeout`**, **`--no-vnc-port`**, and so on.

Here is how the six terminal windows pan out, once we start all the components of the distributed Grid in one machine:

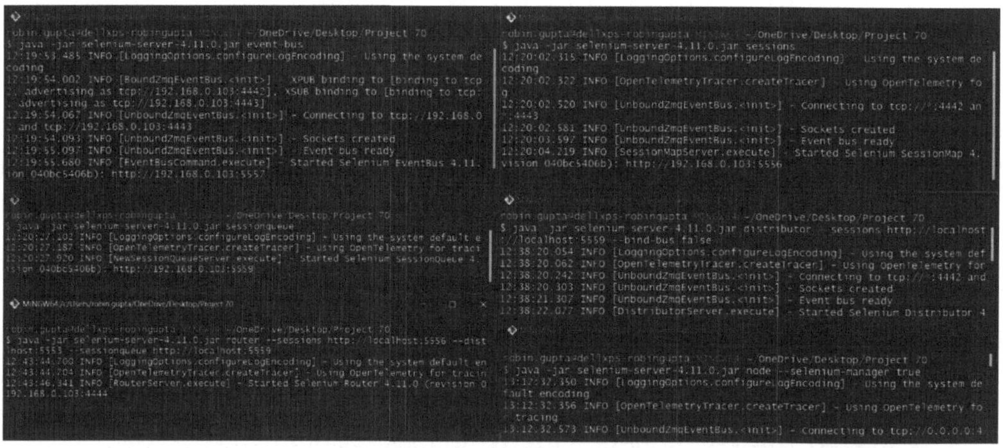

***Figure 6.10**: Terminal windows for components in distributed Grid mode.*

Therefore, this section covers starting a fully distributed Selenium Grid setup with all key components on separate machines. The distributed architecture allows maximum scalability and reliability for large-scale test automation.

Within the domain of Selenium and cross-browser testing, the Selenium Grid emerges as a cornerstone, seamlessly orchestrating the complexities of diverse browser interactions. As we forge ahead into the expansive realm of quality assurance, the integration of observability becomes our compass, guiding us towards unparalleled precision and excellence. In the world of Selenium Grid, cross-browser testing not only meets industry standards but pioneers a future where observability sets the gold standard for testing sophistication and reliability.

- Manoj Kumar Kumar, VP, Developer Relations at LambdaTest.

Note: Once you have grasped the concept of running Grid in various modes, and completed the exercise at the end of this chapter; kindly comment out the Grid-related lines of code in WebDriverFactory and BaseTest, so that we don't have to run Grid components for the remaining chapters.

Security

Did you notice how easily Selenium Grid allows you to run your tests on multiple machines simultaneously? On one hand, this can significantly reduce the execution time, but on the other hand, we must ensure the security of our Grid infrastructure at all costs. For example, here are some security risks which we should account for:

- **Accessible Hub Console**: The hub console at http://localhost:4444/grid/console is accessible by default without any authentication. This allows anyone to access and tamper with the Grid.
- **Unencrypted Traffic**: All traffic between hub, nodes, and tests is unencrypted by default. This allows malicious actors to sniff test details or manipulate traffic.
- **Insecure Hub Port**: The default hub port 4444 is commonly targeted for attacks. Leaving it open invites attackers to discover and access the hub.
- **Browser Exploits**: Outdated or misconfigured browser versions on grid nodes can contain exploits for malware injection into tests.
- **Node Compromise**: Access to a single unsecured node provides a foothold to attack other Grid components from within the trusted network.

Here are some mitigation strategies for the preceding risks:

- **Password Protect Hub**: Require username/password to access the hub console to prevent unauthorized access.
- **Enable TLS**: Use HTTPS with valid certificates for encrypted traffic between grid components.
- **Change Default Ports**: Avoid default ports like `4444` for the hub, `5555` for nodes, and so on, which are commonly targeted.
- **Harden Nodes**: Nodes should only run the browser and Selenium server. No other apps or services should be allowed on nodes to minimize the attack surface.

- **Isolate Grid**: Provision grid in a separate Virtual Private Cloud (VPC) with restricted access only to test machines. Don't connect it directly to the corporate network.
- **Monitor Activity**: Watch logs for signs of exploitation like spikes in traffic, unusual browser versions, and so on.
- **Periodic Scans**: Perform periodic penetration testing on the grid to find weaknesses before attackers do.

By proactively securing your grid infrastructure, protecting access with authentication, and monitoring for suspicious activity, the risk of exploits can be significantly reduced.

Conclusion

In this chapter, we learned about the challenges of cross-browser testing and how to handle browser-specific issues using Selenium. A key takeaway is that testing manually across multiple browsers is very time-consuming. As our web apps grow larger, we need smart solutions to scale browser testing. Whether we want to run 1800 tests or 18000 tests in an automated fashion, Selenium Grid can help us scale automated tests in an easy-to-use fashion. By distributing tests across multiple machines, Selenium Grid makes cross-browser testing faster and easier. We no longer have to run all tests on a single machine! And that too manually!

We covered the components of Selenium Grid architecture like Hub, Nodes, and the configuration of tests. With the Grid, we can run parallel tests on different browsers and operating systems in a simple manner.

In the next chapter, we will explore another important automation area - testing Software-as-a-Service (SaaS) applications. SaaS apps have unique attributes like multi-tenancy that need specialized testing techniques. We will learn how to strategize and scale test automation for modern SaaS apps using the right tools and frameworks.

Exercise

Kindly set up a miniature grid to see distributed testing in action:

1. Launch a Hub on your local machine using the Selenium server JAR in a Hub-Node model. Make note of the Hub URL.

2. Register 3 Node machines with the Hub. These can be on your localhost using different ports.
3. Verify that the nodes are registered in the Hub console.
4. Write a simple Selenium test for navigating to https://google.com.
5. Run 6 copies of the test in parallel. They should be distributed evenly across the nodes in parallel.

Try adding more nodes and running more parallel tests. Notice how the Hub distributes the load. This should give you a feel for how Selenium Grid enables distributed, cross-browser testing, at scale.

CHAPTER 7

SAAS and Non-functional Test Automation

Introduction

As software eats the world, it becomes clear that there is no place for bug-prone or slow software applications. Alongside this evolution, it also becomes clear that SaaS (Software as a Service) applications are eating up the software world.

SaaS applications, exemplified by industry giants such as Salesforce, Workday, and Office 365, have swiftly woven themselves into the fabric of modern enterprises. They offer convenience, accessibility, and scalability that traditional software models struggle to match. However, as organizations increasingly embrace SaaS solutions, a new set of challenges arises in the realm of software testing.

In this chapter, we embark on a journey to unravel the intricacies of effectively testing SaaS applications using the powerful combination of Selenium and Java. Our exploration encompasses a wide array of topics, including comprehending the architecture of SaaS applications and delving into the crucial realms of performance and security testing.

But our quest does not stop there. We go beyond the basics and equip ourselves with the knowledge of best practices for continuous testing, ensuring that our testing processes remain robust and adaptable in the face of evolving software landscapes. With the right approach, we cannot only conquer the unique challenges of testing SaaS applications but also elevate the reliability of modern software. So, let us embark on this journey, aiming to deliver nothing less than impeccable test automation for the contemporary world of modern applications. Do not forget to bring along your water bottle, as this expedition might get a little hot!

Structure

In this chapter, we will discuss the following topics:

- Basics of a SAAS application
- Dissecting web application layers
- Test automation for SAAS
- Performance analysis
- Security testing

Basics of a SAAS Application

Software as a Service (SAAS) represents a cloud computing model facilitating the delivery of diverse software applications through the internet on a subscription basis. It enables users to access software hosted and maintained by providers, granting the advantages of accessibility, scalability, and cost-efficiency.

A notable feature of SAAS lies in its subscription model, where users pay periodic fees, thereby obviating the need for substantial upfront capital investments. Furthermore, SAAS providers shoulder the responsibility of software updates, ensuring users continuously enjoy the latest features and security enhancements.

The inherent accessibility of SAAS applications is also noteworthy, allowing users to access them from any location with an internet connection, fostering flexibility and convenience. Here are some of the key tenets of any SAAS application:

- **Sharing is Caring: Multi-Tenancy**: Imagine you and your friends sharing a playground. In SAAS, it's similar; many people can use the same software, which is efficient and cost-effective. This model optimizes resource utilization and ensures efficient operation.
- **Pay as You Go**: **Subscription Mode**l: In the world of SAAS, the traditional practice of accumulating significant capital to procure software is replaced by a more convenient subscription model. Users make periodic payments, akin to subscribing to magazines or digital streaming services, thus mitigating upfront financial burden.

- **Always Up-to-Date: Automatic Updates**: SAAS providers orchestrate the management of software updates, rendering the software perpetually up-to-date, akin to the seamless evolution of a favorite video game with new levels and bug fixes.
- **Anytime, Anywhere: Accessibility**: An integral aspect of SAAS applications is their omnipresence. Users can access SAAS applications from a diverse array of devices and locations, akin to carrying one's favorite pastime across different venues. Most of the time, this kind of accessibility is provisioned by web applications.

  In the ever-evolving landscape of technology, the Software as a Service (SAAS) industry stands as a formidable force, with its worth surpassing an impressive $195 billion as of 2023. The growth of the SaaS sector has been nothing short of remarkable, having expanded by nearly 500% in just the past seven years.

Note: The preceding data is gathered from https://explodingtopics.com/blog/saas-statistics.

Recognized as a linchpin for achieving success in the world of business, SaaS is hailed as the most critical technology. Within this domain, the United States emerges as a prominent player, boasting approximately eight times more SaaS companies than any other nation.

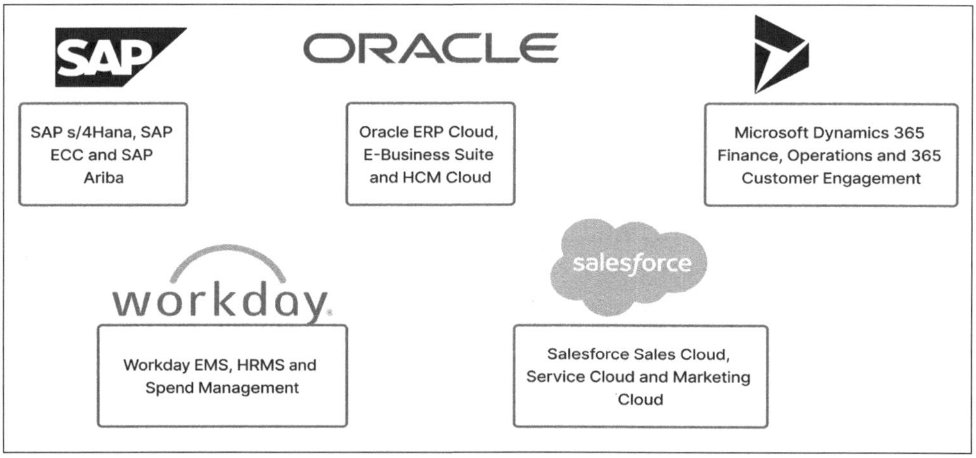

Figure 7.1: *Major enterprise SAAS applications*

Here is a list of some major enterprise-grade SAAS applications:

- **Salesforce**: Salesforce is known for its customer relationship management (CRM) software. Their primary product is "Salesforce CRM." It helps businesses manage their customer relationships, sales processes, and marketing efforts. Salesforce CRM also offers a wide range of tools for analytics, automation, and collaboration.

- **SAP**: SAP offers a suite of enterprise software solutions. Their primary product is "SAP Business Suite." This suite includes applications for enterprise resource planning (ERP), customer relationship management (CRM), supply chain management, and more. It helps businesses streamline their operations and make data-driven decisions.
- **Oracle**: Oracle provides a variety of cloud-based services, but one of their primary products is "Oracle Cloud Applications." These applications cover areas such as finance, human resources, supply chain, and customer experience. Oracle Cloud Applications help organizations run their business processes efficiently and securely.
- **Microsoft Dynamics**: Microsoft Dynamics offers a range of business applications, with "Microsoft Dynamics 365" being their primary product. This product includes various modules for sales, customer service, marketing, and more. It enables businesses to manage customer interactions, automate processes, and gain insights from data.
- **Workday**: Workday specializes in cloud-based human capital management (HCM) and financial management software. Their primary product is "Workday HCM." It helps organizations with tasks like human resources, payroll, workforce planning, and financial management, all in one platform. Workday's solutions aim to streamline HR and financial processes for businesses.

> *Quality can't be an afterthought for any application, more so for SaaS applications. The most successful SaaS applications are the ones which solve a problem to its core, are well-tested, performant and easy to use. You can have the next billion dollar idea and build a SaaS app around it, but if it's poor quality, it's not worth a dime - quality matters and that's where automation tools like Selenium fit in the puzzle.*
>
> - Gaurav Kheterpal, Salesforce MVP Hall of Fame, Mulesoft Ambassador, GDG Cloud Leader and CEO of Vanshiv Technologies.

Many engineering teams don't realize that when we are working with a SAAS application, the one thing which matters more than the technology at hand is the domain it serves. Therefore, engineering folks should be aware of the domain at hand and its paraphernalia, to define the right level of testing and automation

Most of the SAAS applications serve one or more industry domains.

Industry	Details
Banking and financial services	Core banking systems, payment processing systems, and other financial applications.
Healthcare	Electronic health record (EHR) systems, patient portals, and other healthcare applications.
Manufacturing	Manufacturing execution systems (MES), enterprise resource planning (ERP) systems, and other manufacturing applications.
Retail	e-commerce platforms, point-of-sale (POS) systems, and other retail applications.
Telecommunications	Customer relationship management (CRM) systems, and other telecommunications applications.
Education	Learning management systems (LMS), student information systems (SIS), and other educational applications.
Insurance	Policy administration systems, claims management systems, and other insurance applications.
Logistics and transportation	Transportation management systems (MS), warehouse management systems (WMS), and other logistics and transportation applications.
Media and Entertainment	Content management systems (CMS), video streaming platforms, and other media and entertainment applications.
Public sector	Government websites, tax filing systems, and other public sector applications.
Utilities	Utility billing systems, customer relationship management (CRM) systems, and other utility applications.

Table 7.1: *Prominent industries utilizing SAAS applications*

Dissecting Web Application Layers

As a quality engineer, you may wonder - why should I care about application internals and architecture, or its domain? Can't I just automate user workflows without worrying about the underlying code structure? While that approach may work for simple apps, it falls short as applications grow larger and more complex. Without understanding what's under the hood or who it serves, your test automation ends up with gaping blind spots and little visibility of the app's real behavior. It is like trying to navigate a maze blindfolded; you might get lucky and find your way, but chances are you will bump into walls, miss hidden doors, and end up lost in a labyrinth of unexpected customer issues.

By delving into application internals and architecture, you gain a map of the application's structure. You comprehend how data flows, how components interact, and where potential bottlenecks or vulnerabilities might exist. This knowledge empowers you to design more robust and targeted test cases, ensuring that your test automation is not just about ticking off user workflows, but also about uncovering deeper issues that might affect the user experience.

Consider this scenario: You are automating tests for an SAAS e-commerce platform like Magento. Without understanding the application's architecture, you might focus solely on common user paths like product selection, adding items to the cart, and checking out. However, by understanding the architecture, you recognize the importance of thoroughly testing the payment processing module, data security layers, and database transactions. This insight prevents potential issues that could lead to lost orders, security breaches, or data corruption, ultimately safeguarding your users' trust.

Moreover, as SAAS applications evolve, they may adopt different architectural patterns or migrate to cloud-based infrastructures. Staying informed about these changes and how they impact the application is essential for effective testing. For instance, if the e-commerce platform decides to transition to a microservices architecture, your knowledge of the transition can guide your test automation strategy to focus on the integration points between microservices, ensuring they work seamlessly together, and hopefully cut away some User Interface (UI) tests into Application Programming Interface (API) layer.

The steps to leverage layers for better test automation are:

1. **Deconstruct the architecture**: Identify components and layers.
2. **Analyze dependencies**: How layers interact and communicate.
3. **Define test focus areas**: What kinds of testing to do per layer.
4. **Implement layered test suites**: Automated checks per layer.
5. **Combine test types for coverage**: API, UI, unit testing, etc.

While it takes effort upfront, this methodology prevents disjointed, ineffective test automation in the long run.

Let's Get Dissecting!

SAAS applications are often structured into layers, each serving a specific purpose in the software's functionality. Let's explore the three main layers of a web application: Presentation Layer, Application Layer, and Data Layer, along with examples:

- **Presentation Layer:** The Presentation Layer is the front-facing part of a web application that users interact with. It includes the user interface, the graphical elements, and the functionality that enables user interactions. Consider a SAAS project management tool like Trello. The Trello board interface, card layouts, and drag-and-drop functionality represent the Presentation Layer. Users interact with this layer to manage their projects and tasks.
  The Presentation Layer is critical for the user experience. Testing should focus on user interface elements, responsiveness, and usability. Potential bugs include layout issues, broken links, and user interface glitches that can hinder the user experience.
- **Application Layer:** The Application Layer is where the core logic of the web application resides. It handles data processing, business rules, and the application's functionality.
  In a SAAS accounting software like QuickBooks, the Application Layer is responsible for functions such as ledger calculations, tax calculations, and financial reporting. It ensures that all financial operations are accurate and compliant.
  Application Layer testing involves checking the correctness of data processing, calculations, and overall functionality. Bugs in this layer could lead to incorrect calculations, transaction failures, or other critical financial errors.
- **Data Layer:** The Data Layer handles data storage, retrieval, and management. It encompasses databases, data warehouses, and other data sources used to store and access data.
  Salesforce, a SAAS customer relationship management (CRM) application, uses the Data Layer to store and manage customer data, sales leads, and other business-related information. It ensures that user data is stored securely and can be accessed when needed.
  Data Layer testing involves verifying data integrity, data storage, and data retrieval. Potential bugs in this layer include data corruption, data loss, or issues related to data access and storage, which can result in incorrect or incomplete information.

In essence, understanding application internals and architecture equips you with a strategic advantage in your role as a quality engineer. Therefore, in the following section, we will learn how to build a successful test automation strategy for web applications and SAAS systems.

Test automation for SAAS

All good things come with a few not-so-good things. Remember, every rose has its thorns, and SAAS applications could have a few thorny issues with testing and automation. Here are some nice features of SAAS applications, each with a testing risk associated with it.

Highly Configurable: SaaS apps tend to be highly customizable to meet diverse customer needs - custom fields, rules, branding, etc. Testing every unique configuration could be challenging.

For example, an ERP like Workday allows customers to configure complex approval rules. All business scenarios must be covered through automated tests.

Rich Integration Ecosystem: SaaS apps feature extensive APIs and integration capabilities to connect with other systems. Rigorous API testing is required to ensure robust integrations.

For instance, Office 365 provides REST APIs for extension and integration. Tests must validate API behaviors under different scenarios and loads.

Browser-based access: Most SaaS apps are accessed via a web browser. This requires standard web testing across different browsers, devices, and versions.

For example, Salesforce relies heavily on browser-based access. Cross-browser tests must run on all supported Firefox, Chrome, and Safari versions.

Combining the preceding notes and the various layers of a SAAS application (UI, API, Database); it could become notoriously difficult to craft a test strategy for automation testing of SAAS applications.

> *SaaS applications that prioritize quality are light-years ahead of those that don't. Having predictable behavior for your app, being able to identify issues early, and ensuring that merging changes doesn't break existing functionality are invaluable. Investing time today in ensuring quality means saving 100 times that amount of time in the future. Everyone should prioritize that.*
>
> - Alba Rivas, Principal Developer Advocate at Salesforce

Test Pyramid

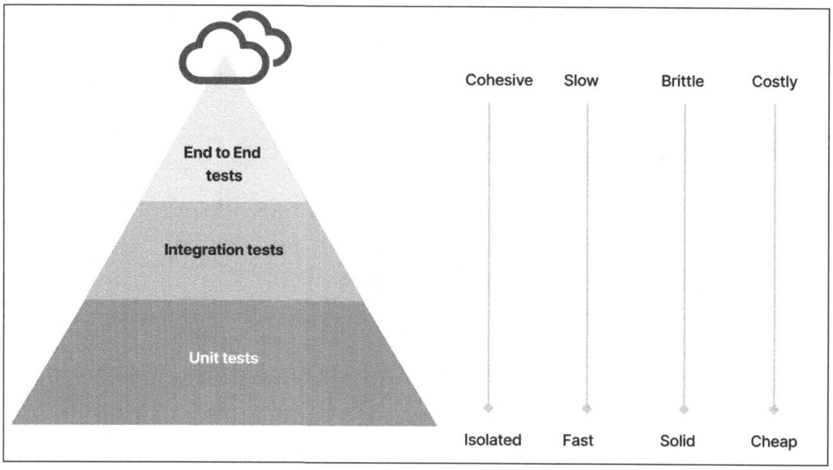

***Figure 7.2**: Software testing pyramid.*

One of the ways, to get started on a test strategy for modern web applications, including SAAS applications, can be understood using the Test pyramid as we can see in *Figure* 7.2.

The software testing pyramid can be used as a guiding principle for determining an appropriate number of tests like UI, system, or unit for each layer of the application.

Unit Tests: Unit tests focus on individual components or functions in isolation. These tests are designed to be cohesive, concentrating on one specific piece of functionality. These tests are designed at the method or the class level in the codebase.

They are isolated from the rest of the application, ensuring that the behavior of a single unit is thoroughly tested. Unit tests are fast, running quickly and providing near-instant feedback. This speed makes them ideal for frequent execution during development. Therefore, they are the base of the pyramid and should represent the majority of the tests.

Unit tests are typically solid and less prone to breakage. They are tightly coupled with the code they test, which can be an advantage, but it can also make them brittle if the code undergoes frequent changes. Unit tests are generally inexpensive to create and maintain. Since they focus on small, isolated pieces of code, they require minimal effort and resources.

Note: Some SAAS platforms like Salesforce mandate a certain unit test percentage as "To deploy Apex or package it for the Salesforce AppExchange, unit tests must cover at least 75% of your Apex code, and those tests must pass".

Integration Tests: Integration tests verify how different components or services work together. They are cohesive in the sense that they ensure the integration and interaction between multiple units. Think of APIs and their tests at this layer. In the context of SAAS applications, this could also relate to integrations with other applications, such as Salesforce-JIRA integration. However, they are not entirely isolated, as they require a broader scope. Integration tests are typically slower than unit tests. They may involve setting up complex mocks, stubs and interactions between components, which can impact execution speed. Integration tests can be more brittle, as they are sensitive to changes in the interactions between components. Maintaining stability in integration tests may require more effort. Integration tests are more resource-intensive than unit tests due to their wider scope. However, they are still less costly than end-to-end tests.

End-to-end Tests: End-to-end tests validate the entire application from the user's perspective. They are cohesive in the sense that they ensure the entire workflow functions as expected, but are not isolated, as they cover a broad range of functionalities. Think of UI tests like creating an Account in Salesforce CRM, or performing a checkout of a product; starting from the home page, as examples.

End-to-end tests are slow, as they simulate real user interactions and involve the entire application stack. They are typically not suitable for frequent execution during development. End-to-end tests can be brittle, especially when they rely on UI elements that may change frequently. Maintaining their stability requires diligent effort, as we have learned in earlier chapters.

End-to-end tests are the costliest to create and maintain due to their comprehensive scope and the need for extensive testing environments.

Note: SAAS applications can provide a lot of UI features like Search, Column sorting, Rich Text format etc. out of the box, and therefore might not require UI test automation for these areas.

The Role of Non-Functional Testing

Oh, did we forget the cloud icons at the top of our summit in *Figure* 7.2? Not at all!

In addition to the three main layers of the Testing Pyramid, it's essential to consider non-functional testing aspects, such as performance testing, security testing, and usability testing.

These tests ensure that your application not only works correctly but also meets performance expectations, is secure, and provides a user-friendly experience.

Limitations and Moving Forward

The Testing Pyramid is a valuable guideline for structuring your testing efforts, but it's not a one-size-fits-all solution. The pyramid's structure may need to be adjusted based on the characteristics of your application.

To move forward, consider the unique needs of your project. Balance the pyramid with non-functional testing and adapt the ratios between layers to match your application's specific requirements. A successful test automation strategy finds the right balance between coverage and efficiency, ultimately delivering a high-quality, reliable software product.

Let's consider some examples and "test" the testing pyramid:

- **E-commerce**: In the case of a SAAS e-commerce platform, merely relying on the traditional pyramid structure may overlook non-functional aspects. For instance, performance testing is crucial to ensure that the system can handle high traffic during peak shopping seasons. To address this limitation, you should incorporate non-functional testing into your strategy. We can implement load testing tools like JMeter to evaluate the application's performance under heavy loads, ensuring it remains responsive and reliable during traffic spikes.
- **CRM**: SAAS CRM (Customer Relationship Management) applications like Salesforce involve a wide range of user interactions, from lead management to customer support. Testing the entire spectrum of user flows solely through end-to-end tests can be time-consuming and cumbersome. Maximizing unit tests and using integration tests for third-party integrations could be crucial in many scenarios. This might result in the test pyramid being remodeled as a cuboid.
- **Project management**: If you are building a third-party application (For example, a Time management application) on top of a SAAS product such as JIRA, integration tests might be the most crucial.

While the Testing Pyramid provides a solid structure for test planning, it's essential to recognize that SAAS applications often present unique challenges. Just as a skilled doctor tailors treatment to each patient's unique needs, a comprehensive testing strategy for SAAS should account for performance testing and security testing. These critical aspects help ensure not only functionality but also speed, stability, and protection against potential vulnerabilities. Just as you'd prescribe a specialized treatment plan, it's vital to implement performance and security testing methodologies that match the distinctive requirements of each web application. So that our web applications not only function well, they can function well in any scenario.

When testing how well a SaaS application performs, it's not just about handling lots of users and distributed services. We need to make sure it's safe too. So, we do security testing to check if it protects data and keeps out bad actors. Also, some industries have rules (like GDPR or HIPAA), so we do compliance testing to make sure the app follows those rules and doesn't get anyone into trouble. The app needs to be flexible too, able to handle more users when needed and scale down when things quiet down. That's what elasticity testing is for. And since so many people use apps on their phones, we also check how the app works on different devices through mobile testing. Bringing all these things together in testing makes sure the app is not only fast but also safe, follows the rules, scales well, and works great on mobiles. Based on the context of the application, we can factor in some or all of the above testing types to ensure that our system delivers the desired results for its consumers.

In the following sections, we will explore how we can augment performance and security testing using Selenium WebDriver.

Performance Analysis

As the adoption of SaaS applications accelerates, performance is a key factor impacting user experience and satisfaction. Slow or unreliable SaaS apps can quickly frustrate users and hurt business metrics.

Imagine an expense management SaaS app that takes over 3 minutes to submit an expense report. Users struggle to use it and complain about productivity loss. The business finally loses 20% of its customers to a rival app and risks losing more.

This illustrates the impact of poor SaaS performance. Some key metrics include:

- **Response Time**: The time to load pages or complete requests
- **Throughput**: Requests handled per second
- **Resource Usage**: Memory, CPU, network bandwidth

Leaving the technical aspects aside, would you like to shop for your next pair of sneakers on a website which takes more than ten seconds for each page to load?

Getting back to the technical side of things, performance issues like slow response times, low throughput, and high resource usage cause problems like:

- Outages under high load
- Data loss and inconsistencies
- Lack of availability and reliability
- Poor user experience hurts adoption

Effective performance testing identifies these bottlenecks before customers experience them. Here are some unique considerations for testing SaaS performance:

- **Multi-Tenant Workloads:** SaaS apps serve multiple customer organizations (tenants) from the same application instance. When one tenant experiences a heavy load, it can degrade the performance of other tenants.
- **Internet-Scale Requirements:** SaaS apps designed for internet-scale usage must handle extremely high concurrent users and traffic volumes. Load levels are much higher than traditional on-premise enterprise software. Tests must generate a high load in the thousands or even millions of concurrent virtual users. Therefore, it's important to test at scale before launch to ensure the system can handle projected growth.
- **Distributed Components:** SaaS apps rely on many distributed third-party services and networks. Examples - CDNs, payment gateways, data/ API services, and cloud infrastructure.

Network latencies and outages on dependencies can impact the overall performance of the system. Therefore, testing should cover different types of loads, deployment architectures and failure scenarios.

Note: A tenant is the most fundamental construct of a SaaS environment. As a SaaS provider building an application, you are making this application available to your customers. Any customer that you sign up to use your SaaS environment is one of the tenants of your system.

Effective performance testing for SAAS applications or otherwise identifies these bottlenecks before customers experience them. To comprehensively test these scenarios, we can employ various types of performance testing:

- **Load Testing**: This method involves progressively increasing the number of users and the load on the system to evaluate its performance under typical usage conditions. Load testing allows us to measure how the SAAS application handles increasing traffic, helping us identify performance bottlenecks and ensuring that it remains responsive as user numbers grow. We can execute load testing at the API layer using JMeter, simulating numerous API requests, or at the UI layer using Selenium, which simulates real user interactions.

- **Stress Testing**: Stress testing pushes the system to its limits by testing at peak capacity thresholds. It assesses the SAAS application's stability and reliability under extreme conditions, determining its breaking point. Stress testing helps identify weaknesses in the application and any potential points of failure. Like load testing, stress testing can be conducted both at the API layer using JMeter and at the UI layer using Selenium.
- **Spike Testing**: This type of testing simulates sudden surges in traffic, such as those experienced during marketing campaigns, product launches, or other events that drive a rapid increase in user activity. Spike testing helps assess how well the application scales to meet sudden demands. By combining spike testing at both the API and UI layers, we gain a comprehensive view of the SAAS application's ability to handle unpredictable traffic spikes.
- **Endurance Testing**: Endurance testing focuses on assessing how well the SAAS application performs over a prolonged period under a consistent and expected load. By maintaining a steady level of users and activity over an extended duration, endurance testing helps uncover issues related to resource leaks, memory usage, and system stability. This ensures that the application remains reliable and responsive over time, addressing concerns that may arise during sustained usage.
- **Scalability Testing**: Scalability testing evaluates the SAAS application's ability to scale both vertically and horizontally in response to increased workload or demand. Vertical scalability involves adding resources to a single server, while horizontal scalability involves distributing the load across multiple servers. This type of testing ensures that the application can efficiently grow to accommodate a larger user base without sacrificing performance. Scalability testing can be conducted at both the API and UI layers to comprehensively assess the application's scalability in different aspects.
- **Volume Testing**: Volume testing involves subjecting the SAAS application to a significant amount of data to evaluate its performance and stability in large data volumes. This type of testing helps identify how the application handles data storage, retrieval, and processing as the volume of data increases. By conducting volume testing at both the API and UI layers, we gain insights into the application's capacity to manage substantial data loads, ensuring optimal performance even with extensive datasets.

Conducting these performance tests at multiple layers, including the API layer with JMeter and the UI layer with Selenium, allows us to gather a comprehensive perspective on the SAAS application's performance under various conditions. This ensures that both the back-end logic and the front-end user interface perform optimally, providing users with a seamless and responsive experience, even during challenging scenarios.

Installation

Let us go deeper into the topic by automating a load-testing scenario using JMeter and Selenium. Time to roll up our sleeves again and set up the pre-requisites:

1. Download and extract JMeter: Start by downloading Apache JMeter, an open-source performance testing tool. You can get it from the official website: https://jmeter.apache.org/download_jmeter.cgi.
2. Navigate to the **`/bin`** folder.
3. Run jmeter.bat on Windows or Jmeter on Linux/macOS to launch Jmeter.
4. Next, we should install the **"`Selenium/WebDriver`"** plugin using the JMeter plugin manager.
5. Download the **`Gecko driver/Chrome driver`** binaries in the system.

The preceding steps would result in the JMeter home page as follows:

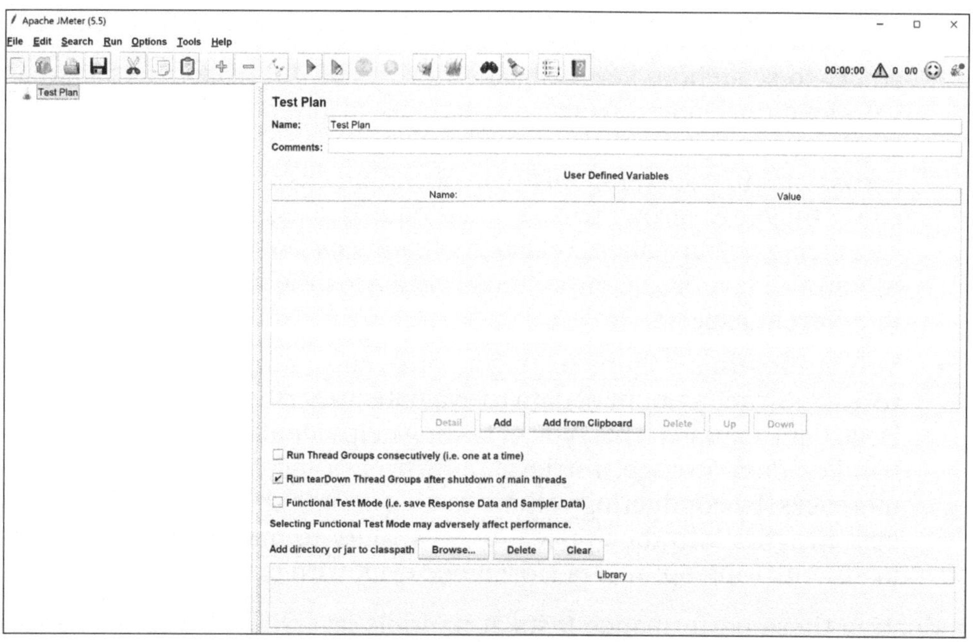

***Figure 7.3**: JMeter home page*

Now that you are on the JMeter UI, let's look at basic JMeter components:

- **Test Plan**: The root element that contains the test definition
- **Thread Groups**: To model users and load patterns
- **Samplers:** Adds requests like HTTP requests to simulate load
- **Listeners**: Displays metrics and graphs from a test run

Test Authoring and execution

The functional scenario we will try to simulate is navigation to https://orangeava.com/, and noting the page load times, with increasing load.

Now, let's create a JMeter Project to configure and test it. We'll create a Thread Group that will have a Selenium Web Driver Sampler instance. We'll include a Selenium script in this sampler and then execute it. First, we can add a simple **`Thread Group`** by clicking **`Test Plan`** and selecting the **`Thread Group`** from the **`Add`** menu as follows:

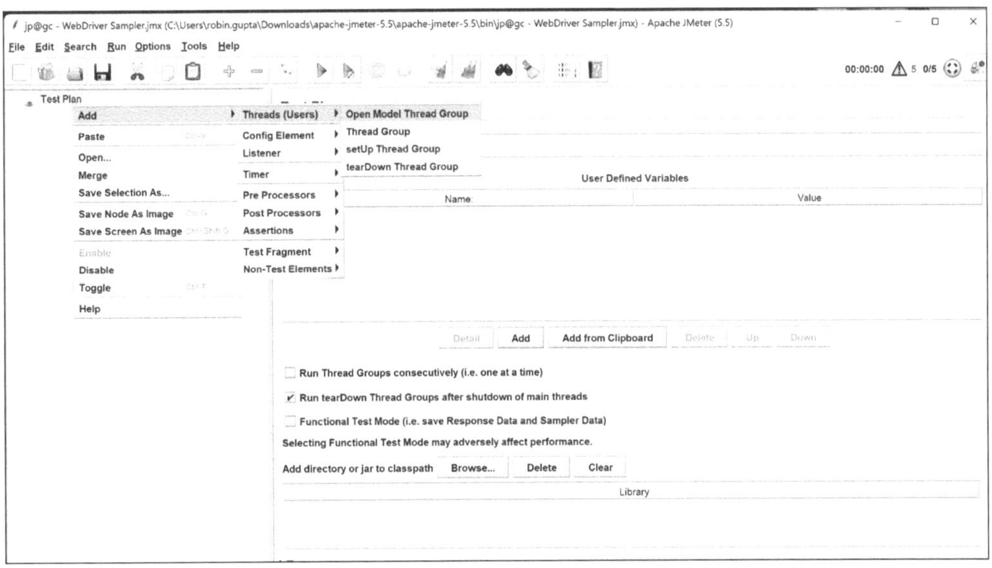

Figure 7.4: *Adding Thread Group*

Then we add the ChromeDriver config as shown in the following figure, and add the **`Path to Chrome Driver`**, pointing to the location of the **`chromedriver`** file:

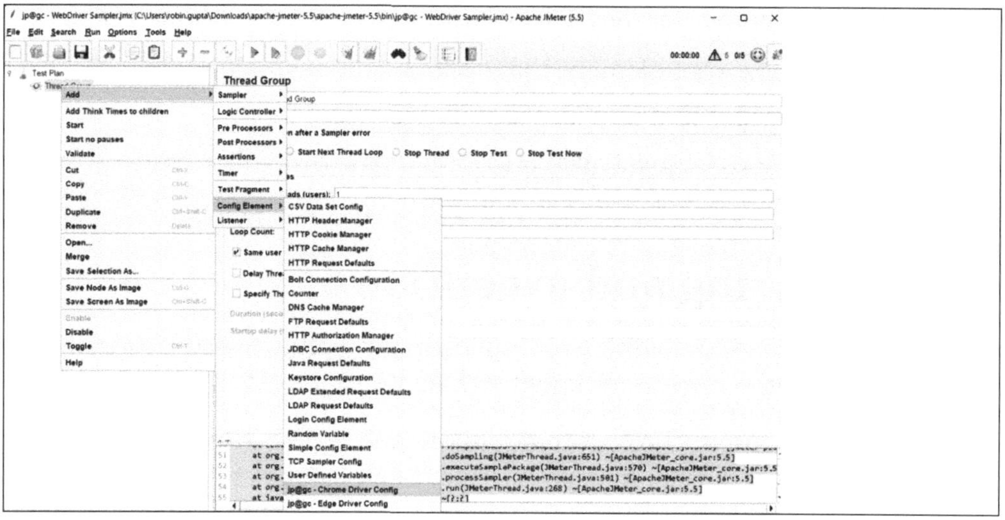

***Figure 7.5**: Adding Chrome Driver Configuration*

Note: If you notice that Chrome Driver configuration is not available, then kindly ensure that the WebDriver plugin is installed correctly.

Additionally, it's crucial to ensure that the version of the Chrome browser aligns with the version of the **Chromedrive.exe** for the script to execute without issues.

Kindly add **--remote-allow-origins=*** to the **Additional arguments** under the **Options** tab. Following this, we should include the web driver sampler **jp@gc-WebDriver Sampler** in the thread group:

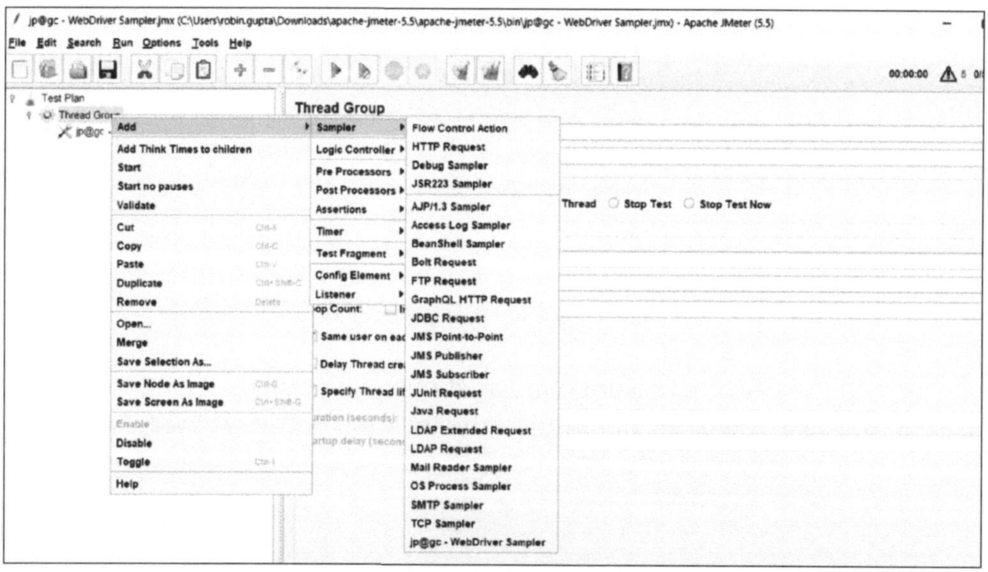

***Figure 7.6**: Adding WebDriver Sampler to the Thread Group*

Here we can add the WebDriver script we want to run as part of our load test:

```
WDS.sampleResult.sampleStart()
WDS.browser.get('https://orangeava.com/')
WDS.sampleResult.sampleEnd()
```

Kindly change the **`Script Language`** to **`groovy`**, and then it should look as follows:

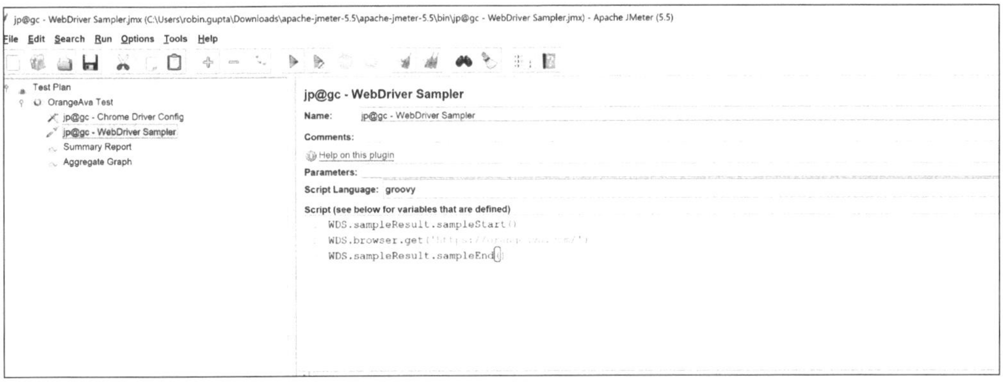

Figure 7.7: *Sampler code in groovy*

Finally, let's add a **`View Results Tree`** listener to the Thread group so that we can view the results of the script execution.

Now hit the play button at the top toolbar to execute the test. This will execute the test and if we navigate to the **`View Results Tree`** node, then we can observe the results as follows:

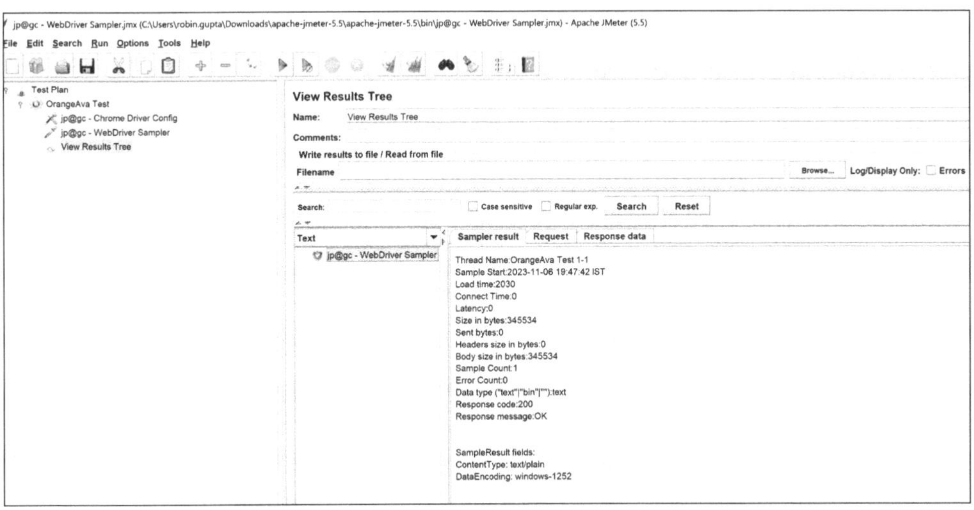

Figure 7.8: *JMeter results from the test execution*

As we can observe, the load time is 2030 milliseconds and 345534 bytes were sent for the body. Let's increase our tests to run 10 browsers with a ramp-up time of 1 second in between. This can be achieved from the Thread Group configuration as follows:

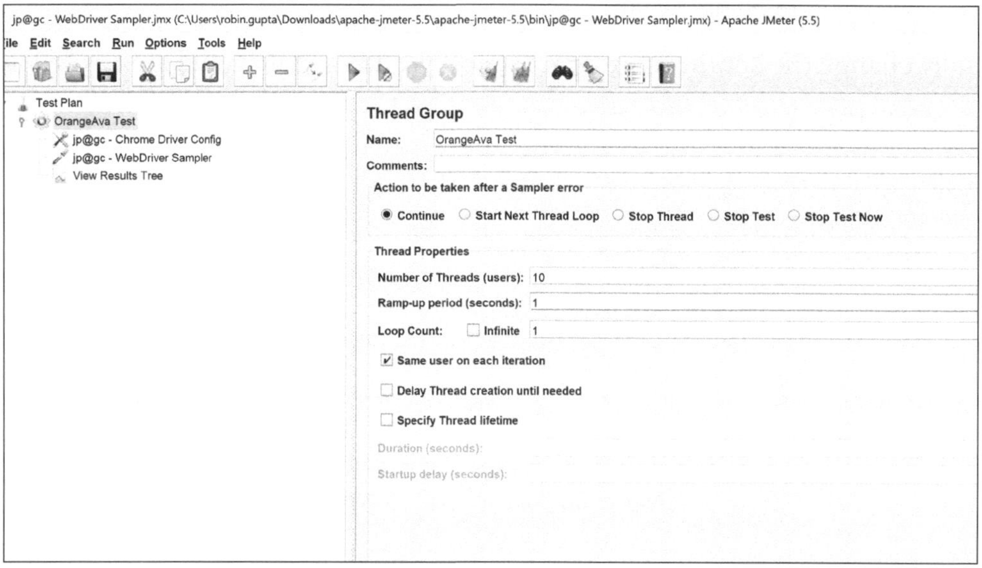

***Figure 7.9**: Configuration for simulating a load of 10 users.*

Using the same analogy, we can upscale the users to 100 or even 1000, based on our load-testing scenario. This setup can be scaled infinitely in theory, using the concepts of GRID, as we learned in the last chapter.

Users can also import the `jmx` file for the aforementioned test plan from `src/test/java/chapter7` as the `OrangeAvaTestPlan.jmx` file. This can be imported into JMeter for usage and experimentation.

Note: The use of Selenium is not recommended for Performance testing, unless the scenario vouches for UI interactions on real browsers, for an end-to-end flow.

Security Testing

In our increasingly digital world, web applications have become an integral part of our lives. From online shopping and social media to online banking and e-learning, we rely on web apps for convenience and accessibility. But, just like in the physical world, security is vital in the digital realm. Web application security is the shield that protects our online experiences and ensures that our data remains confidential and safe.

Web application security involves safeguarding these applications from a wide range of threats, including data breaches, hacking attempts, and phishing schemes. Ensuring the security of web applications is crucial, not only for the users who entrust them with personal information but also for the developers and organizations responsible for creating and maintaining them.

Before diving into security testing, it's essential to understand the common threats that web applications face. These threats are the adversaries that security measures aim to thwart. For example, data breaches can occur when an unauthorized party gains access to sensitive user information. This could lead to financial losses and reputational damage. Hacking, another common threat, involves exploiting vulnerabilities in an application's code to gain unauthorized access or control. In contrast, phishing schemes deceive users into revealing confidential information, often by impersonating trusted entities.

To put these threats into perspective, consider a real-life example: the Equifax data breach in 2017. In this incident, the personal information of 143 million individuals was compromised, highlighting the significant impact of a security breach. Equifax, a major credit reporting agency, suffered a severe blow to its reputation and faced legal consequences. This case emphasizes the importance of robust web application security measures.

OWASP and ZAP

The Open Web Application Security Project (OWASP) plays a crucial role in enhancing web application security. OWASP is not just an organization but a community of security experts who collaborate to make the Internet a safer place.

Their work revolves around promoting a transparent, open-source methodology for conducting security audits. These audits involve periodic inspections of projects to identify and mitigate vulnerabilities and errors, thus strengthening web application security. OWASP is like the guardian of the digital realm, and one of its most valuable tools is OWASP ZAP or Zed Attack Proxy.

ZAP helps identify and fix security issues in web applications. It's like having a vigilant sentinel that tirelessly scans and safeguards the digital fortresses of our online world.

In a time when technology is a double-edged sword—promising innovation but also posing risks—the work of OWASP is paramount. According to the World Economic Forum's Global Risks Report 2023, technology will "exacerbate inequalities" while "cybersecurity risks will remain a constant concern" over the next 10 years.

Note: Global Risks Report 2023 can be found here: https://www3.weforum.org/docs/WEF_Global_Risks_Report_2023.pdf

With a foundation in web application security, it's time to explore the world of security testing. Security testing is the practice of evaluating a web application to identify vulnerabilities and weaknesses that could be exploited by malicious actors. It's like a set of security drills, checking the locks and gates to ensure your fortress is well-protected.

There are different types of security testing, each with its specific focus and purpose. These include penetration testing, vulnerability scanning, and code review, among others. Penetration testing, often called ethical hacking, simulates an attack to find and fix vulnerabilities before attackers can exploit them. Vulnerability scanning involves using tools to scan an application for known vulnerabilities, much like scanning a fortress's walls for weak spots. Code review examines the application's source code to find potential security issues that could be exploited. Each type of security testing serves as a different line of defense, working together to ensure comprehensive security.

To get started with security testing, you need the right tools and a clear plan. Various tools and resources are available for conducting security tests, such as OWASP ZAP, Burp Suite, and Nmap.

These tools help you analyze web applications and detect potential security issues. It's like having a set of special instruments to inspect your fortress for hidden vulnerabilities. The process of security testing generally involves the following steps:

1. **Planning**: Define the scope and objectives of the security test. Determine which aspects of the web application will be tested and what types of security vulnerabilities are of concern.

2. **Scanning and Testing**: Use security testing tools to scan the web application for vulnerabilities. This may involve performing penetration tests, scanning for known vulnerabilities, and reviewing the source code.

3. **Analysis**: Examine the results of the security tests to identify vulnerabilities and potential risks.

4. **Reporting**: Create a comprehensive report that documents the findings, including the identified vulnerabilities and recommendations for remediation.
5. **Remediation**: Work with developers to fix the identified vulnerabilities and improve the security of the web application.

Let us walk through the usage of Selenium with OWASP ZAP to perform a basic security scan to cement our understanding.

ZAP and Selenium

ZAP is the world's most widely used web scanner. Not only is it free and open source, its actively maintained by a dedicated international team of volunteers. ZAP creates a man-in-the-middle proxy server and makes our website traffic pass through that server. It comprises auto scanners that help us identify the vulnerabilities in the applications under test.

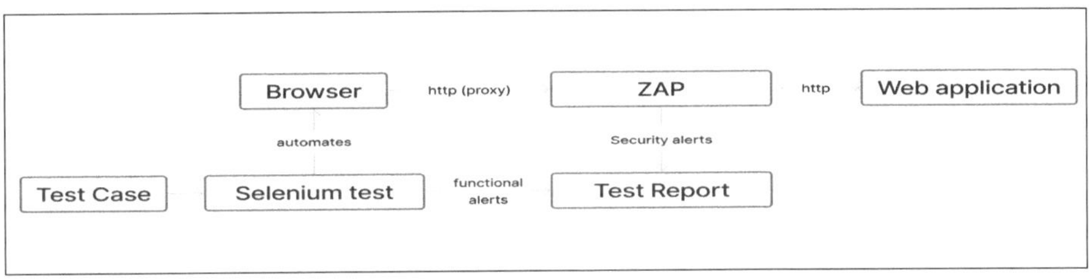

***Figure 7.10**: Test automation with ZAP and Selenium*

ZAP can be run in one of the three modes as follows:

- **Spider** is used to discover new resources (URLs) on a web app automatically. Spider visits these URLs to identify all the hyperlinks on the page and adds them to the list of URLs to visit and the process continues recursively until new resources are found.
- **Passive scan** checks the requests and responses sent to a web app and creates alerts for detected vulnerabilities. Passive scan only examines the HTTP requests and responses, making it good at finding vulnerabilities, such as missing security headers or missing anti-CSRF tokens.
- **Active scan** actively modifies the recorded requests and responses to determine further vulnerabilities. This helps us in finding vulnerabilities such as SQL Injection and XSS (cross-site scripting).

Setup and Pre-requisites

We can add OWASP ZAP to our framework using the maven dependency as follows:

```
<dependency>
    <groupId>org.zaproxy</groupId>
    <artifactId>zap-clientapi</artifactId>
    <version>1.12.0</version>
</dependency>
```

For our usage, it has already been added to the pom.xml file in our project. Next, we need to download and set up the ZAP desktop client for running the proxy. The latest binaries can be downloaded and installed from https://www.zaproxy.org/download/.

Once you have downloaded and installed the ZAP client, kindly run it, and select "No, I do not want to persist this session at this moment in time" on the welcome screen as follows:

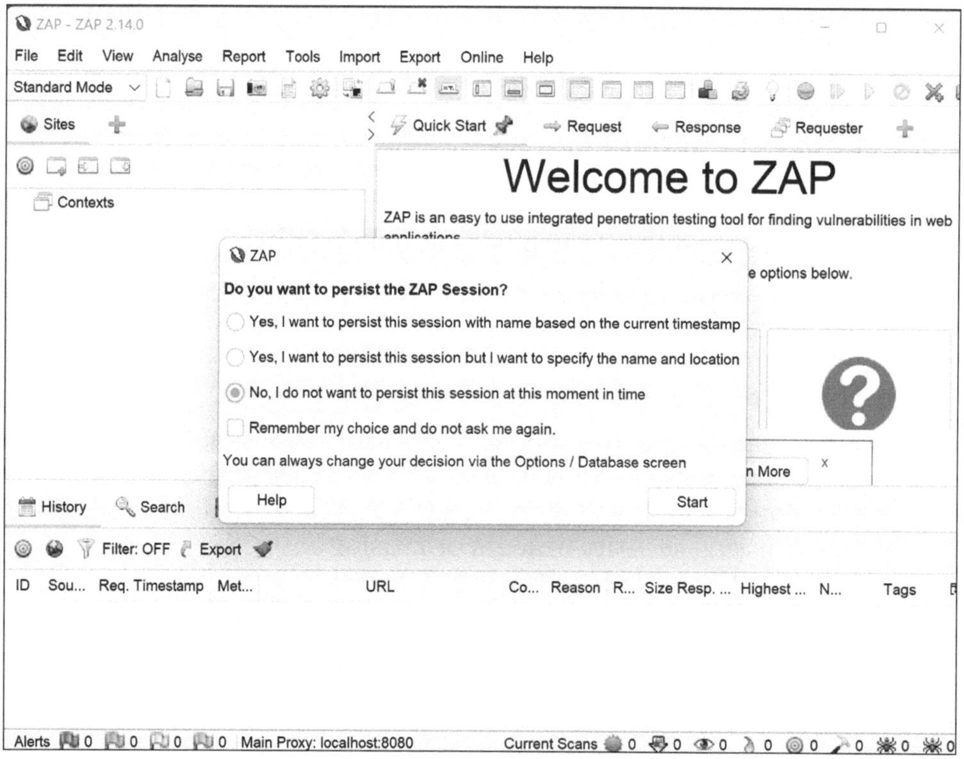

Figure 7.11: *ZAP Desktop client configuration.*

Note: If you get an error for starting the main proxy on port 8080, that should be fine, and you can use the next available port, and note down the value for using it in our code.

Once you have the ZAP client up and running, navigate to **`Tools>Options>API`** and copy the API key as follows:

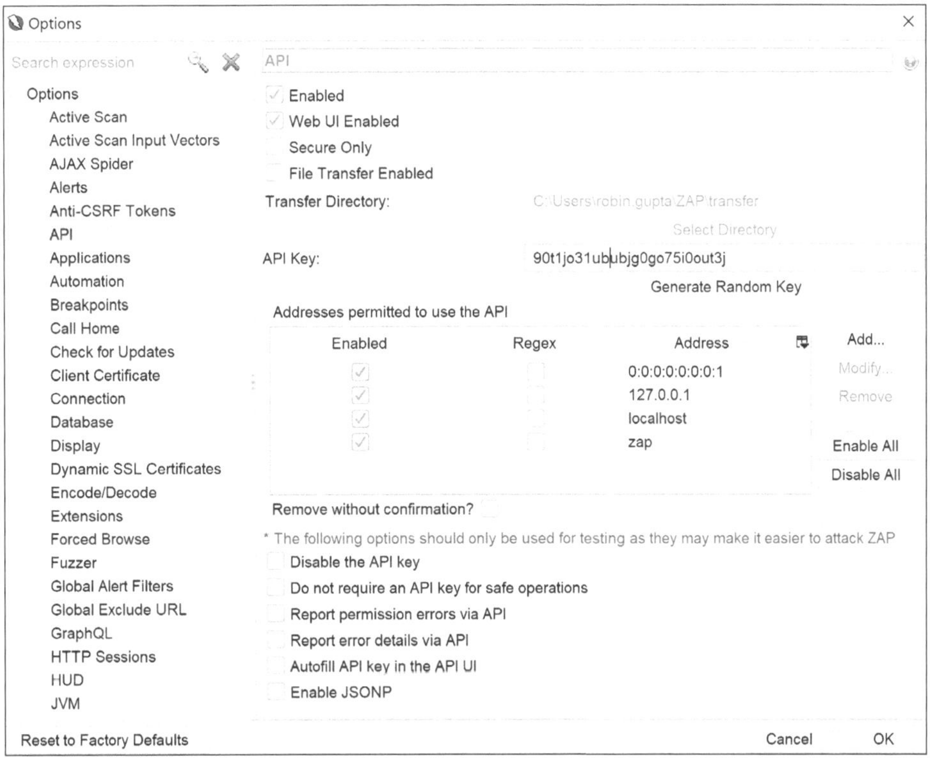

***Figure 7.12**: ZAP API key location in options*

Note: Kindly comment out the GRID-related code from previous chapters, or you might have to set up a GRID-related configuration such as "hubURL", for running these tests.

Now that our setup is complete, let us dive into some code. Kindly open **`Chapter07_ZAPTest`** java test class at **`src/test/java/chapter7`** location as follows:

```
public class Chapter07_ZAPTest {
      static final String ZAP_API_KEY = "90t1jo31ububjg0go75i0out3j";
      static final int ZAP_PROXY_PORT = 8081; // This is the port on which ZAP is running
      static final String ZAP_PROXY_ADDRESS = "localhost";
```

```
	public WebDriver driver;
	public ClientApi clientapi;
	@BeforeMethod
	public void proxySetup() {
		String proxyserverURL = "http://" + ZAP_PROXY_ADDRESS +
":" + ZAP_PROXY_PORT;
		Proxy = new Proxy(); // This dependency is being utilized
from Selenium
		proxy.setHttpProxy(proxyserverURL);
		proxy.setSslProxy(proxyserverURL);
		ChromeOptions options = new ChromeOptions();
		options.setProxy(proxy);
		options.setAcceptInsecureCerts(true);
		driver = new ChromeDriver(options);
		clientapi = new ClientApi(ZAP_PROXY_ADDRESS, ZAP_PROXY_
PORT, ZAP_API_KEY);
	}
	@Test
	public void seleniumSecurityTest() {
		driver.get("https://www.selenium.dev/");
	}
	@AfterMethod
	public void TearDown() throws ClientApiException {
		if (clientapi != null) {
			String reporttitle = "Selenium website ZAP Report";
			String template = "traditional-html";
			String description = "OWASP ZAP report for https://
www.selenium.dev/";
			String reportfilename = "selenium-zap-report.html";
			String targetfolder = System.getProperty("user.dir");
			System.out.println("Report is generated at this
folder " + targetfolder);
			ApiResponse apiresponse =
clientapi.reports.generate(reporttitle, template, null, description,
null, null,
```

```
                                null, null, null, reportfilename, null,
targetfolder, null);

System.out.println("Check the ZAP report at this location " + apire-
sponse.toString());
                    driver.quit();
            }
      }
}
```

This script sets up a proxy for the Chrome WebDriver, allowing traffic to be intercepted and analyzed by OWASP ZAP to identify potential security vulnerabilities.

In the **proxySetup** method, a proxy server is configured to intercept and forward HTTP and HTTPS traffic to OWASP ZAP, running on the local machine at port 8081. The Chrome WebDriver is configured to use this proxy. Additionally, the script sets **AcceptInsecureCerts** to true to enable the WebDriver to accept self-signed SSL certificates. This is particularly useful when testing applications with self-signed certificates. By using this configuration, any web traffic initiated by the WebDriver, such as navigating to a website, will be routed through the ZAP proxy for security analysis.

In the **seleniumSecurityTest** method, the script navigates to the official Selenium website (https://www.selenium.dev/). During this navigation, all web traffic passes through the ZAP proxy, which inspects the traffic for security issues.

In the **TearDown** method (executed after the test), the script generates a security test report using OWASP ZAP's API. It specifies report details, such as the title, report template, and description. The report is then generated and saved as an HTML file, and the location of the report file is printed to the console. Finally, the WebDriver is closed using **driver.quit().**

This script automates the process of setting up a security testing environment using Selenium and OWASP ZAP, navigating to a web application, and generating a security test report for analysis. It's a practical example of how Selenium can be used to perform security testing within a testing framework.

Oh, were you wondering, where are the reports? And what do they look like?

The reports can be found in the specified location in the following code:

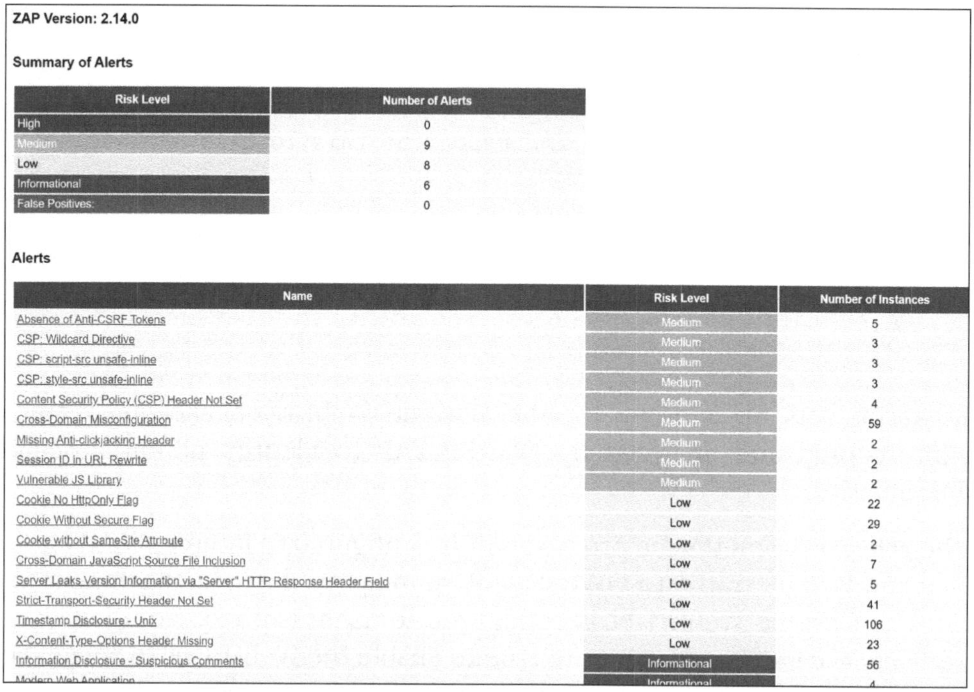

ZAP Version: 2.14.0

Summary of Alerts

Risk Level	Number of Alerts
High	0
Medium	9
Low	8
Informational	6
False Positives:	0

Alerts

Name	Risk Level	Number of Instances
Absence of Anti-CSRF Tokens	Medium	5
CSP: Wildcard Directive	Medium	3
CSP: script-src unsafe-inline	Medium	3
CSP: style-src unsafe-inline	Medium	3
Content Security Policy (CSP) Header Not Set	Medium	4
Cross-Domain Misconfiguration	Medium	59
Missing Anti-clickjacking Header	Medium	2
Session ID in URL Rewrite	Medium	2
Vulnerable JS Library	Medium	2
Cookie No HttpOnly Flag	Low	22
Cookie Without Secure Flag	Low	29
Cookie without SameSite Attribute	Low	2
Cross-Domain JavaScript Source File Inclusion	Low	7
Server Leaks Version Information via "Server" HTTP Response Header Field	Low	5
Strict-Transport-Security Header Not Set	Low	41
Timestamp Disclosure - Unix	Low	106
X-Content-Type-Options Header Missing	Low	23
Information Disclosure - Suspicious Comments	Informational	56

***Figure 7.13**: ZAP report for Selenium's official website.*

Apart from the colors, what we can appreciate about these reports are:

- A quick summary with risk levels of alerts
- Hyperlinked names for each risk
- Full payload and attack vector details for baselining and fixing the issues

This report is like a treasure map, pointing out where the hidden dangers lie. Armed with this knowledge, developers and security experts can reinforce their applications, ensuring that they are as impenetrable as a well-fortified castle. By automating security testing with this dynamic duo, the process becomes not only faster but also smarter. Testers can uncover security vulnerabilities swiftly, which is like discovering weak spots in a fortress's defenses early on. This proactive approach not only saves time and resources but also ensures that applications are robustly secure.

As we observed, integrating Selenium with OWASP ZAP is a straightforward process, much like fitting two puzzle pieces together. It does not demand complex acrobatics, making it accessible to testers from different backgrounds. Once they are joined, these tools become a powerful pair, enabling testers to weave security checks into their web application testing routine, like adding an extra layer of armor to their digital fortresses.

Note: We can also use the "headless" option for security testing, for faster test execution. This can also help in the separation of concerns between UI, Performance and Security tests.

Conclusion

In conclusion, our journey through the world of testing Software as a Service (SaaS) applications with the potent combination of JMeter and OWASP ZAP has shed light on the essential aspects of ensuring the quality and reliability of modern software. As we have explored the intricacies of SaaS application architecture, dissected the various web application layers, and delved into the nuances of test automation for SaaS, we have armed ourselves with the knowledge and tools needed to navigate the challenges of this evolving software landscape.

Modern web applications, such as SAAS systems, have undeniably transformed the way businesses operate, offering unparalleled convenience, scalability, and accessibility. Yet, this transformation has also introduced a new set of challenges, particularly in the domains of performance and security testing. Through our journey, we have not only uncovered these challenges but also developed a deep understanding of best practices for testing and automation, ensuring that our pyramid stays balanced in the face of ever-changing software ecosystems.

But guess what? Our adventure does not end here! There is a new chapter waiting for us just around the corner. In the upcoming chapter, titled "BDD with Selenium" we'll dive into the world of Behavior-Driven Development (BDD). We will learn how to make the most of Cucumber, a nifty BDD tool, combined with Selenium. Together, we will discover how to create feature-rich and easily readable test scripts.

Buckle up, because this voyage is like a summer road trip–it's going to be hot out there, but the sights at our destination will be sizzling, and our tests will be cool as cucumber.

Exercise

In this hands-on exercise, you will apply the concepts discussed in this chapter to automate performance and security testing for a SAAS application.

1. Load testing:
    a. Automate the navigation for the OrangeAva home page at: https://orangeava.com/.
    b. Run this automated test via JMeter with one user in the Thread Group to note down the base load times.
    c. Run the same automated test with 10 users with a ramp-up period of 0 seconds and a Loop Count of 10.
    d. Note down the data points such as times and data exchanged, and compare with the base data from step 1.a.
2. Security testing:
    a. Automate the security audit of the following scenario using OWASP ZAP:
        i. Login to OrangeHRM : https://opensource-demo.orangehrmlive.com/web/index.php/auth/login
        ii. Click on the `Admin` button on the left navigation panel.
    b. Run this automated test and generate the report.
    c. Analyze the report results for "High, Medium, Low" risks.

Chapter 8
BDD with Selenium

Introduction

Navigating the intricate balance between business objectives and technical implementation is a crucial challenge in software development. This chapter is a gateway to exploring the concepts of Behavior Driven Development (BDD) and Selenium, weaving together strategies for creating adaptable, business-centric test suites.

To start, we uncover the core principles of BDD. It's more than a methodology for software testing; it's a way to shape software development by understanding behaviors through a business lens. Picture it as a collaborative effort, where stakeholders, developers, and testers communicate using clear and relatable examples.

Then, we delve into the mechanics of Cucumber, a pivotal tool in the BDD toolkit. Exploring its language and structure, we showcase how it bridges the gap between non-technical stakeholders and the world of automated testing. By the end of this chapter, you will possess the groundwork to seamlessly merge BDD principles with Selenium, crafting tests that not only function effectively but also resonate with the core objectives of the business. Oh, and these technical tests would be readable by non-technical team members too! Adding collaboration, efficiency, and team work across the board.

Structure

In this chapter, we will discuss the following topics:

- Behavior Driven Development
- Gherkin and Cucumber

Behavior Driven Development

Behavior Driven Development (BDD) is a way of developing software that focuses on describing how the software should behave from the user's perspective.

For example, imagine you are developing a login feature for a website. Instead of writing technical code tests, such as "password field should accept minimum 8 characters", you would write a test scenario in simple language as follows:

"User should be able to login with valid username and password. When user enters a password less than 8 characters, they should see an error message."

This test scenario reads like a specification or user story. It describes the expected behavior without technical jargon. The development team can then write code to make this test scenario pass. The magic here is that everyone involved, from developers to non-tech stakeholders, can understand this scenario. BDD acts as a universal translator, ensuring that the story of your software is crystal clear. Now, why do we need this storytelling approach in development? Well, it is a game-changer for collaboration. BDD bridges the gap between technical and non-technical teams, aligning everyone on a shared narrative. It keeps the focus on the end user, creating software that not only works but also meets the real needs of those interacting with it. It also serves as living documentation for the software behavior.

The key is to write specifications and test scenarios that focus on the user perspective and business value, rather than technical details. This helps ensure the software meets the actual user needs.

BDD uses a simple and natural language called Gherkin to write test scenarios that are understandable by both technical and non-technical stakeholders. It also helps to bridge the communication gap between developers, testers, and business analysts.

BDD is derived from Test Driven Development (TDD), which is a software development process that relies on writing automated tests before writing the actual code. TDD ensures that the code meets the requirements and design specifications, and facilitates refactoring and maintenance. However, TDD has some limitations, such as:

- TDD tests are often written in a technical language that is not accessible to non-developers.
- TDD tests are focused on the implementation details of the code, rather than the business value and user needs.

- TDD tests can become obsolete or irrelevant as the code evolves and changes, and therefore the maintenance effort might become a bottleneck for delivery pipeline.
- TDD requires upfront design and implementation for both automation framework and team's delivery process.
- TDD methodology requires a steep learning curve and could be a mindset shift for the team and the management.
- Refactoring larger TDD projects can potentially create a bottleneck in code coverage, as modifications to the code may introduce new code that lacks corresponding tests.

BDD addresses these limitations by shifting the focus from testing to behavior. BDD tests are written in a business-readable language that describes the desired outcomes and scenarios of the system.

Additionally, BDD tests are aligned with the user stories and acceptance criteria, which are the main artifacts of Agile software development. These tests can serve as a living documentation of the system as well as a verification tool.

BDD was first introduced by Dan North in 2006, who was a Java developer and a coach for Agile teams. He noticed that some of his students had difficulties with learning and applying TDD, especially with naming and structuring the tests. He also observed that the word "test" had a negative connotation for some people, who associated it with failure and pressure. As a result, he decided to experiment with a different approach where he replaced the word "test" with "behavior" and used a simple template to write the test scenarios. He called this approach "Behavior Driven Development", and published an article about it in 2006.

BDD is based on some principles and practices from other software development methodologies, such as:

- **Domain Driven Design (DDD)**: It is a software design approach that emphasizes the use of a common language and model to represent the domain and the business logic of the system.
- **Acceptance Test Driven Development (ATDD)**: It is a software development process that involves writing acceptance tests before writing the code, and collaborating with the customers and stakeholders to define the requirements and expectations of the system.
- **Specification by Example (SBE):** It is a software development technique that uses concrete examples and scenarios to illustrate and validate the behavior and functionality of the system.

BDD is supported by various tools and frameworks that allow the execution of the test scenarios written in Gherkin. Some of the most popular tools are as follows:

- **Cucumber**: It is a cross-platform tool that can be integrated with various programming languages and testing frameworks, such as Java, Ruby, Python, C#, Selenium, and more.
- **SpecFlow**: It is a tool for .NET platform that can be used with Visual Studio and NUnit, MSTest, or xUnit testing frameworks.
- **Jbehave**: It is a tool for Java platform that can be used with JUnit, TestNG, or Maven testing frameworks.

BDD has many benefits for software development teams, such as:

- Improving the collaboration and communication among the team members and the stakeholders by using a common language and format to describe the behavior of the system.
- Enhancing the quality and reliability of the software by ensuring that the code meets the user needs and business goals, and by detecting and preventing defects early in the development cycle.
- Reducing the maintenance and documentation costs by having a single source of truth for the behavior and requirements of the system, and by keeping the test scenarios up to date and relevant.

Behavior Driven Development (BDD) is a way of testing software applications by describing how the software should work from an end user's perspective. Let's take some examples of BDD tests:

E-commerce Website

- **User Registration**: This test checks that a new user can create an account on the website by entering their details such as name, email address, and password. The password they enter should be at least 8 characters long.
- **Search**: This test verifies that a user can search for products on the website by keyword, product category, or by applying filters like price range, average rating, and more. If the user searches for something that does not exist, they should see a "No results found" message.
- **Checkout**: This test validates that a user must be logged in to their account to be able to checkout. At checkout, they should be able to enter the shipping address, billing information, select a shipping method and make a payment. If they enter an invalid coupon code, it should display an error.

Banking Application

- **Login**: This test checks that users can log in to their bank account by entering a valid username and password. If wrong credentials are entered, appropriate error messages should be displayed.
- **Money Transfer**: This verifies that a logged-in user can transfer money between two of their own accounts. They should have a sufficient balance in the source account to complete the transfer. If the balance is low, an alert should be displayed.
- **Account Statement**: This test checks that users can generate monthly statements that display all transactions and current account balance.

BDD tests, as noted above, explain the expected behavior from an end-user standpoint without technical jargon. This helps software teams build applications that meet real business and user needs.

> *I believe that using tools like Cucumber and SpecFlow for automated checks is not the same as practicing BDD. These tools, while helpful, are often misused in a way that leads to unclear testing scenarios and does not foster the intended collaboration. I've noticed a trend of using these tools for their perceived readability or popularity, but this misses their true purpose. I advocate for using these tools thoughtfully, ensuring that test scenarios are clear and meaningful. When misused you end up with more code, that code needs maintaining, not to mention the increase in code complexity. If the context suits it, use these tools, otherwise make sure they are adding value to your solution in the short and long term.*
>
> - Richard Bradshaw, Senior Architect at Slalom Build and Community Builder.

However, all roses come with thorns, and similarly, BDD comes with its own set of challenges and considerations for successful adoption, as follows:

- **Cultural and Mindset Shift**: Adopting BDD requires a major cultural change for many teams who are used to traditional waterfall development. Developers and testers must shift their mindsets from writing technical code tests to describing user behaviors.

  For example, at a fictitious company, the QA team was used to creating detailed test cases in spreadsheet templates, including inputs, expected results, actual results, and more. With BDD, they had to learn to write tests in plain English focused on user needs. This change was uncomfortable initially, and the teams required ramp-up time and education to make the right moves. Similarly, product managers had to let go of large requirements documents and embrace agile user stories. Through coaching and management direction, the team was able to eventually adopt the collaborative BDD approach.

- **Finding the Right Level of Detail**: Writing BDD scenarios that are neither too vague nor too specific is an art that takes practice. If they are too vague, they lack the detail to develop and test against. On the other hand, if they are too detailed, they lose business focus and read like traditional test cases. For instance, a scenario like "User should be able to login" is incomplete. A more detailed one, such as "System should validate user ID and password, check user status and permissions, log all successful and failed attempts" loses the user perspective. The right level could be "User should be able to login with valid credentials. Invalid user ID or password should display appropriate error." Why did we say "could be"? Because the right level would be dependent on the stage of the team and project to work out the details.
- **Tool Integration Challenges**: BDD tools like Cucumber must be integrated with testing frameworks like Selenium and programming languages like Java and Ruby to give a body to the proverbial soul. Setting this up and getting the tools to work well together can take significant effort in large enterprises with complex systems.

In summary, while BDD has many benefits, adopting it requires changes in culture, perspective, and tools from teams. With management direction and commitment, teams can overcome these challenges.

Gherkin and Cucumber

Behavior Driven Development (BDD) is an Agile software development approach that aims to bridge the communication gap between technical and non-technical teams by allowing them to collaborate on describing the expected behavior of the system in a simple, ubiquitous language called Gherkin. Gherkin utilizes a set of keywords like **Feature, Scenario, Given, When, and Then** to define acceptance criteria and scenarios in plain English, understandable by all stakeholders. These scenarios serve as automated tests that are run using the Cucumber framework, which maps steps in Gherkin to code written in languages like Java and Ruby, integrated with testing frameworks like Selenium and JUnit. This enables living documentation that is executable, ensuring the system behavior matches the business needs.

Gherkin

Gherkin was created by the developers of Cucumber, a popular BDD framework. It is named after "gherkins", which are used for pickling cucumbers, matching the Cucumber tool. The need for Gherkin emerged because traditional requirements documents tended to be highly technical and not very readable. Test cases also ended up being too detailed and code-focused. Gherkin became a way to describe behavior in plain language that could be understood by everyone. It allowed non-technical business experts to be involved in defining the product behavior.

Gherkin uses the following keywords to structure the expected behavior:

- **Feature**: High-level description of a functionality
- **Scenario**: Concrete example and test case of the feature
- **Given/When/Then**: Preconditions, events, outcomes of the scenario
- **Background**: Context shared across scenarios
- **And/But**: Logical connections between steps

Alright, now that we know the keywords, let us take an example of making coffee to expand our understanding:

- **Feature**: Imagine you're writing a recipe or a script for a movie. The `Feature` is like the title or the main theme of that story. In our coffee example, the feature could be **`Brewing a Perfect Cup of Coffee`**.
- **Scenario**: Now, think of a **`Scenario`** as a specific scene or situation in your story. In our coffee script, a scenario could be **`Making Morning Coffee`**. It's a concrete example, like a scene from your movie.
- **Given/When/Then**: These are like the script directions for each scene.
    - **Given**: This sets the stage, providing the initial conditions. For coffee, it could be **`Given a bag of freshly ground coffee.`**
    - **When**: This is the action or event. In our coffee script, it might be **`When hot water is poured over the coffee grounds.`**
    - **Then**: This is the expected outcome or result. For our coffee scenario, it could be **`Then a fragrant cup of coffee is brewed.`**
- **Background**: Think of "Background" as the general setting or context that applies to all scenes in your story. In our coffee script, the background could be **`Background: Every morning, you have a clean coffee maker and fresh water ready.`**

- **And/But**: Now, sometimes in your story, you need to connect ideas logically.
    - **And**: This is an additional step that logically follows the previous one. In coffee making, it could be **`And a teaspoon of sugar is added`**.
    - **But**: This introduces a contrasting step. For instance, "But no milk is added."

So, putting it all together, your coffee-making script in Gherkin might look like this:

```
Feature: Brewing a Perfect Cup of Coffee


Background: Every morning, you have a clean coffee maker and fresh water
ready.


Scenario: Making Morning Coffee
  Given a bag of freshly ground coffee
  When hot water is poured over the coffee grounds
  And a teaspoon of sugar is added
  Then a fragrant cup of coffee is brewed


Scenario: Trying Something Different
  Given a bag of freshly ground flavored coffee
  When hot water is poured over the coffee grounds
  And no milk is added
  Then a unique and aromatic cup of coffee is brewed
```

This Gherkin script is like your coffee-making movie script, breaking down the process into scenes (scenarios) with specific directions (Given/When/Then), a shared setting (Background), and logical connections (And/But). If you are not a coffee person, don't worry, here is an example from the web development domain in Gherkin syntax:

```
Feature: Login


Background:
```

```
Given the user is on the website

Scenario: Successful Login
When the user enters valid username and password
Then they should be logged in

Scenario: Failed Login
When the user enters invalid password
Then they should see an error message
```

Let us dive into a few tips for writing effective Gherkin scenarios in a way that's easy to understand.

- **Start with User Stories and Acceptance Criteria**: Think of a "user story" as a short narrative from the user's perspective. It's like telling a friend what you want the software to do. Acceptance criteria are conditions that need to be met for the story to be complete. So, before you start writing your Gherkin scenario, have a clear idea of what you want your software to achieve from the user's point of view.
- **Focus on Primary Happy and Unhappy Paths**: Imagine your scenario as a journey. The "happy path" is the smooth, expected route, such as making a purchase online without any hiccups. The "unhappy paths" are detours or bumps in the road, such as encountering an error during checkout. By focusing on these primary paths, you ensure that your scenarios cover the most critical aspects of your software.
- **Keep Scenarios Small and Test Only One Thing**: Picture your scenario as a single step in a recipe. You wouldn't mix ingredients for a cake and roast a chicken in the same step, right? Similarly, keep your scenarios small and focused. Test one thing at a time to make it easier to understand, maintain, and identify issues.
- **Use Conversational Language and Active Voice**: Gherkin is like a friendly chat with your software. Use everyday language and active voice, as if you're talking directly to the system. Instead of saying "The system should do this," say "When I do this, the system responds like that." It makes your scenarios more engaging and relatable. This also promotes writing acceptance stories with the influence of user personas.
- **Avoid Technical Jargon and Implementation Details**: Imagine explaining your scenario to a friend who is not into tech. That is your goal. Skip the complex tech terms and details. For instance, instead of saying "The system sends a POST request," say "The system submits the form." This

ensures that everyone, regardless of their technical background, can understand what is happening.

- **Use Clear, Expressive Scenario Names**: Your scenario name is like the title of a chapter in a book. Make it clear and expressive so that anyone glancing at it understands what's being tested. If your scenario name is like a movie trailer, enticing and informative, it sets the stage for what's about to unfold.

By following these tips, you're essentially creating a friendly, easy-to-follow script for your software, ensuring that everyone involved understands the story you're trying to tell. Well-written Gherkin serves as excellent documentation and is readable even for a novice.

In a nutshell, Gherkin is like a friendly translator that helps everyone on the team speak the same language. It's a tool that makes sure developers, testers, and even non-tech folks can easily understand what's going on in the software. When you write really good scenarios using Gherkin, it's not just a bunch of rules; it's like creating a storybook about your product.

Imagine your scenarios as living, breathing documents. Instead of buried paperwork, they're like story chapters that vividly describe how your software should behave. So, Gherkin isn't just a code language; it's a storyteller that keeps everyone on the same page, turning your software development journey into a collaborative adventure.

Cucumber

In the previous section, we introduced Gherkin as the language for defining expected software behavior. Now, let's shift our focus to the practical side of things as we explore Cucumber's role in executing Gherkin scenarios against the actual system.

Cucumber serves as a test automation framework, streamlining the process of automating Gherkin scenarios. Think of it as the engine that drives your tests. In this section, we'll delve into the technical aspects, understanding how Cucumber works to automate the scenarios you've defined.

To make Gherkin scenarios executable, we need to map them to code. This process involves translating the human-readable Gherkin syntax into machine-understandable instructions.

Cucumber stands out as an open-source test automation framework, making it possible to run automated tests based on plain-text Gherkin scenarios. Its versatility extends to various programming languages like Java, Ruby, Python, and more.

Here's a breakdown of how Cucumber operates:

1. **Writing Gherkin Scenarios**: Think of Gherkin scenarios like writing a story or script for your software. It's done in feature files, making it easy for everyone, even those who aren't tech experts, to understand what the software is supposed to do.
2. **Creating Step Definitions**: Now, imagine you're telling your computer how to act out each part of your story. This is done by writing step definitions in a programming language (like Java with Selenium). It's like giving behind-the-scenes instructions for each step, telling the computer exactly what to do.
3. **Matching Steps to Definitions**: Cucumber, acting as the director, matches each step in the scenario to its corresponding step definition. It's like ensuring that the script aligns with the instructions you've set in the background.
4. **Executing Code on the Test System**: The code linked to each step definition is executed on the test system. This is where your script comes to life, and the software performs the specified actions. Think of it as the actors following the director's cues during a play.
5. **Reporting Results in Gherkin Format**: Once the script is played out, Cucumber reports back the results in Gherkin format. This report is like the reviews and feedback after a performance, providing a clear and standardized overview of how well the software adhered to the specified behavior.

In essence, Cucumber acts as the conductor, orchestrating the entire testing process and ensuring that your Gherkin scenarios seamlessly translate into executable tests with meaningful outcomes. This enables living documentation that is automated and always up to date! This concept can be summarized using the diagram as follows:

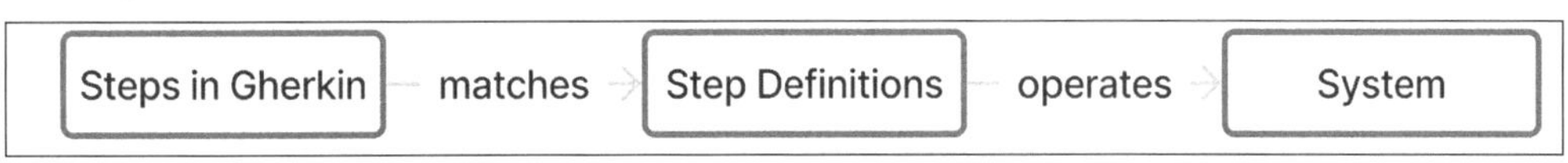

Figure 8.1: *Connecting Gherkin to System level operations*

Cucumber identifies steps in each scenario and calls the matching step definition methods to execute. These methods contain the automation code. As we learned earlier, the automation code operates the system or web application.

Oh, going through all the concepts made time fly away, and we forgot what time it is? It is "Rolling up the sleeves and coding" time. So, let us go deeper by adding Cucumber capabilities to our test automation framework.

Pre-requisites and installation

We can build Cucumber-based tests by adding Cucumber to our Maven **pom.xml** as follows:

```
<!-- https://mvnrepository.com/artifact/io.cucumber/cucumber-java -->
<dependency>
    <groupId>io.cucumber</groupId>
    <artifactId>cucumber-java</artifactId>
    <version>7.14.0</version>
</dependency>
<!-- https://mvnrepository.com/artifact/io.cucumber/cucumber-testng -->
<dependency>
    <groupId>io.cucumber</groupId>
    <artifactId>cucumber-testng</artifactId>
    <version>7.14.0</version>
</dependency>
```

For our convenience, these dependencies have been already added to the pom.xml file in our downloaded code base.

Note: Optionally, you can also add Cucumber plugin from the Eclipse marketplace, or from the plugin marketplace of your IDE. This would enable the IDE to natively understand the Cucumber keywords such as Given, When, Then, and more.

Feature file

In Cucumber, a feature file plays a crucial role as it serves as a user-readable document that outlines the expected behavior of a software feature. Let's break down its role and format. Feature files promote collaboration among team members. They provide a shared space where everyone can contribute to defining and understanding the behavior of the software feature. Think of it as a common ground for effective communication and efficient test automation. While it's a document that humans can read, a feature file also serves as executable documentation. The scenarios outlined in the feature file can be automated to validate that the software behaves as described. This brings the benefit of having living, up-to-date documentation that reflects the current state of the software.

Kindly open the **OrangeHRMLogin.feature** file at **src/test/java/chapter8** location as follows:

```
Feature: Login to HRM Application

  #Background:
  #Given User is on HRMLogin page "https://opensource-demo.orangehrm-
live.com/"
  @ValidCredentials
  Scenario: Login with valid credentials
    Given User is on HRMLogin page "https://opensource-demo.orangehrm-
live.com/"
    When User enters username as "Admin" and password as "admin123"
    Then User should be able to login successfully and land on home page

  @InvalidCredentials
  Scenario Outline: Login with invalid credentials
    Given User is on HRMLogin page "https://opensource-demo.orangehrm-
live.com/"
    When User enters username as "<username>" and password as "<pass-
word>"
    Then User should be able to see error message "<errorMessage>"

    Examples:
      | username | password  | errorMessage        |
      | Admin    | admin12$$ | Invalid credentials |
      | admin$$  | admin123  | Invalid credentials |
      | abc123   | xyz$$     | Invalid credentials |
```

As you can read and easily understand this feature file in Gherkin syntax, the objective here is to validate the login functionality of the OrangeHRM application. This feature file can be explained in three sections as follows:

1. **Feature/Background**: This section outlines the purpose of the feature, which is to log in to the OrangeHRM application. It also includes a

commented-out Background section that, if activated, would set up a common starting point for all scenarios. However, in this case, it's not currently in use.

2. **First scenario**: The first scenario tests the valid login credentials and asserts that the user should land onto the home page. Each feature file contains one or more scenarios, each starting with the Scenario: keyword. A scenario is a specific test case or example that explores a particular aspect of the feature.

3. **Second scenario**: For scenarios with multiple sets of data, you can use the Scenario Outline keyword. It acts like a template for running the same scenario with different inputs. The Examples table provides specific combinations of usernames, passwords, and expected error messages for the outlined scenario. Here, various values of `<username>`, `<password>`, and `<errorMessage>` are dynamically fetched from the table for running a battery of tests against the login page.

Now, how do we implement the Selenium WebDriver methods and TestNG asserts for our feature file?

Appreciate your curiosity and the answer lies in Hooks and Step Definitions.

Note: You can tag scenarios or features with keywords preceded by the @ symbol, such as @ValidCredentials. Tags are useful for organizing and running specific subsets of scenarios.

Hooks

In Cucumber, hooks are essential components that enable the execution of setup and cleanup tasks at specific points in the test execution lifecycle. These tasks are encapsulated within methods annotated with `@Before` and `@After`, allowing you to define actions before and after each scenario, step, or even based on specific tags. For instance**,** `@Before` is commonly used for pre-scenario setup, while @After is employed for post-scenario cleanup. The order of hook execution follows the method order in the hook-annotated class, providing flexibility for customized sequencing. Moreover, hooks support the tagging mechanism, enabling selective execution of setup and cleanup procedures based on scenario or feature tags. Sharing state between hooks and step definitions is facilitated through Cucumber's Scenario Context, allowing seamless information transfer during the test execution process.

Note: In the context of TestNG, the concept of `@BeforeClass and @AfterClass` shares similarities with Cucumber hooks.

Kindly open the **`Hooks.java`** class at **`src/test/java/chapter8`** location as follows:

```
public class Hooks {
	public static WebDriver driver;
	public static OrangeLoginPage loginpage;
	@Before
	public void setUpClass() throws Exception {
		driver = new ChromeDriver();
		loginpage = new OrangeLoginPage(driver);


	}
	@After
	public static void tearDown(Scenario scenario) {
		driver.quit();
	}
}
```

The Hooks Java class uses Cucumber hooks to manage the setup and cleanup of a web application test suite with Selenium WebDriver.

It initializes a static WebDriver and a Page Object for an **`OrangeHRM`** login page before each scenario using the `@Before` annotation. The setup ensures a clean state for testing. After each scenario, the `@After` annotated method, which is static, is executed, quitting the WebDriver session and closing the browser. This systematic approach aids in maintaining a consistent and reliable testing environment, enhancing the efficiency and stability of the automated tests.

Here are some use cases for Cucumber hooks:

- **Setting up Test Data**: Hooks are useful for initializing or resetting test data before scenarios run.
- **Opening and Closing Resources**: Hooks can manage the opening and closing of resources such as databases, browsers, or network connections.
- **Logging and Reporting**: Hooks can log information or perform reporting actions at different stages of the test execution.

In summary, hooks in Cucumber offer a way to execute setup and cleanup tasks at specific points in the test lifecycle. They enhance the modularity and maintainability of your test code by allowing you to define actions before and after scenarios, steps, or even based on specific tags.

Now, that we have the WebDriver instance and a Page Object instance setup, let us dive into the Step Definition and understand the link between Feature files and Step Definitions.

Step Definition

In Cucumber, the Step Definition file is like the translator between human-readable scenarios and the computer's language. It holds the instructions for each step mentioned in scenarios written in plain English (Gherkin). This file is where you put the actual code to make things happen, such as opening a web page or entering data. It's like a recipe book where you define how to perform actions based on the steps outlined in the scenarios. This setup not only makes the automation logic reusable and organized but also lets you pass information between steps. So, while Gherkin scenarios describe what the software should do, Step Definition files tell the computer exactly how to do it, ensuring clear communication between the human and the machine.

Kindly open the **LoginPageDefinitions.java** file at **src/test/java/chatper8** location as follows:

```
public class LoginPageDefinitions {


      @Given("User is on HRMLogin page {string}")
      public void loginTest(String url) {
            Hooks.driver.get(url);


      }


      @When("User enters username as {string} and password as {string}")
      public void login(String userName, String passWord) throws Inter-
ruptedException {


            // login to application
            Hooks.loginpage.login(userName, passWord);
```

```
    }

    @Then("User should be able to login successfully and land on home
page")
    public void verifyLogin() {

        // Verify home page
        String homepageURL = Hooks.driver.getCurrentUrl();
        Assert.assertTrue(homepageURL.contains("dashboard"));

    }

    @Then("User should be able to see error message {string}")
    public void verifyError(String errormessagetext) throws Inter-
ruptedException {
        String expectederror = errormessagetext;
        String actualerror = Hooks.loginpage.getErrorMessage();
        Assert.assertEquals(actualerror, expectederror);
    }

}
```

Let's break down the key components:

- **Given - `loginTest` Method**: This method, annotated with `@Given`, represents the initial state where the user is on the HRMLogin page. The URL of the login page is passed as a parameter. The method uses the WebDriver instance from the Hooks class to navigate to the specified URL.
- **When - `login` Method**: The **`@When`** annotated method, named `login`, corresponds to the step where the user enters a username and password. The method uses the Page Object **`Hooks.loginpage`** to perform the login action by calling the `login` method and passing the provided username and password.
- **Then - verifyLogin Method**: The **`@Then`** annotated method, named **`verifyLogin`**, represents the verification step where it checks if the user

has successfully logged in and landed on the home page. It retrieves the current URL using the WebDriver and asserts that it contains the expected URL component ("dashboard").

- **Then - verifyError Method**: Another `@Then` annotated method, named `verifyError`, handles the scenario where the user should see an error message. It compares the expected error message (passed as a parameter) with the actual error message obtained from the Page Object, asserting their equality.
- **Assertion Using TestNG**: Assertions using TestNG's `Assert` class are employed in both verification methods (`verifyLogin` and `verifyError`) to validate expected outcomes against actual results.
- **Integration with Hooks**: This class relies on the Hooks class, which presumably contains the WebDriver instance `driver` and the Page Object `loginpage`. These are used to interact with the web application during the test.

In summary, this Step Definition file contains methods that define the automation logic for Gherkin steps related to login scenarios. It uses TestNG assertions for verification and integrates with the Hooks class to access the WebDriver and Page Object for interacting with the application.

Cool! Now that we have the Feature file, Hooks, and Step Definitions in place, the next question is how do we run it? The answer is a runner class, as explained in the next section.

Runner

In Cucumber, a runner class acts as the starting point for running your Cucumber scenarios. It's like a central hub that connects your feature files with the actual automation code. This class is annotated to let Cucumber know it's the runner, and it holds key configurations. It specifies where to find your feature files and step definitions (the glue code) and can include additional settings, such as plugins for generating reports. The runner class triggers the execution of your Cucumber tests, reading the scenarios, matching them with step definitions, and making sure everything runs smoothly. It's an essential part of setting up and launching your Cucumber tests, making the process organized and efficient.

Kindly open the **Chapter08_CucumberRunnerTest** at **src/test/java/chatper8** location as follows:

```
@CucumberOptions(plugin = { "pretty",
          "html:target/cucumber" }, features =
```

```
"src\\test\\java\\chapter8\\OrangeHRMLogin.feature", glue = "chapter8")
@Test
public class Chapter08_CucumberRunnerTest extends AbstractTestNGCucumber
Tests {
}
```

Now, isn't this short and sweet? Let's understand its contents:

- The **`@CucumberOptions`** annotation is used to provide various configurations for Cucumber.
- **`plugin`** specifies the formatters or plugins to be used during test execution. In this case, it includes both the **`pretty`** and **`html`** plugins. The **`pretty`** plugin generates human-readable console output, while the html plugin generates HTML-based reports. The reports are stored in the **`target/cucumber`** directory.
- **`features`** points to the directory or file where your Gherkin feature files are located. In this example, it specifies the path to the **`OrangeHRMLogin.feature`** file.
- **`glue`** indicates the package where the Cucumber should look for the step definitions (glue code). Here, it is set to **`chapter8`** package.
- The runner class extends **`AbstractTestNGCucumberTests`**, a Cucumber class that integrates Cucumber with TestNG. This is a standard practice when using Cucumber with TestNG.

Now, by running this file as a TestNG test, we can observe that the tests noted in the Feature file are run to explore the combinations of valid and invalid login scenarios.

Oh! Did you notice a strange entry into your console? It appears as follows:

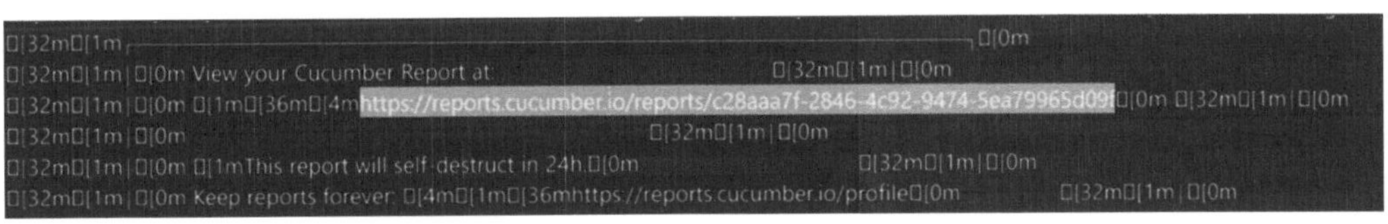

Figure 8.2: *Console log with entry for reports*

Yes, Cucumber can also help us publish reports, as we will explore in the upcoming section.

Cucumber properties file and reports

Cucumber properties files, commonly named `cucumber.properties`, provide a way to configure various settings and parameters for Cucumber test execution.

These files are used to customize the behavior of Cucumber tests and may include settings related to reporting, output formats, parallel execution, or other Cucumber-specific options.

Kindly open the **cucumber.properties** file at **src/test/resources** location as follows:

```
cucumber.publish.enabled = true
cucumber.publish.quiet = true
```

The provided properties in the file suggest configurations related to Cucumber reporting using the Cucumber Publish feature. Let's break down each property:

- **cucumber.publish.enabled = true** : This property indicates whether the Cucumber Publish feature is enabled (**true**) or disabled (**false**). When set to **true**, Cucumber will generate and publish reports using the Cucumber Publish service. Cucumber Publish is a cloud-based service that allows you to store and share your Cucumber test results for collaboration and analysis.
- **cucumber.publish.quiet = true** : This property, when set to **true**, indicates that the Cucumber Publish feature should operate in **quiet** mode. In **quiet** mode, the publishing process is performed with minimal console output or logging. This is useful when you want a more streamlined execution process without extensive logging information.

These settings provide flexibility in tailoring the reporting behavior based on project requirements. So, if we navigate to the URL as per the console logs, we can observe the Cucumber reports as follows:

Figure 8.3: *Online Cucumber report*

The report also displays the details of the cucumber tests as depicted in *Figure* 8.4:

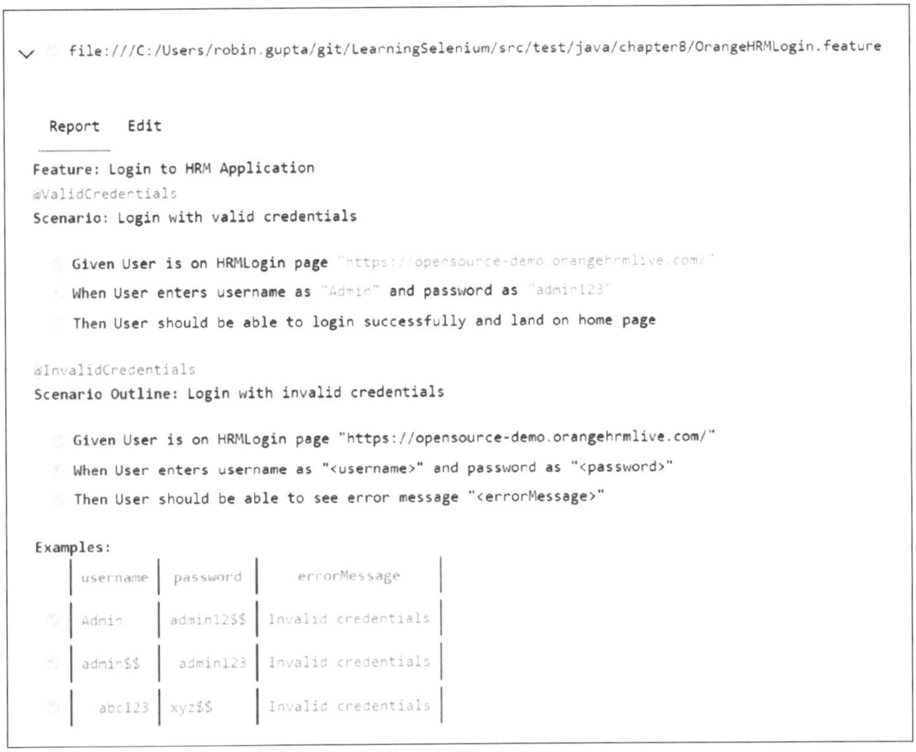

***Figure 8.4:** In-detail online Cucumber report*

Tips for Cucumber

Here are some tips specifically tailored for Cucumber test automation along with simple examples:

- **Use Descriptive Scenario Titles**: Write clear and descriptive titles for your scenarios. This makes it easier to understand the purpose of each scenario. For example:

  ```
  Scenario: User adds a product to the shopping cart
  ```

- **Create Expressive Gherkin Scenarios**: Craft Gherkin scenarios that read like plain English, focusing on user behavior. This enhances collaboration and makes your scenarios more readable. For instance:

  ```
  Given the user is on the product page
  When the user adds a shirt to the shopping cart
  Then the shopping cart should display one item
  ```

- **Organize Step Definitions Using Tags**: Use tags to organize and categorize your step definitions. This helps in managing scenarios and executing specific groups during test runs. For example:

```
@ProductPage
Scenario: User views product details
@Given("the user is on the product page")
public void userIsOnProductPage() {
    // Step definition logic
}
```

- **Reuse Step Definitions with Scenario Outline**: Utilize Scenario Outline to parameterize scenarios and reuse step definitions with different input values. For instance:

```
Scenario Outline: User logs in with valid credentials
  Given the user is on the login page
  When the user enters username "<username>" and password
  "<password>"
  Then the user should be logged in successfully

Examples:
  | username | password |
  | johnDoe   | secret123 |
  | alice     | pass456   |
```

- **Leverage Background for Common Preconditions**: Use the Background keyword to define common preconditions shared across scenarios, reducing redundancy. For example:

```
Background:
  Given the user is on the homepage

Scenario: User navigates to the products page
  When the user clicks on the products link
  Then the products page should be displayed

Scenario: User searches for a product
```

```
  When the user enters "laptop" in the search bar
  Then the search results should be displayed
```

- **Use Regular Expressions for Flexible Step Definitions**: Leverage regular expressions to create flexible step definitions that match a variety of inputs. This allows you to handle dynamic content in your scenarios. For example:

  ```
  #Gherkin
  Scenario: User searches for a product
    When the user enters "<product>" in the search bar
    Then the search results should be displayed
  ```

  This can be implemented with Step Definition as follows:

  ```
  @When("the user enters \"(.*)\" in the search bar")
  public void userEntersProductInSearchBar(String product) {
      // Step definition logic using the dynamic product value
  }
  ```

  Here, the regular expression `\"(.*)\"` captures any text within double quotes, providing flexibility for different product names.

  Using regular expressions in your step definitions allows you to handle various scenarios with a single, adaptable step definition, enhancing the scalability and maintainability of your Cucumber test automation.

These tips aim to improve the readability, maintainability, and efficiency of your Cucumber test automation, making collaboration among team members smoother and test scenarios more expressive.

Conclusion

Imagine Cucumber as the conductor of your software opera. The musical score, written in a Gherkin feature file, lays out the notes and lyrics for each performance. The orchestra, your step definitions, transforms those notes into beautiful music during rehearsals.

Before the grand opera, there are warm-ups and backstage preparations - that's the hooks, setting the stage. The runner is like the conductor's schedule, ensuring each aria and duet unfolds seamlessly.

And the properties file? It's the conductor's notes, deciding if the opera should be recorded, enjoyed quietly, or shared with a wider audience. With Cucumber leading the orchestra, your software opera hits every high note, leaving the audience in awe of the harmonious performance!

BDD allows living documentation in the form of Gherkin scenarios to be automated with frameworks like Cucumber and Selenium. This drives the development of software that meets customer needs and passes acceptance criteria, on time; every time.

Our next chapter is dedicated to new features in Selenium 4. It has a monumental leap in terms of features from Selenium 3, and we will look at some of the glaring ones such as relative locators, Chrome Dev Protocol, Network and Geo-location emulation, and the really big one, adherence to Bidi protocol.

Time to have some water and maybe some real cucumbers to rehydrate and replenish our body and mind.

Exercise

Let's perform a simple exercise to practice the concepts explored earlier in the context of an E-commerce website's checkout flow.

1. Create a Feature file to cover the first scenario of navigating to https://orangeava.com/.
2. The second scenario should be adding a book to the cart.
3. The third scenario should be navigating to the cart page.
4. Write expressive Gherkin scenarios for the outlined tasks above. Ensure they read like plain English and focus on user behavior.
5. Use **`Background`** to avoid duplicate code.
6. Organize your step definitions using tags. For example, tag steps related to the checkout process under the **`@Checkout`** tag.

Run the scenario and observe the result file for details of scenarios that passed or failed from the execution.

CHAPTER 9

New Features in Selenium 4

Introduction

Hey there! Good morning. Oh, do not worry if it's not morning when you are reading this chapter. I wish you a good morning because this chapter is all about the new morning Selenium 4 brings for us, with new core architecture and shiny features. Selenium has come a long way since its beginnings as an internal test tool at ThoughtWorks in 2004. The first major release, Selenium 1, introduced basic web application testing capabilities like navigating to URLs and validating page text. Selenium 2 was a major upgrade, moving to the WebDriver API that gave testers more control over browsers. Selenium 3 focused on keeping pace with changing web technologies like asynchronous JavaScript and headless browsing.

Now, Selenium 4 represents the next evolution with architectural improvements and innovative new features. It builds on learnings and experience from over 15 years of Selenium versions. The major re-architecture aims to deliver better stability, performance, and extensibility. Selenium 4 also introduces highly requested capabilities like relative locators and network emulation to help testers keep up with the trends.

Selenium's journey from its inception in 2004 to the release of Selenium 4 encapsulates a narrative of continuous innovation and adaptation. This evolution reflects Selenium's commitment to aligning with the ever-changing landscape of web application testing, positioning Selenium 4 as a robust, efficient, and versatile tool for modern web development challenges.

Structure

In this chapter, we will discuss the following topics:

- History of Selenium (again)
- Support for BiDi and CDP
- DOM mutation
- Browsing context
- Console logs
- Network interception
- Website performance metrics
- Relative locators
- Geolocation emulation
- Crucial updates

History of Selenium (again)

"Once upon a time, there was an engineer named Jason; who wanted to automate a boring part of his job....". Yes, I know that we have heard this legendary story about the inception of Selenium in our earlier chapters. So, as per the tradition of storytelling; let us briefly revisit the history of Selenium; before we dive into its new features and futuristic aspects.

Jason Huggins kick-started Selenium in 2004 while at ThoughtWorks, building the Core mode as "JavaScriptTestRunner" for the testing of an internal Time and Expenses application. It began as a tool just for their use, but they decided to share it with the world. Paul Hammant joined the team and played a key role in developing what we now know as Selenium Remote Control (RC). Shinya Kasatani in Japan became interested in Selenium and realized that he could wrap the core code into an IDE module in the Firefox browser, and be able to record tests as well as play them back in the same plugin. Lo and behold Selenium IDE is born from this effort.

Fast forward to 2007, and Huggins is now at Google, working with Jennifer Bevan and others to enhance Selenium RC. Around the same time, Simon Stewart, also from ThoughtWorks, was crafting WebDriver, another browser automation tool. In a twist of fate, in 2009, the Selenium and WebDriver teams met and decided to combine their powers, creating Selenium WebDriver, also known as Selenium 2.0.

Meanwhile, Pat Lightbody and Jennifer Bevan contributed towards creating the first version of Selenium Grid. This nifty tool allowed for running multiple Selenium tests at the same time on different machines, speeding up the whole process. This was a game-changer, like what Google was doing internally for Selenium RC.

While working on browser automation for various tools, the Selenium team realized that there should be a standard for web browser automation. This thought culminated in the W3C standard for WebDriver, ensuring consistency across browsers. Fast forward to 2018, Selenium 3.0 was launched which focused on WebDriver API and deprecated RC. Two years later, Selenium 4 Alpha is released with stabler Grid and support for modern web technologies.

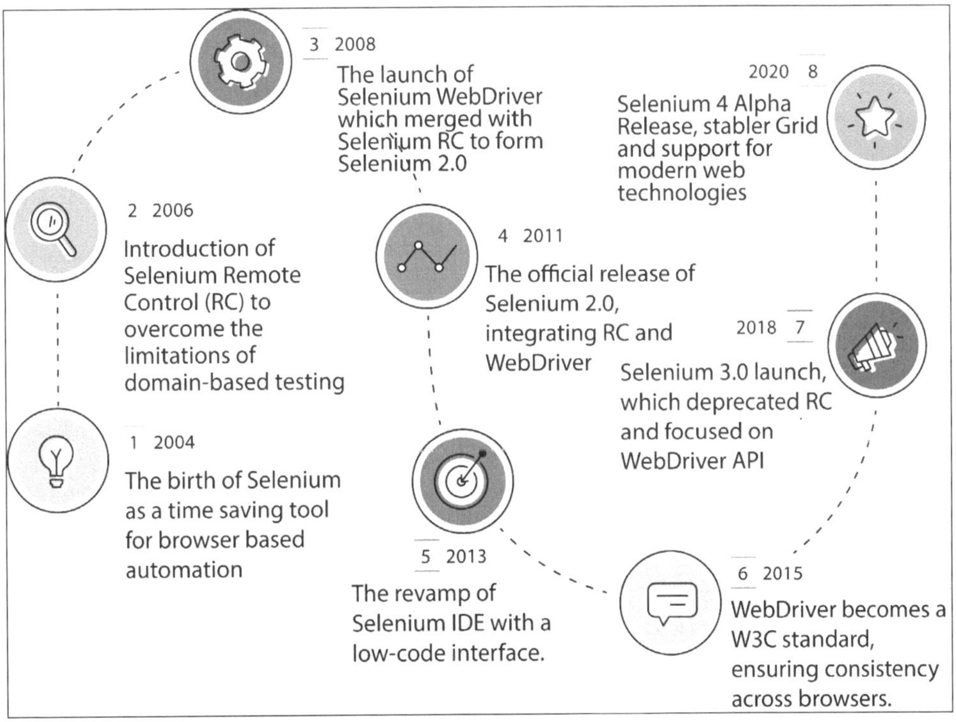

Figure 9.1: *History of Selenium*

Up until Selenium 3, Selenium primarily used JSON wire protocol for most parts of communicating with the Browser drivers. You can think of the JSON wire protocol as a one-way street where your Selenium commands travel to the browser, but the browser cannot talk back. You send commands; the browser executes them, and that is the end of the conversation. It is straightforward, but somewhat limited.

Enter Bidirectional communication (BiDi), the game-changer as part of Selenium 4. Imagine BiDi as a bustling two-way street, where information flows back and forth between your tests and the browser. It's like having a dialogue with the browser, where you can not only send commands but also listen to what's happening inside it, in real-time. This two-way communication opens new possibilities for more responsive and insightful testing. Think of it as calling up your friend on the phone and talking about a task at hand, with a free-flowing conversation back and forth.

BiDi in Selenium 4 brings several advantages that revolutionize web testing. Firstly, it allows for real-time monitoring of browser events, providing an immediate understanding of how a web page behaves in response to different stimuli. This leads to more accurate and efficient debugging. Secondly, BiDi enhances the automation capabilities of Selenium, allowing testers to interact with the browser in more sophisticated ways, such as capturing console logs or network requests. This enables more comprehensive testing scenarios, closely mimicking user interactions and leading to higher-quality web applications. In essence, BiDi empowers testers with deeper insights and control, elevating the overall testing strategy.

And BiDi is not the only advancement in Selenium 4. Selenium IDE, Grid and its UI, WebDriver's monitoring capabilities, Selenium project's documentation and locator strategies underwent major upgrades as well.

Support for BiDi and CDP

Imagine a scenario where a team is assigned to automate tests for a sophisticated SAAS application. At first, everything appears to be going smoothly. However, as they delve deeper, they encounter a unique challenge: during their tests, clicking a button in the application causes new elements to dynamically appear on the page. The issue is that their automation scripts, not anticipating this change, continue to interact with the page as if it were still in its original state, leading to failures.

In an effort to resolve this, the team decided to explore the inner workings of how Selenium interacts with web browsers. Through their investigation, they discovered that older versions of Selenium was using an outdated JSON wire protocol, which only allowed one-way communication. This meant their scripts could send commands to the browser but were unable to receive real-time updates about changes occurring on the page. This revelation was a turning point in addressing the challenges they faced in their test automation process.

Going deeper into the Selenium architecture, we discover BiDirectional (BiDi) protocol, Selenium 4's new bidirectional communication protocol. Instead of just sending commands, our tests can now also register event listeners for browser events using JavaScript callbacks.

In a nutshell, bidirectional communication, often referred to as BiDi, is a breakthrough in Selenium's capabilities. It's like having a two-way conversation with your web browser. You can ask questions (send commands) and listen (receive events) in real-time. This functionality overcomes the limitations of the traditional one-way Selenium commands from older versions.

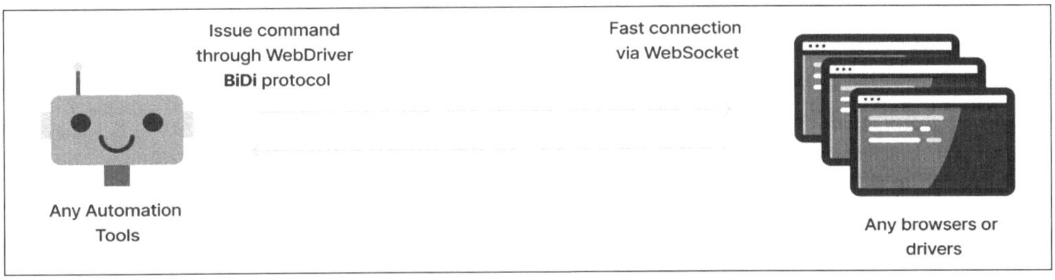

Figure 9.2: *Vision behind WebDriver Bidi*

Note: WebSockets in programming are like a two-way walkie-talkie connection between a web browser and a server. Normally, a web page must ask the server to send new information, which can be slow and inefficient. With WebSockets, once the connection is established, the server and browser can send information to each other directly and instantly.

This is great for real-time applications like online games, chat applications, or live sports updates, where you want to receive new information without constantly asking (or refreshing) the server for it. In essence, WebSockets keep the line of communication open for immediate and continuous data exchange.

The integration of the W3C BiDi protocol is pivotal for Selenium. By leveraging WebSockets, BiDi establishes a bidirectional, efficient line of communication. This allows for the inclusion of the event-driven nature of browsers, exposing granular browser functionality to provide users with extensive control over browser behavior from an automation standpoint. As BiDi gradually integrates the full scope of W3C WebDriver classic APIs, it will no longer be an extension, but the primary implementation method in Selenium. W3C BiDi sets the stage for Selenium's future, where testing is all about adapting to standards, improved performance, and comprehensive browser control.

- Puja Jagani, Open-source contributor at the Selenium Project and Team Lead at Browserstack.

BiDi's introduction to Selenium 4 opens a plethora of possibilities for testing web applications more effectively. Here is a snapshot of what you can do:

- **Checking Browser Console Logs**: Imagine you are testing a web application and want to know what's happening under the hood. With BiDi, you can easily access the browser's console logs, allowing you to understand and assert the behavior of your application during tests.
- **Intercepting and Inspecting Network Requests**: BiDi allows you to act like a traffic controller, observing and even modifying network requests. This can be invaluable for mocking backends or simulating different network conditions.
- **Mutation Observation**: Think of this as a watchdog for your DOM. Previously, you might have needed to continuously poll an element to see if it changes. Now, BiDi lets you observe changes in the DOM and react when they occur, making your tests more efficient and less prone to errors. This ties back to the personal anecdote mentioned earlier.
- **Handling Authentication**: Bypassing authentication prompts becomes smoother with BiDi. You can programmatically provide credentials, streamlining your testing process for sites that require login.

The preceding capabilities might spark a curious question: Who is responsible for building the BiDi protocol?

BiDi protocol is being built as per the World Wide Web Consortium(W3C) WebDriver specification. Now based on the specification, browsers are implementing the WebDriver specification, and the Selenium team is implementing features as per the protocol.

The WebDriver BiDi (Bidirectional) protocol is being developed as a significant upgrade in browser automation, aiming to integrate the best features of the classic WebDriver and Chrome DevTools Protocol (CDP). It facilitates bidirectional communication, enabling faster and more control-intensive operations. The WebDriver BiDi Working Group, part of the W3C, is overseeing its development. This group comprises a diverse group of browser vendors, open-source browser automation projects, and companies offering browser automation solutions. This collaboration ensures a promising future for browser automation.

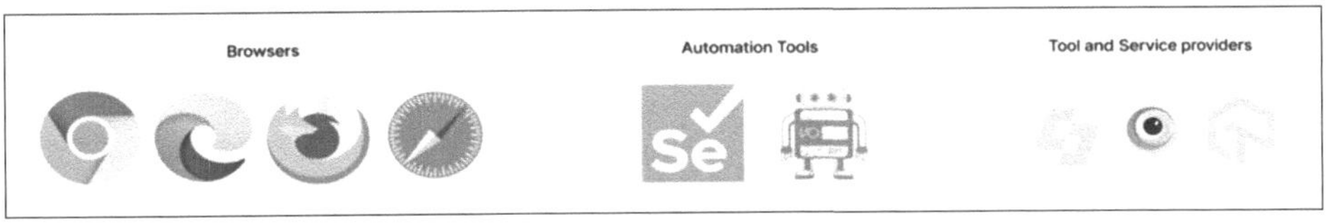

Figure 9.3: *WebDriver BiDi Working Group*

Chrome DevTools Protocol

DevTools are integrated tools in modern browsers that assist developers in debugging web applications and analyzing page performance. They are like a Swiss Army knife for anyone looking to understand and improve how a website behaves. Within Google Chrome's DevTools lies a special communication method known as the Chrome DevTools Protocol (CDP).

It's a set of rules and guidelines that allows Chrome to interact with web applications for tasks like inspecting network activity or manipulating page elements. However, CDP is unique to Chrome and changes with each browser version, making it a bit rigid as per the browser version at times.

The WebDriver BiDirectional Protocol is the next generation of the W3C WebDriver protocol and aims to provide a stable API implemented by all browsers, but it's not yet complete.

Until it is, Selenium provides access to the CDP for those browsers that implement it (such as Google Chrome, Microsoft Edge, and Firefox), allowing you to enhance your tests in interesting ways.

There are primarily three ways to interact with Chrome DevTools through Selenium:

- **Using the CDP Endpoint**: This method is straightforward but limited. It's suitable for simple tasks, such as modifying browser settings or retrieving basic information. However, it requires familiarity with specific command strings, which can be complex.
- **Employing the CDP API:** This approach is an upgrade from using the endpoint directly. It allows for asynchronous operations and provides a more user-friendly way to access Chrome's DevTools functionalities. While this method offers more control than the CDP Endpoint, it is still a temporary solution within Selenium.
- **Opting for the BiDi API:** This is the most future-proof method. The BiDi API abstracts away the complexities of CDP and is designed to be compatible with the upcoming WebDriver-BiDi. This makes it the most recommended approach for long-term projects.

Here are some of the use cases for CDP:

- Setting geolocation for location-aware testing
- Capturing performance metrics like page load timings
- Intercepting and mocking network calls
- Overriding device display parameters like user-agent string

The Chrome DevTools Protocol (CDP) provides a powerful way for Selenium to interact with web browsers, offering advanced capabilities for testing. However, understanding its nuances and the different ways to access it through Selenium is crucial for effective utilization. While some features might have limitations, CDP remains a valuable tool in the arsenal of web testers and developers.

Note: While CDP opens up a range of possibilities for testing, some of its uses have practical limitations. For example, emulating geolocation might not always yield accurate results, as many websites use IP addresses to determine location. Similarly, trying to emulate mobile devices can be more effectively achieved through Chrome's built-in options for mobile emulation, rather than using CDP.

In the following sections, we will explore some of these additional capabilities enabled by the newer versions of Selenium, utilizing modern web protocols, Bidi and CDP.

DOM mutation

A common difficulty with modern web apps is that the document object model (DOM) frequently updates in the background, causing automation scripts to get out of sync.

As web applications continue to evolve and add sophisticated capabilities, test automation challenges grow proportionally. Modern front-end frameworks rely heavily on dynamic JavaScript to update page content asynchronously, without full page reloads. Such single-page applications break traditional website testing approaches.

Mutation observation in Selenium 4 allows for monitoring such changes in the Document Object Model (DOM) of a web page. Previously, one would repeatedly query the DOM to detect changes, which were inefficient. Selenium 4 introduces a more dynamic approach using BiDi.

To consider the hands-on code example for observing DOM mutations, kindly open https://ava-orange-education.github.io/Ultimate-Selenium-WebDriver-for-Test-Automation/docs/Chapter3_Waits.html from *Chapter* 3 in the browser and click on the **`Wait 1 second to get an input box`** button. This is a simple example of DOM mutation, where a user input causes the DOM to change on the fly.

Now open the DOM mutation observation code in the **`Chapter09_DOMMutationObserver.java`** class at **`src/test/java/chapter9`** location as follows and run it:

```
public class Chapter09_DOMMutationObserver {
	public static void main(String[] args) throws Exception {
		WebDriver driver = new ChromeDriver();
		WebDriverWait wait = new WebDriverWait(driver, Duration.
ofSeconds(10));
	driver.get("https://ava-orange-education.github.io/Ultimate-Sele-
nium-WebDriver-for-Test-Automation/docs/Chapter3_Waits.html");
		CopyOnWriteArrayList<WebElement> mutations = new
CopyOnWriteArrayList<>();
		((HasLogEvents) driver).onLogEvent(domMutation(e ->
mutations.add(e.getElement())));
		driver.findElement(By.id("implicitbutton")).click();
		wait.until(_d -> !mutations.isEmpty());
		System.out.println("Number of DOM mutations observed is " +
mutations.size());
		driver.quit();
	}


}
```

The WebDriver instance enables log event handling via the **`HasLogEvents`** interface. We register a mutation observer callback via **`onLogEvent(domMutation(...)).`** This callback will fire whenever a DOM mutation occurs and add the changed element to the mutations list. When we click the button with ID **`implicitbutton`**, it dynamically adds new elements to the page asynchronously. But our preceding mutation observer detects these new elements being added and stores them in the list. We wait until at least one mutation is observed before proceeding, indicating the async DOM update is finished. Finally, we print out the number of detected DOM changes to confirm the mutation callback worked as expected. In essence, the mutation observer acts as an automated synchronization point for dynamic page updates. This prevents fragile, broken tests that assume static content.

Note: A callback in programming is like giving someone a phone number to call you back when they're done with a task. In the world of coding, a callback is a function you provide as an argument to another function. After the second function completes its task, it 'calls back' by executing your function. This is especially useful in asynchronous operations, like when you're waiting for a file to download or a database query to complete. Instead of sitting and waiting, you can proceed with other tasks, and the callback function gets activated once the operation is complete, allowing you to handle the result or next steps.

Browsing Context

A browsing context is an environment in which a browser displays a document. In modern browsers, it usually is a tab but can be a window or even only parts of a page, like a frame or an iframe. Each browsing context has an origin (that of the active document) and an ordered history of previously displayed documents.

Imagine you are using a web browser and you have multiple tabs open. Each tab represents a separate browsing context. Let's say in one tab, you are logged into a social media site, and in another tab, you are reading a news article.

These two tabs (browsing contexts) are independent of each other. Actions you perform in one tab (like scrolling through your social media feed) do not affect what happens in the other tab (the news article remains static). Each tab has its own document (webpage), history, and session. Our use case is to automate the test for the live posting of items from the news site to the social media site. In this case, we can use browsing contexts to open two sessions and automate the end-to-end test at hand.

However, the preceding use case is an artificial example and can be solved by other means as well. Browsingcontexts can be instrumental in isolating browser sessions.

Kindly open the **`Chapter09_BrowsingContextTest.java`** class at **`src/test/java/chapter9`** location as follows, for the hands-on practice:

```
public class Chapter09_BrowsingContextTest {

      public static void main(String[] args) {
            FirefoxOptions options = new FirefoxOptions();
```

```
            // Note here that we set the WebSocket capability as true
            options.setCapability("webSocketUrl", true);
            WebDriver driver = new FirefoxDriver(options);
            String id = driver.getWindowHandle();
            // Creating a new browsing context
            BrowsingContext browsingContext = new BrowsingContext(driver,
            id);
            System.out.println("ID for the browsing context is " +
browsingContext.getId());
            // Create a new tab using BrowsingContext
            BrowsingContext tabBrowsingContext = new BrowsingContext
(driver, WindowType.TAB);
            System.out.println("ID for the new tab is " + tabBrowsing-
Context.getId());
      }
```

In the provided Java code, the process begins by configuring a Firefox browser for automation using Selenium WebDriver. It initiates by setting up **FirefoxOptions** and enabling a specific capability **webSocketUrl** essential for BiDirectional interactions. Subsequently, a **FirefoxDriver** is instantiated with these options, representing the automated browser. The code then retrieves the identifier of the current browser window, known as the window handle. Utilizing this, identifier creates a **BrowsingContext** for the current window. Additionally, it demonstrates how to open a new tab by creating another **BrowsingContext** with a specific parameter indicating a tab. Finally, the code prints the identifiers of both the original and new tab browsing contexts, showcasing how to manage and reference multiple browser tabs programmatically in Selenium, a key aspect of automated web testing that involves multi-browser interactions.

Console logs

Capturing console logs and errors in web applications is an essential aspect of debugging and quality assurance. Selenium 4 provides advanced capabilities to capture these logs efficiently. This feature is particularly useful in identifying JavaScript errors, network issues, and other browser-related events that occur during the execution of automated tests.

Consider an e-commerce web application that occasionally fails to load product details. This intermittent issue is difficult to replicate manually. By utilizing Selenium 4 to capture console logs, testers can automate the browsing process and gather logs at moments of failure. These logs might reveal JavaScript errors or network issues that occur only under certain conditions, which manual testing might miss. This ability to capture and analyze console outputs enables a more targeted approach to debugging, leading to quicker resolutions of such elusive issues.

First, let us explore a sample HTML file, which can help us simulate the console errors and logs. Navigate to the URL https://ava-orange-education.github.io/Ultimate-Selenium-WebDriver-for-Test-Automation/docs/Chapter9_ConsoleLogs.html, and open the Chrome developer console. Now press the **`Click me for generating a console log`** button and the **`Click me for generating a console error`** button. This would lead to the console logs as follows:

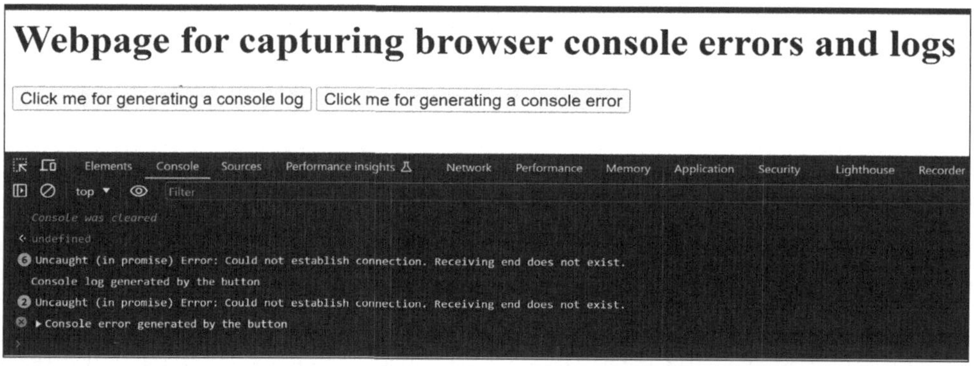

Figure 9.4: *Console log examples*

Now kindly open and run the hands-on example of **`Chapter09_ConsoleLogTest.java`** class at **`src/test/java/chapter9`** location as follows:

```
public class Chapter09_ConsoleLogTest {


      public static void main(String[] args) throws InterruptedException,
ExecutionException, TimeoutException {
            WebDriver driver = new ChromeDriver();
      driver.get("https://ava-orange-education.github.io/Ultimate-
Selenium-WebDriver-for-Test-Automation/docs/Chapter9_ConsoleLogs.html");
            driver.findElement(By.id("consoleLog")).click();
            driver.findElement(By.id("consoleError")).click();
            LogEntries logEntries = driver.manage().logs().get("browser");
```

```
            for (org.openqa.selenium.logging.LogEntry entry : logEntries)
{
                        System.out.println(new Date(entry.getTimestamp()) +
“ “ + entry.getLevel() + “ “ + entry.getMessage());
                        String errorLogType = entry.getLevel().toString();
                        String errorLog = entry.getMessage().toString();
                        System.out.println(“Error LogType: “ + errorLogType
+ “ Error Log message: “ + errorLog);


            }driver.quit();
    }}
```

The Java program utilizes Selenium WebDriver to capture and analyze console logs from a web page. It starts by initializing a Chrome browser session and navigates to a specified URL. **`driver.manage().logs().get(“browser”)`** retrieves all the console logs from the browser's console. The program then simulates user interactions by clicking on elements identified by specific IDs, likely triggering console logs and errors on the webpage. The **`for`** loop iterates through each `LogEntry` object in logEntries.

For every entry, the program extracts and prints the timestamp, severity level, and the log message to the console. Additionally, it categorizes and prints the severity and content of each log, providing detailed insight into the browser's console activity, which is invaluable for debugging purposes.

When we run the preceding example, we can observe that the logs like the Chrome developer console are printed in the IDE's console as follows:

```
Wed Feb 07 12:52:12 IST 2024 WARNING security - Error with Permissions-Policy header: Origin trial controlled feature no
Error LogType: WARNING Error Log message: security - Error with Permissions-Policy header: Origin trial controlled feature
Wed Feb 07 12:52:12 IST 2024 SEVERE chrome-extension://invalid/ - Failed to load resource: net::ERR_FAILED
Error LogType: SEVERE Error Log message: chrome-extension://invalid/ - Failed to load resource: net::ERR_FAILED
Wed Feb 07 12:52:12 IST 2024 SEVERE https://ava-orange-education.github.io/Ultimate-Selenium-WebDriver-for-Test-Aut
Error LogType: SEVERE Error Log message: https://ava-orange-education.github.io/Ultimate-Selenium-WebDriver-for-Test-
```

Figure 9.5: *Console logs recorded by Selenium*

Capturing console logs and errors using Selenium 4 offers a deeper understanding of the web applications under test. It enables testers to go beyond surface-level testing and dive into the underlying causes of UI malfunctions, JavaScript errors, and other critical issues. This feature is not just a debugging aid but a powerful enhancement to the overall quality assurance strategy, ensuring more stable and reliable web applications.

Network Interception

In modern web development, analyzing network responses is key to understanding how web applications communicate with servers. As more and more applications migrate to a service-oriented architecture, Selenium 4 introduces advanced capabilities to capture these network communications directly within automated tests.

This feature is invaluable for debugging API calls, inspecting returned data, and ensuring that web applications interact correctly with backend services.

For instance, consider an e-commerce website where users occasionally face issues during checkout. By using Selenium 4 to capture network responses, testers can automate the checkout process and closely monitor the interactions between the web application and its servers, or third-party payment servers. This approach can help in pinpointing issues like failed API calls or unexpected server responses that occur during the transaction process, which might not be evident through front-end testing alone.

This enhanced capability provided by Selenium 4 is particularly useful in scenarios where understanding the back-and-forth of network requests and responses is key to ensuring the functionality and reliability of web applications.

Kindly open and run the **`Chapter09_CaptureResponseTest.java`** class at the **`src/test/java/chapter9`** location as follows:

```
public class Chapter09_CaptureResponseTest {
      public static void main(String[] args) {
            WebDriver driver = new ChromeDriver();
            DevTools devTools = ((ChromeDriver) driver).getDevTools();
            devTools.createSession();
            // Kindly ensure that the Devtools version for the imports
are as per your
            // browser version, to correctly use Network libraries
            devTools.send(Network.enable(Optional.empty(), Optional.
empty(), Optional.empty()));
            devTools.addListener(Network.responseReceived(), response
Receieved -> {
                  System.out.println("Response Url => " + response
Receieved.getResponse().getUrl());
                  System.out.println("Response Status => " + response
```

```
Receieved.getResponse().getStatus());
                    System.out.println("Response Headers => " + response
Receieved.getResponse().getHeaders().toString());
                    System.out.println("Response MIME Type => " +
responseReceieved.getResponse().getMimeType().toString());
                    System.out.print-
ln("------------------------------------------------------");
            });

            driver.get("http://google.com");
            driver.close();
      }
}
```

In the provided Java code, Selenium WebDriver is used in conjunction with Chrome's `DevTools` to capture network responses. The code initializes a `ChromeDriver` and creates a `DevTools` session. It then enables network monitoring using the `Network.enable` method. The key aspect is the lambda function passed to `devTools.addListener`, which is triggered on each network response. This function extracts and prints details such as the URL, status, headers, and MIME type of each response. This setup is particularly effective for monitoring and analyzing the network interactions of the webpage navigated to, in this case, "http://google.com".

The use of the lambda function here simplifies the process of defining a response handler, leading to cleaner and more readable code. This script is particularly useful for examining the network traffic generated by web applications, offering insights into server-client interactions.

Note: **`Network.enable()`** method is provided by import org.openqa.selenium.devtools.v115.network.Network, therefore, kindly update the import's version based on your browser and chromedriver version.

If you are unsure of terms, such as Headers and MIME Type, don't worry as we have got you covered:

- **URL (Uniform Resource Locator):** It's like an address for a location on the internet. Just as you need an address to visit someone's house, you need a URL to visit a specific webpage.

- **Status:** This is like a response code from a website. It tells you if your request to visit the webpage was successful if there was an error, or if the page was moved somewhere else.
- **Headers:** These are like the additional information or instructions that come with a webpage. They can tell your browser how to display the content or provide other details, like when the page was last updated.
- **MIME Type (Multipurpose Internet Mail Extensions type):** This is a way to label the kind of content a file contains. It helps your browser understand how to process and display the file, whether it's an image, a video, a PDF, or a webpage.

Capturing network responses in Selenium 4 is a powerful tool for web application testing. It allows testers and developers to gain deep insights into how web applications interact with servers and helps in identifying potential issues in data transfer or API integrations. This level of detail is crucial for thorough testing and efficient debugging of complex web applications.

Website Performance Metrics

With the advent of high-speed internet and instant gratification, the performance of a website is a critical factor for user satisfaction and business success. Measuring website performance metrics has become an essential part of web development and testing. Selenium 4 offers native features to capture these metrics, aiding in the assessment of various aspects like load time, responsiveness, and resource usage.

Here are some of the key website performance metrics we can capture using Selenium 4's capabilities:

- **Time to First Byte (TTFB):** TTFB measures the time from the start of the page load to when the first piece of data is received from the server. It's crucial to understand the server's responsiveness. A long TTFB indicates server delays, possibly due to slow server processing or network issues.
- **First Contentful Paint (FCP):** FCP marks the time at which the first text or image is painted on the screen during page load. It's a key metric for user perception, as it indicates when content starts becoming visible to the user.
- **Largest Contentful Paint (LCP):** LCP measures the time taken for the largest content element on the page (like an image or text block) to fully render. This metric is a good indicator of perceived loading experience since the largest elements often catch the user's attention.

- **First Input Delay (FID):** FID quantifies the time from when a user first interacts with a page (like clicking a link) to the time when the browser is able to respond to that interaction. It helps in understanding the real-world interactivity of a page.
- **Time to Interactive (TTI):** TTI is the time it takes for a page to become fully interactive. This includes elements being displayed and the page responding to user interactions without noticeable delay. It's critical for understanding the usability of a page.
- **Total Blocking Time (TBT):** TBT measures the total amount of time between FCP and TTI where the main thread was blocked, preventing user input. High TBT values can mean a frustrating experience for users, as the page appears loaded but isn't responsive.
- **Cumulative Layout Shift (CLS):** CLS quantifies the sum of all individual layout shift scores for every unexpected layout shift that occurs during the entire lifespan of the page. It's used to measure the visual stability of a page, with high CLS indicating a high chance of content shifting while the page is being viewed.

Kindly open and run the **`Chapter09_DevToolsPerformanceTest.java`** class at the **`src/test/java/chapter9`** location as follows:

```
public class Chapter09_DevToolsPerformanceTest {
      public static void main(String[] args) {
            ChromeDriver driver = new ChromeDriver();
            DevTools devTools = driver.getDevTools();
            devTools.createSession();
            devTools.send(Performance.enable(Optional.empty()));
            driver.get("https://www.google.org");
            List<Metric> metrics = devTools.send(Performance.
getMetrics());
            List<String> metricNames = metrics.stream().map(o ->
o.getName()).collect(Collectors.toList());
            devTools.send(Performance.disable());
            List<String> metricsToCheck = Arrays.asList("Timestamp",
"Documents", "Frames", "JSEventListeners",
                        "LayoutObjects", "MediaKeySessions", "Nodes",
"Resources", "DomContentLoaded", "NavigationStart");
            metricsToCheck.forEach(
```

```
                        metric -> System.out.println(metric + " is :
" + metrics.get(metricNames.indexOf(metric)).getValue()));
            driver.close();
    }
}
```

This code is getting performance data about a webpage load using Chrome developer tools. Specifically, it wants to know how long it takes for the DOM content to completely load. When you first open a webpage, the browser does a lot of work behind the scenes. It must make network requests to fetch all resources like HTML, CSS, JavaScript, etc. Then it must construct the DOM tree and render the page visually.

We want to measure how long just the DOM construction takes. Because that tells us when the main content has loaded and is visible to the user. So first the code opens up a special developer tools connection to Chrome using Selenium. This allows accessing performance data that is usually only visible in the Chrome dev console. When we load a new page now, Chrome will track various metrics under the hood automatically. Things like:

- Timestamp when page load started
- When DOM finished building
- Number of CSS resources loaded
- Count of JS event listeners, etc.

The code uses Java's Stream API to transform the metrics list into **`metricNames`**. The **`map()`** function, with a lambda expression **`o -> o.getName()`**, extracts the name of each metric. After the page finishes loading, the code retrieves all those performance metrics that were tracked in the background into a list. It specifically looks for the `DomContentLoaded` entry. This is a timestamp metric that tells us exactly when the DOM was fully constructed. A list of desired metrics **`metricsToCheck`** is defined, including `DomContentLoaded`. The code iterates over **`metricsToCheck`** using **`forEach`**, another lambda function. For each metric, it prints the name and value.

The value of each metric is retrieved using `metrics.get(metricNames.indexOf(metric)).getValue()`.

This gets the index of the metric from **`metricNames`** and then uses it to fetch the corresponding metric value from metrics. Finally, we print out this timestamp to see how long the DOM took to load. By monitoring this number across test runs, we can catch any regressions in page load efficiency. So in essence, it allows the use of built-in Chrome tools to extract key webpage performance data in our automated tests.

Note: Selenium is not generally recommended for deep performance analysis of web applications. We should augment tools like JMeter with Selenium to complete performance analysis of web applications.

Relative locators

Selenium 4 introduces relative locators, an innovative feature for locating web elements based on their spatial relationship to other elements. These locators provide a more intuitive approach to element identification, mimicking how humans visually interact with web pages.

Traditionally, locators like CSS Selector, XPath, ID, etc., have been used to interact with various web elements such as radio buttons, text boxes, and drop-downs. However, these methods sometimes fall short in dynamic web environments where elements' positions are not fixed but their spatial relationships remain consistent. Selenium 4 addresses this gap by introducing Relative Locators, which allow locating elements based on their visual position relative to other elements in the Document Object Model (DOM)

Selenium 4's relative locator methods are designed to identify elements based on their spatial relationship to a specified element, including:

- **above**: Finds elements located above a fixed element.
- **below:** Identifies elements located below a fixed element.
- **toLeftOf**: Locates elements to the left of a fixed element.
- **toRightOf**: Identifies elements to the right of a fixed element.
- **near:** Finds elements within 50 pixels of a specified element.

Some of the practical examples of using relative locators could be:

Checking for the position of elements: A typical use case involves regression testing for an icon or button's relative location with regard to another web element on the screen. For instance, locating a cart icon to the right of a search icon in the following screenshot from an e-commerce website. This could be achieved using the withTagName method along with the toRightOf locator.

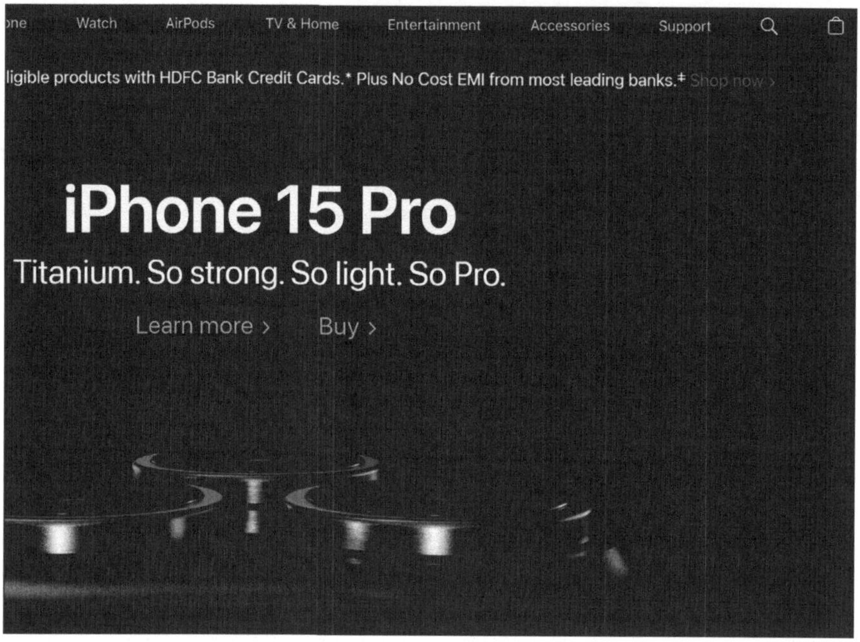

***Figure 9.6**: Sample image of e-commerce website: https://www.apple.com/.*

Stable locators by chaining multiple locators: Another scenario is retrieving specific text located above a button and to the right of a checkbox. For example, we can craft a stable locator for the Shop Now link in *Figure* 9.6, by chaining "`above`" and "`toRightof`" locators with respect to the text "iPhone 15 Pro".

These methods work by leveraging a JavaScript method called **`getBoundingClientRect`**, which helps in calculating the relative positions of elements.

Selenium 4's relative locators are versatile and can accept either `WebElement` or `By` locator as an argument. This flexibility aids in creating robust test scripts for automated cross-browser testing.

Let us deepen our understanding of the relative locators with some hands-on examples. Kindly open and run the **`Chapter09_RelativeLocatorsTest.java`** class at **`src/test/java/chapter9`** location as follows:

```
public class Chapter09_RelativeLocatorsTest extends BaseTest {
      @Test
      public void relativeLocatorTest() {
            driver.get("https://www.apple.com/in/");
```

```
            // Using relative locator to find a webelement for scenarios
like regression testing
            By carticonlocator = RelativeLocator.with(By.id("globalnav
-bag"))
                        .toRightOf(By.xpath("//li[@data-topnav-flyout
-label='Search apple.com']"));
            WebElement carticon = driver.findElement(carticonlocator);
            Assert.assertTrue(carticon.isDisplayed());
      }
      @Test
      public void chainingLocatorTest() {
            driver.get("https://www.apple.com/in/");
            // Chaining relative locators to create a stable locator


            By searchiconlocator = RelativeLocator.with(By.xpath("//*[@
data-topnav-flyout-label='Search apple.com']"))
                        .toRightOf(By.xpath("//a[@aria-
label='Support']//span[@class='globalnav-link-text-container']"));
            WebElement carticon = driver.findElement(searchiconlocator);
            Assert.assertTrue(carticon.isDisplayed());
      }


}
```

In this Java code using Selenium 4, two tests are implemented to demonstrate the use of relative locators. The first test, **`relativeLocatorTest`**, navigates to the Apple India website and utilizes a relative locator to find the shopping cart icon. This is achieved by locating the icon to the right of the Search element, identified by its XPath. The second test, **`chainingLocatorTest`**, also navigates to the same website and showcases the chaining of relative locators. It aims to identify the search icon by placing it to the right of the Support link, again using XPath for identification. In both cases, the presence of the located elements is asserted to ensure they are displayed, exemplifying the practical application of relative locators in scenarios like regression testing, where stability and precision in element location are crucial.

In the dynamic world of web automation, the introduction of Relative Locators in Selenium 4 is a game-changer, especially across diverse sectors like e-commerce, CRM, banking, and healthcare.

In e-commerce, for example, locating a product's **`'Add to Cart'`** button relative to its image or description can streamline testing despite frequent layout changes. For CRM systems, finding a **`'Submit'`** button next to a dynamically positioned form field becomes simpler. In banking applications, identifying security alert messages above transaction fields enhances test reliability. Likewise, in healthcare web applications, accurately locating patient data input fields relative to labels or icons, regardless of interface updates, ensures consistent functionality and user experience.

These examples illustrate how Selenium 4's Relative Locators significantly enhance the adaptability and efficiency of test scripts, reflecting a major advancement in web testing tools, tailored to the varied and evolving needs of different industry web applications.

Geolocation Emulation

Geolocation testing holds high importance in today's diverse digital environment. Many applications, including e-commerce platforms offering location-specific deals, weather apps providing localized forecasts, and travel apps with regional insights, rely heavily on geolocation data. Selenium 4, recognizing this need, introduces robust support for emulating geolocation, enabling developers and testers to simulate various geographic locations. This feature is crucial for verifying that geolocation-dependent functionalities perform flawlessly across different regions.

Emulating geolocation in Selenium 4 is beneficial for:

- E-commerce websites to test location-based product recommendations.
- Weather applications to verify local weather updates for different regions.
- Travel applications to ensure accurate navigation and local service offerings.
- Testing social media platforms' location-tagging features.

Kindly open and run the Chapter09_GeolocationTest.java class at **`src/test/java/chapter9`** location, as follows, to gain hands-on experience with Geolocation tests:

```
public class Chapter09_GeolocationTest {
      @Test
      public void locationSettingTest() {
            WebDriver driver = new ChromeDriver();
            DevTools devTools = ((ChromeDriver) driver).getDevTools();
            devTools.createSession();
            Map<String, Object> coordinates = new HashMap<>();
            coordinates.put("latitude", 48.858093);
            coordinates.put("longitude", 2.2945);
            coordinates.put("accuracy", 100);
            ((ChromeDriver)
driver).executeCdpCommand("Emulation.setGeolocationOverride", coordinates);
            driver.get("https://whatmylocation.com/");
            WebElement shareablelocation =
driver.findElement(By.id("latitude"));
      Assert.assertTrue(shareablelocation.getText().contains("48.858093"));
            driver.close();
      }
}
```

In the provided Java code, the method **`locationSettingTest`** demonstrates how to emulate a specific geographical location in a Selenium test using the Chrome DevTools Protocol (CDP) command. After initializing a **`ChromeDriver`** instance and creating a **`DevTools`** session, a HashMap named coordinates is created and populated with specific latitude, longitude, and accuracy values representing a location. The key line **`driver.executeCdpCommand("Emulation.setGeolocationOverride", coordinates)`** sends a command to the browser to override its default geolocation settings with the specified coordinates. This functionality is used to test how a website, in this case, "https://whatmylocation.com/", responds to the emulated location. The code then verifies if the website correctly reflects the latitude value set through geolocation emulation, demonstrating the effective simulation of a user's physical location.

Note: Many sites use the IP address to determine physical location, so setting an emulated geolocation might not have the desired effect.

Crucial updates

Selenium 4 marks a significant milestone in the evolution of web automation, bringing forth a host of new features and improvements. However, with these advancements, some APIs have been deprecated or modified to align with modern testing needs and enhance the framework's efficiency. Understanding these changes is crucial for developers and testers to smoothly transition from Selenium 3 to Selenium 4.

- **Deprecation of Desired Capabilities**: Selenium 4 marks the deprecation of the **`DesiredCapabilities`** class. Previously used extensively with **`RemoteWebDriver`**, this class is now replaced with browser-specific **`Options`** objects like **`ChromeOptions`**, **`FirefoxOptions`**, **`InternetExplorerOptions`**, **`SafariOptions`**, and **`EdgeOptions`**. These options are used to set browser capabilities and are passed directly to the Driver constructor.
- **Changes in the Actions Class:** The `Actions` class, which facilitates complex user gestures like mouse movements and keyboard actions, has been enhanced with new methods. These include **`click(WebElement)`**, **`clickAndHold(WebElement)`**, **`contextClick(WebElement)`**, **`doubleClick(WebElement)`**, and **`release()`**. These methods simplify and streamline the process of emulating user actions on web elements.
- **Modifications to the FluentWait Class:** The **`FluentWait`** class has undergone changes in Selenium 4. The **`withTimeout()`** and **`pollingEvery()`** methods now accept a single **`java.time.Duration`** parameter, replacing the previous two-parameter approach (integer and TimeUnit). This change leads to a more straightforward and flexible implementation of wait functionality.
- **Driver Constructors' Modifications:** Driver constructors that previously accepted **`Capabilities`** objects have been deprecated in favor of those accepting `Options`. This change necessitates the creation of specific Options `objects` for each driver class and passing these objects to the driver constructor. This modification applies to **`ChromeDriver`**, **`FirefoxDriver`**, **`EdgeDriver`**, **`SafariDriver`**, and **`InternetExplorerDriver`**.
- **Deprecation of FindsBy Interfaces:** The **`FindsBy`** interfaces, part of the **`org.openqa.selenium.internal`** package, are deprecated in Selenium 4. This change, though internal, is significant for those developing tools or products on top of Selenium APIs. However, the standard **`findElement(By)`** and **`findElements(By)`** methods continue to be available for end users.

The deprecations and changes introduced in Selenium 4 reflect a commitment to streamlining and modernizing the Selenium framework, over a decade of concentrated focus. These updates are designed to improve the overall efficiency and adaptability of the tool, making it more aligned with the current trends and needs of web automation. For developers and testers, understanding these changes is crucial for leveraging the full potential of Selenium 4 in their automation projects.

In addition to the above; Selenium IDE, Grid and its UI, WebDriver's monitoring capabilities and the project's documentation underwent major upgrades; thanks to the open-source contributors across the world.

Conclusion

As we conclude this chapter on Selenium 4, we reflect on the significant strides made in web automation. Selenium 4 marks a pivotal evolution in the Selenium journey, introducing remarkable features and architectural improvements that cater to the modern demands of web application testing. This version is not just an update; it's a testament to Selenium's commitment to innovation and adaptability in the fast-paced world of web development.

The introduction of features like Bidirectional communication (BiDi), Chrome DevTools Protocol (CDP), enhanced network interception, and relative locators, among others, underscores Selenium 4's focus on providing a more responsive, insightful, and intuitive testing experience.

These capabilities bridge the gap between traditional automation limitations and the complexities of modern web applications, offering testers more control and efficiency.

Moreover, Selenium 4's support for emulating geolocation and capturing website performance metrics adds layers of versatility, enabling testers to simulate a wide range of user scenarios and interactions. This aligns Selenium more closely with real-world web browsing experiences, ensuring that web applications are robust, efficient, and user-friendly.

As Selenium continues to evolve, it remains a critical tool for testers and developers, adapting to changing technologies and user expectations. In summary, Selenium 4 is not just an upgrade; it is a leap towards more sophisticated, reliable, and user-centric web application testing. The future of Selenium looks promising, with a continued focus on innovation and excellence in web automation.

Next up, we are diving into the thrilling world of Test Maintenance, Data-Driven, and Keyword-Driven frameworks. Think of it as a grand adventure where each framework is a weapon in your arsenal, empowering you to conquer the universe of web testing!

But wait, there is more! We are not just stopping at web testing. We will extend our superpowers to emails and Excel, making sure that no stone is unturned. We will be casting spells over emails and spreadsheets, automating checks, balances, and tasks beyond the browser.

For the grand finale, we will explore how Test Automation can team up with Artificial Intelligence (AI), creating a dynamic duo like Batman and Robin!

Exercise

For this chapter's exercise, we will automate an end-to-end scenario, while covering multiple concepts as follows:

1. Set the coordinates for ChromeDriver to Latitude as 20.593683, and Longitude as 78.962883.
2. Set up the Browsing context for a new window and navigate to https://orangeava.com/products/ultimate-chatgpt-handbook-for-enterprises.
3. Use the concept of relative locators to click on the `ADD TO CART` button above the `Buy with PayPal` button.
4. Create a DOM Mutation observer as per the code in this chapter and note the changes in DOM due to the action performed in the preceding step.
5. Intercept the network traffic and write it to a text file.
6. Record the website performance for each page navigation, as per the code provided in this chapter.
7. Record all console logs throughout the preceding test and write them to a text file.

CHAPTER 10
Conclusion

Introduction

We started this journey together back in *Chapter 1: Introduction to Selenium Test Automation*, just you and me, like two strangers standing at a trailhead pointing off into the woods. From mastering locators to maneuvering through complex AJAX calls, we've covered a lot of ground when it comes to using Selenium for test automation. Now here we stand, at the end of the trail, looking out over the valley we've traversed. Take a moment to soak it all in. Enjoy that feeling of accomplishment, like a cool breeze after a long hike. Let it recharge you.

But just because we've finished this trail doesn't mean the adventure is over! Far from it. Think of this last chapter as a cozy basecamp from which exciting new trails branch out to explore topics like test maintenance best practices, calculating that ever-important automation ROI, pushing the proverbial envelope with cool stuff like Excel automation, more robust frameworks like data-driven and keyword-driven approaches, and blue-sky musings over what the wizards at Selenium HQ might cook up for us in future versions.

So set down your pack for a bit and grab a cup of trail mix. This chapter awaits as our journey continues, my friend! No need to go it alone – We'll be blazing those Selenium trails together, conquering each step as a team. Onward and upward!

Structure

In this chapter, we will discuss the following topics:

- Test Maintenance
- ROI for Test Automation
- Extending Selenium with Excel
- Data-driven frameworks

- Keyword-driven frameworks
- Hybrid Frameworks
- Roadmap for Selenium

Test Maintenance

As we turn the final pages of our journey through Selenium Test Automation, let's pause for a moment. Picture this: you've been diligently building and refining your test suites, akin to a gardener perfecting a landscape. But as with any great art, the beauty lies not just in the creation but in the maintenance. Imagine these tests as your garden; they need regular tending, or else the weeds of obsolescence will take over. It's not just about making it work; it's about keeping it working, and beautifully so.

Let us take an example. Salesforce is a SAAS (Software as a Service) CRM (Customer Relationship Management) product, which offers thrice a year updates to its software platform. While these updates bring crucial updates to functions across the product, by making it better for the end customers, these changes generally change the UI elements, as well; causing UI test automation scripts to break.

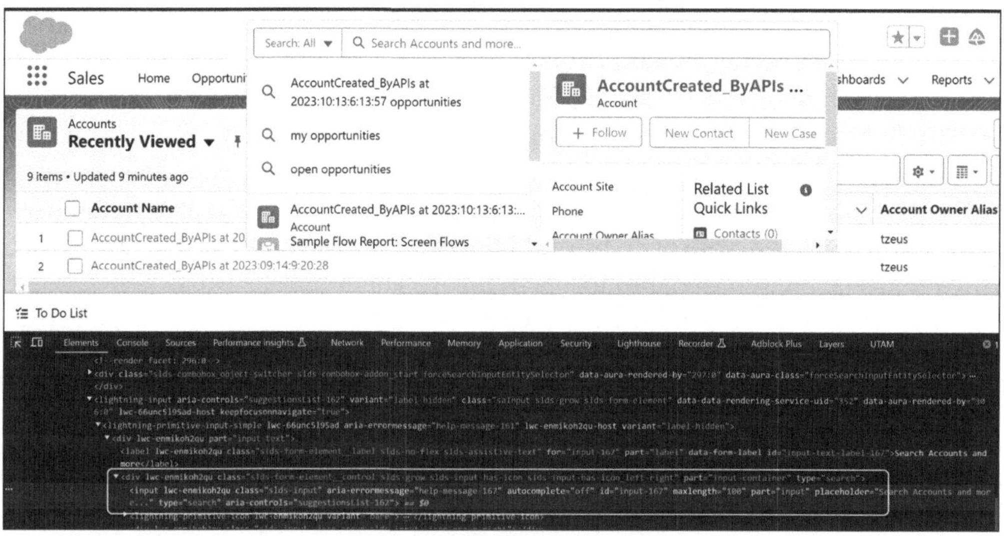

Figure 10.1: *DOM example for Salesforce Search*

In *Figure* 10.1, we see the Search Field for Salesforce. Interestingly, with the advancement of frontline technologies, this Search field has been modernized with contextual results and Artificial Intelligence (AI) related features. This means easier search for the users.

On the other hand, the advancement of these UI features for Search also means DOM-related updates across the page structure. And if our locators and synchronization techniques are not adequate, then these changes would cause our UI automation tests to break. For example: If our locators for the Search box are too tightly integrated with the attribute as **`aria-errormessage="help-message-167"`**, then our automation scripts could break if the numerical identifier changes between the releases, or across pages.

Figure 10.2: *DOM example for e-commerce website – https://in.puma.com/in/en*

Here is another example from an e-commerce website related to the fashion industry. Fashion is typically split into four seasons: Spring/Summer, Fall/Winter, Resort, and Pre-Fall. The two main seasons, however, are Spring/Summer and Autumn/Winter and are always shown at Fashion Week in London, Milan, New York, and Paris. Spring/Summer starts in January and extends to around June. With each season, a new catalog is curated at the ecommerce website, potentially with a new visual layout. This would result in multiple changes throughout the year. In addition to this, if we look closely at the preceding screenshot for *Figure* 10.2, we can observe that the e-commerce retailer is also running a time-bound deal. Fashion retailers across the globe run similar deals throughout the year, on various occasions, such as Thanksgiving, Christmas, Diwali, New Year, and Eid. While these functional changes are advantageous for businesses and customers, these could result in a regression spiral for the test automation codebase.

Similar examples can be found in the Healthcare industry with compliance changes, Ed-Tech (Education Technology) with the advent of new learning modules and formats, and other industries.

Henceforth, we can conclude that the ever-evolving dimensions of business can lead to application changes, which might not be very conducive to the automation codebase.

In addition to business-related changes, internal technical changes can also lead to maintenance efforts for the test automation codebase. For example, assume an application moving from Spring Hibernate technology to a Mongo-Ember-Angular-Node (MEAN) stack. This would result in the front-end technology stack being updated for the application, leading to a direct impact on the test automation suite. Similarly, an e-commerce platform's migration from Bootstrap to custom CSS could crash half the regression pack with ambiguous "unable to locate element" errors across the board.

To cope with these challenges, test automation engineers need to adopt some best practices and strategies to maintain their test automation codebase. Some of these include using design patterns, modularizing the code, following coding standards, implementing version control, performing code reviews, and updating the test cases regularly. These practices can help to improve the readability, reusability, maintainability, and scalability of the test automation codebase.

Let's face it, maintenance isn't the most glamorous part of test automation. You might have dreamt of a triumphant end to your scripting journey, riding off into a glorious sunset. But then, reality strikes. Software updates come crashing in, throwing a wrench in the works. We've all been there, right? But don't worry! It's like brushing your teeth twice a day, so that they remain pristine and you can still have candy, hopefully twice a day for many youthful years.

With some good old-fashioned care and smart strategies, your test suite cannot only survive but thrive amidst these constant changes. Let's dive into some practical tips to keep your test automation framework agile and robust.

Avoid Blocking Sleep Calls: In test automation, the use of blocking sleep calls, like `Thread.sleep` in Java, is a common but inefficient practice. These commands force the entire test to pause for a specified duration, regardless of whether the page or element is ready. This is akin to waiting for a bus that might arrive early or late; you're essentially guessing how long to wait.

Instead, Selenium offers more intelligent waiting mechanisms, namely Implicit and Explicit waits. Implicit waits allow the script to pause for a defined time, but will move on as soon as the element is located. Explicit waits are even more sophisticated; they wait for a specific condition to be met (like an element becoming clickable) before proceeding. It's a bit like having a smart assistant who watches for the bus and notifies you the moment it arrives, saving you from needless waiting.

Implementing these waits requires understanding the typical load times and behaviors of your web application, and setting waits that reflect these. This not only makes your tests faster but also more reliable, as they dynamically adapt to the actual performance of the web application.

Name Test Cases and Suites Appropriately: Naming in test automation is more than a mere formality; it's a critical practice for maintainability and clarity. A well-named test case or suite immediately conveys its purpose and functionality, much like a well-titled book gives you an idea of its content. This is particularly valuable in collaborative environments where multiple team members might work on or review the same tests.

The key is to be descriptive yet concise. For example, a test for a login function might be named **`testLoginWithValidCredentials`** rather than just **`testLogin.`** This specific naming helps in quickly identifying the test's purpose, especially when scanning through a long list of tests. Naming conventions also aid significantly during troubleshooting and debugging. When a test fails, its name should give a clear indication of what functionality might be broken. This is especially helpful for teams practicing Continuous Integration/Continuous Deployment (CI/CD), where test results directly impact the deployment pipeline.

Choose the Best-Suited Web Locator: Web locators are the compass of Selenium tests, guiding the automation script to the correct web elements. The choice of locator can greatly impact the robustness and maintenance of your tests. Common locators include ID, Name, Link text, XPath, and CSS Selector. Each has its own strengths, and the key is to choose the one that provides stability and resistance to UI changes.

For example, while XPath offers powerful and flexible ways to locate elements, it can be brittle if not used carefully. A small change in the page structure might render an XPath locator invalid. Conversely, IDs and Classes, when used consistently, offer a more stable way of locating elements, as they are less likely to change with UI updates.

The best practice here is to understand the structure and design of your web application and choose locators that complement it. For instance, if your application uses dynamic content, CSS Selectors or Relative XPath might be more appropriate than static IDs.

Chain findElement calls: In Selenium WebDriver, chaining `findElement` calls is a powerful technique to locate a web element within another web element. This approach can be particularly useful when dealing with complex page structures or when you want to narrow down the search context to a specific part of the webpage.

Here's an example in Java that demonstrates how to use this technique:

```
// Locate the parent element
            WebElement parentElement = driver.findElement(By.id("search-
            BoxId"));
            // Now chain findElement to locate a child element within the
            parent
            WebElement childElement = parentElement.findElement(By.id("-
magnifierIconID"));
            // Interact with the child element, e.g., click, getText,
            etc.
            childElement.click();


            // ... additional actions or verifications ...
```

Using Hard and Soft Asserts in TestNG

In test automation, asserting conditions is vital for verifying the correctness of the application under test. However, the way a test responds to a failed assertion can significantly impact the test flow. TestNG comes with a solution for easing the maintenance issues with Hard and Soft asserts as follows:

- **Hard Asserts**: In the case of Hard Asserts, test execution fails and ends if the condition provided in the Assert is not met. Use Hard Asserts when a failure indicates a critical issue and further test steps are irrelevant or might lead to misleading results.
- **Soft Asserts**: In the case of Soft Asserts, if the condition provided in the Assert clause is not met, then it's recorded as a failure, and the Test Execution continues to the end. After the complete test is executed, all of these pass/fail results are collated and presented in the console and report. Use Soft Asserts in scenarios where it's essential to run the test to completion to gather information about multiple failures.

So far, we have used Hard Asserts in our examples such as `Assert.assertEquals(actualTitle, expectedTitle, "Title mismatch")`.

TestNG also provides us with Soft Asserts, to maintain the flow of test execution and reduce the maintenance effort. Consider a scenario where we are testing an e-commerce website. We need to validate multiple elements on a product page, such as the product title, price, description, and reviews. Using soft asserts allows us to check all these elements in a single test execution, even if one or more checks fail.

Kindly open and run the **Chapter10_SoftAssertTest.java** class at **src/test/java/chapter10** package as follows:

```
public void testGoogleSearchElements() throws InterruptedException {
            WebDriver driver = new ChromeDriver();
            SoftAssert softAssert = new SoftAssert();
            driver.get("https://www.google.com");
            // Check if the search bar is present
            WebElement searchBar = driver.findElement(By.name("q"));
            softAssert.assertNotNull(searchBar, "Search bar is not
present");
            // Check if the Google Search button is present
            WebElement searchButton = driver.findElement(By.
            name("btnK"));
            softAssert.assertNotNull(searchButton, "Search button is
            not present");
            // Perform a search operation
            searchBar.sendKeys("Selenium WebDriver");
            // Simulating the press of Enter key to trigger search
            searchBar.sendKeys(Keys.ENTER);
            // searchButton.click();
            // Verify if the first search result is relevant
            Thread.sleep(3000);
            WebElement searchResult = driver.findElement(By.id("search"));
            String expectedTextInFirstResult = "WebDriver";
      softAssert.assertTrue(searchResult.getAttribute("innerHTML").con-
tains(expectedTextInFirstResult),
                        "First search result is not relevant");
            // Finalize the test with assertAll to report all soft
assert failures
```

```
            softAssert.assertAll();
        }
}
```

The provided Java code exemplifies the use of **`SoftAssert`** in Selenium WebDriver for a web testing scenario, specifically for testing Google's search functionality. The process begins with initializing a **`WebDriver`** instance to interact with the Chrome browser, followed by creating a **`SoftAssert`** instance for performing non-abrupt assertions. The driver navigates to Google's homepage, and the code includes checks to ensure the presence of key elements like the search bar and the Google Search button, using the **`assertNotNull`** method of **`SoftAssert.`** These soft assertions verify the existence of these elements without halting the test execution in case of failure. The test proceeds to perform a search operation by sending keys to the search bar and simulating an **`Enter`** key press.

After a brief pause to allow search results to load, the code verifies the relevance of the first search result, checking if it contains a specified text. This is achieved through the **`assertTrue`** method, again a soft assertion, ensuring the test continues even if this check fails. The critical aspect of this code is the use of **`SoftAssert`**, which allows the entire test to run to completion, regardless of individual assertion failures. The **`assertAll`** method, called at the end, is crucial as it aggregates and reports all the failures from the soft assertions made throughout the test. This approach is particularly beneficial in scenarios where collecting comprehensive failure data from a test is more valuable than stopping the test at the first sign of trouble.

Choosing between hard and soft asserts in TestNG for Selenium automation depends on the specific requirements of each test scenario. Hard asserts are best for critical checks, while soft asserts are ideal for comprehensive tests where multiple failures need to be captured. By judiciously using both types of asserts, testers can enhance their test scripts' effectiveness and reliability.

As we can see Test maintenance is like tending the gardens. Yes, it requires effort, but just like every well-maintained garden, it provides quality air, or in our case, the air of "Quality".

And before we move on to the next section, here's the biggest trick for maintaining your test suites: **Walk in sync with your business stakeholders**. It's like being in a band where the business folks are the songwriters, setting the overall direction and goals. Your job on the tech team is to bring their vision to life, like musicians playing the tune. Make sure to chat regularly with the business side and understand their priorities and upcoming changes. This way, you can focus your testing efforts on what really matters to the business. By aligning your technical work with the business goals, you ensure that your testing not only works well technically, but also adds real value to the company. So, keep the lines of communication open; it'll make maintaining your test suites much easier and more effective.

ROI for Test Automation

In all my years of industry experience, I believe that if we had to give the award for "The most disputed" metric in the field of test automation, it would be ROI (Return On Investment) for Test Automation. Let us take an example of it. Assume that we have 20 smoke test scenarios for a certain application. These scenarios need to be run twice to be run every week, and whenever they are run, it takes one person 4 hours. And if we automate these scenarios, what is the ROI for Test Automation? If we do simple math, we will save 160 hours of manual execution. So, 160 x 52 weeks = 8320 hours saved in an average year. It's all good so far, but some folks have started taking the wrong turn here. They start equating surface-level automated checks to the deep testing an actual human can accomplish. And some folks assign a dollar value to the hours saved and might come up with a Dollar saved in Testing. While these approaches are correct mathematically, they beg a question: Are we measuring the value delivered to our customers correctly?

Test automation, by replacing repetitive manual testing tasks with automated scripts, offers significant benefits in terms of speed, accuracy, and cost-effectiveness. However, understanding and quantifying its ROI can be complex, as it is dependent on the stage of the team, test maturity and definition of value for the customers. For example, even if we did save a million hours of manual test execution, but failed to deliver the value which customers expect, then we have not been able to satisfy our roles as an engineering team.

To measure the ROI of test automation, consider factors like the reduction in manual validation hours, the decrease in bugs reaching production, and the overall improvement in software quality. For example, if a manual testing process takes 10 hours and is prone to human error, automating this process might reduce it to 1 hour with significantly fewer errors. This time saving translates directly into cost savings, as well as indirect benefits like increased customer satisfaction due to higher quality products.

Moreover, the scalability of test automation allows teams to cover more ground in less time, which is especially beneficial in agile and continuous deployment environments. In such cases, the ROI can be measured in terms of the increased number of deployments or the faster delivery of features to the market.

Another aspect to consider is the reduction in time-to-market for new features or products. Automated testing can significantly accelerate the development cycle, allowing companies to launch updates or new products faster, gaining a competitive edge in the market.

> *Effective automation should deliver rapid feedback on the quality of software while mitigating the need for repetitive manual testing efforts. If your metrics aren't shedding light on the current quality landscape or pinpointing potential challenges, bottlenecks, and inefficiencies, it may indicate a misstep in your automation strategy. It's crucial to understand that insights derived from metrics hold different significance for various roles. Therefore, selecting metrics that align with each role's requirements is paramount, enabling swift and informed decision-making for continuous improvement initiatives.*
>
> -Anand Bagmar, Quality Evangelist & Solution Architect at Applitools.

In conclusion, the ROI of test automation is multifaceted, encompassing not just direct cost savings but also improvements in product quality, customer satisfaction, and market responsiveness. While the initial investment in setting up automated testing might be significant, the long-term benefits in terms of efficiency, scalability, and speed offer a compelling case for its adoption. Another factor worth consideration is the effort spent on maintenance and updates for test automation scripts. Test Automation code base can accrue technical debt, like any other codebase, so we must be mindful of building it correctly and measuring its impact. This comprehensive view, considering both technical and business perspectives, solidifies the case for investing in test automation as a strategic tool for software development success.

Extending Selenium with Excel

Test automation is a critical part of delivering high-quality software at speed and enterprise scale. Selenium has become the de facto standard for automating web applications due to its flexibility and cross-browser support. However, Selenium on its own falls short when tests require complex datasets or validation of data in Excel files, which are commonly used in enterprises. Tests often need to validate dynamic datasets in Excel or import test data from Excel sheets during runtime. For example, you may need to:

- Read pricing data from Excel to verify pricing calculations on the website
- Import a new test data set in each iteration based on parameters in Excel
- Extract reports from the application and verify data against Excel

These use cases are difficult to implement using vanilla Selenium, requiring complex workarounds. Excel integration bridges this gap, enabling you to incorporate spreadsheet data in your automation framework elegantly.

While there are many ways to add Excel capabilities to a Test Automation framework, Apache POI is the most prominent library for integrating Selenium with Excel in Java. This library efficiently handles both XLS and XLSX file formats. Alongside Apache POI, other libraries such as JExcel and Fastexcel also offer functionalities for working with Excel spreadsheets in Java applications.

Apache POI is an open-source Java library often utilized to create and handle Microsoft Office-based files. Users can leverage POI to perform various operations (modify, create, display, read) on specific file formats (Excel files being one of them).

Apache POI can perform reading or writing data from multiple external resources. Some of these are as follows:

- **POIFS** (Poor Obfuscation Implementation File System): This component reads and writes Microsoft's OLE 2 Compound document format. Since all Microsoft Office files are OLE 2 files, this component is the basic building block of all the other POI elements.
- **HSSF** (Horrible Spreadsheet Format): Reads and writes Microsoft Excel (XLS) format files. It can read files written by Excel 97 onwards; this file format is known as the BIFF 8 format. As the Excel file format is complex and contains a number of tricky characteristics, some of the more advanced features cannot be read.
- **XSSF** (XML Spreadsheet Format): Reads and writes Office Open XML (XLSX) format files. Similar feature set to HSSF, but for Office Open XML files.

Apache POI was originally an acronym for "Poor Obfuscation Implementation", referring humorously to the fact that the file formats seemed to be deliberately obfuscated, but poorly since they were successfully reverse-engineered. This explanation – and those of the similar names for the various sub-projects – were removed from the official web pages later to better market the tools to businesses who would not consider such humor appropriate.

To create or maintain Excel Workbooks, Apache POI provides a **`Workbook`** as a super-interface for all classes. It belongs to **`org.apache.poi.ss.usermodel`** package. It uses the **`WorkbookFactory`** class to create the appropriate workbook (that is **`HSSFWorkbook`** or **`XSSFWorkbook`**). The two classes which implement the **`Workbook`** interface are as follows:

- **`HSSFWorkbook`**: Methods of this class are used to read or write data to Microsoft Excel files in .xls format.
- **`XSSFWorkbook`**: Methods of this class are used to read/write data to Microsoft Excel and OpenOffice XML files in .xls or .xlsx format.

Apache POI Installation

Apache POI can be downloaded as a JAR and added to the build path for the project, or it can be added as a Maven dependency to the project. We have added Apache POI to the pom.xml as follows:

```
    <!-- https://mvnrepository.com/artifact/org.apache.poi/poi -->
<dependency>
    <groupId>org.apache.poi</groupId>
    <artifactId>poi</artifactId>
    <version>5.2.3</version>
</dependency>
<dependency>
    <groupId>org.apache.poi</groupId>
    <artifactId>poi-ooxml</artifactId>
    <version>5.2.3</version>
</dependency>
```

Note: We will need a commons-io library for the working of Apache POI, so it has been added to the **`pom.xml`** as well.

Reading Values from Excel

Now that we have the dependencies set, we can create methods as follows in BaseTest.java class, for reading values from an Excel sheet.

```
public static String excelValueReader(int row, int column) throws
FileNotFoundException {
// Path of the excel file
```

```
FileInputStream fs = new FileInputStream("src\\main\\resources\\Excel
DemoFile.xlsx");
        try (// Creating a workbook
                XSSFWorkbook workbook = new XSSFWorkbook(fs)) {
                XSSFSheet sheet = workbook.getSheetAt(0);
                Row excelrow = sheet.getRow(row);
                Cell cell = excelrow.getCell(column);
                String cellval = cell.getStringCellValue();
                return cellval;
                } catch (IOException e) {
                        // TODO Replace with logging if required
                System.out.println("Exception occured in excelValueReader" +
e.getMessage());
                return null;
                }
        }
```

The provided Java method, **excelValueReader**, is designed to read a specific cell value from an Excel file. It takes two parameters: **row** and **column**, which specify the location of the cell in the Excel sheet. The method begins by creating a **FileInputStream** to read the specified Excel file at **src\\main\\resources\\ExcelDemoFile.xlsx**. It then uses this stream to create an **XSSFWorkbook** object, representing the entire Excel workbook.

Within the **try** block, the method accesses the first sheet of the workbook **getSheetAt(0)** and retrieves the specified row **getRow(row).** From this row, it then gets the cell at the specified column **getCell(column).** The value of this cell is extracted as a string using **getStringCellValue(),** and this value is returned by the method.

If an **IOException** occurs during this process, the catch block is executed, printing an error message with details of the exception. In such a case, the method returns **null,** indicating that it was unable to read the cell value. This exception handling ensures that the program does not crash and provides information about what went wrong, which can be useful for debugging.

Writing Values to Excel

Isn't it too simple to read values from Excel using Apache POI? Now, let's look at writing values into Excel cells. It is like reading with a few additional steps.

Here is how we have implemented the method for writing values into Excel in the **BaseTest.java** file:

```
public static void excelValueWriter(int row, int column, String value)
throws FileNotFoundException {
        String path = "src\\main\\resources\\ExcelDemoFile.xlsx";
        FileInputStream fs = new FileInputStream(path);
        try (// Creating a workbook
            XSSFWorkbook workbook = new XSSFWorkbook(fs)) {
            XSSFSheet sheet = workbook.getSheetAt(0);
            Row excelrow = sheet.getRow(row);
            Cell cell = excelrow.getCell(column);
            cell.setCellValue(value);
            FileOutputStream fos = new FileOutputStream(path);
            workbook.write(fos);
            fos.close();
        } catch (IOException e) {
            // TODO Replace with logging if required
            System.out.println("Exception occured in excelValue
Reader" + e.getMessage());


        }
    }
```

The Java method **excelValueWriter** is designed to write a specified value into a cell in an Excel file. It accepts three parameters: **row** and **column** to identify the target cell and **value**, and the string to be written into that cell. The process begins with the method specifying the path to the Excel file and creating a **FileInputStream** to read this file.

Inside the **try** block, an **XSSFWorkbook** object is instantiated using the file stream, representing the workbook. The method then accesses the first sheet of this workbook using **getSheetAt(0)**. It retrieves the specified row **getRow(row)** within this sheet. From this row, the target cell is obtained **getCell(column)**. The value provided as a parameter is then set into this cell using the **setCellValue(value)** method.

After modifying the cell, the method creates a **FileOutputStream** to write back to the Excel file. It writes the updated workbook to the file using **workbook.**

write(fos). The file output stream is then closed to ensure no resources are leaked.

In the case of an **IOException** during this process, the catch block captures the exception and prints an error message, including the exception's details. This can help in diagnosing what went wrong during the file-writing process.

The simple print statement should ideally be replaced with more robust logging for better error handling and tracking in production environments.

Sample Test Case

We have utilized both methods in the **Chapter10_ExcelTest.java** class at the **src/test/java** location for reference as follows:

```
public class Chapter10_ExcelTest extends BaseTest {
	@Test
	public void excelReadTest() throws InterruptedException,
FileNotFoundException {
		System.out.println("Value from specified file is " +
excelValueReader(0, 0));
	}
	@Test
	public void excelWriteTest() throws InterruptedException,
FileNotFoundException {
		String testdata1 = String.valueOf(Math.random());
		System.out.println("Value written is " + testdata1);
		excelValueWriter(0, 0, testdata1);
	}
}
```

We can run the test and verify that a mathematically random value is written and read from the first row and column, from the provided Excel file.

Also, just zoom out for a bit in the preceding section, we integrated Selenium's web automation capabilities with Excel automation. As expert automation engineers, we might frequently need such capabilities, where integration with various libraries, such as Appium, Optical Character Recognition (OCR), Databases and Emails, is needed for widening the net of our test automation projects. For widening the net of our test automation projects. With the superpower of Maven under our belt, it should be no different from adding the relevant Maven dependencies and utilizing the power of the corresponding library.

Data-driven Frameworks

As a Selenium WebDriver user, you know the challenges of keeping up with the fast pace of test automation for a myriad of data combinations. This is where the magic of Data-Driven Testing (DDT) comes in. It's like having a secret weapon that simplifies your testing life. Imagine not having to juggle your test scripts every time there's a slight change in test data.

Or running the login test case with hundreds of valid and invalid username and password combinations. That's what DDT does – it externalizes the test data from your scripts.

Think of it as keeping all your test ingredients (data) in separate, easily accessible bottles (like Excel, CSV, or XML files), away from your cooking recipe (test script). This means you can change the ingredients as needed without rewriting the recipe! It's a game changer, especially when dealing with applications that demand a variety of input scenarios. With DDT in Selenium WebDriver, you're not just testing efficiently; you're testing smartly, adapting swiftly to different data needs without getting bogged down in code tweaks.

Let us assume that we must automate the scenario for a login page with valid and invalid combinations of user credentials. And this test needs to be executed across Chrome, Firefox, and Edge browsers. Here is how we can design the Excel data table for the test case:

User ID	Password	Browser
Valid	Invalid	Chrome
Invalid	Valid	Firefox
Valid	Valid	Edge

Table 10.1: *Sample data set for Data-driven framework*

While this is a small subset of the possible combinations, the idea here is that using the principles of Apache POI, we can easily externalize the test data from the test script, and scale the test automation.

Another example would be in e-commerce platforms, DDT enables testing of various user transactions with different payment methods and user details efficiently.

Embracing Data-Driven Frameworks is all about smart management and foresight. Data Driven Framework might not be the optimal choice when the test data is simple and does not require multiple data sets. Think of it as tending to a garden where your test data files are the plants needing regular care. Keep them tidy and up-to-date, and don't forget to back them up – it's like insurance against unforeseen digital disasters. Proper documentation is your roadmap here, guiding you and your team smoothly through the complexities of framework setup and usage, making everyone's life easier.

Avoiding shortcuts, like hardcoding file paths or overlooking error handling in test scripts, is crucial. These might seem like time-savers initially, but they can lead to future problems. Data-driven frameworks in Selenium are like trusty multi-tools in the ever-evolving landscape of test automation – adaptable, reliable, and incredibly versatile. They may come with their own set of challenges, but the benefits of flexibility, maintainability, and efficiency they offer are undeniable, making them indispensable in adapting to new testing trends and technologies.

Keyword-driven Frameworks

The Keyword Driven Framework is a method of test automation that separates the test script logic from the actual test steps and data. This separation is achieved by using keywords, which are human-readable words or phrases representing actions to be performed on the application under test. For instance, '**`navigate`**', '**`click`**', or '**`enter text`**' are typical keywords. This approach not only enhances the readability of test scripts, but also simplifies maintenance and updates.

Does it sound familiar? Yes, we have covered some of these approaches in the chapters around BDD and Screenplay patterns.

In the context of the Keyword Driven Framework, keywords represent actions. Each keyword corresponds to a specific operation, like clicking a button or entering text in a field. These keywords are then mapped to actual Selenium commands that execute these operations. Here is a quick refresher on this concept from our chapter on BDD:

```
@InvalidCredentials
Scenario Outline: Login with invalid credentials
  Given User is on HRMLogin page "https://opensource-demo.orangehrmlive.com/"
  When User enters username as "<username>" and password as "<password>"
  Then User should be able to see error message "<errorMessage>"
```

Figure 10.3: *Sample Keyword-driven Test case using BDD*

Keyword-driven test automation scripts help you write clear, reusable tests without needing to be a coding whiz. It works by separating the technical stuff from the test steps, using human-friendly keywords like "`User enters username`" and "`User should see error message`." This makes tests easier to write, understand, and maintain, even for people who don't code. Plus, you can easily test different scenarios by plugging in different data, like different usernames and passwords. While setting it up takes some effort, the long-term benefits of easier maintenance and clearer tests are worth it.

All good things come with their limitations. The keyword-driven framework in software testing too has several disadvantages. Firstly, it can lead to a high initial cost and effort due to the need for developing and maintaining a comprehensive set of keywords and associated scripts. This complexity can make it less suitable for smaller projects or teams with limited resources. Secondly, this framework often requires a significant level of technical skill and understanding of the underlying automation tools, which can be a barrier for team members who are not programmers.

Thirdly, the abstraction layer created by keywords can sometimes obscure the actual functionality being tested, making it difficult to diagnose and fix issues in the test scripts or the application under test.

Hybrid Frameworks

The Hybrid Test Automation Framework is a methodology in software testing that combines the best features of various established frameworks, such as keyword-driven, data-driven, and modular frameworks. This integrated approach allows testers to leverage the strengths of each framework type, enhancing flexibility, scalability, and efficiency in automated testing. In a hybrid framework, testers can use a data-driven approach to manage test data, employ keyword-driven techniques for better readability and maintenance of test scripts, and use a modular structure to break down the application under test into logical and manageable sections. This amalgamation enables testers to tailor their testing strategy to the specific needs of the project, facilitating easier maintenance, better reusability of code, and more effective handling of complex test scenarios. The hybrid framework is especially useful in large-scale projects where different parts of the application might require different testing approaches. Therefore, a lot of modern engineering teams, prefer a Hybrid framework for test automation using Selenium.

Imagine you're building a house. You need different tools and materials, right? The Hybrid framework for test automation works similarly. Here's a breakdown of its key components:

- **The Driver Script**: This is like your foreman, overseeing the entire construction process. It reads instructions (test data and keywords) from blueprints (external files) and tells other workers (keywords) what to do. It also checks if everything is built as planned (verifies results).
- **Object Repository**: This is your toolbox, holding all the tools (locators) needed to interact with the house's elements (UI elements). Each tool has a label for easy identification (locators are stored centrally). This way, the workers (keywords) know exactly which tool to use without searching everywhere.
- **Keyword Library**: Think of this as a collection of skilled workers (functions) with specific tasks. They can paint walls (user enters username), install doors (user clicks button), and more (different user actions and assertions). This library helps avoid doing the same work repeatedly, just like skilled workers save time on the job.
- **Test Data**: This is your blueprint containing specifications and details for the house (test cases). It includes usernames, passwords, and expected outcomes (different data sets for different test scenarios). This blueprint allows you to build different variations of the house (run tests with different data).
- **Application Under Test (AUT)**: This is the house itself, the software being tested. The workers (keywords) interact with the house's features (UI elements) using the provided tools (locators) and instructions (keywords).

Bonus Components

- **Function Library**: This is like a specialized toolkit for repetitive tasks, like hammering nails (common operations).
- **Test Case Template Design:** This is a pre-defined layout for your blueprints, ensuring consistency and clarity in your instructions (test cases).
- **Excel Sheet with Keywords**: This is an alternative to the Keyword Library, storing worker instructions (keywords) directly within the blueprint (test data spreadsheet).

In summary, the foreman (Driver Script) reads the blueprint (test data) and tells the workers (keywords) what to do (invokes functions). Each worker uses the right tool (locator) from the toolbox (Object Repository) to follow instructions (keywords). The foreman then checks if the house is built correctly (verifies results).

The hybrid framework clearly has the following advantages over DDT or Keyword driven frameworks:

- **Reuse what works**: Tools and instructions can be used repeatedly, making testing faster and easier.
- **Easy maintenance:** If something needs fixing, you only adjust the instructions or tools, not rebuild the entire house.
- **Clear understanding**: Simple language in instructions makes it easy for everyone, even non-experts, to understand the construction process.
- **Testing flexibility**: Different blueprints allow you to test various house variations with ease.
- **Teamwork makes the dream work**: Both technical and non-technical people can contribute to building the house (test automation).

The Hybrid Test Automation Framework is a game-changer for in-sprint automation in agile software development. Its mix-and-match approach, combining data-driven, keyword-driven, and modular frameworks, makes it super adaptable. This flexibility is a boon during sprints, allowing test cases to be quickly tweaked or expanded as development evolves. Plus, its modular setup with reusable components like a keyword library means setting up new tests is a breeze, keeping pace with the sprint's rapid development.

Collaboration between developers and testers gets a big boost with the Hybrid framework. Its structured, easy-to-understand test scripts make it easier for both sides to work together efficiently. This is crucial in sprints, where teamwork is key to quickly addressing and testing new features or changes. Also, the framework's layered design means adapting to these changes is fast and doesn't require redoing the entire test suite.

Finally, the Hybrid framework's ability to play nice with popular tools like Selenium is a real asset for in-sprint automation. It fits seamlessly into the continuous integration/continuous deployment pipeline, aligning testing with the sprint's development and deployment rhythm. This integration ensures thorough and robust testing within the tight timelines of agile sprints, making the framework a reliable ally in maintaining quality while keeping up with fast-paced development cycles. Overall, the Hybrid framework is like a well-equipped construction team, working together to build and test your software efficiently.

Roadmap for Selenium

Selenium has been continuously evolving, with each version bringing new features and improvements. Key areas of focus have traditionally included enhancing browser automation capabilities, support for new web technologies, and improving the ease of use and efficiency of the automation process.

Selenium is an open-source project, so its contributors include a diverse and global community of developers and testers who voluntarily dedicate their time and skills to develop and enhance its features. As Selenium is an Open-Source project, therefore it's tough to nail down the exact features which would be released in Selenium 5 or 6, so we will try to enumerate the strategic and tactical goals for the Selenium project in upcoming releases.

First and foremost, let us focus on one of the biggest changes to Selenium recently, Selenium Manager. Earlier Selenium users had to download the ChromeDriver, or other browser drivers, and configure them as part of the build path, for interacting with the browser. With the current versions of Selenium (4.6 onwards); we only need to have the browsers installed, and Selenium Manager takes care of the browser driver management. This had been a long-time issue for Selenium users, and with the help of open-source contributions, this feature has been delivered. As Selenium evolves, Selenium Manager will be integrated deeper into the framework, so that it becomes the default option for users, and browser driver management becomes easier.

Another key change is that the Selenium project is driving more and more of its APIs towards BiDi implementation. Selenium is refining its approach to browser interaction by moving away from a heavy reliance on the Chrome DevTools Protocol (CDP). While CDP is a powerful debugger protocol, it's intricately tied to specific browser versions and can be verbose due to its nature as a debug tool. Selenium aims to enhance the testing experience by decoupling from CDP versions and browser versions, thus providing a more stable and version-independent testing environment.

Bi-directional (BiDi) communication is a vital part of modern Selenium. Currently, Java, JavaScript, and Ruby bindings have substantial coverage for BiDi, and the focus is now shifting to extend this to .NET and Python. The implementation will include comprehensive APIs and Event-driven design, moving towards a unified BiDi approach across all bindings.

In Selenium 4, network interception capabilities are based on CDP. Future updates will replace this dependency with BiDi, aligning with the broader goal of reducing reliance on CDP. This change promises a more consistent and browser-agnostic approach to network interception in web application testing.

Selenium plans to promote other open-source frameworks in the ecosystem. This move indicates a commitment to supporting a broader range of tools within the Selenium ecosystem, catering to the various needs and preferences of developers and testers.

Recognizing the importance of accessible and comprehensive documentation, efforts are underway to improve Selenium's documentation. This enhancement will benefit new and existing users alike, providing clearer guidance and support, and ultimately contributing to a more user-friendly experience.

Selenium project is also focused on the improvements for its build process. Some key tasks involve making tests runnable on Windows, adopting new build tools, and adding source generator support for .NET. Efforts are also focused on creating scripts to set up a complete development environment on Windows, creating Bazel files for better build system management, and streamlining the release process with one-command updates. Additionally, there is a focus on improving the Selenium Manager for Rust on Windows and managing Selenium Manager binaries for continuous integration. These improvements reflect a broader initiative to simplify the development process and maintain the project's compatibility with evolving technologies.

The future of the Selenium project is marked by a series of innovative changes and enhancements aimed at improving efficiency, expanding capabilities, and ensuring compatibility with evolving web technologies.

Conclusion

As we reach the end of this chapter of our Selenium adventure, it feels like we're standing atop a mountain, looking back at the path we've traversed. We've not only learned the ropes of Selenium but also delved into the art of nurturing and evolving our test suites, much like a gardener who lovingly tends to their plants.

Remember how we compared maintaining test automation to gardening? That's because it truly is an ongoing process. Think of the frequent updates in applications like Salesforce or the seasonal changes in e-commerce websites. They can really shake things up in our test environment. But fear not! We discussed strategies like smart waits, meaningful naming conventions, and the magic of avoiding hardcoded values to keep our tests running smoothly.

When it comes to the ROI of test automation, it's a bit like peeling an onion – there are layers to it. Sure, there's the obvious time and cost savings, but it's so much more. It's about the better quality of software we deliver and the satisfaction of our users. We also learned that equating automated checks with the depth of human testing is a no-go. It's about understanding the broader impact.

Who would have thought Selenium and Excel could work so well together? Using libraries like Apache POI, we explored how to read and write data in Excel.

This integration significantly amps up Selenium's capabilities, especially when dealing with complex datasets. We dived into Data-Driven Testing, where we keep our test data separate from the scripts. It's like having a well-organized pantry where everything is within reach but doesn't clutter the kitchen. Then there's the Keyword-Driven approach, making our tests readable and easy to maintain, though it does come with its own set of challenges. And for those who want the best of both worlds, we looked at Hybrid Frameworks. These are like Swiss Army knives, versatile and adaptable to various testing scenarios, especially in complex projects.

We took a moment to gaze into the crystal ball for Selenium's future. The upcoming Selenium versions sound exciting with features like Selenium Manager, making browser driver management a breeze, and the shift towards Bi-directional communication. There's also a focus on making Selenium's documentation more user-friendly and improving the overall build process.

As we close this chapter, it's not the end, but a new beginning. With the foundations laid and skills honed, the world of Selenium test automation is ours to explore and conquer. So, here's to more learning, testing, and automation in the future!

Exercise

Time to roll up your sleeves, one more time and get your coding hat on. In this exercise, we will be pulling together lessons learned in this chapter and a few from earlier chapters to really solidify the learning experience.

We need to automate the scenario of checking out a book from the OrangeAVA website. Our task is to automate two test scenarios as follows:

1. Fetching the list of all books
    a. Navigate to https://orangeava.com/collections/new-release.
    b. Fetch the title of all books and write them in the first column of an Excel sheet named **`Booklist.xlsx.`**
    c. Fetch the prices of all books and write them in the second column in **`Booklist.xlsx.`**
2. Validating the checkout process
    a. Navigate to https://orangeava.com/collections/new-release.
    b. Go to the list of books.

c. Define a method named **`Bookbuyer,`** as part of the framework. This method will take the title of the book as input, and perform the action of navigating to its page, and then adding it to the cart. After adding the book to the cart, the method returns to https://orangeava.com/collections/new-release .

d. Iterate through all the books in **`Booklist.xlsx`** from the 1.c step, and add them to the cart using the **`Bookbuyer`** method defined earlier.

e. Navigate to the cart page.

f. Validate that the cart total is equal to the sum of prices for each book.

CHAPTER 11
Way Forward

Introduction

Welcome to the final chapter of our journey through the fascinating world of Selenium test automation! As we reach the end of this book, it's not just about closing a chapter–it's about opening a door to new possibilities and adventures in the ever-evolving landscape of test automation. Think of this chapter as your personal toolbox, packed with the latest trends, tools, and techniques that will not only keep you ahead in the game but also ignite your passion for learning more. First, we're going to take a peek into the future by exploring the exciting intersection of AI and test automation, with a special focus on how tools like ChatGPT are changing the game. And to accelerate your learning, we will also look at prompt engineering, so that you can be conversant with Large Language Models. Next, we'll dive into the nitty-gritty of GIT basics, making sure you're equipped to handle your code like a pro. And of course, we can't forget about Selenium's vibrant open-source community, which is the heartbeat of its success. This vibrant community is a melting pot of software developers, testers, and enthusiasts from around the world, each contributing their unique skills and perspectives. They collaboratively work to develop, refine, and enhance Selenium, ensuring it remains not only relevant but also at the forefront of web testing technologies. And by being a part of it, you can symbiotically grow your skills and network.

So, grab your favorite beverage, find a comfy spot, boot up your computer and let's embark on this final leg of our journey together. Whether you're a seasoned pro or just starting out, there's something in here for everyone. Let's make this learning experience not just informative but inspiring as well. Here's to the many more lines of code, tests, and innovations that lie ahead of us!

Structure

In this chapter, we will discuss the following topics:

- Usage of AI in Test Automation
- GIT Basics
- Open-source community of Selenium

Usage of AI in Test Automation

The rise of artificial intelligence (AI) is transforming many industries, including software testing and test automation. AI promises to make test automation faster, easier, and more powerful by assisting human testers. Let's explore how AI like ChatGPT can enhance test automation processes. Traditional test automation relies on human testers writing rigid test scripts that attempt to simulate user behavior. It is time and labor intensive. The integration of Artificial Intelligence (AI) in test automation is like opening a treasure trove of possibilities. AI isn't just transforming our tools; it's reshaping our thinking and approach towards testing. Overall, AI enables creative destruction of traditional testing limits through machine learning and natural language processing. Humans can focus more on high-value exploratory testing while AI handles repetitive test case execution.

Some key AI applications in test automation include:

- **Natural Language Test Case Recommendations**: Imagine scribbling down your desired test scenarios in plain English, and presto! AI spits out a detailed test plan, pinpointing potential issues and edge cases you might have missed. This capability is not only a huge time-saver but also makes test case generation more accessible to those who may not have deep expertise. AI algorithms can analyze the natural language input, understand the underlying requirements, and then recommend comprehensive test cases covering various aspects of the functionality. This approach ensures that the test cases are aligned with real-world usage scenarios, enhancing the effectiveness of testing efforts.
- **Automatic Test Code Generation**: Automatic test code generation is a breakthrough in reducing manual effort in the testing process. AI tools can now generate executable test scripts from high-level descriptions or existing test cases. This automation significantly speeds up the test development process and reduces the likelihood of human error. AI's ability to generate code also standardizes test scripts, ensuring consistency and adherence to best practices. Testers can focus more

on complex test scenarios and leave the routine coding tasks to AI, enhancing overall productivity and efficiency.

- **Test suite augmentation and optimization**: Existing test suites can be optimized by applying AI to analyze code coverage, redundancy, relevance, and other metrics to identify gaps needing new test cases or unnecessary test cases to remove. AI can also mutate existing test cases to generate additional relevant cases providing improved test suite coverage and effectiveness.
- **Defect Prediction Based on Historical Data**: Defect prediction using historical data is a prime example of AI's predictive capabilities in test automation. By analyzing past test results and project data, AI tools can identify patterns and predict potential areas where defects are likely to occur. This foresight enables teams to proactively focus their testing efforts on high-risk areas, potentially reducing the number of defects that make it to production. Such predictive analytics not only streamline the testing process but also contribute to higher software quality and better resource allocation, making testing efforts more strategic and results-driven. This area would also enable proactive testing efforts.
- **Intelligent Test data management:** AI can help in creating and managing test data by understanding patterns and requirements, ensuring efficient and effective data usage in tests. AI can automatically generate test data that meets specific criteria or conditions, which is especially useful in situations where sensitive data (like personal information) cannot be used. This synthetic data generation ensures privacy compliance while still providing robust datasets for testing.

As we can see, AI can help quality engineering on multiple fronts. So, the logical next question is: "How can we utilize AI in our day-to-day work?"

Here are some key AI applications which can be useful in the work of software testing and automation:

- **ChatGPT**: Created by OpenAI, ChatGPT is an impressively capable conversational AI chatbot that can answer questions, explain concepts, summarize texts and more. It demonstrates strong language skills but has some limitations around accuracy and objectivity.
- **Google Bard**: Google Bard aims to serve as a conversational AI service integrated into Google's search engine. Early demos faced criticism but Bard promises to be grounded in facts and provide transparent sourcing.
- **Anthropic Claude**: Claude is focused on being helpful, harmless, and honest. Created by AI safety company Anthropic to serve as an assistant,

Claude has limitations to prevent potential harms. Its model stresses constitutional AI principles to provide reliable and trustworthy support to users.

Figure 11.1: *Various AI products*

All the AI products depicted in *Figure 11.1* are Large Language Model (LLM) based AI products, which can help us in day-to-day tasks efficiently.

Selenium stands as the gold standard of tools for software testers and engineers worldwide, anchoring a vast ecosystem of resources, expertise, and infrastructure. With the advent of AI shaping the next frontier in test automation, Selenium's open nature ensures it remains adaptive and future-proof. This adaptability, combined with its flexibility to seamlessly blend with emerging technologies, cements its relevance for the innovations of tomorrow.

- Jason Arbon. (CEO at Checkie.ai.)

Prompt Engineering

In the evolving landscape of AI and software testing, "Prompt Engineering" is emerging as a crucial skill. But what exactly is prompt engineering, and why should software testers care? Let's dive in, explore this concept, and understand how it can be a game-changer in your testing strategies.

Prompt engineering is the art and science of crafting inputs (prompts) to effectively communicate with AI models, like ChatGPT or code generation tools. It's about asking the right questions or giving precise instructions to get the most useful and accurate responses. In the context of AI applications for software testing, prompt engineering becomes a tool to extract maximum value from AI, whether it's generating test cases, debugging code, or automating routine tasks.

The quality of your prompt can make or break the AI's output. A well-crafted prompt leads to responses that are more accurate, relevant, and useful, while a poorly framed prompt can result in vague, incorrect, or unhelpful answers. It's not just about what you ask; it's about how you ask it. The right prompt can be the difference between an AI tool delivering valuable insights or going off on a tangent.

Let's look at two examples to understand this better, as you can try the following on ChatGPT, Bard or Claude and observe the difference:

- Bad Prompt: "Selenium test for a web application."

This prompt is too vague. The AI might not understand whether you want to create a Selenium test, troubleshoot an existing one, or learn about Selenium testing in general.

Good Prompt: "Generate a Selenium test script for a login page with fields for username and password and a submit button."

This prompt is clear, specific, and actionable. The AI understands exactly what is needed and can generate a relevant test script.

- Bad Prompt: "Write test cases for an app."

Again, this is too broad and lacks context. The AI won't know what kind of app or what features to focus on.

Good Prompt: "Create detailed test cases for a mobile shopping app focusing on the checkout process, including error handling for invalid payment methods."

This prompt provides specific details about the app type, the feature to be tested, and even includes a particular scenario (error handling), leading to more targeted and useful test cases.

To solidify our understanding, here are a few guidelines for writing better prompts for any Large Language Model (LLM)-based application:

- Be Specific: Clearly define what you need. Include details like the type of application, specific functionalities, or particular issues you're addressing.
- Provide Context: Context helps AI understand the scenario better. If you're working on a web app, mention it. If you need test cases for a specific feature, specify it.
- Use Clear and Concise Language: Avoid ambiguous or overly complex phrasing. The goal is to communicate your needs as straightforwardly as possible.
- Set the Scope: Define the limits of what you're asking. If you need a script for a particular browser or a test for a specific environment, mention it.
- Iterate and Refine: If the first response isn't perfect, use it as a learning opportunity. Refine your prompt and try again.

Let's put our prompt engineering skills into practice with examples tailored for software testers:

- "Draft a comprehensive test plan for a cross-platform mobile application that includes both functional and non-functional testing elements."
- "Provide a step-by-step guide to automate regression testing in a CI/CD pipeline using Jenkins and Selenium for a web application."
- "Suggest a strategy to perform load testing on a cloud-based microservices architecture, focusing on peak traffic handling and response time optimization."

Incorporating these examples and prompt engineering techniques in your interactions with AI will not only enhance the quality of the outcomes but also save you time and effort, making your testing process more efficient and effective. As AI continues to integrate into various aspects of software testing, mastering the art of prompt engineering will undoubtedly become an essential skill for every software tester.

Note: More strategies for Prompt engineering can be found at: https://platform.openai.com/docs/guides/prompt-engineering/six-strategies-for-getting-better-results.

Impact of AI in the field of Test Automation

In the early 1870s, construction of the Chesapeake and Ohio Railway along the Greenbrier and New Rivers employed thousands of workers. The process of building a tunnel in the 1870s was slow and difficult work. Holes were drilled into the layers of rock using a hand drill and hammer. Holes were then filled with powder and blasted in order to make the rock small enough to remove from the tunnel. The drill was held by a "shaker" who turned it slightly after each blow and gave it a shake to flip the rock dust out of the hole. The "steel driver" swung the hammer as hard and as often as he could, pounding the drill into the rock.

As the story goes, John Henry was hired as a steel driver for the railroad. Later, the railroad company brought in a steam drill to speed up work on the tunnel. It was said that the steam drill could drill faster than any man. The challenge was on, "*man against machine*." John Henry was known as the strongest, the fastest, and the most powerful man working on the railroad. He went up against the steam drill to prove that the black worker could drill a hole through the rock farther and faster than the drill could.

Using two 10-pound hammers, one in each hand, he pounded the drill so fast and so hard that he drilled a 14-foot hole into the rock. The legend says that the drill was only able to drill nine feet. *John Henry beat the steam drill and later died of exhaustion.*

The moral of the story here is that we should not think of the advancements in AI as "Man versus Machine". Imagine, what could be the combined output of "Man and Machine". And isn't that the narrative of automating test cases? Where human testers check the detailed features, and use machines, or Selenium in our case to automate the boring repetitive work.

We should think of AI and LLM based technologies, similarly as machines. When humans and AI collaborate, the output is substantially enhanced. Testers can focus on more complex, creative aspects of testing, leaving the routine, time-consuming tasks to AI. This collaboration not only increases efficiency but also leads to more thorough and effective testing processes. Moreover, AI's role in test automation isn't about replacing human testers but rather augmenting their capabilities. It's about using AI to handle what it does best, thereby freeing up human testers to leverage their unique skills more effectively.

In essence, the story of AI in test automation is not a tale of competition but one of collaboration. It's a partnership where each party brings its strengths to the table, resulting in a combined output that neither could achieve alone. This approach, where "Man and Machine" work together, is the true essence of innovation and progress in the field of test automation.

AI is poised to revolutionize test automation, bringing unprecedented efficiency and accuracy to the process. By leveraging advanced algorithms for test case generation, predictive analytics, and intelligent maintenance, AI will enable testers to focus on more complex and creative aspects of software quality assurance.

1. Advanced Test Generation: AI will automate test case generation, creating more comprehensive and efficient test suites. AI will reduce human effort in writing and maintaining tests.

2. Intelligent Test Maintenance: AI will detect application changes and automatically update tests, significantly reducing the maintenance burden.

3. Predictive Analytics: AI will predict potential defects and areas of high risk in the software, guiding testers on where to focus their efforts.

4. Enhanced Debugging: AI will aid in identifying the root cause of defects more quickly, improving the debugging process.

5. Automated Test Execution Analysis: AI will analyze test results, providing insights and recommendations for improvement.

To prepare for these changes:

Upskill in AI and Machine Learning: Acquire AI and machine learning skills to understand and leverage these technologies in test automation.

Adopt Agile and Continuous Testing Practices: Embrace agile methodologies and continuous testing to integrate AI-driven testing seamlessly into the development process.

Invest in AI-Enabled Testing Tools: Explore and invest in AI-powered testing tools to stay ahead of the curve.

Collaborate with AI Experts: Collaborate with AI experts to tailor AI solutions to specific testing needs.

Stay Informed: Keep abreast of the latest AI and test automation developments through continuous learning and community engagement.

- Nikolay Advolodkin, founder of UltimateQA and Senior Developer Advocate at Sauce Labs

---

Git Basics

In our digital era, where code is the backbone of technology, Git stands as a fundamental tool in software development. As a distributed version control system, Git is critical for managing and tracking code changes across versions and projects, streamlining collaboration, and increasing efficiency.

Created by Linus Torvalds in 2005, Git revolutionized version control with its distributed nature and efficiency. Designed initially for managing the Linux kernel, Git enables each developer to have a complete history of the code, fostering speed and flexible workflow management, a leap from centralized systems like SVN.

Git's integration into CI/CD pipelines and its role in collaborative and open-source projects underscore its modern relevance. Its adaptability across various programming environments and its support for non-linear development via branching and merging make it indispensable for today's software development.

Key Concepts of Git

The key concepts of Git are as follows:

- **Repository**: The heart of Git, a repository (or "repo"), is where project files and their history are stored. Repositories can be local (on a developer's computer) or remote (on a server or platform like GitHub).
- **Commit**: Commits are snapshots of your repository at specific points. They're checkpoints to which you can revert your project if needed.
- **Branch**: Branching allows developers to diverge from the main codebase to work on new features or fixes without affecting the main project.
- **Merge**: Merging brings changes from one branch (like a feature branch) into another (typically the main branch), integrating different development paths.
- **Pull Requests** and Code Reviews: In collaborative environments, pull requests are proposals to merge one branch into another, often used alongside code reviews to ensure quality and consistency.

Essential Git Commands and their Usage

Some essential Git commands and their usage are as follows:

- **`git init`**: This command initializes a new Git repository. It's the first step in creating a new project under Git's version control.
- **`git clone [url]`**: To start working on an existing repository, use **`git clone`** followed by the repository's URL. This command creates a local copy of the repository on your machine.
- **`git add [file]`**: Before committing changes, you need to stage them using **`git add`**. This command adds files to your staging area, preparing them for a commit.
- **`git commit -m "[commit message]"`**: After staging changes, use **`git commit`** to save them to your local repository. The `-m` flag allows you to add a descriptive message for context.
- **`git push [remote] [branch]`**: To update the remote repository with your local changes, use git push, specifying the remote's name (often 'origin') and the branch you're pushing.

- **`git pull [remote] [branch]`:** This command updates your local branch with changes from its remote counterpart, merging updates automatically if possible.
- **`git branch [branch-name]`:** To create a new branch, use **`git branch`** with the desired branch name. This allows you to work on different aspects of your project simultaneously.
- **`git merge [branch]`:** Use **`git merge`** to combine the changes from one branch (like a feature branch) into another (like 'main' or 'master').
- **`git log`**: This command displays the commit history, helping you track changes and navigate through the development process.

Git Workflow

Imagine you're an artist with a sketchpad, your working tree, where you draw your pictures. When you have a sketch you like, you pin it up on a board, your staging area, to decide if it's ready to be part of your portfolio. Once you're sure, you add it to your portfolio with a note on the back, which in Git is like committing your changes with a message that explains what you did. Your portfolio at home is like your local repository, where all your finished pieces are kept safe and sound.

Now, suppose you want to show your art to the world, you'd take it to a gallery. In the Git world, this gallery is like your remote repository, a place like GitHub where everyone can see your work. When you're ready to share a new piece, you push it from your portfolio to the gallery, and now it's out there for everyone to enjoy. If you want to see if there are new pieces in the gallery that other artists have added, you fetch to look at them without bringing them home just yet. If you love what you see and want to add it to your local portfolio, you pull it, which is like fetching and then immediately hanging it up in your home.

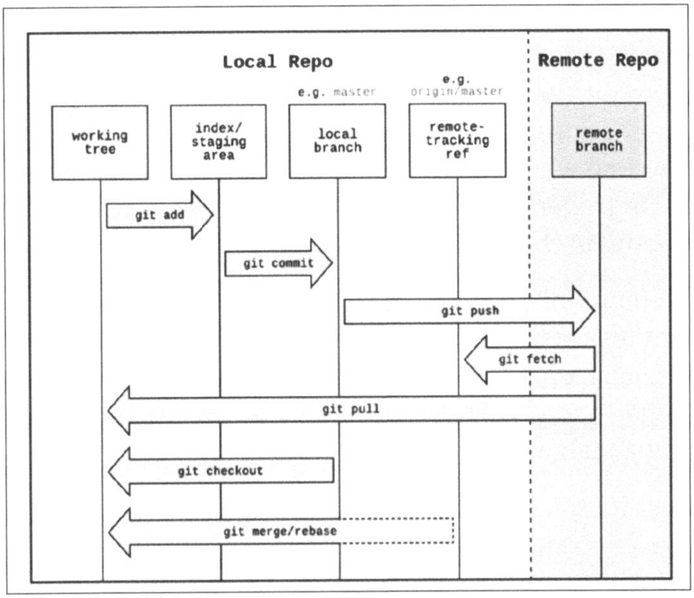

Figure 11.2: *Basic flow of Git commands*

Sometimes, you might want to create a whole new series of art without messing up your main portfolio, which you can do by starting a new branch. It's like having a separate folder for a specific project. When you're done and want to include this series back into your main portfolio, you merge or rebase. Merging is like putting the pages from your project folder into your main portfolio, mixing them in with your other art. Rebasing is more like rearranging your portfolio to include your project work in a new, tidy order. Either way, your art evolves, and your portfolio grows in a way that makes sense to you and your audience.

Mastering Git is a crucial skill in software development. Its robustness and flexibility in handling project versions and collaborations make it an essential tool for developers. Practice, exploration, and continued learning are key to becoming proficient with Git.

Open-Source Community of Selenium

Selenium, an open-source project under the Software Freedom Conservancy (SFC), stands as a testament to collaborative innovation in web automation. This project, more than just a suite of tools, is driven by a global community passionate about advancing web testing. The SFC plays a pivotal role, handling the legal and financial aspects, allowing the community to focus on technological advancements.

Selenium is an Apache 2.0 licensed open-source project. The Apache License 2.0 is like a permission slip that lets you freely use, modify, and share software, as long as you credit the original creators and include the same license when you redistribute the software. It's a promise that you won't blame the creators if anything goes wrong while using their software. Also, you can't use the original creators' names or trademarks without their permission. It's a way to keep things open and respectful in the world of software.

The Selenium community is a diverse and inclusive gathering of developers, testers, and enthusiasts. Governed by a structure that includes the Project Leadership Committee and the Technical Leadership Committee, the project ensures fair and open participation, inviting contributions from anyone interested in enhancing web automation

Whether it's through reporting bugs, suggesting new features, enhancing documentation, or contributing code, there's a place for everyone in the Selenium project. The community values each form of contribution, from small documentation updates to major code enhancements. Engaging with the community through forums and discussions not only strengthens the project but also expands your horizons in software engineering. Joining the Selenium community is straightforward. Start by connecting with other contributors through chat channels and forums to understand the project's current focus. Explore the GitHub repository to find areas that match your skills and interests, and don't hesitate to start small - every contribution, no matter its size, is a step towards collective progress in web automation.

I am a firm believer that getting involved in open source isn't just good for software innovation and the community, but also just breeds good karma. As a former social worker that eventually would build community programs for developers and automation engineers, I attended my first open-source meetup thinking everyone understood the value of building quality software. Together. Years (RIP Selenium IDE) and eventually running the SF Selenium meetup group, I still believe more than ever that everyone can benefit from contributing to open source be it opening issues, minor code changes, sponsoring projects, improving documentation, amplifying open-source projects, and/or even hosting events, you only have to gain personally and professionally by getting involved in open source. Open source

> *sits at the intersections of innovation, good karma, and building better software for your community and by your community.*
>
> - Tristan Lombard, Software Quality Advocate and Community Builder

Technical Contributions

If you're technically inclined, consider contributing code. Start simple - you don't need to engineer a new feature right off the bat. A great entry point is to improve the documentation. That's how a lot of us began our journey to open source contributions.

Documentation is the roadmap that guides users through the intricacies of the software, and ensuring its clarity and accuracy is a noble contribution.

Ready for more? Take the initiative to raise a Pull Request (PR) with your improvements. Perhaps you've spotted a bug while working on your project; this is your cue to switch roles from user to contributor. Delve into the issue, propose a fix, and submit your PR. Your proactive approach will not only enhance the tool but also refine your skills as a developer.

Testing reported issues is another crucial area where technical contributors shine. Verify bugs, explore edge cases, and work alongside others to fortify Selenium's reliability. Each bug squashed is a step towards a more robust tool for everyone.

These contributions can be made at: https://github.com/SeleniumHQ

Beyond Tech: Enriching the Community in Varied Ways

Selenium's strength lies not only in its code but also in its vibrant community. The Selenium Open Space Conference is a testament to this, where ideas and experiences are exchanged in an open, informal setting. It's a melting pot of perspectives, and your voice matters here. Share your experiences, learn from others, and watch as the project grows through communal knowledge. If you prefer something more in-person, Selenium project hosts regional conferences across the world, and you are welcome to contribute as a speaker or audience. More details about these events can be found at: https://www.selenium.dev/blog/

For those who prefer the written word, the Selenium Slack group is a bustling digital space where users and contributors converge. Answering questions and offering guidance here can be as impactful as submitting code. Your insights can help users overcome hurdles, smoothing their path to success. You can join the group following the following link: https://www.selenium.dev/support/

Financial contributions are equally important. Open-source projects thrive on the support of their users, and Selenium is no exception. By donating, you're not just funding the software; you're investing in a tool that empowers people and organizations around the globe. Here you can contribute financially to the project: https://opencollective.com/selenium

Contributing to Selenium means nurturing a project that's pivotal to the tech industry. Whether through coding, community engagement, or financial support, your involvement pushes the envelope of what's possible in the open-source world. Remember, every contribution, big or small, weaves into the larger tapestry of Selenium's success. So, take that first step, and be part of something transformative.

Conclusion

As we close the book on Selenium test automation, let's open our minds to the myriad of opportunities that await us. This isn't just the end of a chapter; it's the start of a thrilling adventure in the dynamic world of testing. Armed with the latest tools and knowledge, from mastering Selenium's nuanced features to navigating the essentials of GIT, or using AI; you're now ready to elevate your test scripts and manage your code like a seasoned pro.

We began with Selenium IDE and the advantages it brings to the test automation table. With each subsequent chapter, like pieces of a puzzle, we added depth to our understanding. The WebDriver fundamentals laid the foundation, while advanced techniques added finesse to our automation skills. The exploration of frameworks showed us how to build robust, scalable systems. And as we delved into distributed test automation and the nuances of SaaS applications, we appreciated Selenium's versatility in handling diverse testing scenarios.

The exploration of Behavior Driven Development, with its human-readable approach, not only showcased a shift towards more collaborative testing but also echoed the essence of team work - making complex concepts accessible and action-able.

Selenium's latest features, introduced in its fourth iteration, marked a significant leap, highlighting the tool's relentless evolution to keep pace with the ever-changing web development landscape.

But it's in this concluding chapter where our journey takes a truly exciting turn. The discussion about the integration of AI in test automation opens a window to a future where the efficiency, accuracy, and scope of testing are bound to expand exponentially.

And the emphasis on the Selenium open-source community underscores a world of continuous learning, sharing, and innovation.

As we look ahead, the road is replete with opportunities for growth, collaboration, and discovery. Whether you're a novice setting out on your first automation project or a seasoned professional looking to stay ahead of the curve, Selenium Test Automation is your gateway to a world where your skills can not only thrive but also make a tangible difference in the quality of software products.

So, as we close this chapter, let's carry forward the spirit of exploration, the eagerness to learn, and the commitment to create. The world of Selenium Test Automation is vast and ever-evolving, and it awaits your unique contributions.

Let's step forward with confidence and curiosity, ready to shape the future of quality.

Index

C

D

E

F

G

H

I

J

T